WOMEN in FOREIGN POLICY

WOMEN IN FOREIGN POLICY

THE INSIDERS

NANCY E. McGLEN AND MEREDITH REID SARKEES

ROUTLEDGE   NEW YORK   LONDON

Published in 1993 by

Routledge
29 West 35th Street
New York, NY 10001

Published in Great Britain by

Routledge
11 New Fetter Lane
London EC4P 4EE

Library of Congress Cataloging-in-Publication Data

McGlen, Nancy E., 1947–
    Women in foreign policy : the insiders / Nancy E. McGlen and
Meredith Reid Sarkees.
        p.   cm.
    Includes interviews with ten women active in foreign policy.
    Includes bibliographical references and index.
    ISBN 0-415-90511-7 (HB) — ISBN 0-415-90512-5 (PB)
    1. Women diplomats—United States. 2. United States—Diplomatic
and consular service. 3. Women diplomats—United States—
Interviews.   I. Sarkees, Meredith Reid, 1950–   .   II. Title.
JX1706.Z7M34   1993
353.0089'082—dc20   92-41704
                                                              CIP

British Library Cataloguing-in-Publication Data also available.

To
Joseph Gadawski
and
John Sarkees

whose support makes all things possible

Contents

Acknowledgments

Most worthwhile things in life can be accomplished only with the assistance of many others, and we would like to take this opportunity to express our gratitude to those who have helped us in this project. We would especially like to thank the women and men in the foreign policy arena who so generously gave us their opinions and insights during our interviews. Their willingness to sacrifice time from their already demanding schedules and subject themselves to an extensive array of questions reflects a dedication to their careers and an appreciation of the pursuit of knowledge, which is the basis of studies like ours.

We would also like to thank those who assisted us in our search for information, including, but not limited to: Maryann Jacob, Air Force; Sharon Bobb, Senior Executive Service; Carmen Arrowood and Mike Duggin, Navy; Maria Melchiorre, State Department; Gwynn Johnson and Bob Zenda, Army; Charles Vaughan, Andrew Klugh, and Ken Darlymple, Office of Personnel Management; Fran Burwell, Women in International Security; and Monica Wagner, esq., Terris, Edgecombe, Hecker, & Wayne. We are particularly grateful to Georgiana Prince and Alison Palmer, who shared much of their accumulated information and insight with us.

We also owe a special debt to the Center for the American Woman and Politics, at the Eagleton Institute, Rutgers University, which provided the inspiration to begin, and the grant which enabled us to undertake, this project. Thanks also go to Niagara University for its support of our research with several Academic Year Research grants.

Intellectually, the ideas for this book benefited from the suggestions and criticisms of Georgia Duerst-Lahti, Susan Carroll, Debra Dodson, and Ruth Mandel who helped us formulate the early stages of our research and/or have reviewed versions of some of the following chapters when they were presented as papers. Thanks also have to go to our editor, Cecelia A. Cancellaro who encouraged us to develop our research into a book.

The actual writing of this book was made possible only with the transcribing and word-processing assistance of Lois Reid, Emily Reid, Barbara Hiller, Richard DiBella, Anita Phelps, and the student aides in Timon Hall. We also benefited from the computer assistance of Regina Kernin.

As in all such endeavors, the credit for what follows can be shared with those we have acknowledged; any omissions are ours.

Introduction

> International Politics, like all politics is a struggle for power. ... It is
> sufficient to state that the struggle for power is universal in time and
> space and is an undeniable fact of experience.
>
> *Hans Morgenthau*[1]

> In a world where a number of sovereign states compete with and
> oppose each other for power, the foreign policies of all nations must
> necessarily refer to their survival as their minimum requirement.
>
> *Hans Morgenthau*[2]

As Morgenthau has indicated, international politics (or foreign affairs)
is about conflicting nation-states locked in a power struggle where the
minimum requirement of a nation-state's foreign policy is the survival of
the nation-state itself. In contrast to earlier predictions, the recent age of
international relations has witnessed a resurgence of nationalism, and an
ever-increasing concern with the creation of, and/or continued existence
of, nation-states. Moreover, in an increasingly interdependent world, the
conduct of foreign affairs has become even more critical to the success
and continued existence of the nation-state. Correspondingly, the persons
responsible for the development and implementation of a country's foreign policy have seen their power magnified. Their decisions not only
influence the fate of their own nation-state, but also have increasingly
significant repercussions throughout the world. As a result, the ranks of
the foreign policy elite have come to be seen as more dominant, prestigious, and exclusive than perhaps ever before. Consequently, the issue of
whether and to what degree women have a role in the process of foreign
policy formulation has also become more crucial.

Women and Foreign Policy

> We still have not let women into the war and peace debate. We still
> have not let them into the arms control debate or how we're going to
> allocate the defense resources or anything else. That is the power
> issue! Now, we see ourselves as the most powerful nation and Wash-
> ington as the most powerful capital of the most powerful nation in

1

the free world. And this is the most powerful issue. War and peace
and tanks and missiles and guns.

Representative Patricia Schroeder[3]

In the United States, and in most other countries as well, women have
generally been excluded from the institutions that make and implement
foreign policy and conduct war. This near ostracism from the centers of
power and the agencies responsible for foreign affairs has meant that
women are rarely present when the most critical decisions a nation-state
faces have been made, especially the decision of whether to engage in
armed conflict. This restriction on the influence of women has deep
historical roots. When Greek city-states invaded their neighbors, when
the Romans conquered most of the known world, when the United Colo-
nies broke their ties with Great Britain, when the United States chose to
enter World Wars I and II, and when troops were sent to Vietnam and the
Persian Gulf, it was men who made the decisions. Similarly when the
Treaty of Paris, the Treaty of Versailles, or the Camp David Accords were
signed, hardly a woman was found at the peace or negotiating tables.

However, women have been, and still are, deeply affected by all these
foreign endeavors. Some women have sacrificed their lives, and many
have lost family members in the multitude of ancient and modern wars.
Others supported the military policies of their country by signing up to
work in munitions plants, rolling bandages, or being camp followers.[4]
Even women who have never participated in a war, or supported or
opposed an international conflict, have experienced the influence of foreign policy decisions in their lives. For instance, those favoring desirable
social policies like a national health care plan or better funding for schools
find that these goals are impossible to implement when a significant
portion of a nation's budget, and the attention of a nation's leaders, are
directed toward defense and international issues. As a result, women
have desired a role in influencing foreign policy.

There have been many instances in which individual women, or women
organized as a group, have attempted to challenge or channel a nation's
dealings with other nations. Even though they were excluded from the
decision-making process, women's voices were sometimes heard by those
in leadership positions. Edward P. Crapol has edited a volume which
recounts the efforts of such women as Lydia Marie Child, who opposed
slavery and worked for recognition of Haiti; Eleanor Roosevelt, who is
credited with getting the United Nations to adopt the Universal Declara-
tion of Human Rights; and Jane Fonda, who vocalized opposition to the
Vietnam War.[5] Other instances of women attempting to shape United
States' foreign policy include the Women's Peace March of 1914, which
its organizers hoped would help convince the United States to avoid

participating in World War I,[6] and the efforts of the Women's Strike for Peace in 1963, which President Kennedy claimed affected his decision to negotiate an above-ground nuclear test ban treaty with the Soviet Union.[7]

As is clear from these few examples, most of the influence that has been exerted by women on foreign policy has come from "outside" the process. However, there have been, and are today, a number of women who have operated on the "inside," who have been able to break into, and succeed within the foreign policy establishment. Particularly, unknown to most Americans, there have been a number of women who have operated at the highest decision-making levels in the foreign policy institutions, having a decisive impact on the direction and conduct of American foreign policy. This book is particularly about these women on the inside of the foreign policy process, the factors which have conditioned their behavior, and the ways in which they have had an impact on foreign policy formulation. The first question, however, is why should we care whether women are included in the process? What are the arguments or the grounds upon which we could argue that it is necessary that women be involved?

A Voice for Women in Foreign Policy

Women have a right to participation and leadership in American foreign policy-making as a matter of simple equity. Although women cannot be expected to speak with one voice or have identical beliefs or interests, we believe that if the time comes when we progress from tokenism to the presence of a "critical mass" of women (as many as men) in government and public institutions, we will have foreign policies more rooted in the reality of people's needs, and our nation and the world will be a safer, healthier and better place in which to live.

Women's Foreign Policy Council[8]

We believe that common security cannot be achieved without the leadership of women—who are the majority of the human species. Women have not had an equal voice in decisions on these issues. It is time for us to speak out and be heeded.

Women for Meaningful Summits, Statement of Purpose[9]

Throughout the 1980s and 1990s, a chorus of women's groups has become increasingly vocal in demanding a role for women in the critical decisions concerning war and peace. Bella Abzug's organization, the Women's Foreign Policy Council, probably best exemplifies these new pressures. Formed in 1985, the Women's Foreign Policy Council has the expressed purpose of increasing the visibility of women in foreign policy debates. To this end, it has established a directory of women knowledgeable about foreign affairs and willing to address these issues in public forums. Several other women's organizations established in the early 1980s, including Women for Meaningful Summits and the Jane Addams Conference, also had as their primary goal the interjecting of women into the foreign policy debate.

A 1987 survey of major women's peace groups discovered that high on the list of priorities for most of these organizations was increasing the role of women in politics and international affairs.[10] The arguments they use to justify this demand for a political role for women in foreign policy are not new. At the beginning of this century, many of the feminists in the Suffrage Movement, for instance, argued for the vote for women on the basis that if women were given the vote and allowed to intervene in the creation of foreign policy, peace and an end to war would soon follow. As a leading member of the Suffrage Movement exhorted, "Let us do our utmost to hasten the day when the wishes of mothers shall have their due weight in public affairs, knowing that by doing so we hasten the day when wars shall be no more."[11] More recently, many of the leaders of the women's peace groups have buttressed their claim for the inclusion of women in foreign affairs along the lines of the earlier feminists. They posit that compared to men women are more peaceful, less aggressive, less willing to use nuclear weapons or nuclear threats, and more likely to emphasize human rights and humanitarian concerns in dealing with other countries.[12] Allowing women to come inside the foreign policy establishment, or influence its output, they argue, would reduce the war making and war preparation that seem to characterize current United States foreign policy. Exemplifying this line of reasoning is Helen Caldicott, founder of Women's Action for Nuclear Disarmament (WAND), who wrote:

> Women have a very important role to play in the world today. . . . If we don't stand up and rapidly become elected to the highest offices in the country and change America's national policies from those of death to those of life, we will all be exterminated. I don't mean that in doing this women should abrogate their positive feminine principle of nurturing, loving, caring, and emotions. . . . I mean they should tenaciously preserve these values but also learn to find and use their incredible power. The positive feminine principle must become the guiding moral principle in world politics.[13]

For the suffragists and some of the leaders of the peace groups, the source of women's peacefulness, and thus their better preparation to decide foreign policy, has biological roots in women's ability to bear and rear children. Ironically, the arguments of the suffragists, along with

Caldicott and some of the women's peace groups, are based on character-izations of women not dissimilar from those used historically to keep women *out* of the political process and *out* of international relations. The "males are warriors, thus they alone should be citizens and rulers" argument of the political philosophers of past centuries is not rejected but accepted and turned on its head by these women leaders. Rather than being a positive or necessary attribute for successful citizenship, men's ability to engage in conflict becomes, in the view of these activists, a liability to the continued existence of the world, and women's peace-fulness its salvation. The following quote from Linda Smith, founder of Mothers Embracing Nuclear Disarmament (MEND), exemplifies this line of thinking. "Women might just be genetically coded to save this species. When we feel threatened, when we know our young are threatened, ... we're going to stand up and be counted and cause a change to save our children's lives."[14]

While Smith's views are not atypical (see the writings of Helen Caldi-cott[15]) other women's groups reject a biologically based peacefulness in favor of a culturally based connection (although still often linked to mater-nal urges).[16] Betty Bumpers, founder of Peace Links, for instance, is quoted as saying, "Women have been socialized to think about the nurturing aspect. Their young are at jeopardy, they don't want their children to be the last generation."[17]

Not all those arguing for the inclusion of women in the foreign policy process take the position that women are innately or by socialization more peaceful than men. Rather they contend that, *as citizens*, women should be allowed to participate in the decisions affecting their lives and the futures of their country and the world. All women and all men have the *constitutional right* to hold any elected, appointed or civil service job in the government including those dealing with foreign relations. Organizations like the National Organization for Women (NOW), a rights feminist group, even argue women should have the "right" to be drafted and to serve in combat. They reason that military service is intimately linked to citizenship. To deny women the right to be drafted prevents them from being complete citizens.[18] Pat Reuss, Executive Director of the Women's Equity Action League at the time of the 1980 debate over drafting women, exemplified the position of women making this argument, "We look to Congress to put aside outdated versions of women's role in society and to declare through appropriate legislation that women shall have equal responsibility to participate in our national defense effort."[19] A simi-lar stand has been taken by feminists like Representative Patricia Schroeder in arguing for allowing women to assume combat positions.[20] For rights feminists like Reuss and Schroeder, whether women, once included, will differ from men in their policy positions is irrelevant. In all likelihood they will not. The issue is that they be allowed in on an equal footing with men.

Thus, there is a sharp contrast in outlook between those who argue women should be included in the foreign policy arena because they are different from men and those who reason women have a right to participate as citizens. The debate between the two positions has wide-ranging implications. Not only do proponents of both sides disagree about why women should be allowed into the international arena, but they also differ on what impact we can anticipate women will have on foreign policy once included.

The Debate Among Feminists: Maximizers versus Minimizers

> What is at stake in the current debates is not only the meaning and aims of feminism, but whether we might move beyond a discourse dominated by war and its necessary antithesis, peace.
>
> *Jean Bethke Elshtain*[21]

> It has been possible to isolate two main sources of a distinctive women's position on organized violence: the experience of maternity on the part of the vast majority of women and women's historical exclusion from public power. ... Consequently, from these two perspectives, feminists have posited conflicting theories on women's relation to war and peace and women have, according to changing historical circumstances, responded to warmongering and peace movements in a great variety of ways.
>
> *Ruth Roach Pierson*[22]

The claims of women peace activists concerning the "natural" peacefulness of women have contributed to an historic debate among feminists. Catherine Stimpson has labeled the two sides of this feminist controversy the minimizers and the maximizers.[23] Ann Snitow describes these two groups: "the minimizers are the feminists who want to undermine the category 'women' to minimize the meaning of sex differences. ... The maximizers want to keep the category (or feel they can't do otherwise), but they want to change its meaning, to reclaim and further elaborate the social being woman, and to empower her."[24] The debate between the two camps of feminists is an old one and has been fought under many guises. The earliest maximizers were the suffragists who argued that maternal urges of women differentiated them from men. More recently cultural feminists in the 1960s posited a biological basis for women's separation from men.[25] The maximizer view was developed further by essentialists like Barbara Deming and Andrea Dworkin who believe biological differences determine gender.[26] In the 1980s and 1990s the maximizer position has been articulated by those fitting loosely under the label of moral feminists or women's values feminists.[27] The maximizers agree with the peace activists, arguing that peace is a feminist issue and women must be part of the foreign policy apparatus, or at least women's voices must be heeded by those in positions of influence. The assumption is that were women included in the foreign policy process, international politics and its policies would be radically different.

The foundations for many of the feminists and activists who take the maximizer position are the works of Nancy Chodorow and Carol Gilligan. In her book, *The Reproduction of Mothering*, Chodorow argues that psycho-social conditioning produces mothers and daughters who have a capacity for emotional connections to other humans. Men's upbringing does not allow them to fully develop these relationships. For Chodorow, women are emotional, tied to other human beings; men are distant and untied.[28] Following a similar line of reasoning, Carol Gilligan posits that women are innately or culturally less conflict-oriented. She contends that women's psycho-socialization leads them to an ethic of care or an ethic of responsibility, while men are raised to adopt an ethic of justice or an ethic of rights. Women's moral judgments will take others into account, men's will rely on universal standards of equality or fairness without concern for the involved individuals.[29] She summarizes her argument as follows:

> Thus in the transition from adolescence to adulthood, the dilemma itself is the same for both sexes, a conflict between integrity and care. But approached from different perspectives, this dilemma generates the recognition of opposite truths. These different perspectives are reflected in two different moral ideologies. . . .
>
> The morality of rights is predicated on equality and centered on the understanding of fairness, while the ethic of responsibility relies on the concept of equity, the recognition of differences in need. While the ethic of rights is a manifestation of equal respect, balancing the claims of other and self, the ethic of responsibility rests on an understanding that gives rise to compassion and care.[30]

Feminists relying on Chodorow and Gilligan have argued that the ethic of responsibility or care provides the basis for women's more peaceful nature. Sara Ruddick's work probably best exemplifies this school of thought. In her numerous writings she argues that maternal practice (or the exposure to it as a daughter) gives rise to preservative love,[31] or maternal thinking,[32] or an ethic of care.[33] In all its guises, the focus of women is on the preservation of life and concern with others. This concern becomes the basis for greater peacefulness on the part of women. For Ruddick, it is but a small step to pacifism. She explains:

The conventional and symbolic association between women and peace has a real basis in maternal practice. Out of maternal practice a distinctive kind of reasoning arises that is incompatible with military strategy but consonant with pacifist commitment to non-violence. The peacefulness of mothers, however, is not now a reliable source of peace. In order for motherly peacefulness to be publicly significant, maternal practice must respect and extend its pacifism. For this to happen, maternal thinking would have to be transformed by feminist politics.[34]

Taking the ethic of care into the world of foreign affairs (which is now governed by militarism), according to Ruddick, would transform the situation, in that the rationality of care might alter the direction of international relations.[35] From a slightly different perspective, Nancy C. M. Hartsock argues that it is men's fixation on war, as a way of affirming their manhood, that distinguishes men from women.[36] Men, as a result, are the more aggressively violent, having abandoned the "natural" peacefulness of humans in an attempt to conquer their fear of death.[37] "Human survival," Hartsock posits, "may well depend on breaking the linkage of masculinity with both military capacity and death."[38] Other feminist and peace scholars draw similar models of women's natural peacefulness and/or men's aggressiveness and the need to infuse the interaction between nations with a women's point of view.[39] In the same vein, feminist scholars who study international politics have argued for the transformation of international relations theory by the inclusion of the women's perspective.[40] In contrast, some feminists, also allied with the maximizers' school, are hesitant about including women in all aspects of international affairs. They reason that women should be kept *out* of certain institutions of foreign policy in order to preserve women's nature. More specifically, they express deep concerns about the possible impact of military training and combat on women's unique traits. Maintaining women's special character and the ethic of care is seen as more problematic if women are prepared for, and engage in, armed conflict.[41]

Not all feminists and feminist scholars accept the logic of the peace activists and their intellectual sisters, the maximizers. These other feminists, the minimizers, reject the view that women are innately different from men. Included in the camp of the minimizers are those who contend that the present culture or social system constructs an image of women that is false (poststructural feminists, or deconstructionists); those who believe the present differences between women and men are transitory, a function of inequitable treatment of women (rights feminists); and those who think the present economic system of capitalism restricts women's development as equal persons (socialist feminists).[42] Indeed some feminists have argued quite persuasively about the need to reject the moral-mother model of Gilligan and Ruddick. For instance, Joan Tronto reasons that adopting the logic of the ethic of care will produce a double moral standard with women's moral values coming in second to men's. She writes:

> The equation of "care" with "female" is questionable because the evidence to support the link between gender differences and different moral perspectives is inadequate. It is a strategically dangerous position for feminists because the simple assertion of gender differences in a social context that identifies the male as normal contains an implication of the inferiority of the distinctly female.[43]

Linda Kerber also cautions against accepting Gilligan uncritically:

> But let us not be in haste to conclude that most or all of what have been called the characteristics of separate spheres emerge naturally from women's own distinctive psychology, biologically rooted in patterns of maturation. Much, perhaps most, of it may well be rooted in the distinctive socialization of young girls in a culture which has always rested on the sexual division of labor, which has long ascribed some social tasks to men and others to women, and which has served as a mechanism by which a patriarchal society excludes one segment of the population from certain roles and therefore makes easier the task of producing hegemonic consensus.[44]

In addition, Micaela di Leonardo fears that this reinvigorated image of women as more peaceful will have disastrous consequences for the Women's Movement which seeks equality for women with men.[45] She proposes, "We *should* fight to 'junk all received notions of traditional femininity and motherhood,' because they cannot be transformed, and will always be used against women to push them back into full responsibility for home and children—and second-class citizenship."[46] Similarly, in a tightly reasoned essay, Janet Radcliffe Richards disagrees with the logic that says peace is a part of feminism.[47] She expresses a deep concern that accepting the position that women are by nature or socialization more peaceful than men plays into the hands of those who would keep men and women in separate spheres and limit women's equality. She writes:

> Unless an adequate justification can be given, it must be assumed that feminist ideas of this kind [those that restrict peace to a women's issue] depend on nothing better than the separate spheres of patriarchal tradition, which have been the main tools of women's oppression. The women's values kind of feminism seems to rest on the unsupported assumptions and deeply flawed arguments of feminism's opponents, and to accept the very divide men originally instituted for their own benefit.[48]

Richards does not reject peace as a goal, but only the proposition that peace is a women's or feminist issue. Women (and men) who wish to work for peace may do so, but they must *not* do so "*as* feminists, or *as* women, but simply as people concerned with peace, and willing whenever possible to join forces with anyone else who shares those concerns."[49]

For feminists like Richards, and many of the minimizers, the rationale for including women in the foreign policy arena becomes a matter of basic human and constitutional rights. Women who hold views like these, moreover, expect that the policy views of women will not be homogeneous. Indeed, they reason, some women, given the opportunity to participate in the military and in foreign affairs decision-making, will be every bit as aggressive and good at war-mongering and war fighting as men.[50]

Are Women and Men Different?

Remaining male-female political behavioral differences may parallel sexual differences that the disciplines strongly suggest are biological in origin.

Dean Jaros and Elizabeth S. White[51]

We know more about how social forces create gender distinctions than ever before, although those writers who believe gender distinctions to be inborn dismiss much of this knowledge.

Cynthia Fuchs Epstein[52]

The discussion between representatives from the two sides of feminism, maximizers and minimizers, over whether we should include more women in the foreign policy arena *because* women are more peaceful than men, or *because* women have a right as citizens to participate, is grounded in the fundamental argument of whether women are indeed *different* from men.[53] Are women genetically programmed, or culturally inculcated, to act or believe in ways distinct from the ways of men?[54] Ann Snitow, who has reviewed the history of the maximizer-minimizer debate, cautions against a belief that the issues between the two positions are easily resolved. She notes, "a common divide keeps forming in both feminist thought and action between the need to build the identity 'woman' and give it solid political meaning and the need to tear down the very category woman and dismantle its all too solid history."[55] Those who adopt the position that women are indeed different include, in addition to the maximizer feminists, a disparate collection of male chauvinists, conservatives, and some scientists.

Male chauvinists believe men are better equipped to lead the country, protect us from our enemies, manage the corporations, determine our relations with other countries, and in general to run the show. Conservatives, including many religious leaders, might not agree that men are better, but they do accept that there are differences between men and women and that these differences lead to men being better equipped, or anointed by God, to head the family, work outside the home, run the churches and generally have the prestigious positions in government and business. The scientists who fall into this camp contend that as a result of biological factors, women have certain skills that men do not have and similarly men have some greater abilities than women. Labeled sociobiologists, these scientists generally identify such traits as aggression, math, and spatial skills as sex-linked.[56] The implication of these "results" is that men are better equipped to engage in politics and military conflict.

The maximizer feminists, as we have seen, reject the negative implications of any gender differences, arguing that these differences, rather than making women less suited to manage foreign affairs, make them more qualified than men. In contrast, the minimizer feminists dismiss the existence of differences, arguing that women (and men) both have a right to make foreign policy decisions, and we should not expect women to necessarily approach these issues differently than men.

Recently, Cynthia Fuchs Epstein has attacked head-on the debate between those who argue for, and those who argue against, men-women differences.[57] After a comprehensive examination of the research on gender distinctions in the fields of biology, sociology, psychology, and the social sciences generally, Epstein concludes that the empirical foundation of the maximizers' school is weak and rests on the faulty assumption that feminine-masculine distinctions have an empirical reality. Her research shows that most of the studies which have found differences between men and women are flawed, and serve merely to rationalize, justify, and even create inequality.[58] In contrast, she concludes that specific gender differentiation is best explained as a social construct, or an artifact of a culture and social order that assigns women to positions of inferiority, low status, and little power. The movement toward a culture where women and men are not treated in a hierarchical, biased manner will eliminate the few remaining artificial differences. She concludes:

> The mounting evidence cited and collected in this book, however, makes it increasingly difficult to obscure the overwhelming similarities between men and women. The studies gathered here bring to light the processes by which the powerful continue to create, emphasize, and maintain gender differences. ... Although people manage reality and make imagined things real, scholars and activists are discovering a non-dichotomous reality that may one day put an end to the self-fulfilling prophecy of differences between men and women.[59]

Obviously, this controversy between the minimizers, who enthusiastically accept the work of Epstein, and the maximizers, who believe differences between women and men will and should persist, is critical to our own topic of women inside the foreign policy process. If the maximizers are correct, including women in the conduct of foreign affairs should result in a reformulation of United States' strategy vis-à-vis the rest of the world. Minimizers, however, would argue that even though it is the right of women to be allowed on the inside, we should not necessarily expect the inclusion of women to shift the direction of foreign affairs.

Locating Women on the Inside of the Foreign Policy Process

Our book will contribute to the ongoing debate between maximizers and minimizers concerning the impact of women on foreign policy by focusing upon women who are in policy-making positions within the institutions where international politics is crafted. In the United States, the institution which in the past almost exclusively controlled this preserve was the State Department. Organized around the Foreign Service and the nation's ambassadors, the State Department was uniquely suited to formulate and implement our nation's foreign policy. However, recent developments have led to a decline in the Department's influence, and a corresponding rise in power of the White House and the Pentagon. Much of this trend has been attributed to the personalities of recent Presidents, such as Nixon, Carter, Reagan, and Bush. However, it can also be seen as a result of the function of the State Department itself, with its relatively passive role of observation, reporting, negotiation, and advisement, as compared to the Defense Department's primary function of action.[60] Particularly during internationally activist administrations, the military has consequently become the largest implementer of foreign policy decisions. Additionally, recent reorganizational measures, which have consolidated five of the nine intelligence agencies within the Department of Defense, have made the Pentagon into the largest gatherer and supplier of information for the foreign policy formulation process.[61] As a result, the postwar record of U.S. foreign policy is replete with evidence of a military approach to foreign affairs. "Although Vietnam may have challenged the supremacy of the military, the security culture of the 1980s points toward a resurgence of military thinking about political problems to which Vietnam itself stands as a monument."[62] Desert Shield and Desert Storm are recent evidence of this trend. Thus today both the Department of State and Department of Defense are major foreign policy agencies, and consequently we have elected to focus our study of foreign policy participants, the Insiders, within these two agencies.

We then needed to identify the women in these Departments who were in positions of influence, who would have a significant impact on policy-making. We chose to include women (and a companion sample of men) who are political appointees or career civil service employees in the *upper echelons* of both Departments (Senior Executive Service and Senior Foreign Service). Although as most of our respondents noted, policy is influenced below the level of Senior Executive/Senior Foreign Service, most significant policy is made at these levels or higher. Identifying the women in those positions we wanted to interview was not always easy. While the Department of Defense and its military branches were generally cooperative in sending along names, addresses and sometimes phone numbers (only the Army's came too late to be included), the Department of State defied almost all our efforts to obtain the information. We suspect our difficulties and those of others who have sought this information stem from the numerous legal challenges the Department has faced for sex discrimination. However, by the time we conducted our interviews in the summer of 1988 (toward the end of the Reagan administration), we had the names of 55 women in the Department of Defense and the Department of State who fulfilled our criteria. We were able to interview 34 of these women.

We also conducted interviews with 22 men, selected randomly from the same lists used to identify the women. Additional mail surveys were sent to women and men working abroad or who were unable to meet with us. Twenty-three responses were received from the mail portion of the study. Thus our final sample consisted of 79 persons, 38 men and 41 women. This group is the primary basis for the discussion to follow. We have supplemented this sample with in-depth interviews conducted in January 1991 with women who have served, or are currently serving, in the higher ranks of both Departments. Portions of this second set of interviews are presented at the end of each chapter in order to highlight the specific attributes of the women who most clearly typify "the Insiders" and their impact on foreign policy. The men and women in our two samples include Assistant Secretaries, Under Secretaries, Deputy Assistant Secretaries, Principal Deputy Assistant Secretaries, Assistant Deputy Under Secretaries, Directors, Deputy General Counsels, Assistant General Counsels, Ambassadors, Consul Generals, Chiefs of Mission and Deputy Chiefs of Mission. Their areas of expertise encompass nuclear weapons technology, narcotics, intelligences, human rights, arms control, supply, personnel, legal affairs, the United Nations, affirmative action, protocol, regional affairs management, and a host of other areas. Collectively, the people in our samples represent the elite of the foreign policy establishment.

Structure of the Argument

Our research focus concerning women in the foreign policy process has been shaped by the maximizer-minimizer debate, specifically in terms of the following issues: the degree women differ from men; whether the source of these difference(s) is innate, socially constructed, lasting, or temporary; and what impact any difference that may exist has on foreign policy. In attempting to address these complex issues, we have organized our discussion around two fundamental questions: what factors influence the women in the foreign policy process; and do these women make a difference in the way in which foreign policy is formulated? These two questions are related by a number of complex interactions. The first question centers upon the variables which impact upon women, while the second question looks at the ways in which women policy-makers have influence, again often conditioned by these same variables. In attempting to address the first question, the structure of our inquiry relies heavily upon the theoretical contributions made by Georgia Duerst-Lahti and Gary Powell.[63] Duerst-Lahti has done research on the status and influence of women in positions of authority in state bureaucracies, while Powell has examined people in managerial positions in the corporate realm. We hope to apply the research in these complementary fields to our much more narrow topic of individuals in policy-making positions in the Departments of State and Defense.

Both of the above-mentioned theorists have demonstrated that, in order to study persons functioning within organizations, one must actually examine three different sets of variables to develop a comprehensive picture. These variables encompass societal, organizational, and individual factors. Following this logic, in attempting to answer our first question, our strategy will be to individually examine the impact of each of these three major sets of variables: societal factors; organizational factors; and individualistic factors. Our discussion will adopt the following sequence: we shall discuss each of these variables in greater detail; and then we shall explore how each factor has conditioned our sample of foreign policy decision-makers.

The second section of our inquiry switches from examining the factors which impact upon foreign policy-makers to an investigation of the role of the policy-makers themselves. Do women have power in their Departments, and if the answer is yes, what types of influence do they have? It is here that our findings will be most applicable to the maximizer-minimizer debate. If women are exercising authority, is it fundamentally different from that of their male colleagues?

The questions we shall pose as we look at these Insiders in the foreign policy arena are thus as follows:

I   What factors influence the Insiders?

A. What societal or cultural factors impact upon women in foreign policy? (Chapter 1)

B. What particular problems do the women on the inside confront as women operating in largely male institutions? Are the State and Defense Departments gendered masculine, in other words, are they, or have they been, so inhospitable to women as to limit the influence of women or a women's perspective if one exists? (Chapter 2)

C. Who are the women on the inside? What types of individual factors influence them? How did they come to be where only men or mostly men have been? What do these women and their paths to the inner sanctum of foreign affairs tell us about the innate differences between men and women or the culture that determines who is on the inside? (Chapter 3)

II   And to the heart of the issue, does adding women to international politics make a difference?

A. Do women on the inside have different policy priorities from men on the inside? (Chapter 4)

B. Do women view the foreign policy process, the way decisions are made in the United States, differently from men? (Chapter 5)

C. Do women manage the affairs of their divisions or agencies in ways unlike those of their male contemporaries? In other words, do women make policy, including foreign policy, in ways distinct from the ways of men? (Chapter 6)

III   The implications of our findings will be discussed in the Conclusion.

In crafting our answers to these questions, we will rely primarily on the data from the 79 anonymous surveys. We have also included in each chapter an interview with one of a select group of women who have had significant influence in the foreign policy establishment. Their comments give us a glimpse into their perceptions of their careers and the situations in which women function.

It is hoped that these complementary data sets and our discussion of the answers to these questions will contribute to our understanding of the role of women on the inside of the foreign policy establishment. We also expect our data will add to the debate among feminist and activists on what *should* be the position of women in shaping the direction of United States' relations with other nation-states.

Interview
MARY S. OLMSTED
A Pioneer for Women's Rights

In 1945, the State Department administered two sets of examinations for admittance into the Foreign Service Officer program. As a result of the first exam, one woman was admitted to the Department, and following the second, five additional women officers were selected. One of these women was Mary S. Olmsted. The narration of her career, which culminated in her being selected as the first American Ambassador to Papua New Guinea, includes many elements which are common to the general experiences of women at State. The culture and practices of the State Department led her in 1970 to become a member of the Ad Hoc Committee to Improve the Status of Women in Foreign Affairs Agencies, and subsequently to serve as President of the Women's Action Organization. Both of these groups were instrumental in encouraging the State Department to discontinue discriminatory practices against women.

When I was in college, I really didn't give any thought to government service. I worked in New York for four years, first in one of the big banks, and then in an economic research organization. A friend of mine had gone down to Washington to take a job, a wartime job with the government, and she wrote glowing letters about how much she was enjoying life and how much more interesting it was than New York. So I decided I'd look into it. . . . The first interview that I asked for was with the Department of State, not that it was my first preference. Actually, I thought I had very little chance, as a woman, getting into the Department of State. Its biases were well known. The reason I put it first was I thought it would be useful to get some experience with a government interview, and see what kind of questions they asked, and what they wanted to know.

I had filled out several copies of Form 57, which all applicants for jobs with the government had to fill out. The copy that was most blotted, the most written over, I decided to give to the State Department, because I didn't have any hopes of getting a job there.

To my surprise, they were interested in me. I went back to New York, and in a few weeks, I got a letter offering me a job in Montreal as a junior economic analyst in the foreign service auxiliary, which was the wartime branch of the Foreign Service. . . . Some months after I arrived in Montreal, I learned that the Foreign Service examination for a tenured position, a career position in the Foreign Service, would be offered. I decided that I would take the examination, I did so and I passed it.

A few months later, I got my first career appointment, which was to Amsterdam as a vice consul in the American Consulate General there. In the beginning, I did some commercial work and then was transferred into a rotational program. I did citizenship work for a while and then visas. After that I was assigned to Reykjavik, Iceland, to our Legation as second secretary and political officer. I had an interesting job in reporting on political developments at a time when the United States was trying to persuade Iceland to establish a NATO air base, to which there was considerable objection.

After I left Reykjavik, I was transferred to Vienna as second secretary in the economic section of the embassy. At first, I was doing commercial work, but then was transferred into another part of the economic section, in which I was reporting on the economic relations between Austria and the Soviet bloc. This was during the time of the four-power occupation of Austria, and it was a very interesting position and one that I enjoyed very much. When the Austrian State Treaty was signed in 1955, I was transferred from Austria back to Washington.

First I was sent for a year of academic training at the Fletcher School of Law and Diplomacy, and that was the beginning of my interest in the Third World. Up until that time I had been thinking mainly about Europe as my career. But some of the courses I took there attracted me to the Third World. My initial assignment after the Fletcher School was in the Bureau of Intelligence and Research. Subsequently, I had a brief tour in the Department of Commerce and then I got a job I really enjoyed, which was economic officer working on Indonesian affairs in the Bureau of Far Eastern Affairs. Policy was very, very vague toward Indonesia at that time because an effort had been made to oust Sukarno, but it had failed and nobody knew what to do next.

After that assignment, in 1960, I was assigned to New Delhi as first secretary in the economic section, and I arrived there on New Year's Day of 1961. It was a very large embassy, and like most newcomers, I started at the bottom and worked my way up. My first assignment was essentially doing the work that other people did not want to do. I quickly discovered that India's economy was very different from any other economy that I had had experience with, and that it was very complex and with many nuances and subtleties. I realized that I would have to learn a great deal, and that the learning process was going to be a long one. So I settled in and did the odd jobs in the various parts of the economic section, and then eventually I got to the point where they made me deputy to the economic counselor. I concentrated on the economic developments under the third five-year plan with particular reference to the political implications of the problems India was encountering.

After that assignment I was returned to Washington again. I spent a year in the Senior Seminar (advanced training for FSOs), and then I began to work in the Bureau of Near Eastern and South Asian Affairs as the Senior Economic Analyst for India. That was during the second year of a two-year drought. A lot of people in the government were getting awfully tired of hearing about the starving Indians. It was a very difficult and frustrating job, but I thought I accomplished something. Following that, I spent a year in the Office of Economic Opportunity, in an out-of-agency assignment, as they call it, and then went back to the Department of State as Deputy Examiner for the Board of Examiners of the Foreign Service and from that, I was asked to take one of the senior positions in the Office of Personnel.

> By this time, Ms. Olmsted had become increasingly aware of many of the obstacles facing women in the State Department. As a result, she became involved in the Women's Action Organization (WAO), which had as its goal the improvement of conditions for women in the State Department.

I might mention that during that time, I had become very active in the Women's Movement in the Department of State and was president of Women's Action Organization, and those activities brought me to the attention of some of the senior people of the Department of State. The Department of State was having severe morale problems, and the Office of Personnel was in a condition of crisis. The leadership wanted to bring in new faces, people not associated with the old way of doing things, and I was one of the new people who was brought in. The disadvantage to me was that I had no experience in personnel work, it was a brand new field for me, and I had to start at a very high level. . . . I had to get on top of a lot of very complicated matters within a short time. Not only complicated, but very controversial as there were lots and lots of disputes and arguments, protests over the personnel system. . . .

I think that in the beginning the Women's Action Organization made people focus on what was really an appalling array of discriminatory attitudes and policies against women. A lot of people who were not in any way feminists had to admit that women were getting a very raw deal. . . . Assignments to positions illustrate the point. I found as I was coming up in the ranks that I usually had to accept a position at a grade lower than my personal grade, whereas men usually did not have to. When I went out to India as a Class 3 officer, I had to take a Class 4 officer's job, but while I was there, I worked myself up into a Class 2 officer's job. I once asked for an assignment as economic counselor in Beirut. This was back when Beirut was still a lovely city, and assignments there were sought after. The person who was handling Lebanese affairs in the geographic bureau at the time said that over his dead body would the Department send a woman to Beirut. Hence I did not get the assignment. My name was put forward as Ambassador to Bangladesh, and there was considerable objection to that, although a woman got the job several years later. I am sure that I was the first woman ever proposed for that position and I was turned down cold....

It used to be that women were not assigned to certain posts, Moscow for instance. It was very, very rare to have a woman on a selection board up until the time WAO started protesting about that issue. It was hard for a woman to get university training. We broke down the ban against women Foreign Service Officers being married. Another problem WAO tackled was cone assignments, or assignments to functional specialties. Each foreign service officer goes into one of four cones: administrative, consular, economic or political, and the cone into which officers go affects assignments, promotions, and the possibility of reaching senior levels in the service. Traditionally, women officers were concentrated in the consular and administrative cones, although a limited number, myself included, spent their careers in the economic or political cones. WAO brought attention to the situation to pressure the management of the Department to equalize opportunities and to encourage women to seek admission to economic and political cones. WAO also worked to improve the status of secretaries. Further, WAO pressed for better housing overseas and improved shipping allowances for single people (mostly women).

> Ms. Olmsted's next career move is the one for which she is perhaps most noted. She became the first American Ambassador appointed to Papua New Guinea when it gained its independence.

In 1974 I asked for, and got the appointment to open a new post in Port Moresby, Papua New Guinea. As part of my responsibilities in the Office of Personnel, I had to clear (process) a request from the Bureau of East Asian Affairs to open a new post in Papua New Guinea, and that's how I knew about it. The country was about to become independent and it was decided that a new post would be opened as a consulate general, and then it would be elevated to an embassy at independence. When I saw the request for permission to open a new post, I became very interested and I thought I would love to have that experience. So I tossed my hat into the ring and said I would like to be considered for the assignment. ... There was objection particularly on the part of one individual to sending a woman to Port Moresby as consul general, but eventually that officer and I became friends. ...

In June 1974, I arrived in Port Moresby. Until that time, developments in Papua New Guinea had been covered by one of our officers in Australia. But there had been no official American presence in Papua New Guinea since General MacArthur left during World War II. I was Consul General in Port Moresby for fifteen months, and then after independence, I became Ambassador. I stayed there in all for five years. It was a tremendously interesting assignment watching a country emerge from the Neolithic period into the twentieth century. I did a lot of traveling, went out to the countryside. I took a great trip in a dugout canoe on the Sepik River, accompanied by an anthropologist friend, spending seven nights in little villages along the river, looking at local artwork, and talking to the villagers. Just a fascinating experience. In 1978, I became Ambassador to the Solomon Islands, which had become independent. I had been covering the Solomon Islands from Port Moresby, usually taking four trips a year to the Solomons. I usually made it a point to visit Honiara, the capital, and then arranged a trip to one of the other islands.

Papua New Guinea is a small country, three million people. It is a long, long way from the U.S., and American interest in it was not great; we saw Australia as the primary country in the region and expected Australia to take the lead in aid and in other matters as well. I saw my job as largely being public relations, and I made a point of going out to see and to be seen. I entertained very widely, not just top levels of government, but I entertained university students, women's groups, artists, athletes, business people, etc. ... A lot of people got to see the inside of the official residence. I tried to make it clear that the United States had a sympathetic interest in Papua New Guinea. Some of the government leadership was a bit afraid of the United States, they had heard about the CIA, they or their parents had heard about our military might in World War II. They knew we were a very large and very powerful country. I felt that it was important to reassure them that our interest in them was of the most benign sort and that we wanted to be friends.

People told me after I left Port Moresby that the government leaders and the diplomatic corps said for years that the first American ambassador there was the best. I was very pleased when they named a street after me. M. Olmsted Street is on a hillside with a lovely view of the Coral Sea.

I

Factors That Influence Women
in the Foreign Policy Process

As mentioned in the Introduction, Duerst-Lahti and Powell claim that one must evaluate the effects of three types of variables upon individuals in organizations: societal, organizational, and individual. In her work, Georgia Duerst-Lahti describes these variables as: the links with the societal system in which they operate; the structure of the organizations themselves; and the social, social psychological, and individualistic elements.[1] In terms of the societal system, organizations operate within the larger system, a system within which dominant societal values structure reality. Individuals come to the organization with ingrained beliefs, which will impact upon the organization and the people within it.[2] In terms of examining the organization itself, the culture of an organization embodies its characteristics and its practices. Its culture, and its accompanying gender ethos, are shaped by its purpose, clientele, formal structure, past and present leadership, and its decision process.[3] Finally, the social, psychological, and individualistic elements focus upon the individuals within the organization. Similarly, in his examination of management within corporations, Gary Powell created a model of career development which identified the factors which he considered to have the most effect upon career patterns: societal factors; organizational factors; decisions by the organization; family factors; personal factors; and actions by the individual.[4]

> People, however, are influenced in their decisions about work by several factors.... First, they are influenced by society's norms about who should or should not work.... According to traditional norms, however, women have been discouraged from entering the workplace. Second, people are influenced by others' expectations of their interests and capabilities. Third, they are influenced by the choices that the marketplace presents as they consider various occupations. Fourth, they are influenced by the decisions made by organizations about their applications for employment. ... Choices also are influenced by the personal characteristics, backgrounds, and life situations of the individuals themselves. ... [5]

Powell argued that these factors are particularly salient in studying women managers, since women face barriers above and beyond those encountered by men.[6] "According to many people now entering the work force, or anticipating entry, the days when women had trouble getting into jobs compared to men are long past."[7] However, "Gender issues have not entirely disappeared from the workplace. ... What hasn't changed is that women are concentrated in the lower levels of management and hold positions with less authority overall than men."[8] Powell's conclusion was based on the observation that even though many employees are bringing new attitudes about male-female roles to their jobs, considerable resistance remains to the shifting of economic roles between the sexes. Hence problems will arise in male-female work relationships, and it is his conclusion that the sources of these problems, societal, organizational, and individual, need to be considered.

Though we intend to discuss each of these three sets of factors separately, we shall see that these variables are interrelated. Figure 1 is an adaptation of an influence diagram utilized by Gary Powell, and it indi-

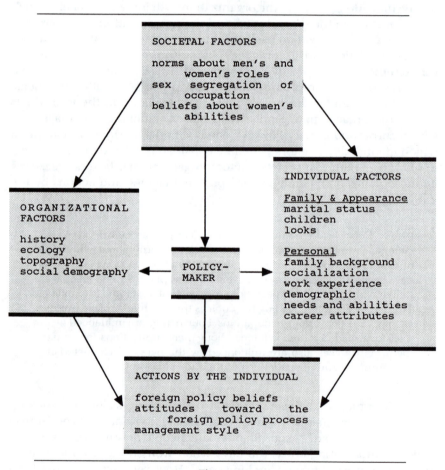

Figure 1

Adapted from Gary N. Powell, *Women & Men in Management* (Beverly Hills: Sage, 1988), 189.

cates the pattern of variable interrelationships. Societal factors, as is clear from the figure, play a dominant role, affecting both the policy-maker and the other sets of factors (organizational and individual). In this way, societal factors both directly and indirectly impact upon and influence the policy-maker. Organizational factors and individual factors impact on each other and on the policy-maker as well, again producing indirect and direct effects. The policy-maker, as the product of these three sets of variables, in turn, adopts specific attitudes and beliefs and undertake certain management actions.

Translating this diagram into the foreign policy arena, we expect that societal norms about women's and men's roles in general, and public views specifically concerning women's abilities in government and foreign affairs, will condition our women policy-makers directly, and indirectly via the organizations in which they have to function, and through their own attitudes and individual life situations which they bring to the work-place. Similarly, we anticipate that the State and Defense Departments' organizational histories and configurations will impinge on the women Insiders, conditioning how they act and what they believe. Individual factors, encompassing family and personal variables, will, we expect, dis-tinguish our women policy-makers from their male counterparts, particu-larly in terms of their career paths and how they manage their positions. We further predict that all three sets of factors will, in turn, impact on how the women and men in State and Defense choose their foreign policy goals, view the foreign policy process, and manage their own sectors of the foreign policy arena.

In the remainder of Section I we shall explore each of the three sets of factors, societal, organizational and individual, mindful of their interaction and the priority assigned to societal factors. We will start our discussion with societal factors in Chapter 1, examine organizational factors in Chap-ter 2 and individual factors in Chapter 3. Section II shifts the focus to an investigation of the foreign policy beliefs and management styles of the women in our sample, while continuing to explore their connection to societal, organizational and individual variables.

1

Societal Factors:
Sex Roles and Stereotypes

What everyone knows to be true often turns out not to be true at all.
Robert K. Merton[1]

As mentioned in the introduction to Section I, organizations operate within the larger societal system, within which the dominant societal values structure reality.[2] Though there are a multitude of societal values, the ones with which we are particularly concerned are those which influence the relations between the sexes. Georgia Duerst-Lahti refers to these relations as "gender power relations."

> Gender relations then can more correctly be named gender power relations. In American society, at least, all avenues of public power—political, financial, technical, coercive, forced—and the organizations used in their administration have been controlled by males. An important byproduct of men's dominant institutional power is their ability to allocate social values and, as many would argue, a self-justifying ideology. That is, the male hegemonic position has enabled them to structure institutions, create laws, establish moral codes, and shape culture in ways which perpetuate their power over women.[3]

The central value of these gender power relations is, of course, the notion of male superiority, with its emphasis on the dichotomous elements of the relations between the two sexes. Moreover, Western civilization has been constructed upon the idea of a patriarchy, or a social system in which the male dominates the female. The entire social system has been centered upon men's "preordained" suitability to lead all society.

> The structure of societal domination refers to the fabric of rules, systems of values, and interests and norms which have been defined as correct

and ingrained in individuals through socialization. Patriarchy has been the predominant instrument in the construction of American society. Few women have participated in the definition process, but when they did, it was under pre-existing conditions established by dominant men. So organizations, which operate within society, do so within the parameters of patriarchy—"The whole system of male authority."[4]

Thus a central and accepted societal belief (created by men) is that men should hold dominant positions, both in society and in its organizations. A consequence of such a structure, as Erika Apfelbaum has noted, is that the dominant groups emphasize the disparity between themselves and others, particularly highlighting the inferiority of others in order to justify the dominant group's control and the dependency of the subordinate group.[5] Men are portrayed as aggressive and fit to lead, thus women must be the opposite, or peaceful and not fit for leadership. Women who attempt to exercise power must confront the ingrained belief that men should dominate women, and thus must overcome the resulting behaviors and resentment.[6]

Many of these beliefs have changed little over time, and, in general, men and their attributes are still more valued by the entire society than women and their supposed unique skills. Two specific aspects of this social bifurcation are the similar, but not equivalent, practices of sex roles and gender stereotypes (or social norms). Sex roles refer to male-female differences which are generally seen as biologically determined, while gender stereotypes are beliefs about the consequences of sex differences, beliefs which are culturally or socially determined, and which lead to social codes of appropriate behavior for, and attitudes about, each gender.

Sex Roles

Sex role stereotypes include two large categories: (1) personality traits associated with and considered appropriate for men or for women; and (2) behaviors associated with and considered appropriate for men or for women.

Constantina Safilios-Rothschild[7]

Traditional sex roles emphasize the differences rather than similarities between women and men, and they have had a profound impact upon relations between women and men in all spheres of life. These differences are typically assumed to be biologically determined, or innate.

First and foremost in this spectrum of beliefs has been the insistence on the basic and pervasive difference between men and women—that reproductive differences should be the main basis for the classification of all traits. . . . Sociobiologists, like social philosophers, churchmen, and others before them, argue that the division of labor by sex is a biological rather than a social response.[8]

This emphasis on biologically determined sex roles has been called "essentialism" by Ann Snitow.[9] Virginia Sapiro has provided a more detailed description of these sex roles:

> It is common for people to talk about male and female "biological roles" in the family. "Biological role" generally refers to a wide variety of behaviors encompassing sexual and reproductive behavior as well as the tendency for women to do the bulk of childraising and to de-emphasize other economic roles, and the tendency for men to specialize in other economic roles and do comparatively little childcare.[10]

As Betty Friedan noted, in the years after World War II this conception of sex roles, or the "feminine mystique," became the cherished and self-perpetuating core of contemporary American culture.

> The feminine mystique says that the highest value and the only commitment for women is the fulfillment of their own femininity. . . . It says this femininity is so mysterious and intuitive and close to the creation and origin of life that man-made science may never be able to understand it. . . . The mistake, says the mystique, the root of women's troubles in the past is that women envied men, women tried to be like men, instead of accepting their own nature, which can find fulfillment only in sexual passivity, male domination, and nurturing maternal love.[11]

While Friedan's own book challenged this cultural view, most women clung to it during the 1950s, apparently willing to let men have all the power in the public world outside the home.[12]

Sociobiologists have recently updated the feminine mystique to argue that men are more suited, biologically, to be business leaders and politicians. Drawing on cross-cultural research, studies of nonhuman primates, and endocrinology, sociobiologists argue that male aggressiveness and female passivity and a host of other gender-linked differences are to be expected biologically.[13] Dean Jaros and Elizabeth S. White, for instance, posit that hormones might be behind males' greater willingness to support wars, to be politically active, and to focus on national and international politics.[14] Others have relied on the research of sociobiologists to explain the greater success of men in achieving political office and of women in being the primary parent. Glendon Schubert, for instance, claims:

The attitudes and associated behaviors relating to both aggressiveness and sexual potency in primate males are transactionalized in the brain in complex ways that we are only beginning to understand. The male attitudes and behaviors that define the major problems of both international and domestic politics, on a global basis, are mixed up with male aggressiveness and sexuality as well as with the bifurcation in structure and function of the male brain.[15]

However, as was noted in the Introduction, this concept of innate sex roles has been challenged on a number of fronts. One such area is anthropology. Based on studies of sex roles across different cultures and different periods, many authors have concluded that sex roles have not been the same, and thus they have challenged the notion that most sex roles are biologically determined.[16] As Virginia Sapiro concluded: "In fact, the only strictly biological portion of this entire system is that only women can bear children and lactate. All of the rest are at least largely social conventions and institutional arrangements. . . ."[17] Cynthia Fuchs Epstein reasoned further that if roles were biologically determined, then sex role assignments would not have to be coercive.[18] Similarly, others, including Gary Powell, have also agreed that these Western roles are not innate, but moreover, that they have been specifically economically determined. Early American society, Powell and others have argued, did not function with separate sex roles. Men and women both worked on the family farm, often sharing responsibility for growing the food and raising the children. Only with the Industrial Revolution did sex roles become distinct, with men going out of the home to work and women staying at home with the prime family responsibility for housekeeping and childbearing. This sex-role division, adopted by middle-class families who could afford a wife who was not working, thus became over time the basis for "traditional" sex roles. [19]

Likewise, in rejecting many of the beliefs about sex roles, a psychological study by Maccoby and Jacklin found only three major possibly innate sex differences: boys' greater mathematical and visual-spatial ability; girls' greater verbal ability; and boys' greater aggression. Theoretically, these differences could influence the kinds of occupations that boys and girls choose and their behavior within these careers.[20] Additional analysis of this category of research over time, however, suggests that the magnitude of even these limited discrepancies is declining.[21] Moreover, many scholars have argued that even these limited differences may not be biologically determined. Janet Shibley Hyde, for instance, reports that meta-analysis of numerous studies of gender differences does not always support Maccoby and Jacklin's early research. More specifically, gender discrepancies in cognitive abilities are generally found to be minimal, with only some limited aspects of spatial and mathematical ability showing any modest disparities between men and women, and verbal ability differences tending to be insignificant.[22] Additionally, differences in aggression and helping behaviors turn out to be more a reflection of the study, the researcher (male researchers find more differences), and the methods used to measure the behaviors than any real sex differences. Still other researchers have criticized the methodological biases of many of the studies that have claimed to have discovered a biological basis for sex roles. Denise Baer and David Bositis, for instance, have systematically dismantled the research and the results of endocrine-based explanations (male androgens and menstruation) on the political behavior patterns of men and women.[23]

After a careful analysis of the data, other scholars have suggested that the disparities that exist could just as easily be explained by socialization differences. Powell, for instance, raised the question as to whether females' greater communication skills could be a result of the fact that they tend to have lower status. Forced into weaker positions, women have to monitor others' reactions to them in order to survive. He thus reasoned that even when sex differences exist, they might frequently be accounted for by situational factors other than sex.[24] Similarly, Cynthia Fuchs Epstein concluded in her review of sex differences in aggression "that aggressive and nonaggressive behaviors are tied to social roles," not biological differences.[25]

While many researchers who study male-female differences thus doubt the biological or sex-role basis of any disparities, feminists themselves, as we saw in the discussion of the debate between minimizers and maximizers, are often split over whether differences in aggression are transitory social products, or more permanent traits to be nurtured and maintained. Although most feminists, even the maximizers, are doubtful about the biological origins of differences between men and women and favor an explanation that relies on a psycho-socialization begun early in life, often their discussion seems indistinguishable from a biological-based discussion of sex roles.

Gender Stereotypes/Social Norms

Women encounter problems "based largely on nonconscious beliefs and attitudes about them as a group which guide behavior and cloud perceptions of women as individuals."

Georgia Duerst-Lahti[26]

Stereotypes create a self-fulfilling prophecy in that others' behavior is mediated by the expectation created by the stereotype.

Cynthia Fuchs Epstein[27]

Even if one rejects the significance of most biologically determined sex differences between women and men, one is still left with the issue of gender stereotypes, or the sociologically determined beliefs about gender differences. These beliefs about sex differences include a much wider range of characteristics than actual sex differences, and have a much larger effect, particularly in terms of formation of occupational aspirations, expectations and success.[28] As Georgia Duerst-Lahti has noted, the entire fabric of society has been organized around gender stereotypes, and these stereotypes set the parameters within which individuals function by establishing differing patterns of behavior which are acceptable for men and women. Similarly, Epstein argues:

> Socialization contributes to sex segregation by creating in males and females specific orientations, preferences, and competencies for occupations that have been defined as sex-appropriate, while leaving men and women disinclined toward or ignorant of opportunities to pursue other occupations.[29]

Though gender stereotypes include a number of elements, we shall limit our discussion to the three which are most applicable to our topic: the relationship of women to work; views on the suitability of foreign policy and its related fields for women; and society's expectations about men's and women's interests and capabilities.

Women and Work

As Powell, who is quoted in the introduction to Section I indicated, one of the critical gender stereotypes or social norms which impacts on women's careers is the prevailing view concerning the acceptability or desirability of women working outside the home. It is often hard, in the late twentieth century when close to 60 percent of all women work, to remember that this phenomenon is relatively new and its acceptance by American society even more recent. Young women thinking about their future in the 1930s would have been immersed in a culture that strongly opposed women, especially wives, working. A poll taken in 1936, for instance, indicated that only 15 percent of a national sample accepted a married woman having a full-time job outside the home.[30] In 1938, 81 percent of men and 75 percent women did not approve of a married woman working if she had a husband capable of supporting her.[31] In the same era, Norman Cousins even advocated this cure for the nation's economic problems: "Simply fire the women, who shouldn't be working anyway, and hire the men. Presto! No unemployment, No relief rolls. No depression."[32] Many officials agreed with Cousins. For example, in 1940 "three-fourths of the school systems refused to hire married women as teachers. Lawmakers in 26 states debated whether to bar them from state jobs. Nor could they expect a hand from organized labor."[33]

While the percentage of the population accepting married women's employment rose dramatically in the 1940s as a result of World War II (by 1945, 38.1 percent of all women were in the civilian labor force, accounting for more than one third of all workers),[34] public views were slow to change. As late as 1972, 37 percent of all men and 31 percent of all women interviewed still were against a married women working if she had a husband capable of supporting her.[35] The Women's Movement directly challenged limitations on women wishing to work, and the public increasingly accepted a place for women in the marketplace. Yet more than a fifth of the public (21 percent of men and 23 percent of women) surveyed in 1986 still disapproved of a married woman working if her husband could support her.[36] Because the public's views have changed only recently on this issue, most people currently in the work force were raised and socialized to relegate women to the home.[37] Moreover, although in the 1990s only a minority overtly object to a married woman working, there is still a strong belief that it would be preferable if a woman placed her husband's wishes and her children's needs ahead of her career. For instance, in a 1989 national poll, 62 percent of all women and 55 percent of all men responded that a wife should quit her job if the husband was transferred.[38] On the other hand, only 29 percent of the women and 28 percent of the men in the same national sample felt a husband should quit his job and relocate if his wife was offered a very good job in another city.[39] Relatedly, 64 percent of the population in a 1990 national poll felt it was better for the children if the mother stayed home and the father worked, and 41 percent thought it would be better for everyone involved if the man was the achiever outside the home and the woman took care of the home and family.[40] Correspondingly, employed women's devalued status is also reflected in the salary differential between women and men. In 1990, a white, college-educated female earned an average of $27,440, while the males earned $41,090. White women without a college degree earned $16,910, while men earned $26,510.[41]

Confronted by these views about the restricted and distinctly secondary place work is supposed to have in their lives, many women in the past chose not to work. Today, fewer women have the option of not working due to the rising costs of having a family and a home. A 1989 *New York Times Poll*, for instance, reported that 48 percent of all women with full-time jobs indicated that the loss of their job would have a major financial impact on their families. Additionally, 60 percent said they worked primarily to support themselves or their family.[42] The push to stay home or focus on family needs, however, results in many women not working (more than 40 percent), and a considerable number of all women (35 percent) preferring a life-style which does not involve a career.[43] Those who are employed, moreover, are more likely than men to see their employment as "jobs" not "careers."[44] Additionally, those women who wish to pursue a life as a professional may expect to encounter difficulties being accepted in the workplace, and managing family and work responsibilities. Indeed, a national sample of working men and women interviewed in 1989 reported that women who worked still took on the major responsibility for food shopping, cooking, housecleaning, paying bills, and taking care of dependent children.[45] Not surprisingly, 43 percent of the women surveyed in this same poll felt their spouse had more free time for themselves than they did.[46] While we might assume that the conflict between work and family would have been even more of a problem in the decades before the Women's Movement, the persistent stereotypes about the place of work in women's lives suggest that even younger women should anticipate some problems.

Women and Occupational Stereotyping

The second, and perhaps more interesting, facet of gender stereotyping is the issue of the suitability of women for certain types of occupations. Just as there has been hostility toward women working, there has also been the belief that women were not sufficiently capable for certain types of occupations. Women's opportunities have been particularly restricted in areas customarily dominated by men, especially those conferring high status and significant rewards. "In the occupational sphere, where men clearly hold power, the exclusion of women has been most clear-cut and severe in cases of jobs that men prize."[47] Politics especially has been seen as an area of utmost importance and thus has been prized, and dominated, by men. Even more than politics in general, foreign policy in particular has been seen as the preserve of men. It has been assumed that only men can serve as diplomats for the king or government, and diplomacy has been portrayed as the job of men in high hats and striped pants. For example, in the 1930s, more than half of the public did not approve of women being appointed to Roosevelt's cabinet or serving as a senator, governor, or member of the Supreme Court.[48] In 1949, the public was asked specifically about a woman being appointed as an ambassador, and 34 percent disapproved (39 percent of the men and 28 percent of the women).[49] More recent polls have shown a growing acceptance of women holding positions of authority in government, yet large minorities of the public would not vote for a woman for President or other high public office and many have doubts about the ability of women to manage the demands of an important government position (see below). Thus, we need to ask why women have been seen as so unsuited to foreign affairs.

Jean Bethke Elshtain has written extensively on this question. In her seminal work, *Women and War*, she contends that the exclusion of women from war, and by extension the crafting of foreign policy, can be traced to cultural stereotypes of women as "beautiful souls" and men as "just warriors."[50] Women, Elshtain proposes, have since at least the eighteenth century been portrayed in Western culture as nonaggressive, peace-loving, and incapable of military action. Men, in contrast, are depicted as possessing the characteristics necessary for military leadership and fighting.[51] Elshtain describes the situation as follows:

> We in the West are heirs to a tradition that assumes an affinity between women and peace, between men and war, a tradition that consists of culturally constructed and transmitted myths and memories. Thus, in time of war, real men and women . . . take . . . the personas of Just Warriors and Beautiful Souls. Men construed as violent, whether eagerly and inevitably or reluctantly and tragically; women as nonviolent, offering succor and compassion: these tropes . . . do not denote what men and women *really* are in time of war, but function instead to re-create and secure women's location as noncombatants and men's as warriors.[52]

As Elshtain notes these stereotypes are often oversimplifications, as many women have fought in and supported their nation's wars, while some men have been pacifists and vocal opponents of armed conflict. Moreover as Antonia Fraser describes in her book *The Warrior Queens*, in virtually every culture there have been examples of fictional or factual sovereign women who have led their nations in war, though these are relatively rare. When such women appear, they represent a paradox, consisting of public admiration and enthusiasm on one hand, versus disgust and fear on the other. This "frisson" is partially caused by the fact that the "concept of the Warrior Queen cuts across not only man's view of woman's traditional weakness but also woman's view of her own ordained role as a peacemaker."[53] Thus the public response to these remarkable women is to emphasize their uniqueness, their difference from other women: "this woman is not like other women, runs the refrain; this being so, her strangeness should be established from the start."[54] This cultural view that only men have the ability to confront the enemy in battle is the underpinning of the exclusion of women from the conduct of foreign affairs, because the practices of soldiership and citizenship have been intimately linked. More specifically, the right to participate in the making of a country's foreign policy has been conditioned by the ability to fight in a country's wars.

This connection began with the Greeks who were frequently engaged in conflict with neighboring city-states. For them war was politics and politics was war.[55] Given this equation, warriors were the best citizens and rulers. Even though Plato's vision of the guardian-warrior included women, subsequent political philosophers with few exceptions (such as John Stuart Mill) developed a model of citizenship and political leadership which equated these roles with the ability to physically defend the republic or nation-state.[56] Writers as diverse as Machiavelli, Rousseau, and Hegel drew a picture of the ideal citizen which left out women since they could not fulfill the requirements needed to be a warrior. Elshtain explains, "Men alone, for civic republicans like Machiavelli and Rousseau, have the bodies of defenders; they alone can serve as soldiers."[57] For Machiavelli, women lacked the proper nature to engage in war and politics.[58] Rousseau limited women's role to raising sons who would be sufficiently attached to the state to defend it with their lives. Women, in Rousseau's politics, should be patriotic but they could not be patriots.[59] Hegel, the originator of the modern idea of loyalty to the nation-state, also drew linkages between the willingness to go to war for one's country, citizenship and maleness.[60]

The founders of the United States drew heavily on this philosophical tradition in drafting the new constitution, and thus they too believed in the tie between citizenship and war fighting. Sarah Livingston Jay, wife of John Jay, prepared the following toast for the new nation which embodied the logic of its intellectual forebearers: "May all our Citizens be Soldiers, and all our Soldiers Citizens."[61] While people like Abigail Adams argued that women also should be given full citizen rights in the new republic, most women accepted the view that politics, war and by extension foreign policy were properly the arena for men.[62]

Americans in the twentieth century have not completely rid themselves of this philosophical foundation. Even though the advent of the Women's Movement has instigated dramatic improvements in the public's notions about what jobs women can hold, stereotypes still persist, often most strongly, about women in defense and foreign affairs positions. For instance, a 1989 survey asked a national sample if women in public office could do a better, worse, or just as good a job as men in several select areas. As Table 1-1 indicates, 58 percent of men and 42 percent of women thought a woman would do a worse job than a man in directing the military, 23 percent of men and 17 percent of women thought a woman would not be as good as a man in conducting diplomatic relations with other nations, and 37 percent of men and 24 percent of women believed a woman would be worse in making decisions about going to war. Interest-

Table 1-1. Percentage of the public who report women in public office would do a better or worse job than men in selected areas of public policy[a]

Area	% Women (Men) believing women would do a better job than men	% Women (Men) believing women would do a worse job than men
Directing the military	6 (3)	42 (58)
Conducting diplomatic relations with other countries	14 (10)	17 (23)
Making decisions on whether or not to go to war	18 (12)	24 (37)
Working for peace in the world	38 (32)	5 (8)
Maintaining honesty and integrity in government	38 (31)	5 (7)
Negotiating with our trading partners, such as Western Europe, Canada and Japan	10 (6)	15 (25)
Protecting the environment	30 (31)	7 (8)
Assisting the poor	49 (46)	4 (5)
Improving our educational system	48 (46)	3 (4)

Data from the 1990 Virginia Slims American Women's Opinion Poll. Survey conducted by The Roper Organization. Data provided by The Roper Center for Public Opinion Research.

[a] The question asked was as follows: "When it comes to _____, do you feel that women in public office would do a better job than men, a worse job than men, or just as good as job as men in public office?" Figures represent the percentage of women (men) who indicate women would do a better or worse job than men.

ingly, 38 percent of women and 32 percent of men surveyed thought women in public office would do a better job than men working for peace in the world. Nearly identical proportions (38 percent and 31 percent respectively for women and men) responded that women would be better at maintaining honesty and integrity in government. Women were also expected to do a good job in managing domestic concerns like education, the environment, and helping the poor.[63]

Thus, it is not politics per se for which women are perceived as ill equipped but politics in which conflict or the use of force would be involved, which is the very essence of international relations in the twentieth century. This table is compelling evidence of the persistence of stereotypes about the supposedly more peaceful, domestic nature of women and their inability to engage in aggressive behavior.

Further support for the existence of these stereotypes can be seen in the recent controversy about allowing women, or forcing women, to be drafted or to serve in military combat. A 1982 poll conducted during a national debate on the draft found 53.4 percent of the public agreed that if a draft were reinstituted young women as well as young men should be drafted.[64] In this same survey, however, only 34.7 percent of the people questioned thought women in the military should be assigned to positions as soldiers in hand-to-hand combat.[65] Many more were willing, however, to allow women to be crew members on combat ships (57.4 percent), commander of a large base (58.7 percent), missile gunner (59.2 percent), jet fighter pilot (62.4 percent), and jet transport pilot (72.7 percent). Not surprisingly, virtually everyone was willing to let women serve as military truck mechanics (83.4 percent), nurses in combat zones (93.7 percent), and typists in the Pentagon (97.4 percent).[66]

In the aftermath of the invasion of Panama and of Operation Desert Storm there has been considerable discussion about the combat role of women in the military. Reporters covering both conflicts wrote of the key roles played by women in the modern military. Moreover, while 63 percent of the public approved of women being involved in combat in Panama, at the beginning of hostilities in the Persian Gulf only 47 percent thought women should participate if the ground fighting began.[67] After the war was over, however, the issue of combat exclusion was taken up by some members of Congress, notably Representative Patricia Schroeder, who said that the policy of excluding women from combat was an anachronism. She introduced legislation to open up some formerly closed job titles, potentially involving women in combat. The resulting opposition from the public, politicians, and military leaders was testimony to the deep-seated beliefs about women, men and war. While only 44 percent of the public, in one poll, rejected the assignment of women to ground combat units, a majority believed only women who wanted such assignments should be given them.[68] Moreover, 89 percent expressed concern about women leaving small children at home, 53 percent doubted women would be able to perform at the same level as men, and 51 percent thought allowing women to serve as infantry soldiers would be a burden on the military.[69] A leading male politician who opposed women in combat was quoted as saying. "If I had 200 fighter pilots and Amelia Earhart came along ... I would still pick the men."[70] Other politicians were willing to allow women to fly combat missions but were reluctant to place women in ground combat positions. Senator John McCain, a former test pilot, was among the leading opponents of extending combat to women. He argued, "We're proud of the role women played in the Persian Gulf War."[71] However, he claimed, unlike pilots, "the overwhelming majority of enlisted women in the Army and Marine Corps do not wish to be in combat."[72]

The men from the Pentagon representing the various branches of the military were in agreement that lifting the combat exclusion would not be a good idea, arguing the "current policy is sound."[73] A presidential commission to make recommendations on whether the combat exclusion rules should be changed was established by the 1992 defense authorization bill. Its report was to be issued in late 1992.[74] Until the policy is changed, however, negative attitudes about women's combat abilities, in addition to the congressionally imposed limitations on women in combat, will continue to severely restrict women's progress in the military and, as we shall see, their ability to wield authority in the Department of Defense.

In yet another example of how these stereotypes limit women in politics, Shelia Tobias examined the electoral success of veterans of wars (men) and women candidates running for Congress in the aftermath of World War II, the Korean conflict, and the Vietnam War. Tobias found that male candidates with experience in the wars were able to win over incumbent women members of Congress and women running for the first time for Congress. Her research thus showed quite convincingly that the voters act as if they believe that war fighting, especially in a popular war, will make the male veterans better public officials.[75] The durability of this stereotype was also in evidence during the 1992 Presidential campaign, throughout which the Republican party attempted to argue that President Bush's service in World War II made him a more fit leader than Bill Clinton, who had avoided military service in Vietnam.

Society's perceptions of foreign policy as a career unsuited to women is furthered by the general belief that women are less knowledgeable than men about foreign affairs. Public opinion polls have generally found much higher levels of information and opinion on foreign policy issues among men than women, and as a result, both the public and policy-makers tend to assume that all women are less knowledgeable than men. This attitude was perhaps most succinctly revealed in comments by Donald Regan, Ronald Reagan's Chief of Staff. At the first summit meeting between Reagan and Gorbachev at Geneva, he told reporters that women would rather read the "human interest stuff" about Nancy and Raisa, and would not "understand throw weights or what is happening in Afghanistan or what is happening in human rights."[76] California Assemblywoman Maxine Waters was quick to note that opinions like Regan's are clearly detrimental to women wishing to influence diplomatic policy. "To indicate that women don't have the intellectual capability to understand what's happening here is certainly an insult. It means someone is trying to make us believe we don't know enough to be involved and it would be a sad state of affairs if people really believe the myth."[77] Unfortunately, of course, many citizens and public officials do believe "the myth." This belief is augmented by the cultural stereotype that women lack an aggressive demeanor, and thus the ability to negotiate with, or stand up to, an enemy. Geraldine Ferraro encountered these stereotypes when she ran for Vice President. In her 1984 televised debate with George Bush, she was asked:

> Congresswoman Ferraro, you have little or no experience in military matters and yet you might some day find yourself Commander-in-Chief of the Armed Forces. How can you convince the American people and the potential enemy that you would know what to do to protect this nation's security, and do you think in any way that the Soviets might be tempted to try to take advantage of you simply because you are a woman?[78]

The questioner was voicing the doubts of millions of Americans. The president, as Commander-in-Chief of the military and *de facto* head of the foreign policy apparatus, must be able to commit the nation to war and/or face down an enemy who wants to engage in armed conflict. Ferraro's questioner and a sizable sector of the public seem to doubt that a woman could fill these roles.[79] A 1990 national survey, for instance, found 33 percent of all men and 21 percent of all women claimed they would be *less* likely to vote for the woman candidate for President of the United States if two people of equal qualifications were running for this office.[80] Similarly, when asked to list the major reasons why there are so few women in high public office like senator or governor, the single most important reason was that many Americans are not ready to elect a woman to higher office, cited by 65 percent of the women and 61 percent of the men polled.[81] Thus, while attitudes are changing we still have a long way to go, and women seeking careers in foreign policy will continue to find themselves hampered by persistent stereotypes about the appropriateness of careers in this field for women.

Women and Their Work Abilities

The final area of gender stereotyping of particular interest in looking at women in foreign policy concerns societal expectations about women's interpersonal skills, or capabilities as managers. Women's historical and philosophical disqualification from citizenship, and thus from participation in international issues, has been supplemented by other cultural stereotypes, often endorsed by psychologists, pseudo-psychologists, and sociobiologists concerning women's abilities to hold high positions and direct other people. Gender stereotypes have led to conclusions about differing patterns of behavior between men and women. Traditional stereotypes suggest that women should behave in a "feminine" manner, in accordance with these presumed feminine attributes; and that men should behave in a "masculine" manner, in accordance with their presumed masculine attributes.[82] Most authors have synthesized these gender stereotypes into the conclusions that women are more nurturant, or that men are better leaders.[83] For example, women have been regarded as the "social specialists" or the more expressive members of society, whereas men have been regarded as the "task specialists," or the more instrumental group members, since males are seen as more competent at tasks than females. Correspondingly, women have also been regarded by many people as possessing a special ability to sense the feelings and thoughts of others ("women's intuition"). Powell disputed this stereotype by noting that in at least one study, women had no advantage over men in sensitivity to others. Instead, he argued that individuals in the subordinate role, regardless of sex, were more sensitive to leaders than leaders were to subordinates. He reasoned that because women have been in the subordinate role in our society more frequently than men, what has been called "women's intuition" might more appropriately be called "subordinates' intuition."[84] However, the stereotype of women as more successful in relationships than at tasks persists.

Strongly held negative stereotypes about women managers is a particular problem for women who seek positions in the upper echelons of the government. In 1946, for instance, a national poll found 50 percent of men (32 percent of women) believed women had less ability to make decisions than men. Nearly as large percentages (44 percent and 28 percent, respectively, for men and women) also felt women would be less likely to handle people well.[85] Surveys taken in the 1950s and 1970s found large majorities of men and women, if given a choice, preferred a man rather than a woman as a boss. In 1975, for instance 63 percent of men and 60 percent of women preferred a man, while only 4 percent and 10 percent respectively chose a woman boss.[86] While these figures improved in the 1980s, as recently as 1987, 37 percent of all women and 29 percent of all men preferred a man as a boss.[87] A Virginia Slims Poll conducted in 1989 asked people to indicate whether they associated certain traits with a female or male boss, or top manager. Among those seeing a difference between men and women bosses (generally over 40 percent of the sample), men thought men bosses or managers would be better than women bosses or managers on ten of the 14 attributes. Even women gave men the advantage on seven of the items.[88] As Table 1-2 reveals, men were generally seen as tougher, more well informed, more decisive, better in dealing with competitors and unions, and more respected by those who report to them. Women bosses were given the advantage in the areas of honesty, concern with workers rights and employees' personal problems.

These stereotypes about the management abilities of women and men correspond rather closely to those we encountered earlier, relative to

Table 1-2.   Percentage of women (and men) who associate certain characteristics with a female or male boss or top manager[a]

Characteristic	Associated with female boss % women (% men)	Associated with male boss % women (% men)
Hard worker	22 (10)	18 (33)
Toughness	10 (6)	47 (59)
Honesty	35 (26)	7 (10)
Intelligence	18 (11)	7 (14)
Concerned about workers rights	38 (31)	9 (14)
Well-informed on business issues	9 (6)	30 (36)
Sensitive to employees' personal problems	49 (45)	7 (11)
Effective in dealing with competitors	10 (6)	31 (40)
Decisive	14 (7)	25 (38)
Loyal to their employees	29 (22)	9 (17)
Effective in dealing with labor unions	8 (5)	41 (49)
Able to delegate responsibility	15 (7)	20 (32)
Respected by the people who report to them	12 (18)	26 (34)
Take a long-term view of things	19 (12)	18 (27)

Data from the 1990 Virginia Slims American Women's Opinion Poll. Survey conducted by the Roper Organization. Data provided by the Roper Center for Public Opinion Research.

[a] The question asked was as follows: "Now I'm going to read you a list of words and phrases. Thinking about the business world, for each one, would you tell me if you associate it more with a female boss or top manager, or more with a male boss or top manager?" Figures indicate the percentage of women (men) who respond they associated the trait more with a female or male boss.

women in public affairs. They indicate that the public perceives women as better equipped to handle the "soft" issues in politics and management (poverty and employees' personal issues), but not the "hard" issues involving conflict (managing the military or dealing with competitors and labor unions). Interestingly, many women and men (48 percent and 63 percent, respectively, in a national poll), believe that when women get into positions of authority in business and industry, they will not change the way business is conducted, nor make it more gentle.[89] Indeed, both men and women agree that if women are to be as successful on the job as men, they will need to adopt a management style similar to that of men. In this vein, a 1989 New York Times Poll found 63 percent of the women and 70 percent of the men agreeing that when women hold positions of real authority, they have to be just as tough as men to succeed.[90] Yet if they do, then they no longer fit the "feminine" stereotype. Supreme Court Justice Brennan summarized this dilemma, "Women are out of a job if they behave aggressively and out of a job if they don't."[91] The effects of these managerial stereotypes can be seen throughout the business world, which restricts women's access to leadership positions. In 1989, only 39.8 percent of all executive, administrative, and managerial positions in the United States were held by women, up from 32.4 percent in 1983.[92] Even though the trend is positive, since women managers are often concentrated in traditional women's fields (education, health, personnel), it still means that in many settings there are very few women at the management level to serve as models and mentors. (This is especially true in the foreign policy arena as we shall see in Chapter 2.) Rosabeth Moss Kanter's research suggests that when women are placed in isolated management positions or have "token" status, they are often subject to the most extreme forms of stereotyping.[93] The consequence of these views of women's management abilities is that women at work often feel they are not treated fairly or with respect. Indeed, a national survey found 53 percent of women (38 percent of men) agreeing with the statement that "at work, most men don't take women seriously."[94] Similarly, 57 percent of women (41 percent of men) still believe that "men still run everything and usually don't include women when important decisions are made."[95]

In conclusion, sex roles and gender stereotypes have emphasized the notions that: women should not work outside the home, or at least women should place family and spouse before work; foreign policy is not a suitable field for women; women are less knowledgeable about foreign affairs; and males are better managers, while females have better social or nurturant skills. The culmination of these views is widespread discrimination against women seeking jobs in government and managerial positions. A national survey in 1990, for instance, found that when presented with a list of 11 areas where women faced discrimination, more than half of the women claimed women faced problems in obtaining jobs in government (64 percent), executive positions in business (61 percent), top jobs in the professions (58 percent), and top jobs in the military services (55 percent). Just under 50 percent of the same sample claimed women also faced discrimination when they tried to assume leadership responsibility in groups of men and women.[96] Indeed, 90 percent of the women in the same poll believed major changes (45 percent) or some changes (45 percent) were needed with respect to opportunities for women for leadership positions in government in the next ten years.[97] These attitudes suggest the parameters under which the women managers at State and Defense must function. We should expect to find that women who seek management positions in foreign policy face a double set of stereotypes. Neither their policy expertise nor their management abilities are seen by large segments of the population as preparing them for successfully conducting the affairs of the nation-state.

The Impact of Societal Factors
on Women in Foreign Policy Formulation

> My influence at this time is not the same as a man's influence. There are the normal set of attitudes. They are not held by everybody, by any means, but they still exist. There is the attitude that there is an inability of women to quite understand the military side of life. There is an attitude that it is somewhat unnatural for women to be working. There is an attitude that one's prestige with one's male colleagues is negatively affected by working with or for a woman. There is an attitude that it is OK to hold these attitudes. This is the particular piece of the culture in which I work. It is by no means the majority of men I am talking about, it is just a few but they still exist and are tolerated at my level of government. Some of them are very nice people, but they are not going to change where they are coming from.
>
> *Woman interviewed at the Pentagon*

As the quote above makes clear, for women at State and Defense, the societal attitudes we have reviewed are very much a part of the workplace. However, in reference to sex role stereotypes, we found little evidence in the responses of the men and women we interviewed at the State and Defense Departments to support the view that women and men are biologically or innately different. Specifically, we asked each of our women interviewees if there were any special traits that she, *as a woman*, had that affected her influence on foreign policy. A parallel question was asked of men regarding any special traits that they might have, *as men*, that would shape their influence on foreign policy. While 74.4 percent of the women and 44.1 percent of the men claimed they had special traits, about one third of the responses described the trait as an *individual* trait, and not as a *female* or a *male* trait, and about ten percent specifically claimed that the traits that were necessary for success were not gender specific. Moreover, of the remainder who did see gender differences (about half of the women and half of the men who listed a trait), none referred to the difference as a product of biology or innate differences, and indeed a couple people noted that whatever special traits existed were a product of socialization, not hormones or genetics. One woman at Defense, for instance, commenting on her better listening and communication skills reasoned that these were probably traceable to her mother, "Better listening skills and communication skills, not inherent in women but social-ization. . . . My mother had good communication skills. Thinking about it, my brothers probably have equally good communication skills as I do." Moreover, two-thirds of the men who cited a gender trait discussed their military background, clearly a product of a socialization experience. Though our respondents rejected most sex roles, the belief in the preor-dained role of men to lead, and in the subordinate status of women, was not entirely absent. The annual evaluation of one of our respondents reflected not only her superior's concern with her innate characteristics, but also the conclusion that merely being a woman was detrimental.

> She is well proportioned, attractive, and somewhat shorter than average. As with all female Foreign Service Officers, she feels keenly the fact that in her career she is constantly competing with men, and I think this factor is basic to any assessment of any officer of her sex in the foreign service. In my opinion, she wears this *albatross* as well as most of her counterparts in the service.

While acceptance of sex role stereotyping as innate biological difference was minimal, we saw more influence of gender stereotypes or social norms. Though the majority of our respondents did not accept the validity of these stereotypes, they acknowledged the impact that these stereotypes have had on them. Recalling that the first stereotype we examined dealt with the view that women should not work, or at least that their career should take second place to marriage or family, we found little evidence of this attitude among our respondents. Most of the women in our sample began their work in government at an early age, generally right after graduation from college, and have stayed on the job ever since, even while starting a family. As we shall see in Chapter 3, many of these women were attracted to government *because* it allowed them to work in a professional position. They chose to have a career rather than to stay at home, prefer-ring the demands of that position to the other alternatives available.

However, several of the women in our sample indicated that they en-dured resistance to their working based on the stereotype that they should be staying home. This dilemma was described by one woman in response to a question asking whether she had experienced discrimi-nation.

> It will almost sound silly, but when I first came back to work, I guess my job interview would never pass muster today. I was told "The women who work here aren't, in large number, very good. What makes you think you'll be able to work the overtime?" At the time I had two small children and subsequent to that I was working very long hours, the same person,

> my boss, said to me, "You must be a terrible wife and mother because
> you are here all the time."

Obviously this woman faced a difficult time, not only in balancing her
career and family obligations, but also in confronting the negative views
of her superior regarding her dual roles. Even though our sample of
women ignored stereotypes about working, the subsidiary expectation,
that women should subordinate their careers to the needs of their spouse
and children, did impact on them. One political appointee was quick to
admit, for instance, that she delayed the high-powered stage of her career
while her children were young.

> I would not have done this [taken the appointment] if they [her children]
> had been younger. My husband was the greatest supporter. . . . If they
> [the children] were young he would have probably said, "You go, I'll raise
> them." But there is a certain point when you wouldn't have done that,
> when they were little. I just couldn't do it.

In Chapter 3 we shall specifically discuss how women have managed the
problems of combining parenthood and career priorities.

The second stereotype, the conception of women as unsuited for certain types of occupations, especially politics and military service, has
certainly kept some women out of foreign policy, and has had a significant
impact upon the Insider women within the process. Individuals tend to
make choices from among the socially structured alternatives available.
As Epstein noted, men have recognized that they derive an advantage
from the general exclusion of women from spheres in which they might
accumulate resources, or that would give them the basis for independence.[98] Politics is such a realm. As was discussed earlier, many women
have been deterred from even considering a career in foreign affairs by
the general stereotypes of this as a career unsuitable for women. In the
next chapter, we shall explore the specific means men have adopted
to ensure that women would not be allowed into the foreign policy
establishments. The result of both of these barriers is that the percentage
of women in positions of authority in both Departments has remained
very low.

Moreover, the stereotype of foreign policy as a male preserve, coupled
with the notion that women are not knowledgeable about foreign affairs,
were the societal factors which created the most difficulties for the women
in our foreign policy sample. In terms of the latter, we asked respondents
if they thought that the public believed women knew as much, more, or
less about foreign policy than men (results reported in Table 1-3).

Both women and men indicated that the public generally stereotyped

Table 1-3. Attitudes toward women's knowledge of foreign affairs[a]

	Women	Men
Percent agreeing that the *public* believes women know less about foreign affairs	94.3	71.9
Percent stating that *they* believe women know less about foreign affairs	22.2	11.1
Percent agreeing that the public's view about women's knowledge of foreign affairs limits their own influence/ or influence of women in their Department	27.8	20.6

[a] Responses are based on the following questions:

Do you think *the public* believes women know as much about foreign affairs as men, or do you think the public believes women know more about foreign affairs, or less about foreign affairs than men?

Do you believe that women, in general, know as much about foreign affairs as men, or do women know more about foreign affairs, or less about foreign affairs than men?

(Women only) Do you think the public views about women's knowledge of foreign affairs conditions your own ability to influence policy decisions in the Department?

(Men only) Do you think the public's views about women's knowledge of foreign affairs condition the ability of your women colleagues to influence policy decisions in the Department?

women as knowing less about foreign affairs. No one said the public believed women knew more, rather almost all the women and 72 percent of the men said the public believed women knew less. For the whole sample, if we remove those who said they did not know the public's view, the percentage identifying the public stereotype that women know less than men about foreign affairs increases to over 80 percent. Interestingly, young women and men were more likely to think these stereotypes about women's abilities existed among the public. Indeed, more than 87 percent of the women and 100 percent of the men under 40 claimed the public believes women know less about foreign affairs. Unfortunately, this would seem to indicate that the influence of these stereotypes is not declining.

Perhaps surprisingly, many of the women and men we interviewed at State and Defense themselves also believed that women in general know less about foreign affairs then men. (See Table 1-3.) Often reluctantly, several women argued that most women know less. "I think they know less. I hate to say it, I think people relationships are more important to women than global concepts." Another responded, "I have a mixed comment. I think there is a keen interest, but I have personally found men to be more interested. I would qualify that by saying that women who are interested are very well versed." Another noted the changes among women as a result of the Peace Movement: "Women are interested in foreign policy. They have never really been focusing on this, but recently there has been a big upsurge because they realize this is important for human survival. As a result, women are very involved in the Peace Movement." One of the male respondents was sophisticated enough to note the stereotype was dependent not so much on ability but on access to information. "A question of opportunity. It's not a question of women's ability, it's of opportunity to have access to information." A man working in intelligence in the State Department denied any difference between men's and women's knowledge of foreign affairs, but perhaps reflected a related stereotype when he commented, "I'm still a little amazed when women come to talk about some issues. The spy area is not where I expect women." One woman political appointee at the Defense Department noted women may know the same about foreign policy but they know less about the military, "in military affairs women may be, and I may be, less knowledgeable."

Given this widespread view of women's general lack of knowledge about foreign affairs, we would expect the women in the State and Defense Departments to feel that these stereotypes would limit their own effectiveness. To establish if this were so, we asked our interviewees whether the public's view of women's knowledge influenced their own ability (or that of their women colleagues) to be effective. Most said no. Only 20.6 percent of the men and 27.8 percent of the women specifically believed that this public perception of women's lack of knowledge limited the ability of women to have influence in this arena of politics (see Table 1-3). When we asked how the influence was manifested, the respondents listed a number of ways. For example, the public's view of women's knowledge was evident to one Insider in the reactions she encountered when she gave talks about foreign policy topics to community groups around the country.

> They're always startled to discover that women might know something about foreign policy. I do a lot of State Department Speaking Series talks and I get the same reaction all the time. A lot of people come because they've never before seen a woman doing something like this. They're expecting two heads. They're always surprised to discover women speakers know what they're talking about, and that it made sense.

Another woman also noticed the influence of the stereotype when she tried to address foreign policy before an all-male audience:

> I was asked to speak at a men's club by a friend of mine, a surgeon in Belgium. It was an international meeting and a Frenchman interrupted

and asked, "Can you cook?" I looked at him, and I said, "Of course I can, monsieur, can you compute?" Believe me I have used that line since. That is the answer for those characters.

Several respondents drew the connection between this stereotype and their own problems in establishing credibility in a masculine field, not only in dealing with the public, but also within the foreign policy establishment itself. A respondent in Defense noted that as a result of this stereotype: "There is a natural tendency of people on meeting a woman in the Defense Department to assume that she is a secretary, or of low level, until there is evidence to the contrary." Interestingly, a woman at Defense identified the impact of the stereotype as being reflected in Donald Regan's put down of women's lack of knowledge about throw weights. (See page 39.) "I hate the whole thing about throw weights. I've used that term in speeches ever since. I was at a commissioning speech that year, and I made sure I used 'throw weight' in the speech twice." In describing the culture at the Defense Department, a woman directly attributed it to the view that women are not as knowledgeable as men.

> It establishes a culture. It establishes a mind set. Especially, I work in the military, and women are making inroads into the military services. But I have been here long enough that I have watched the first woman in the military to be *allowed* to become a general, and then she was the head of the nurses. They just recently heralded that the Marine Corps now has a lady general down at Quantico. She is in charge of the post, administration operation of the post. She is not making major command decisions. But that was really heralded. When I came to [this Defense Department division], I was told, "you know you are the first woman we have hired in this organization. We'll hire you and see how it works out." There is still a lot of that attitude.

Elaborating on this idea, a woman whose expertise is in nuclear weapons commented, "It doesn't matter internally because I'm a known quantity. But when I go out of house and have to deal with new admirals, I have to establish my credibility to convince them." When asked if her area of expertise made this a particular problem she answered, "Yes because it is very technical; it is very masculine, it is very macho. What can be more macho than nuclear warheads exploding?" Several of the men were also aware of how the public stereotype shaped the ability of their women colleagues to have influence. Of these, most thought the effect was only limiting when a woman first started a job. "I think inevitably and unfortunately. Initial impact only. Initial assumptions are fairly easily overcome by demonstration. If a man or woman demonstrates competence, most people's attitudes will change quickly."

While a majority rejected the limiting influence of this stereotype, often their answers seemed to suggest otherwise. One of the senior women at State, while denigrating the influence of the public stereotype, revealed her dismay over women peace activists' attempts to develop a women's point of view on foreign policy.

> For one, I think women do know less. It is not just a perception. I think women have traditionally set foreign affairs, security, defense, uniforms, all these kinds of things to the side. So they do tend to be less informed. Women have very little impact, I can tell you. If someone came in and said that N.O.W. [the National Organization for Women] had just completed a study on our nuclear posture, and believed that this is the way to go, "as women," as if there were not a national security agenda, they would be totally disqualified, and no one would pay any attention to them. Women have to really inform themselves. Until they do, forget it. I sit on a major policy group and I can't state a policy "as a woman."

Thus, while she dismissed the implication that the stereotype about women's knowledge has an impact on her, her comments seemed to reflect that they do. She has to clearly and unequivocally reject the role as spokesperson for an uninformed (her characterization) group, women. She does not want to be seen as speaking "as a woman."

The Defense Department seemed to be particularly hostile to women as a result of the assumption that men are more knowledgeable about military matters. One respondent presented the dimensions of the problem as follows:

> In a military area most people see women as ignorant and unable to relate to military matters as clearly as men, either because they haven't had access or experience. So every time you start a new position or run into new people, you have to start again to prove yourself again. Men don't have to prove themselves.

As the quote indicates, stereotypes about women's knowledge and capabilities presented some unique problems for the women who are in management positions in the two Departments. Chapter 6 will include a discussion of the specific tactics women have adopted to overcome initial perceptions of the inabilities of woman. This need to "prove yourself," to show competence where none or little is assumed, is a management-leadership problem of particular import to the women in State and Defense who find themselves making decisions for which the public, and many of their colleagues, still believe men, as men, have the better qualifications. This problem is made all the more severe, as we shall discover in the next chapter, by the specific organizational configurations, especially the gender ratios, within both Departments.

In terms of the final stereotype concerning interpersonal capabilities, one could perhaps argue that the view of women as having better communication skills and of being intuitive should give women an edge in negotiations, which are a major facet of foreign affairs. However, this has always been offset by the stereotype of women's emotionality, or inability to "stand tough." Women's supposed emotionality is also seen as a definite hindrance in areas of war, in which women are perceived as being unable to handle the stress of combat. To examine how pervasive these views were, we asked the women (and men) in our sample if there were any views about women in general that limited their ability (or their women colleagues' ability) to influence policy decisions in their Department. Of those responding to this question, over 70 percent of the women and 49 percent of the men said there were such views. Typical was this response from a high-ranking woman in the State Department:

> They tend to be mostly behavioral views. The fear of the shrieker. The fear of a woman's uncontrolled anger. It's in the area of not being confident about how a women would play the game. I'm confident that when I took this job three years ago there was great skepticism as to whether I would fit in. Because women bring a new element to the physical appearance of a meeting. It changes and it's upsetting. Are you going to make things difficult for them? Or are you going to be a great show? Are you going to be a bitch to deal with? There is usually an effort to handle that problem by cutting you out.

Another woman explained the influence of management stereotypes about women as follows:

> Every woman is always aware of the stereotype: that she is going to be more emotional, perhaps less steady, and softer on the issues. I think a lot of women in positions of importance have to be aware that that is there. Perhaps they compensate, perhaps they don't. They have to be aware that a comparison with men is going to be made. She's a woman, and therefore she is going to be softer or more unclear on the issues.

Correspondingly, women's social skills were seen as a detriment in an atmosphere in which men are stereotyped as task oriented, and are thus seen as able to get crucial and necessary jobs done.

Conclusion

Foreign policy is thus not seen as a career to which women are suited. Cultural norms about the place of work in women's lives, traditions tying

citizenship and war-fighting ability with maleness, and cultural stereotypes about women's and men's nature, have served in the past to limit
women's access to the circle of foreign policy-makers and to inhibit the
influence of those few women who make it into the inner sanctum. Given
these pervasive cultural stereotypes about women, it is a wonder that the
women in our sample chose the careers they did. However, while public
attitudes are still often depressingly negative about women's abilities, the
period from the mid-1960s on has witnessed great advancements in public
thinking. Women growing up in the last three decades, therefore, might
be expected to be less affected by these limiting societal values than
women who came of age in an earlier era. However, as we shall see in the
next chapter, women contemplating careers in either the military or
diplomatic arena would not only have discovered a public who doubted
their ability, but two organizations at the Defense and State Departments
that employed few women and discriminated, often legally, against those
in their employ.

Interview
JEANE KIRKPATRICK
The Mouse Who Roared

Jeane Kirkpatrick has undoubtedly been the most visible woman in the United States foreign policy arena. From her unique position as both United States Ambassador to the United Nations and a member of the inner coterie of President Reagan's foreign policy advisors, Ambassador Kirkpatrick had an incalculable impact on American foreign policy extending far beyond the United Nations. Yet, in becoming so successful, Ambassador Kirkpatrick was influenced by the same societal stereotypes which confront all women who attempt to achieve influence in the foreign policy process.[99]

There came a day, as the lawyers say, when I think I focused in, really for the first time, on the facts. I was probably the only woman who had ever made it into the inner circles of foreign policy-making in the U.S. government. That may not be accurate and I certainly don't say it in a self-aggrandizing way, I say it in a moment of realization. When I understood just how nontraditional the sex role was: curiously on a day that there was a NSPG [National Security Policy Group] meeting. NSPG, as you probably know, was the inner, inner circle of Reagan administration foreign policy making, the inner circle of the NSC [National Security Council], and it was very active during the first term through 1985. It was the President, Vice President, Secretary of State, Defense, CIA, NSC, in my days me, and the Chair of the Joint Chiefs, about eight people. The President presided and it was a principles only meeting. It was small and it met in the Situation Room around a small table. The Situation Room was in the basement of the White House and it has special security protection and heavy doors and special locks. We were in the middle of an NSPG meeting when someone said "it's a mouse." I said: "A mouse in the Situation Room?" We all looked and there was indeed a mouse in the Situation Room. The mouse was sitting across the room and he looked at us, walked across the floor, and disappeared. Now someone else said "it must be the first time there has ever been a mouse in the Situation Room." For some reason something clicked in my head and I thought to myself that day that the mouse was really no stranger a creature to find in the Situation Room than I was. It must have been about the first time that a creature such as I had ever been in the Situation Room too.

I think that is probably true and it is interesting in that regard to note that I was not there in one of the positions that was *ex officio*. It was not as though I were a secretary of a major foreign policy department. I wasn't. I was there because the current UN representative job is an ambiguous one, and the President asked me to be there. Basically the group consisted of whomever the President asked plus the Secretaries of State and Defense, President, Vice President and so on. I mention it only to say that there has been very, very, very little participation by women at the really top policy levels of our government. The foreign policy field is one of the areas which really remains male exclusive. Not only in the U.S. government, I think, but in all governments. I think in Britain probably Margaret Thatcher is the only exception. It's interesting. It's interesting to me because I never had really thought about it when I was writing *Political Women*. I never sort of zeroed in on the question of foreign policy, diplomacy, defense as sort of discreet issues that might involve some sex role factors. I suppose the first time I thought about the diplomatic corps, as an exclusive male preserve, was when I was at the UN and realized that not only was I the first woman ever to represent the United States at the United Nations, I was the first woman ever to represent any major power, any European, Western country. There had only been three, four, five women who had ever headed missions to the UN anyway. They were from Liberia, from Sri Lanka, Ghana, they weren't what you would call mainstream countries. A Liberian was there as head of mission when I got there. There was never a woman as ambassador of the Soviet Mission when I was there, although there were eleven other Soviet ambassadors; no woman from Britain. There was no woman at the policy level at the Secretariat of the United Nations, and there is no doubt that my appointment came as a great, and unwelcome, surprise to a lot of people. When I was appointed I think people found it so incredible, they began to expect incredible things of me.

> Ambassador Kirkpatrick's entrée into the foreign policy arena was not typical. Unlike the careerists, she had not worked her way up through the foreign policy bureaucracy, but unlike most appointees, she had not received her position as a reward for political activities, but on the basis of her knowledge and views about foreign policy.

The article on "Dictatorships and Double Standards" was an article which I had written during a period of a couple of months in France over the summer. I had written it, actually not in the spirit of polemics, but for my own purposes, trying to figure out what I thought was going on in U.S. foreign policy and in the world. I tried to think about those developments in the kind of political scientist terms in which I had become accustomed to thinking. I didn't even intend to publish the article when I wrote it. I probably never would have published it had it not been for my husband's nagging me about it. This is kind of interesting, they're kind of reversed sex roles, I guess you could say, because I read some of the article, as I was writing it, to my husband and a friend who was with us in France and they found it very interesting. I knew that it was going to be a highly controversial article, and I didn't really care to get involved in that kind of controversy, frankly. I was writing it for my own purposes. I really didn't intend to do anything with it and put it in the drawer after I finished it. My husband asked me from time to time what was I going to do with it. I said maybe nothing, I didn't know. I was going to keep it for a while, and he would say "let somebody take a look at it" and finally he persuaded me "to let Norman [Podhoretz] take a look at it and then decide, see what he thinks." I am absolutely certain that if my husband had not been repeatedly, really almost nagging me about the article, I would not have published it. It would have been there in the drawer. I wouldn't have been in this office, though I would have been in a smaller office on another floor, not in a nice corner office with a couple of windows and you wouldn't be interviewing me for a profile. Instead Norman read it, published it in *Commentary*.

Ronald Reagan read it and wrote to me about it, much to my surprise. I didn't know Ronald Reagan read things like that. I wasn't particularly thrilled about that. I was never a Reagan fan, I was an active Democrat at the time, as I had been throughout my adult life, an active frustrated Democrat. I didn't think particularly about it. After two or three weeks I wrote him a letter and said "thanks very much. I would be happy to talk to you sometime if you are in Washington." Six months later they called me. April Fool's Day I got a call from Richard Allen asking me if I'd be willing to meet with Reagan in Washington. I met him and after a few meetings I agreed to go on his foreign policy advisory task force. Then after a few more meetings, he was elected President. He made the point to move me almost immediately into his senior group of advisors, foreign policy advisors. Almost everybody in the group was either a former Republican [party activist] or in the Cabinet. Then he asked me to become the UN ambassador and I didn't do anything besides that. I was somewhat active in that campaign. I had been somewhat active in Democratic politics at the presidential level particularly before that, never very active. I didn't do anything at all, to this day I have never done anything to advance a political career.

Similarly to most of our women respondents, Ambassador Kirkpatrick sees herself as having been successful in her position and as having had a significant influence on U.S. foreign policy.

I used to say that my goal was to achieve a situation in which the United States and its interests could be treated with as much respect and concern as any small Third World country. And I meant that too. The fact is that the United States was in something close to a pariah status at the UN in January 1981. That was not entirely the fault of my predecessors. It had a lot to do with trends that had been developing in the UN from the mid-sixties, when nobody had really tried to take on the Chairman....

I had a really good team which I was able to recruit, mainly because the President, within some limits, supported the choices that I made. So with my team I think we changed, substantially changed, the role of the United States in the United Nations. We managed to move into a situation in which American interests were, in fact, given the decent consideration which they hadn't been: a situation in which the United States was no longer the whipping boy of the world. We made these issues, we talked about them, we took a campaign to accomplish them, and we accomplished them. I think we demonstrated too that there is another way to represent the United States in the United Nations, somewhat more assertive but also more effective. It didn't make things worse as the State Department had predicted, it made things better. By the time I left the UN and the administration, there was general agreement in the UN, around the UN, and in a lot of the media that followed the UN, that we had been successful in fact in accomplishing these goals....

There were a number of specific accomplishments. One was simply bringing about an effective end to a situation in which the United States was continually attacked or attributed with the responsibility for most of what was wrong with the world. You may say that that's not very important, but the United Nations is of course the place of symbolism. Its business is symbolic output. It's what one political scientist who has written on the UN has called collective legitimization of deal generalization. I think that we dramatically strengthened the influence of the United States in the United Nations, and because we strengthened the influence of the United States in the United Nations, we were able to have an impact on a good many specific policies. For example, we got back onto the agenda of the United Nations consideration of free market strategies of development, which were considered wholly out of date. Really no one considered free-market strategies of development as even a possibility for the least developed countries' development policy in 1981. Nobody had in more than a decade.

Another thing we did was to get much more serious and much more evenhanded consideration of human rights issues by the UN. Actually we made a lot of progress toward the restoration of the UN Human Rights Commission from what it had become, which was a political playground, run by the Communist Bloc for example, into an arena in which there was some consideration, fair chance of consideration, of really the most clear-cut human rights abuses on their own merits. I think that was an accomplishment.

I think we were able to influence the Security Council to cease its obsessive preoccupation with attacks on Israel and to instead devote somewhat more attention to crisis areas in the world as they appeared. Although that was limited progress, very limited, we got a start on it. We didn't achieve it, but we got a start on it. As I said before, I think we created a situation in which the U.S. and its interests were treated with more respect.

> Ambassador Kirkpatrick saw a number of reasons for her success, several of which, like the need to work harder, reflect a common thread in women's experience.

If I have any specific traits, I guess I think in terms of comments that others have made, you know recurring comments. In the UN, it certainly was very important to people that I'd be willing to "stand up," and what they meant was "stand up" for the United States. It wasn't just that the people liked the fact that I stood up and had an argument, but that I had evidence, that I made a case they found persuasive. They liked that, you know. I also worked harder. People told me at the U.S. Mission that there had never been a permanent representative who worked as hard as I did. I'm not sure that that's true, maybe there was one who worked as hard as I did. But I worked hard and I'm sure that probably helped me a lot doing my job.

It helped to have been a university professor in political science. I can't imagine trying to understand that institution without having been a political scientist, frankly, because it's a highly political institution which can really, in my judgment, only be understood in terms of its political interactions or power processes. I also think it was enormously helpful, this is part of working hard, being a university professor was helpful in orienting me toward doing a tremendous amount of reading to keep abreast of issues. So that I was informed. I mean, why would they include me in their meetings? Well, partly because they thought I was very well informed. If there were personal qualities, those are it. I've always thought so and I still think so that you have to work harder and probably have to be a little better.

> Emphasis on these traits demonstrates the problem women have in establishing credibility. In essence, Ambassador Kirkpatrick began with one strike against her: she was a woman. This made it more difficult to establish credibility and led to resistance within the establishment to her inclusion.

Resistance is different than hostility. Resistance is just a barrier, a kind of reluctance to full inclusion. One never knows moreover, whether any such case is a consequence of a personal attribute, something about you quite personally and specifically, or a sex-based attitude. . . . I have heard it said that one top White House person, opposing my appointment to a higher-level job at one point, said, "at the end of the day when people sit around with their feet up, she just isn't one of the boys." That wasn't said in my presence, obviously, so it's hearsay, but it's hearsay from very close sources.

So I think that there was some kind of resistance inside at the very top of the Reagan Administration. Actually, I think not really with the President. Interestingly enough, I think Ronald Reagan is really quite prepared to deal with women seriously, professionally. How do I know? Well, women feel things like this. I think he was, more so than some of these other people around him, most of whom, I think, you know, were people who were in the Bohemian Club [an exclusive male social club], that kind of men. But you know, I've been one of the few women around who have had a pretty good look at top levels of the political parties. Anybody who thinks that there is a significant difference in the role and openness to women in the parties is, rather seriously, deluding themselves. I think there is much more in common there than is usually thought to be the case. . . . I used to sometimes think that there was something, I call to myself "the Marine factor." (There were a lot of Marines in the Reagan Administration at the top.) I'm not wholly sure what all I thought was involved in the Marine factor, but it had something to do with macho concerns about not being or seeming less willing to use force than anybody else that was present. I sometimes felt that being a woman just removed me entirely from that particular set of concerns and left me freer to examine or raise questions about the various options and so forth. I'm not sure, however, how much this had to do with male-female differences. . . . You get the feeling that you are under continuous scrutiny of a critical nature. It's true, I think.

Now are women under more pressures? I don't know, it's very hard to be sure about that. I think so, but I am not sure. I think, I have said, I believed there was a little more resistance to accepting women as experts. I noticed this a lot about Margaret Thatcher, a lot of a tendency to suggest that if a woman is strong, she's seen as tough. If she's strong enough to be in the job, then she's tough, which is never a compliment. But if she's not strong, she's not strong enough to be in the job. If you are assertive enough to demonstrate expertise, you are likely to be charged with lecturing or being schoolmarmish. But if you are not, then you're likely to be regarded as not a factor, not sufficiently either expert or strong enough to be a factor. I think that there are a number of this kind of "double binds" for women in public life.

> Despite these elements of societal resistance, Ambassador Kirkpatrick is very optimistic that changes have occurred in society, whereby the public has become more accepting of women in foreign policy, partially as a result of having had her in such a visible position.

My own experience has led me to feel more strongly than I did that there is very broad public acceptance of women today in top policy roles and I think that's true for foreign policy as well. I have had enormously positive public response to my occupancy of one of the top foreign policy roles. Just tremendously positive. And I mean the broad public too. I mean people in airports who saw me, thanking me for what I've done for the United States, and asking if I would like to run for President. This kind of thing which clearly, anyway you define it, represents approval. So I have to say that my own personal experience really has to be treated as strong evidence that there isn't much public resistance to women in top roles.

Organizational Factors:
Tokens in Diplomacy and War–Making

A woman explained the struggle to survive within a male-dominated office, where she received jobs that others did not want or had failed at. She was the subject of character assassination through gossip (in which her boss participated, often intentionally within earshot) and frequent sexual advances. She feels she can document and easily win an EEO complaint, but does not want to pursue this. She desperately wants a career with the Department of State, and feels that "to file a complaint is to cut your throat. The organization wants only apple polishers and yes-men."

W. V. Rouse[1]

As previously mentioned, our discussion of organizations borrows heavily from the work of Georgia Duerst-Lahti and her research on the status and influence of women in positions of authority in state bureaucracies.[2] Duerst-Lahti has argued that the organizational culture of a bureaucracy or department will influence the attitudes and behaviors of the members of that organization, and thus the relative power and influence of women within the organization. In her terminology, organizations are cultured, and the culture embodies the characteristics and practices of the organization, including the organization's gender ethos. Gender ethos is defined as "distinctive characteristics of an organization and attitudes of actors within it which affect relations between the sexes and women's ability to gain and use power."[3] Though Duerst-Lahti does not claim a strict causal relationship between the formal structural variables and the organization's culture and gender ethos, she contends that an organization's culture emerges on four domains: its historical forces, ecological context, internal topography, and social demography. Historical forces refers to past organizational policies, and how these policies have shaped the institution to be either an unfavorable or favorable environment for women. The argument here parallels that of Gary Powell, who in his examination of corporate managers contended that individuals and their careers will be influenced by the decisions of the organization, which reflect its willingness to welcome certain types of workers and not others.[4] Ecological context focuses on the present organizational structure and women's location within this organizational hierarchy. Internal topography examines the formal and informal cleavages based on policy areas; the task segregation within an agency, and where women are located relative to the primary policy tasks of the department. Social demography looks at the interests, expectations, and characteristics of the employees, particularly relative to the extent to which women are seen to fit into the job of the agency.

It has generally been assumed that government agencies have been, and continue to be, organizations which are more hospitable to women. Since the government makes the laws concerning employment standards, including affirmative action and sex equity, the government, as an employer, is under some pressure to implement these same regulations itself.[5] For example, the 1967 Executive Order, which added sex to the other prohibited forms of discrimination in the federal government, led to the creation of the Federal Women's Program in 1969. In fact, the government's record in this area is mixed. It was not until 1972 that the Equal Employment Opportunity Act brought federal employees under the equal employment provisions applied to others by the 1964 Civil Rights Act.[6] Additionally, government commitment to equal opportunity has not been applied equally in all government agencies, and has shown significant variation over time. As we shall see, support for equal opportunity and openness to women have not been overwhelming in the foreign policy establishment. As was noted, societal values have considered the realm of foreign relations as the preserve of men, and this perception has been reinforced by organizational factors within the foreign policy apparatus. Consequently, it is the authors' contention that the four factors that define the culture and gender ethos of both the Departments of State and Defense have restricted and continue to restrict women's ability to fully participate in the foreign policy process. In order to examine this hypothesis we shall discuss each of the four dimensions of culture and ethos (historical forces, ecological context, internal topography, and social demography) separately, and then relative to each Department.

Historical Forces

Recruitment efforts suffered from an image of the Foreign Service as elitist, self-satisfied, a walled-in barony populated by smug white males, an old-boy system in which women and minorities cannot possibly hope to be treated with equity in such matters as promotions and senior level responsibilities.

Commission on Civil Rights[7]

Historical forces refer to past organizational policies, and in particular to the ways in which these policies have made the organization into a favorable or unfavorable environment for women. Policies can be adopted which either encourage or discourage women's inclusion. As we shall see, the histories of both the Departments of State and Defense are replete with examples of explicit policies adopted with the expressed purpose of prohibiting women from entering the Departments, or restricting the influence and opportunities of those women who were finally admitted. The Defense Department and its military branches virtually excluded women until very recently, and are still wrestling with the implications of the policies which prohibit women from most combat positions.[8] Similarly, the State Department's policies concerning women have been the target of several recent lawsuits, seeking to eliminate and redress the Department's discriminatory practices in hiring, promotions, and assignments (most recently, *Palmer v. Baker*). The Court has generally found the Department to be liable, and pursuant to court orders the State Department has been revising the Foreign Service exam, as well as its appointment, review, and promotion processes.

Historical Forces: State Department

> If I hadn't fought it, widespread discrimination would have continued forever. I would have been ashamed.
> *Alison Palmer*[9]

> You have essentially a glacial case of progress, which will not get better for a while yet.
> *Torey Williams, State Department Bureau of Personnel*[10]

In contrast to Duerst-Lahti's forementioned optimism about the supportive relationship between government and women, Homer Calkin[11] concluded that in general the government has been slower than industry in employing women, and that the field of foreign policy, and in particular the State Department, has been especially inhospitable. For many decades the Foreign Service remained a male preserve. It was only in 1922 that the United States appointed Lucile Atcherson as the first woman Foreign Service Officer. At that time, women were seen as representing a problem for the Department due to their perceived inability to fulfill all the functions of a Foreign Service Officer.[12] Therefore, Wilbur J. Carr, the Director of the Consular Service suggested that, since he did not feel the Department could make a rule excluding women, instead it should use the entrance examination as a means of keeping them out.[13] As an alternative, the Personnel Board at the time even suggested to the Secretary of State, Charles Evans Hughes, that he apply for an Executive Order excluding women, minorities and naturalized citizens from the Department. Hughes, to his credit, declined.[14] Between 1926 and 1929, four women were appointed to the Foreign Service, constituting 5.5 percent of those women who had taken the exam; however from 1930 to 1941, no women were admitted.[15] The general attitudes towards women officers, and the justifications the Department had for not hiring them, hardly changed from 1924 to 1944. Obstacles continued to be: the issue of marriage, which, it was assumed, would sooner or later make women leave their posts; the unfavorable climatic conditions in various parts of the world, with which women were assumed to be unable to cope; and "foreign" cultural prejudices against women as government representatives.[16]

A major policy shift took place in 1946 with the passage of the Foreign Service Act, which established the goal that the Foreign Service should be broadly representative of the American people. As a result, during the 1950s and 1960s, more women were admitted to State. However the Department continued to be perceived as discriminatory, despite its attempts to assure women that it did not discriminate. For example, in 1964 the Department cited figures to demonstrate that its ratio of women to men in grades 12 and above was more than five times the government average.[17] In reality, however, from 1960 to 1970, the percentage of women in State declined from 9.2 percent of Foreign Service Officers to 4.8 percent.[18] In 1963 Secretary of State Dean Rusk launched the State Department's first affirmative action efforts by inviting civil rights leaders to Washington to discuss the need to increase the number of minorities in the Foreign Service.[19] In 1964, the Civil Rights Act passed, but it was not until 1972 that Congress amended the Civil Rights Act of 1964 to require federal agencies to develop and implement affirmative action programs.[20] In 1970, the Ad Hoc Committee to Improve the Status of Women in Foreign Affairs Agencies was created with the goal of ending discrimination against women in the State Department, AID (Agency for International Development) and USIA (U.S. Information Agency). This group later became known as the Women's Action Organization (WAO) and was instrumental in encouraging the Department to provide more training for women, and to take steps to encourage the recruitment of qualified women. The WAO also was instrumental in persuading the State Department in August 1971 to overturn the ban on married women having a Foreign Service Career and to allow tandem couple appointments.[21]

Also in August 1971, the first major sex discrimination case filed against the State Department was decided in favor of Foreign Service Officer Alison Palmer, who had claimed that she had been discriminated against because of her sex in assignments abroad. Specifically, she was denied appointment as a political officer by the U.S. Ambassadors in Ethiopia, Tanzania, and Uganda, who all claimed to prefer a male officer.[22] In compensation, Ms. Palmer was awarded a promotion, back pay, and a desired assignment to the National War College.[23] The Deputy Under Secretary at the time, William B. Macomber, Jr., conceded that there had been discrimination in the past, but promised that changes would be made, so that diplomats could no longer request to exclude women from certain assignments.[24] Throughout the 1970s, the State Department professed a willingness to help women, with Secretary Cyrus Vance in particular urging the Department to make a special effort to hire qualified women.[25] Shortly after taking office in early 1977, Secretary of State Vance announced his strong commitment to affirmative action progress in the Foreign Service: "We, of the Department of State, working at home and abroad, are obliged to set an example of equality and human dignity for all peoples."[26] Vance also created a committee, the Executive Level Task Force on Affirmative Action, with Ambassador Philip C. Habib as Chairman, to review the recruitment and examination procedures in the State Department, . The committee made recommendations designed to ensure that the Service become "truly representative of American diversity."[27] Dissatisfied with State's progress toward this goal, Congress passed the Foreign Service Act of 1980, which required the Department of State to take steps to increase equal opportunity for women and minorities. This legislation represented the first time Congress had required specific affirmative action steps of a specific federal department or agency.[28] The Commission on Civil Rights found:

> Foreign Service ranks have been filled almost exclusively by white males, particularly at the middle and upper levels. Its complex and lengthy entrance procedures, its relatively small size, and what some identify as traditional elitist attitudes have combined to limit severely employment opportunities for women and minorities in the Foreign Service.[29]

The Commission recommended a number of steps to be taken along these lines.

In terms of the organizational structure, an Office of Women's Affairs had been created in 1971. In 1975 it was combined with the Office of Equal Employment Opportunity, which was changed in the 1980s to the Office of Equal Employment Opportunity and Civil Rights (EEOCR). However, despite these institutional mechanisms, an outside consultant concluded that there was little support for EEOCR within the Department. "The concept of equal employment has little or no influence on the operationalization of issues important to equal employment, such as recruitment, hiring, training, assignment, and promotions."[30] A second study, seven years later, found the situation little changed: "top-level commitment to the principles of equal employment opportunity had never been strong enough for a period long enough to break through the general apathy on the subject that appears to prevail throughout the Department of State."[31] This study observed that EEOCR had continually been hampered by personnel shortages and the assignment of semi-qualified personnel. Its computer data base had proven to be unable to provide the information and statistics necessary for promoting equal employment.[32]

The 1980 Foreign Service Act and the 1982–1986 Multi-Year Plan for Affirmative Action were implemented with the goal of making the Foreign Service more representative of the American populace.[33] These programs have made some progress in increasing the number of women at State. However, as the study by Olmsted et al., concluded, "the progress in the improvement in the status of women in the Department continues to be agonizingly slow. If this rate should continue, it will be decades into the 21st century before women can expect to be represented equitably and to play a significant role in foreign affairs."[34]

It is thus not too surprising that there have been a large number of formal discrimination complaints filed against the State Department in recent years: 25 in 1983; 24 in 1984; 39 in 1985; 29 in 1986; and 32 in 1987.[35] Two earlier lawsuits have been particularly important. In 1976 Alison Palmer filed her second lawsuit, a class action suit, joined by the Women's Action Organization, and in 1977, an additional class action was filed, *Cooper v. Baker*. These lawsuits, which were consolidated, alleged that the State Department discriminated against women Foreign Service Officers in hiring, assignments, performance ratings, and awards.[36] A 1985 decision in the Federal District Court went against Ms. Palmer. However, in 1987 the Court of Appeals reversed the decision and sent the case back to the District Court.[37] The decision on remand by the United States District Court for the District of Columbia (which will be discussed in greater detail later) held that the Department violated Title VII of the Civil Rights Act of 1964. The State Department was found to have engaged in gender discrimination in a wide range of activities including the Foreign Service exam, assignments, evaluations, and awards.[38] As a result of this case, two independent experts were to examine Department processes and suggest modifications in its personnel system. The Department canceled the 1989 Foreign Service exam, since the "traditional written examination, scored neutrally, has been found to have an adverse impact on women and minority candidates."[39] The Department also notified 601 women that they might be entitled to relief.[40] As of August 1992, compensatory relief measures had been provided to over 200 women.[41] In a subsequent case after twelve years of litigation, the Voice of America and its parent organization, USIA, were found to have been guilty of sex discrimination and ordered to compensate the victims.[42]

Thus in examining the historical forces, or past organizational policies, one must conclude that the State Department has a history of attempting to exclude women. This historical force continues to impact the effectiveness of women in foreign policy making. Indeed, two 1989 studies (one by a five-member commission authorized by Congress, the other an internal State Department study) both concluded that the Department was still failing to recruit sufficient women and minorities.[43]

Historical Forces: Department of Defense

> Women's participation in the military is not, as many believe, of recent origin—it goes back to our nation's beginnings. The extent of their involvement and the degree to which they have been "militarized" and integrated into the services are, however, significant departures from the past and have become major subjects of controversy in recent years.
>
> *Jeanne Holm, Maj. Gen. USAF (Ret.)*[44]

As Maj. Gen. Jeanne Holm, USAF (Ret.) described in her comprehensive history of women in the military, the situation of women in Defense is similar to, but perhaps even more difficult than, that faced by the women in State. "The story of women's progress is a marvelous tale of persistence, courage, and foresight in the face of repeated frustrations and the built-in institutional resistance of the tradition-bound military subculture."[45] Though women have long been interested in committing themselves to military activity, the military did not welcome them, and thus they have had to be particularly ingenious in their attempts to figure out ways in which they could demonstrate their commitment. While most of these women were content with auxiliary civilian status, others were determined to have an active military role. Women such as "Molly Pitcher," who began by serving water to Washington's troops, but who took over a gun position when needed, and others who masqueraded as men, such as Lucy Brewer, who ultimately became recognized as the first woman Marine in the War of 1812, confronted a military establishment and a social climate which did not see women's participation as suitable.[46] However, during the Civil War, many of these restrictions and social conventions were set aside or ignored due to the demanding nature of that war. As a result, not only did women serve in the traditional capacities of cooking and foraging for supplies, but many women also served as saboteurs, scouts, and couriers.[47] For instance, noted abolitionist Harriet Tubman served as a nurse, spy, scout, and guide for Union forces.[48] Probably the most significant contributions women made during this war and the Spanish-American War were in the fields of health care and nursing. The activities of those such as Clara Barton are well known. Yet at that time, the social conventions which have throughout the history of the military emphasized a double standard for women were evident. "To serve as a nurse, a woman had to be over thirty, very plain looking, and wear plain brown or black dresses."[49] Despite these women's contributions to the military, they still had no regular organizational structure. The breakthrough came in 1901, when Congress established the Nurse Corps as an auxiliary of the Army. The nurses' dubious status was reflected in the fact that the women nurses had no military rank, nor did they receive any of the other military benefits.[50]

> The military was a male institution whose social and occupational context was permeated by the cult of masculinity. So it was in 1900. So it was in 1917. And so it is to a great extent in 1982. Acceptance of women as full and equal role participants in this masculine milieu is seen by many as the ultimate test of society's willingness to compromise with long-established traditions.[51]

By World War I, women were needed not only as nurses, but for clerical positions as well. In general, the beginnings of the twentieth century witnessed the feminization of office work, but the War Department initially resisted employing civilian women in any positions other than nurses. It was only after commanders who were faced with severe personnel shortages pleaded with the War Department, that they were authorized to employ civilian women in other positions, "as long as they were of mature age and high moral character."[52] In 1917 the Navy authorized the enrollment of women other than nurses to free men for sea, and to ease shortages of personnel for clerical positions. The Army did not enlist women in World War I, but employed them as civilians under contract.[53] By the end of the war, 34,000 women had served in the Army and Navy Nurse Corps, the Navy, the Marines and the Coast Guard.[54] However, the concept of women serving permanently in the military was still rejected, and the women were deactivated at the end of the war.[55] In fact, in 1925 the Naval Reserve Act of 1916 was even altered to require the employment of male citizens, so that the Navy could not even enlist Yeomanettes again. Needless to say, this rejection of women, despite their contributions, was not popular with many women's groups. In an attempt to pacify them, the War Department in 1920 established a position of Director of Women's Programs, U.S. Army, with the limited purpose of merely serving as a liaison between the War Department and women's organizations. Instead, the director utilized the position to demand that the Army give greater recognition to women, and to begin organizing the Women's Service Corps as an agency with full military status, no longer as just an auxiliary.[56]

Even though World War II saw a much larger expansion of roles for women, the War Department was still unwilling to include women in the regular services. The compromise proposal was for the creation of a women's auxiliary of highly educated women, who also had to have reputations above reproach. "Moreover, this notion that women should be of high moral character and technical competence while no such standards were used for men set the tone for the double standards that were to characterize the women's programs for the next forty years."[57] The Women's Auxiliary Army Corps program was created in 1942, but its auxiliary status was still problematic. This was rectified by the creation of the Women's Army Corps (WAC) in 1943, along with the establishment of the Navy Women's Reserve (WAVES), the Coast Guard Women's Reserve (SPARS), and the Marine Corps Women's Reserve. The Air Force created the civilian Women's Air Service Pilots (WASPS).[58] The women served in a variety of key support functions, reaching a peak wartime force of 220,000 and totaling over 350,000 women serving in the military.[59] Army and Navy nurses, organized separately from the women's corps, were stationed in all theaters of action, with the Army Nurse Corps suffering over two hundred casualties.[60] Yet these women faced continued hostility for invading a male preserve.

> Reception by the men ranged from enthusiasm through amused conde-scension to open hostility. Each found that she had to prove herself each time she went to a new job or had a change in supervisors. Whereas a man was accepted immediately at face value and was assumed to be competent at his job, a woman was always regarded with suspicion. Because it was considered unnatural for a woman to join the military, she was often considered a deviate of some sort.[61]

These women were embarking on a road that would eventually lead to the permanent integration of women into the U.S. armed forces. Since the standards for women officers and enlisted women were higher than those for men, overall, they were better educated, older, and more carefully selected in terms of character and personal backgrounds.[62] Even so, the collective antagonism of the men in the military was soon communicated to the public at large. The women came under increased media attention, and they soon became the objects of gossip and slander, dirty jokes, snide remarks, and obscene cartoons, with the motive of degrading the women and driving them out of a "man's world." In general military men would not accept the possibility that most jobs in the military were not inherently masculine or that they could be performed by women. "Like the male Marine Corps office clerks in World War I who estimated it would take two women to replace one male Marine at a desk, most men genuinely believed the masculine mythology of the military world."[63]

The services conducted studies to determine which jobs women could hold, which ultimately led to increased admittance of women. The most progressive of the military units in accepting women were the aviation units. However, the services generally were unprepared to deal with the influx of women, and as a result were almost "paternal" in treating women like schoolgirls, despite the fact that the women were more mature and better educated than the men. It was not until November 1944 that the law was modified to allow women to serve overseas, and then only on U.S. territories, not foreign soil.[64] The War Department's treatment of African-American women was even worse. It opposed desegregation, urging a policy of "segregation without discrimination." Yet African-American women were not assigned to suitable positions, and most commanders refused them. For example, sixty African-American medical technicians in the WAC were put to work doing cleaning, rather than in their medical specialties. When they began a sit-down strike in protest, they were told "'Black girls' are 'fit only to do the dirtiest type of work' because that's what 'Negro women are used to doing.'"[65]

By the end of the war, acceptance of women was still marginal. Even the wartime directors of the WACs, WAVES, SPARs, and Women Marines assumed that the women's positions were temporary and that women would only serve during the war. Thus even they did not urge a permanent place for women.[66] General Eisenhower was one of the few who wanted to keep the WAC beyond its scheduled demobilization date due to the severe shortage of skilled personnel after the war. He proposed legislation to establish a permanent WAC in the regular and reserve Army, but his proposal was not implemented at that point.

The Department of Defense itself only came into existence after World War II as a result of interagency conflict between the Departments of War and Navy and the emergence of a third branch, the Air Force. The National Security Act of 1947 (and its amendments in 1949) created the Department of Defense, presided over by a civilian secretary, and the Joint Chiefs of Staff, established to advise the President and the Secretary of Defense. The three armed service departments were also headed by civilian secretaries and initially they functioned relatively independently of the Secretary of Defense.[67] Since then, the roles of both the Secretary of Defense and the Joint Chiefs have expanded, while those of the three service secretaries have declined. This can be partially traced to the increase in agencies under the control of the Secretary of Defense. Specifically in reference to foreign policy, the National Security Agency was created in 1952, in 1961 the Defense Intelligence Agency was added, and later the Bureau of International Security Affairs (ISA), often called the "Little State Department" was established. All three agencies promoted the Secretary of Defense's role in foreign policy.[68]

Despite the subordination of the military departments to civilian command, even a casual observer of military policy-making knows that the three branches still have considerable influence in the Pentagon. (For example, note the "need" for the Army, Navy, and Air Force to all have their own sophisticated planes.) The power of the branches has had a direct role in limiting women's influence on policy making in the Department. In 1948, in response perhaps to the Cold War, the Women's Armed Services Integration Act was passed. This opened up the military services to women, but still only in a very limited way. It was actually assumed in 1948 that the Air Force would lead the way in the utilization of women, since it had been the most enthusiastic and innovative utilizer of women during the war.[69] However, the Air Force's earlier theoretical approval was not easily implemented, especially during the period in which the organization itself was undergoing such growing pains. Women were not to constitute more than two percent of the military, and women officers could not be promoted beyond the rank of lieutenant colonel/commander, except for the colonel/captain director of each women's branch.[70] In 1951 DACOWITS (Defense Advisory Committee on Women in the Services) was established, consisting of civilians who were to advise the Secretary of Defense on matters relating to women.[71]

The Korean and Vietnam Wars again raised the nation's military leaders' interest in recruiting women for additional forces, although few real advances were made. Indeed it could in fact be said that women's position in the armed forces had retreated since the enactment of the 1948 Integration Act. Women suffered institutional segregation and "unequal treatment that would shock modern-day civil libertarians."[72] Even though in 1964 President Johnson told DACOWITS that he thought that there should be more women in the armed forces "to play an even more important role," no one was pushing for an expanded role for women.

This policy stagnation changed when, in November 1967, President Johnson signed Public Law 90-130, which was the first major policy change since 1947–48. It was intended to remove restrictions on the careers of female officers in the Army, Navy, Air Force, and Marine Corps by repealing the limits on the percentage of women in the services and barriers to their promotion possibilities.[73] It removed the two-percent ceiling on females imposed in 1948, permitting more women to enter.[74]

Furthermore, women were no longer restricted to the traditional specialties, but were assigned in large numbers to jobs previously considered the exclusive domain of men. However, most military men still could not accept the idea of their serving under a woman general. During the 1970s, the acronyms WAC, WAVES, and WAF were eliminated, symbolizing the commitment to integrate women into the mainstream of the Armed Forces.[75]

Throughout the 1970s women's progress in the military was relatively rapid as many of the old barriers were eliminated as a result of court decisions, the threat of legal action, or executive initiatives. The adoption in 1973 of the All Volunteer Force also expedited the progress of women.[76] However, women were still not allowed into the service academies, though legislation had been introduced to that effect in 1973. Lawsuits on behalf of women applicants began in the courts, and finally in 1974 the Coast Guard Academy announced that it would accept women. The results of these changes were dramatic. In 1972, women constituted 1.9 percent of all active duty military personnel, and by 1985 their participation had increased to 9.8 percent.[77]

At this time the entire perspective of the services concerning women underwent a radical transformation from a policy of exclusion from all but the "women's jobs" to one of programmed inclusion in all but combat and direct combat-support jobs. However, despite this "metamorphosis from 'typewriter soldiers' to mainstream military personnel," women were actually being assigned to only 44 percent of the jobs in the Marine Corps, 63 percent in the Army, 70 percent in the Air Force, and 72 percent in the Navy.[78]

The early 1980s saw the election of Ronald Reagan and a renewed emphasis on preparedness and readiness to do battle. As a consequence, in 1981, Deputy Secretary of Defense Carlucci requested a review of women in the military to be conducted by Lawrence Korb. Korb's report reflected the earlier philosophy that it was preferable to have men rather than women in the services.

> They gave the impression that the Reagan administration values women only as poor substitutes for men rather than as a pool of talents and skills with a useful contribution to make in its own right. While this may not have been Korb's intent, the message conveyed to the military was unmistakable: *the heat on recruiting women is off.*[79]

As a result, all the service branches began to halt the integration of women or even reverse the progress that had been made. The goals for the numbers of women to be recruited were reduced, and some of the positions open to women were closed. In addition to the rising fear of war, a number of factors contributed to this change, including a decline in the economy and increased pay scales for the military, which made recruiting men easier.[80] There is also evidence that many officers and enlisted men were happy to see the end of efforts in a "bizarre experiment in a fraudulent equality."[81] However, this desire to cut back on women was out of sync with the Reagan Administration's overall desire to expand the military. Consequently, on January 14, 1982, Defense Secretary Casper Weinberger sent a memo to the military secretaries reminding them that qualified women were essential to maintain the readiness of their forces and that the administration desired to increase the role of women in the military.

> While we have made much progress, some institutional barriers still exist. . . . This Department must aggressively break down those remaining barriers that prevent us from making the fullest use of the capabilities of women in providing for our national defense.[82]

In 1984, Weinberger also created the Department of Defense Task Force on Equity for Women to examine opportunities for women with an emphasis on equality.[83] However, by the late 1980s, progress toward including women still had a way to go. DACOWITS has continued to push for changes to improve the status and opportunities of women, and in January 1988 the Task Force on Women in the Military issued a report recommending adopting policies that would reduce sexual harassment and increase career opportunities. Yet at the same time the Task Force urged the continuation of the policy of keeping women out of combat.[84] Though, as of now, none of the services expect to increase the number or percentages of women very dramatically, more people are challenging the exclusion of women from combat. Interestingly one of those who is questioning this practice is Lawrence Korb, Assistant Secretary for Manpower and Reserve Affairs during Reagan's first term and chair of the Task Force on Equity for Women. He stated in a *60 Minutes* interview on women in combat that the issue was critical and "This [women in combat] may be the last cultural barrier we have to break down." Women are playing a more active role in the military, as was evidenced in both the Panama exercise and the Gulf War. However, both the military's and the public's continued resistance to including women was still in evidence in the Congressional hearings on women in combat. As we shall see below, this public and organizational bias against women and their corresponding lack of military experience, especially combat experience, is often cited as a key factor in reducing the influence of women in the foreign policy decision-making process.

To summarize, the historical conditions in the Defense Department have not been generally favorable for women. Women have been either excluded or restricted in what positions they could hold. Even today women are kept out of combat and combat-connected positions. In the civilian arena, in part because it draws from the military, women have also not reached the highest ranks. As we shall see, additional barriers, including educational deficiencies, cultural stereotypes, discrimination, and childrearing responsibilities have slowed progress. There are, however, women now poised at the level (GS-14 and 15) where we might expect to see greater numbers of women in decision-making positions in ten or so years.

Ecological Context

I am fully committed to equality between men and women in every area of Government and in every aspect of life.

President Carter[85]

In essence, what theorists like Duerst-Lahti, Powell, and Rosabeth Moss Kanter have argued is that an individual's behavior can be influenced by the structure of the organization within which one functions. In Duerst-Lahti's terminology, ecological context refers to the ways in which the activities of an organization are structured, the degree to which organizations are hierarchical, and the extent to which they reward individualistic behavior.[86] Although Duerst-Lahti discussed a number of structural dimensions, she emphasized the importance of: the division of labor composition in the work force, or the sex ratio of the organization; the degree of centralization and formalization of decision-making, or hierarchical structure and leadership; and policy type.[87] All of these factors contribute to the gender ethos of the organization, which determines whether an organization will be hospitable to women. "Departmental ethos will favor women's power where women have held a larger percentage of professional and upper administrative positions over a longer period of time, the ease with which women were perceived as credible within the policy area, and where a woman has or currently holds the top leadership position."[88]

Sex Ratios

The first ecological element, sex composition or an imbalanced sex ratio, has been a remarkably stable feature of the American workplace. The number of men and women in an organization is significant in itself, but it also over time affects the organizational culture and gender power relations, since organizational power is assumed to be the product of proportional representation.[89] It is probably the most important of the ecological variables in that it affects the other structural elements as well. In her study of this relationship, Rosabeth Moss Kanter identified four types of organizations, depending upon their sex composition or ratio of women to men. Uniform organizations are all male or all female. Balanced groups consist of approximately equal numbers of men and women. Tilted organizations have ratio of males to females or vice versa ranging from 65:35 to 85:15. Finally, skewed groups have a ratio of males to females or vice versa ranging from 85:15 to almost 100:0.[90]

There has been a great deal of attention paid to skewed organizations, particularly focusing upon the role of women in such groups. Within skewed organizations, the members of the larger group are called dominants (because they are seen as controlling the group and its culture), while the other group is referred to as "tokens." Kanter noted that tokens, because of their rarity, are subject to "three perceptual tendencies: visibility, contrast, and assimilation."[91] Tokens are visible to those around them because they stand out, they are unique. Similarly, the uniqueness of tokens results in a contrast with the dominants. The latter in turn "become more aware of their commonalities and their differences from the tokens, and to preserve their commonality, they try to keep the token slightly outside, to offer a boundary for the dominants."[92] Lastly, assimilation, for Kanter implied "the use of stereotypes, or familiar generalizations about a person's social type." Tokens, because they are few in number, find that they are lumped together with others of their group and their characteristics are "distorted to fit the generalizations."[93] Visibility, contrast, and assimilation each create their own problems for tokens. "Visibility tends to create performance pressures on the token. Contrast leads to heightening of dominant cultural boundaries, including isolation of the token. And assimilation results in the token's role encapsulation."[94] In terms of performance pressure, many token women have reported that they have to work twice as hard as men in their groups to have their competence recognized. The token woman has no trouble in having her presence noticed, but she does experience difficulty in having her achievements noticed. Tokens are also constrained from showing disaffection with the organization (unlike men) for this is frequently perceived as disloyalty.[95] Boundary-heightening involves both an exaggeration by the dominants of what they have in common, and a parallel minimization of what they have in common with the tokens. Male camaraderie can involve telling sexist jokes, or talking about sports, hunting, excessive drinking, or their sexual abilities. Other ways of drawing distinctions include pointing out that because women are present, men have to change their normal ways of doing things.[96] Finally, token women have a greater probability of being classified according to the feminine gender stereotypes, whether or not their personal characteristics are consistent with the particular stereotype. This process is called role encapsulation, by which dominants' stereotypes of token women force them into playing limited roles. Such roles benefit men by providing them a familiar context for viewing women, thereby allowing them to make use of familiar forms of behavior. For example, when professional women are mistakenly assumed to be secretaries, they are stereotyped as conforming to a traditionally subordinate female role. They may be further stereotyped by being assigned secretary-like functions in groups or by being given jobs that reflect their presumed feminine capabilities and concerns, such as equal employment opportunity or corporate social responsibility jobs. Other common roles assigned to women are mother, seductress, and pet.[97] Though the impact of sex ratios in themselves will be discussed here, the ways in which women respond to their token status will be addressed more fully in Chapter 6.

Sex Ratios in State and Defense

When we look at both the Department of Defense (DOD) and the Department of State, we find organizations that are largely male. In 1983, women constituted 32.3 percent of all DOD employees, and 37.0 percent of all State Department employees.[98] Out of the total of 68 government agencies, in terms of their composite rankings for the employment of minorities and women, State ranked number 39, Army number 45, Navy number 59, Air Force number 60, and OSD (Office of the Secretary of Defense) number 68.[99] In comparison to the country as a whole, in 1984 the civilian labor force employed 44 percent women, and the federal government had 40 percent female employees, while State had 39 percent women and Defense had 34 percent women.[100] While overall percentages of women increased slightly in 1987 to 34.4 percent and 41.4 percent respectively in Defense and State, this placed Defense below and State just above the federal average of 38.6 percent women in a department or agency.[101] There was some improvement by 1988 as the civilian labor force consisted of 45 percent women, while State had moved up to 41.5 percent women and Defense was 36.2 percent women.[102] More important, for our purposes, are the percentages of women in professional or decision-making positions, where the situation was less optimistic. In 1983, the State Department's professional employees included 19.19 percent women, and the professionals in the entire Defense Department were 13.09 percent female (with Navy at 10.0 percent, Air Force 11.3 percent, Army 15.9 percent and OSD at 6.1 percent which ranked it at seventy-fifth out of 77 government offices).[103]

Sex Ratios at State

The State Department's personnel system is divided into two major elements, the Civil Service and the Foreign Service. The Civil Service manages the logistics and domestic affairs of the Department, and has traditionally been staffed predominantly by women. The Foreign Service is divided into two broad categories, specialists and generalists. The generalists are at the heart of the foreign policy process providing the Foreign

Service Officers (FSOs) who help shape and implement U.S. foreign policy. They represent the U.S. abroad, staffing the foreign embassies and consulates, as well as the State Department offices in Washington. Our discussion of the State Department will focus primarily on FSOs, though a brief description of those in upper level Civil Service positions will also be included. It is the FSO corps which has traditionally been a male bastion, and women have until recently definitely had token status. If one looks exclusively at Foreign Service Officers, in 1957 there were 306 women out of a total of 3,436, or 8.9 percent. After that, the percentage of women officers actually declined to 8.5 percent in 1962. In 1967, there were 194 women out of a total of 3,438 or 5.6 percent and this further declined to 4.8 percent in 1970. By 1977 women rebounded with 337 women out of 3,514 officers or 9.6 percent. By 1987, women finally got past token status of 15 percent when they attained 1006 women out of a total of 4,427 officers or 22.7 percent.[104] By 1990, women constituted 24.3 percent of the 4,954 FSOs.[105] The figures are slightly more promising in terms of recruitment. In 1966, only 7 percent of the incoming Foreign Service candidates were women, a figure which remained constant in 1971. By 1977 the number of women recruits had reached 16 percent, 34 percent in 1982, and 33.6 percent in 1987.[106]

However, as Table 2-1 makes clear, the distribution of women has not been uniform at all ranks of employment. Both the Civil Service and the Foreign Service have ranking systems dividing employees into junior (GS-9 to 12 and FS-4 to 6), middle (GS-13 to 15 and FS-1 to 3), and senior-SES (Senior Executive Service) and SFS (Senior Foreign Service)-levels. In both the Civil Service and the Foreign Service, the senior ranks have consistently

Table 2-1.   Women throughout the Department of State

	12/31/70		12/31/89	
	# women	% women	# women	% women
Civil Service				
Senior (SES)	3	10.3	12	12.1
Middle GS 13–15	208	27.4	399	33.3
Junior GS 9–12	1,010	71.7	1,710	78.9
Foreign Service				
Senior (SFS)	23	2.1	54	6.9
Middle FS 1–3	261	8.2	777	20.4
Junior FS 4–6	1,409	37.9	1,231	34.7

Source: "WAO'S 20th Anniversary: Legacy of the Past-Challenges for the Future" (Washington, DC: Women's Action Organization, 1990), 5.

been male-dominated, with women constituting 12.1 percent of the SES and only 6.9 of the SFS. Women clearly still have token status at these levels. Since the focus of this research is people in policy-making positions, defined as SES and SFS, we might thus expect that for women in these positions, the impact of token status will be significant.

Sex Ratios at Defense

Though women have over time increased their visibility in DOD civilian positions, their admittance into decision-making levels has been severely limited. Civilian employees are classified according to the Civil Service GS rankings, and similarly to State, women tend to be concentrated in the lower wage levels, a situation which has not improved markedly. In 1979, women constituted 76 percent of all employees in ranks GS-1 to 6; in 1986 they were 75.1 percent of these ranks. The inverse of this relationship can be seen if one examines the women in the upper GS ranks (16 to 18), now classified as the Senior Executive Service. In 1979, out of a total of 1,033 executives only 21 or 2.0 percent were women. By 1987 this percentage had increased to 3.9 percent, though this represented only 55 women. There is some fluctuation within the Department, for women constituted 5.4 percent of the executives in the Office of the Secretary of Defense, 4.1 percent in the Army, 3.9 percent in the Air Force and only 2.2 percent in the Navy. This would seem to indicate that the Defense Department has not been a particularly welcome place for women's advancement, in that by 1987 women constituted 8.0 percent of the entire federal senior executive service.[107] Within DOD, many of the policy-making positions are filled by political appointments. Though the Carter presidency included women in several important positions in the Defense Department, including General Counsel, Air Force Under-Secretary, Deputy Under-Secretary of the Navy and Deputy Secretary of Defense for Equal Opportunity, the Reagan Administration generally appointed fewer women to such policy positions.[108] In 1988, only fifteen women were political appointees in the Department.

Using Kanter's definition of tokens being in a minority of less than 15 percent, both the State and Defense Departments at the upper administrative levels present an environment in which women constitute tokens. Since both State and Defense have not significantly increased the number of women policy-makers, it would appear that both organizations will remain skewed into the foreseeable future. Thus we should expect to find evidence of the effects of women's token status. As Kanter hypothesized (and as we shall see in Chapter 6), being a token presents special problems for women and virtually mandates that they adopt alternative coping mechanisms.

Hierarchy, Leadership, Policy Type

> The absence of women and minorities among the upper echelons of
> the Civil Service is an indicator of a lack of real government concern for
> implementing Affirmative Action (AA) policies and Equal Employment
> Opportunity (EEO) policies.[109]

The effects of the ecological element of sex ratio are also reinforced by
the other three structural elements; hierarchy, leadership and policy type.
In terms of hierarchy, it has been found that some types of decision-
making structures are more conducive to women's power than others.
Accordingly, decision structures which: (1) have non-rigid procedures
that downplay rightful participation based on position and include individuals by expertise; (2) tend to de-emphasize and personalize the power
of the secretary; (3) are least centralized and hierarchical; and (4) have
more women involved in communication surrounding decisions; can be
expected to produce more favorable gender ethos for women and improve
women's overall power capacity in decision-making.[110]

One can begin to gauge the extent to which an organization is hierarchical by examining the organizational flow chart, which illustrates formal
reporting relationships and demarcates power based on proximity to the
top. If the chart is linear and rigid, with emphasis on individuals, it is
more hierarchical. The more rigid and hierarchical, the more male. If it is
more congenial, if for example the triad of the top decision-makers is
listed in one box all together, then it is less hierarchical, or more female.
Centralized hierarchical decision structure can generally advantage
women only if women populate the crucial positions.[111] In most instances
hierarchical organizations are seen as impacting negatively upon women,
for a number of reasons: because women generally are not part of the
elite group which dominates these hierarchies; because women are not
seen as having the characteristics necessary to sit at the top of the pyra-
mid; and because of the barriers to women's advancement into the policy-
making levels within organizations.

Government employees in general are structured in hierarchical fashion, as emphasized in the 1979 restructuring of government upper-level
employees. The General Service wage system was revamped by the creation of the Senior Executive Service (SES) to replace the former GS levels
16 to 18. The middle level is GS-12 to 15, junior level GS-7 to 11, and the
support level consists of GS-1 to 6. The SES includes both career and
noncareer officials (those are the Presidential appointments that do not
need Senate confirmation, though noncareer are limited to 10 percent of
the SES).[112] The only positions above SES are the Executive Schedule,
which is the highest level of presidential appointments, requiring Senate
confirmation.[113] As Table 2-2 indicates, there has been a shift of women

Table 2-2. Distribution of women as a percentage of GS (General Service) level employees

GS Levels	1970	1980	1987
1–6	72.2	74.1	74.9
7–10	33.4	46.3	51.4
11–12	9.5	19.3	30.0
13–15	3.0	8.2	14.2
16–18 (SES)	1.4	4.4	6.9
Total percent women	33.1	38.6	48.2

Source: Federal Civilian Employment Statistics (Washington, DC: OPM, 1987), 323.

employees into the SES ranks over time. In 1970, only 1.4 percent of all SES rank equivalents were women, while in 1987 women constituted 6.9 percent of the upper crust of federal employees. A more recent report in 1990 indicated that women were 11.5 percent of the SES.[114] We should point out that 6.9 percent or even 11.5 percent is a minuscule proportion, especially given the fact that nearly half of all federal employees in 1987 were women.

The third structural element, organizational leadership, can be a result of the sex or the conscious behavior of the President and/or the Department secretary. The President can provide leadership to the government as a whole, particularly by encouraging the employment of women. President Carter was seen as providing leadership by nominating more women to senior government positions than any president before him. Thirty-three percent of all his nominees were women.[115] Yet, it is more than just the sex of the leader or the leader's propensity to promote women which impacts on leadership. "Leaders are selected according to the 'fit' between their styles and the agency's culture regardless of sex."[116] Thus organizational leadership is the result of reciprocal influences created by both specific policies adopted by the leaders, and by the ways in which the organizational culture impacts upon the leader. Most organizations are homogeneous, based on shared values and common membership, and they regard anyone whose attributes are different as an outsider.[117] Up to this time, the upper ranks of most organizations have been predominantly male, and the qualifications for managerial positions have been defined in masculine terms. Thus males are seen as more suited to upper-level positions than females. Many studies have documented a bias toward the hiring of male applicants for managerial positions, even when the qualifications of female and male applicants have been equivalent.[118] As discussed in Chapter 1, these results also reflect the influence of gender stereotypes, which suggest that men are more appropriate for leadership roles than women.

Organizational hiring practices also are not only influenced by overt decisions to exclude or categorize people by sex, but can likewise be dominated by the same gender stereotypes that are rampant in society. As Powell has noted, when organizations make hiring decisions, these decisions are generally made with limited information about competence, and under such circumstances these judgments are likely to be influenced by stereotypes. In such instances, gender stereotyping is indicative of the personnel officials within the organization and the organizational situation in general. "Organizations' decisions to hire female or male applicants may be affected by the conscious or unconscious biases of their recruiters and by the steps they take to prevent these biases from determining hiring decisions."[119] Such stereotypes have major ramifications as to who is hired by the organization and who is discriminated against. For example, attractive women are more likely to be judged by stereotypes, which would tend to reduce the credibility of attractive women seeking decision-making positions.[120]

Thus, structural and societal factors work together, resulting in increased discrimination against women.[121] Such prejudices may consist of untested assumptions about women: they are seen as less competitive, less aggressive, less ambitious, and more nurturing; some assume that women "can't hack" the rough-and-tumble of corporate life at the top, that they do not have enough drive, that they will not come back to work after having a baby, or that they make clients uncomfortable. On other occasions, prejudice may be manifested by men at the top openly asserting that they themselves feel uncomfortable with women working beside them. In some instances women are presented with a Catch-22: the woman who is tough is not womanly, while the woman who is not tough is not worth having around. Such a view forces women to choose between being womenly or being successful; this choice between sex role and success is one which men are neither asked, nor expected, to make.[122] As Patricia Thomas has noted, this may be particularly true in the military:

> In the military the behaviors and traits associated with the image of the leader/brave warrior define success. In other fields and professions the traits characterizing success may be different but, with few exceptions, are also masculine. Few women, even those of indisputable talent and competence, are viewed as measuring up to those images.[123]

Duerst-Lahti assumes that women in leadership positions will be able to alter the gender ethos of their departments.[124] However, this presupposes that there have been women in top leadership positions. As we shall see, this conclusion is not applicable to the Departments of State and Defense.

As a result, though women have been increasingly entering professions in all areas, and have made great strides in achieving middle management positions, their opportunity for advancement has been stunted due to hitting the "glass ceiling" of organizational ecology (which is the "invisible barrier, aptly named by the *Wall Street Journal*, which in innumerable cases stands between women and top executive posts").[125] As we have seen, there are a number of factors which contribute to this glass ceiling, but one which has been receiving a lot of attention recently is the practice of mentoring and the lack of mentoring opportunities for women. Mentors in essence assist one up the hierarchical ladder. For women mentoring is limited due to the paucity of female leaders, and thus women are hindered in their advancement.[126] The specific impacts of the lack of mentoring will be discussed in greater detail in Chapter 3.

The final ecological variable of policy type has already been peripherally addressed in terms of general societal variables. Specifically, in terms of organizational structure, it is argued that: "Agencies in which women can more easily achieve credibility as experts will provide more favorable gender ethos for women."[127] Thus, in policy areas, such as foreign policy, where women are perceived to be unsuitable and to have little knowledge, it can be expected that gaining credibility will be a major problem faced by women attempting to gain and use power. Women need to be credible experts to be hired and promoted, and without expertise they will have more problems with subordinates.[128] We shall next examine the extent to which these organizational practices have influenced women in leadership positions in the State and Defense Departments.

State: Hierarchy, Leadership, Policy Type

> Here I was, with my college degree and my Phi Beta Kappa, typing these little three-by-five cards, while men with high school diplomas were hired at higher levels for more responsible work.
>
> *Alison Palmer*

> WAO's [the Women's Action Organization] struggle was far from over. Career women in the foreign affairs agencies still faced the more subtle and difficult problem of negative attitudes about "women's work" and "women's place" held by many personnel officers and supervisors.[129]

> The State Department has hiring, promotion, and assignment policies which have been found to have a negative effect on women and minorities.[130]

The State Department is a hierarchical organization with both the Washington office and the foreign posts having specific chains of command. This hierarchical system is based upon two different ranking systems. In the Civil Service rankings discussed earlier, employees are ranked by GS level. Foreign Service Officers have a similar system, with the highest being the Senior Foreign Service (SFS) (recently renamed the Foreign Service Executives), followed by FSO levels 1 to 9 in descending order of influence. This hierarchical structure impacts upon women in a number of ways.

Firstly, the means by which Foreign Service Officers are selected mediates against women. Though the Foreign Service Act of 1980 required the State Department to develop recruiting strategies to increase female representation, a 1989 GAO study found that State's recruiting plans were inadequate and that women were not being reached.[131] Subsequently, the examination procedure, by which Foreign Service Officers are selected, also has been found to work against women. Of those women taking the written exam in 1971, only 1.8 percent also passed the oral. Among men that year the pass rate was 2.9 percent. In 1976, women's pass rate remained at 1.8 percent, while men's improved to 3.7 percent.[132] By 1987, this situation had improved: of all White males taking the exam the passage rate was 4.3 percent and the White female pass rate had grown to 3.9 percent.[133] The extent to which the exam discriminates against women has been the subject of recent litigation. In the Palmer Case, the Court noted that the disparity in cone assignments (see next section) was caused by the fact that women received lower scores on the political function field exam than men.[134] As a result, the 1989 examination was canceled and the exam procedure was revised.

Secondly, even more than other agencies, the State Department's Foreign Service system rewards individualistic behavior. In contrast to the Civil Service employees, the Foreign Service personnel system is a bottom entry, merit promotion, "up or out" system,[135] with one's rank being determined by one's own status rather than the rank of one's position. This practice has also had a negative impact on women. Progress within the ranks is dependent upon one's service evaluations. The Palmer case ruling concluded that in 1977, for FSOs in classes five and six, women officers received evaluations that were statistically worse that those of male officers.[136] The original finding that there was no overall pattern of discrimination in promotions was also overturned in May 1990 by the U.S. Court of Appeals, which concluded that women were hampered in promotions due to fewer honor awards, service in less prestigious assignments and evaluations.[137] As a result of the ruling in *Palmer v. Baker*, 26 superior honor awards have subsequently been awarded to women who were initially passed over.[138]

This hierarchical ecological context has had another negative effect upon women. Career women at State have had difficulty in reaching decision-making positions, those jobs at the top of the career ladder. Evidence of this glass ceiling abounds. As a 1984 study of the Department concluded, there is an inverse relationship between the proportion of women and level of rank. The higher the rank, the lower the percentage of women.[139] "The circumscribed role of women in foreign affairs is most clearly evident at the senior level, the level from which career ambassadors, deputy chiefs of mission at the larger embassies, assistant secretaries (heads of bureaus), and deputy assistant secretaries are chosen."[140] In 1970, only 2 percent of all senior career officers were women and by 1981 this figure had increased only to 3 percent.[141] As of 1987, out of total of 703 Senior Foreign Service Officers, only 34 or 4.8 percent were women.[142] Looking at it from another angle, in 1970 of all women FSOs, only 1 percent were in senior positions. Almost twenty years later, in 1989, the percentage of all women who were in senior positions had grown only to 2 percent. Similarly, among the women in Civil Service positions, only one half of one percent of the women reached SES positions.[143] The State Department's Affirmative action plans for fiscal years 1985 and 1986 were rejected by the EEOC, which in its evaluation of State's 1987 plan, concluded that State relied on the promotion of entry level FS officers to eliminate under-representation at senior levels, which EEOC did not feel would resolve the problem.[144] The 1988 report by EEOCR also indicated that the percentage of women is unlikely to radically change soon. Of the 135 promotions to the Senior Foreign Service in 1987, only 7 or 5.2 percent were granted to women. In 1989, only 7 percent of the ambassadors were women.[145] This same conclusion was reached by a 1989 GAO study which found that "minorities and women are still significantly underrepresented at the senior levels of the Foreign Service. The State Department has not had an effective affirmative action plan or program for overcoming the underrepresentation in the Foreign Service."[146] This same study concluded that State had not fully complied with EEOC requirements for affirmative action programs.[147]

The 1984 study by Olmsted et al. posited a number of reasons for the small percentage of women in higher levels, several of which relate to this ecological context of the department: the pool from which senior officers can be chosen is small; promotions come more slowly for women; ambassadors choose the deputy chiefs of mission from a short list of FSOs submitted by the Bureau of Personnel, and both career and political ambassadors have been consistently reluctant to accept a woman as a deputy.[148] In *Palmer v. Baker*, it was found that women have been underassigned to Deputy Chief of Mission (DCM) positions. Between 1972 and 1983 out of 586 appointments only 9 women were selected. Based on the number of women in grade levels from which DCMs were chosen, the expected number of appointments would have been 26.8.[149] As a result of the *Palmer* case remedies, eight women have received relief from having been denied DCM assignments in the past.[150] One woman described how the process works against women:

> There certainly are cases when some ambassadors don't want a woman to be the DCM, it's a personal preference. Other women have been very successful women DCMs, some ambassadors don't mind a bit, others do. A friend of mine who went out this past summer to be an ambassador was talking about different candidates he was interviewing for DCM, and he wanted someone with a wife to help his wife share the social aspects. That's terrible but you find that in some individuals. They'll never admit it, but I know it must be true.

Another aspect of progress within this hierarchy are what are known as "stretch assignments," which are the ability of foreign service officers to obtain positions of higher responsibility than their current rank would warrant. Down-stretch assignments are the opposite; when officers are assigned to positions with lesser rankings than their own. These practices have also been used to the disadvantage of women. Again in the Palmer case, the State Department was found to have engaged in discrimination between 1976 and 1981 in that among FSO-4 officers, 32.2 percent of women as compared to 17.6 percent of men received "down-stretch" assignments. The figures for FSO-5 officers were similar, 20.8 percent of women as contrasted to 14.2 percent of men.[151] Conversely, it was also found that the Department discriminated against women Foreign Service Officers by underassigning them to stretch positions. Though the State Department tried to argue that women preferred "down-stretch" assignments, it is clear that these patterns hindered the promotion of women to decision-making levels. This individualistic hierarchy is also reflected in the awards given to officers based on meritorious service. In *Palmer v. Baker* the State Department was also found to have engaged in gender discrimination in that women proportionately received fewer superior honor awards than men, which again hampers their chances for promotion within the hierarchy.

The State Department's hierarchical structure also reinforces the importance of organizational leadership. The Secretary of State has the primary responsibility for all policy matters, including equal opportunity for women. As the Olmsted report concluded "The single most important factor in achieving equal employment opportunity in the Department of State is the commitment demonstrated by the Secretary of State and the Under Secretary for management."[152] Decision-making responsibility itself follows the hierarchical pattern of its organization chart. The most important decisions are made by the Secretary, the Deputy Secretary, and the Under Secretaries, who occupy the 7th floor.[153] The major leadership positions in the Department are the Secretary of State, the Deputy Secretary of State, and the Under Secretary for Political Affairs, none of which has ever been filled by a woman. Thus, as an outside consultant concluded, there has been little support for equal employment opportunity in the top management.[154] For example, the Federal Women's Program and the Equal Employment Opportunity and Civil Rights Office have been hampered by personnel shortages and lack of necessary data.[155] However, as part of the 32 Directives George Shultz signed in September 1986, the EEOCR office was removed from the service of Under Secretary for Management and made independent with direct access to the Secretary of State. Though this move was justified in terms of enhancing its effectiveness in overcoming these ecological origins of discrimination, the move may have been nothing more than cosmetic. In 1989, the General Accounting Office was directed to review the State Department's compliance with equal employment requirements and it found that the State Department still had not collected key data nor analyzed the barriers to equal employment.[156]

DOD: Hierarchy, Leadership, Policy Type

> Despite advances that have taken them far beyond roles envisioned even a decade ago, women's place in the U.S. military of the 1990s remains uncertain—their careers frequently thwarted by institutionalized discrimination, pervasive sexual harassment and the prejudices of tradition—bound institutions. There is widespread discrimination against women in recruiting, training, and promotions—particularly for traditionally male jobs, according to the Pentagon's own internal studies, outside analysts, and dozens of women interviewed for this series.[157]

The organization of the Defense Department is even more hierarchical than the State Department. At the top are the Secretary of Defense and the Deputy Secretary of Defense, under whom are organized the Office of the Secretary of Defense (OSD), the twelve defense agencies, and the three military departments (Army, Navy, and Air Force). Each branch of the uniformed military service is organized as a separate agency in DOD, headed by a Secretary appointed by the President. The combat side of the Department is additionally organized through the Joint Chiefs of Staff (representing the four armed services, Army, Navy, Air Force, and Marine Corps), below which are the Unified and Specified Commands. A Unified Command is made up of forces from two or more military services, and is generally organized on a geographical basis, whereas a Specified Command is organized on a functional basis and is generally composed of only one service. The number of commands varies over time but is presently at ten.[158] This military structure creates a military ethos which extends even to the civilians in DOD. As a result, even civilian leaders develop militaristic traits due to their conditioning experiences, including the belief that foreign policy is a "game of men, somewhat like major sports, in which toughness (associated with military deportment) gains the day."[159] This military ethos obviously negatively impacts upon women, who as we saw in the preceding section have been historically excluded from military service. Currently, on the military side, women are integrated most thoroughly into combat support roles. "No law prohibits women from serving 'in combat.' Laws do prohibit the permanent assignment of Navy, Marine Corps and Air Force women to ships and aircraft engaged in combat mission, and while there is no comparable statutory prohibition for Army women, policies adopted by the Army and the other services further restrict women's roles."[160] As a result, in 1989 the proportion of jobs open to women in each of the services was as follows: Coast Guard, 100 percent; Air Force, 97 percent; Navy, 59 percent; Army, 52 percent; and Marine Corps, 20 percent.[161]

The overriding organizational principal of the Department of Defense is, of course, the notion of a military chain of command. Those at the top make the decisions that those at the bottom are obligated to carry out. As Table 2-3 demonstrates, DOD can be considered hierarchical in that it has even fewer people in the top positions than in other government agencies.

While the presence of civilian personnel in key positions softens this military philosophy somewhat, men with military titles or backgrounds

Table 2-3.   GS grade spread comparison percent of positions by GS grade

	1–4	5–7	8–11	12–13	14–15	16–18
Government wide	22.6	27.8	25.5	17.5	6.0	0.7
Dept. of Defense	25.4	28.1	26.3	16.5	3.6	0.2
Army	26.4	30.4	24.0	16.0	3.1	0.1
Navy	25.6	25.3	25.5	18.7	4.7	0.2
Air Force	25.5	28.8	27.7	15.1	2.8	0.1
Office of Defense Analysis	20.3	24.4	34.3	16.1	4.4	0.5

Source: Defense Manpower Commission, *Defense Manpower: The Keystone of National Security* (Washington, DC: DOD, 1976), 10.

dominate the structure. This is especially true in the combat command. All the Joint Chiefs of Staff are high ranking military officers. Similarly, of the 12 Department of Defense Agencies only four were headed by civilians during the latter stages of the Reagan Administration.[162] This reliance on military personnel obviously limits the opportunities for advancement of women who are less likely than men to have had military experience.

There are several implications of this hierarchical structure on women. To begin, women have a hard time moving up in the ranks. "The women employed within DOD have clustered in jobs in lower grades. As a result, women have found a limited growth potential."[163] Women have made some, albeit limited, gains in entering the policy-making ranks. In 1980, women constituted only 2.6 percent of all DOD SES executives. By 1991, the percentage of women in SES positions had grown to 6.15 percent.[164]

One might also speculate that the prevalence of military personnel in a hierarchical structure would create an atmosphere where women, who generally lack military training or rank, would be uncomfortable and unable to influence the decision-making process. It appears that at Defense women are more likely to be "cut out" by boundary-heightening activities and the reliance of others on stereotypes of women's abilities than at State. The almost universal references to the "military," "macho-military" environment by our women interviewees at Defense leads us to believe that the us-them (male/military versus women/non-military) boundary is reinforced often and with severe consequences for women who aim to influence policy in the Department. The quandary this presents for women was perhaps best described by one of our interviewees as follows:

> The Department of Defense is male dominated. The top positions are all filled by men. It is basically a power club and you don't push your way into that world. They can pull a few of us up. But the major jobs, the more critical jobs, are basically held by men, military and civilian, in the Department of Defense. That attitude makes it difficult to prove the potential you have. The male dominated culture tends to keep women limited in their contributions.

Similarly to the State Department, Defense's hierarchical structure also amplifies the importance of organizational leadership. The notion of the military chain of command ensures that policies or practices set by the leadership will be followed or mimicked throughout the organization. As one woman respondent indicated, the chain of command can have devastating influence on a woman's effectiveness when those military officers in charge decide to discriminate. "Chain of command and what is acceptable in the military is very influenced by what the leader does and if discrimination is acceptable at top it will be mimicked, regardless of what they believe, at lower levels." She noted it also works the other way too:

> I've had a couple of officers who never adjusted to a woman, but their bosses, the group at my level, the admirals who were my counterparts, didn't respond to it, so they [the men who wouldn't accept women] were ineffective. The madder they got, the more isolated they became and eventually they were in trouble with their own bosses. They didn't get with the program.

Another women agreed:

> The hierarchial structure of the military would make it easier to be a woman in that structure because you just do away with a lot of the hundred ways subordinates have to *not* do something you ask them to do, the hundred ways to be nonhelpful.

A woman who worked in the Navy reported an additional benefit of the chain of command when asked if men interrupted her. "Military people don't interrupt." Another noted, "My rank and position means they won't interrupt."

This hierarchical structure creates another problem for women managers in the need to deal directly with military men. In most of the offices, career military officers are assigned as staff persons to the political appointees and career executives. A woman at Defense described the more general climate that results:

> I think it [discrimination] is to be expected. I called a Master Sergeant the other day in charge of the U.S. Army Band. I had a soloist who was going to sing the National Anthem and I wanted her to sing "I'm Proud to be an American." He said, "That's a male song, we don't have any female arrangements and women don't sing that song." And he believed that. That is just one example or small anecdote. But there are belief systems in this building, this culture, this corporate culture, this country. And women believe it about themselves, that there are some things a woman shouldn't do, or they can't do. Sometimes it is not intentional. I see it as sexism, and they see it as well, but it is a matter of interpretation. There is an unreadiness to accept authority of a female boss, a lack of support.

Others indicated the problem was not with those military personnel who worked for them, but with the military officers at or above their level. One woman in the weapons research area was forced to send male couriers to a particular officer who "had trouble dealing with women on military matters." Sometimes it is the military rules that prevent women from exercising all the powers of their position. A woman who dealt with submarine equipment, for instance, was not allowed to spend a week on board ship to test the equipment she helped design. Rather her husband (also in the Navy) had to take the shipboard assignment for her. Other women cited slower promotions, fewer opportunities, and not being allowed to make decisions as results of the military atmosphere.

In terms of type of policy, DOD's military function creates additional problems for women. The double bind of being a token woman and being in an area where women's knowledge is assumed to be limited seems to heighten the need to work harder and prove yourself, especially for the women in Defense. The situation is described most forcefully by a career woman in the Defense Department in response to a question asking whether being a woman limits her influence:

> DOD tends to be a male chauvinistic master. It is very difficult. I was on assignment and I went into this office and they said to me, "This is the most critical project for the Department of Defense. It is much too important for a woman to work here." I stayed there for eight months, and they let me know it every day that I was a woman and couldn't make these decisions. In the Department of Defense, it is much more difficult to be a woman and to be accepted and to have people listen to what you have to say. There is a military macho image, so you have to prove yourself. Before they listen to you, you have to prove yourself, over and over and over again.

Internal Topography

The third element of ethos is internal topography, or the formal and informal cleavages based on policy areas, tasks and territorial segregation. Internal topography describes the means by which women are segregated into positions outside of the policy-making functions, such as clerical jobs. In terms of task segregation, the realms of policy and budget are the most important. At one time, the personnel arena was considered powerful, yet the degree to which it become routinized under civil service has made it less influential. In male bastions, power rests with male incumbents, and women tend to be clustered in weaker service divisions. This task segregation not only limits women's influence by keeping them distant from the primary power positions, but it also hinders their future effectiveness or career opportunities by placing women in positions in which promotions to policy-making positions are more unlikely.

State: Internal Topography

The internal structure of the State Department is fairly complex and this myriad of organizations impacts upon women in a number of significant fashions. The Department of State employees currently fall into three general classifications: Civil Service 33.5 percent; Foreign Service Generalists 36.4 percent; Foreign Service Specialists 30.1 percent.[165] The Civil Service employees are generally located in Washington and are involved in predominantly administrative tasks. It is here that the women in the Department of State have been clustered. In 1960, 60.4 percent of all Civil Service employees were women; in 1970, 64.7 percent were women and in 1990, 62.6 percent of all Civil Service employees were women. In contrast, in 1981 women constituted only 21.6 percent of all Foreign Service Generalists and 34.4 percent of all Foreign Service Specialists. Looking at this from another angle, of all women employed by the State Department in 1987, 53.9 percent were in the Civil Service, 26.2 percent were Foreign Service Specialists, and only 19.9 percent were Foreign Service Generalists (the major component of which is the Foreign Service Officer Corps).[166] These distributions have been further skewed by the previously mentioned hierarchical pattern in which women have rarely been found in the upper echelons. In State, of the Senior Executive Service in Civil Service only 8.3 percent were women. Women constituted only 4.9 percent of the Senior Foreign Service among the Generalists and 4.2 percent among the Specialists.[167] Both of these distribution patterns combine to place women in positions in which they function as support staff, not as foreign policy decision-makers.

Another way in which internal topography has served to limit women FSOs is through the "cone" system. The primary foreign policy-makers in the Department are the Foreign Service Generalists, and they are subdivided into four primary functional areas (in which one generally remains for the duration of one's career). The four areas are political, economic, consular, and administrative, of which the political is the most influential and career-enhancing. Officers from the political cone also experience a higher rate of advancement to and within the Senior Foreign Service.[168] However, women have been assigned less frequently to the political cone and more frequently to the consular cone. In 1986 the percentage of women in each of the cones was as follows: administrative, 25.5 percent; consular, 34.2 percent; economic, 15.0 percent; and political, 13.0 percent. These figures did improve slightly in 1987, with women constituting 15.5 percent of the political cone. However, of all women generalists in 1986, 26.1 percent were assigned to the political cone and 34.4 percent to the consular cone; whereas for all male generalists, 43.2 percent were assigned to the political cone and only 16.4 percent were assigned to the consular cone.[169] Figures such as these for the period 1975 to 1980 led to the Court's decision in the Alison Palmer case that the State Department discriminated against women in original cone assignments. According to their calculations 16.9 percent more females were assigned to the consular cone and 17.6 percent fewer were assigned to the political cone than one would have expected based on their percentage rate of new hires.[170] As a result, of the over 200 relief measures provided as a result of the *Palmer* case, the highest percentage were to remedy these disadvantageous cone assignments.[171] The 1989 GAO study concluded that this same pattern still existed, with women still being disproportionately assigned to administrative and consular work.[172] The difficulty in getting assignments to political cones was exemplified by one woman at State who recounted how she had to keep on insisting on a political cone assignment before she was finally given one:

> At the end of six years I said to my grooming officer, "I would really still like to do political work. You have me answering public correspondence, and I've been a personnel officer and a vice-counsel, but now I've been in for awhile and I still think I'd like to do political work."

Her next assignment was in the political cone but one can assume other women were not as persistent nor as fortunate as she.

Foreign Service Officers are able to move into a cone other than that originally assigned to them through "out-of-cone" assignments. Instead of using these assignments to alleviate the dislocation of women due to past discrimination, the State Department has utilized these assignments to further concentrate women in the consular cone. Again in the Alison Palmer case, it was demonstrated that women were given out-of-cone assignments to the consular cone in a much higher percentage than the men. For example, from the political cone 40.4 percent of the women but only 15.5 percent of the men were assigned to the consular cone. From the economic cone 22.9 percent of women, yet only 11.6 percent of men; and from the administrative, 50.8 percent of women and 32.2 percent of men are assigned to the consular cone.[173] Though the State Department tried to argue that these disparities were due merely to the women's preference for consular work, the Court found that the Department had discriminated against women in such cone assignments. It appears as if the Department may be trying to rectify some of its past practices. In the 1987 hires of generalists, 39.6 percent of those assigned to the political cone were women and only 33.3 percent of those assigned to the consular were women.[174]

In the Civil Service sector, women have tended to be found in non-

policy-making positions, even within the SES. As Mary Lee Garrison testified to Congress in 1987, only nine SESs at State were women:

> Of that nine women, five were assistant legal advisers in the Legal Advis-
> er's Office. These are not mainstream Foreign Service policy-making
> positions. These are not supervisory positions and they are not career-
> ladder positions. These people are very much outside of the mainstream,
> yet that was the bulk of the women in the Senior Executive Service at the
> State Department.[175]

DOD: Internal Topography

As noted in the previous section, the Department of Defense is a complex hierarchical organization, headed by a Secretary and a Deputy Secretary of Defense. Employees within the Department are divided into civilian
and military personnel. Overall, though the percentage of civilian employees is slowly increasing (29.7 percent in 1960, 28.0 percent in 1970, 31.9
percent in 1980, and 33.4 percent in 1987), the vast majority of DOD's
employees are in the military classifications.[176] The locus of women within
the Department has remained fairly stable during the 1980s. Of all women
employed by the Department, just over 60 percent are civilian employees
and under 40 percent are military employees. Concerning military
women, both their numbers and status have increased in the 1980s. In
1980, women constituted 8.4 percent of all active military personnel and
7.7 percent of all officers.[177] By 1987 women constituted 10.3 percent of all
military and 10.4 percent of all officers. Broken down by military branch,
women constituted 10.6 percent of the enlisted personnel of the Army,
9.1 percent of the Navy, 5.1 percent of the Marines, and 12.4 percent of
the Air Force.[178] Among the officers, 10.4 percent Army, 10.1 percent Navy,
3.3 percent Marines, 11.5 percent Air Force were women.[179] Moreover,
women officers tend to be concentrated in the lower ranks. Only eight
women held the position of Brigadier General (or equivalent, none were
higher) in 1986 out of a total of officer force at this rank or above of 1055.[180]

Women's place of power in the military is even more restricted by the
type of positions or specialties they are allowed to hold. The largest
percentage of enlisted women in the services are found in support and
administration, while medical and dental, and communications and intelligence are the next largest categories. The distribution of officers reverses
the order slightly, with the medical field having the most women officers.
Administration is second while intelligence is an area with few women
officers. With the possible exception of communications and intelligence,
therefore, the areas women find themselves in are largely "support," and

given the small percentage of women officers in communications and intelligence (about five percent), one can speculate that women are largely in the support positions, telephone and radar operators, in this field as well. Currently women are not allowed to participate in most combat positions. Thus, they are excluded from the most important and key line jobs in the military. The exclusion of women from combat and the restrictions put on the positions they can assume because of the need to reserve slots for men, limits the upward mobility of women in the military and thus the Department of Defense. As we have seen, many of the critical and important decision-making positions in the Department of Defense are reserved for military brass. Moreover, the experience gained by serving in technical, intelligence and combat positions is often critical for advancement in the area of foreign policy. (Almost all the men we interviewed in intelligence at both the State and Defense Departments had served in Vietnam in intelligence positions.) In addition, the absence of military and combat positions for women was identified by many of the respondents as an important variable in limiting women's credibility, a point we will return to below.

While the position of women in the military is restricted, our primary concern is with civilian employees, which also happens to be where the majority of women are employed. An interview with a former member of the Presidential Personnel Staff at the White House in charge of political appointments during the first term of the Reagan Administration indicated some of the problems she encountered with placing women in the Department of Defense. First, she was under a lot of pressure to get people with a "special view," (for instance, she indicated the Heritage Foundation was busily grooming people for particular jobs). Second, the biggest problem was in the area of technical jobs. There was simply "not a rich pool" of women in the technical areas. She speculated that the reasons for this might be because of women's lack of military service, lack of training or merely that technical areas are not of interest to women. In an attempt to solve the problem, she reported "We salted people at levels to get credentials and this policy bore fruit in the second term."

Even with the help of women in the White House, those women who have made it into the higher ranks of the Department have tended to be concentrated in "staff" positions. For instance, both Carter and Reagan had women General Counsels. The personnel area is also dominated by women. At one point in the Reagan administration, the Deputy Assistant Secretary of the Navy for Personnel and Families was a woman, as were the persons holding similar positions in the Army and in the Office of the Secretary of Defense (OSD). Only Air Force had a man in this area. As one of the career women in Defense observed:

> Most of the women in the Defense Department are in technical staff roles. They are Comptrollers, they are Equal Opportunity officers, they are particularly in Personnel Administration. In the hard core, analytic, key roles that influence policy there are fewer women. My own role has been closer to real strategy than most women are allowed to play.

Of the women we interviewed in the Department, 42 percent were in positions of authority in personnel, manpower, or law. This concentration of women in traditional staff areas does not necessarily mean they are without power in influencing foreign policy. Several of the respondents noted their decisions regarding matters in their immediate area did indirectly or directly impact on the nation's foreign policy. Others, however, were quick to point out that what they did placed them far from the policy process. As an example of the latter, one woman in personnel and manpower noted in reply to what percent of the time she devoted to developing foreign policy: "Ten percent. Questions dealing with reserve forces from other nations." Another woman in a related area made an even more tenuous connection:

> I give advice on issues overseas, with families and dependents overseas. Dependent education is all overseas. Who goes and who stays. But it is generally related to family and dependent issues. But any of our forces overseas I'm involved in if it has anything to do with quality of life.

A woman lawyer in the Department rejected a role in making foreign policy (or any policy) "Doesn't fit lawyers. Kinda reactive. (I spend) lots of time 'tasking' people. . . . Try real hard in giving clients legal advice, though I may give policy advice on top of this."

Not all women in the Defense Department are in positions that prevent them or restrict them from influencing foreign policy. Several of the women who were closely connected with weapons development were able to see how their decisions influenced the foreign policy of the nation. A woman in the Navy noted in regards to influence in foreign policy: "Indirectly. All the products we produce give this nation a capability of war fighting that can impact the flexibility this nation has in making foreign policy." In general, however, few of the women in the Department of Defense felt they were in positions that afforded them a direct opportunity to have a large say in setting our nation's foreign policy.

Social Demography

> Sexual harassment stems from "our own lack of ability to control our careers and our destinies."
>
> *Anita Hill*[181]

To a great extent, social demography within organizations is a reflection of the general societal factors discussed in Chapter 1. "Social demography includes the interest, expectations, and characteristics of the workforce required by organizational functions and the characteristics of its clientele."[182] The characteristics of the workforce will be influenced by the societal values concerning who should work and what types of careers are suitable for certain groups, women in particular. Employees also tend to bring with them the values and stereotypes they have absorbed from society as a whole. However, the functioning and characteristics of the organization can serve to either reinforce or ameliorate these expectations. For example, in her study of women in state bureaucracies, Georgia Duerst-Lahti found that women in higher-ranking positions had higher gender consciousness, yet their organizational experiences had ameliorated the impact of societal values. "These women also tend to hold attitudes about 'proper gender relations' which differ from commonly accepted feminist attitudes" (they tend to believe that women are no different from men in the work setting).[183] In addition, they are not easily offended and are tolerant of being in uncomfortable situations as tokens. After definite proving periods, they appear to be welcomed by most male counterparts.[184] However, as we have already seen, the Departments of State and Defense are different from other organizations, particularly in terms of their mission and their hierarchical structure. They have a distinctive masculine gender ethos. As a result, we would expect that gender would serve "as a critical variable for members of an organization and for organizational structures and processes. Therefore, attitudes and behaviors towards women in the organization will tend to correspond with dominant societal patterns and women will still face more obstacles than men."[185] The culmination of this process may well be a pattern of sexual discrimination and harassment. A 1979 study of federal employees, for instance reported that 35 percent of SES males believed that females were treated better than males, while only 6 percent of the males said that women were treated worse. This contrasts with the opinions of women, only 5 percent of whom concluded that females were treated better than men, and 24 percent of whom claimed that women were treated worse.[186] In the 1980 update of the same study, 29 percent of SES women felt that women were treated worse than men, while 29 percent of the men felt women were treated better. Only 5 percent of the women felt women were treated better, while only 6 percent of the men said women were treated worse.[187]

Additionally, the impact of societal values may be amplified by the organizational culture, creating additional problems and barriers for women in State and Defense. The sex ratio of an organization, particularly if it is also the result of organizational decisions, can also influence the incidence of sexual discrimination. As previously discussed, in a skewed group, the tokens, or minority sex, are more noticeable and thus subject to special attention. In such organizations with skewed sex ratios, there is an increased tendency to utilize gender stereotypes and an increased incidence of "sexual role spillover." "Sexual role spillover" refers to the carryover into the workplace of gender-based expectations that are irrelevant or inappropriate at work.[188] Such gender stereotyping can lead not only to inappropriate behavior (such as off-color jokes or the use of profanity or unwarranted attempts at intimacy), but can subsequently lead to a further decision to avoid or isolate the tokens. For example, male managers in large, male-dominated, industrial organization described their feelings about working with women as follows:

> "They're hard to understand." "It takes a lot of toe testing to be able to communicate." "I'm always making assumptions that turn out to be wrong." Some managers were willing to admit that this was "90 percent my problem, mostly in my head." However, they preferred to deal with people who were similar to themselves. Women as a group were seen as highly dissimilar.[189]

As noted above, skewed sex ratios lead to an increased reliance on gender stereotypes by the dominant group. The focus here is on the extent to which emphasis on these stereotypes leads to discrimination against women. When we examined the types of discrimination the women have encountered, we find a legacy of the past (and sometimes current) images of women held by both Departments. At Defense, as the previous sections on societal and organizational factors made clear, one of the biggest problems confronting women is the stereotype that women know nothing about defense and military matters. As the quotations in those sections revealed, as a result of this stereotype, women often find they are not given a fair hearing for their opinions. As Table 2-4 indicates, our study

Table 2-4.   Percent experiencing discrimination[a]

	Men	Women
All DOD & DOS	5.4	46.3
State	0.0	31.3
Defense	11.1	56.0
State Career	0.0	28.6
Defense Career	6.3	68.8
State Appointees	0.0	33.3
Defense Appointees	50.0	33.3

[a]Figures represent the percent answering yes to the following question: Have you ever experienced any discrimination on account of your sex since you've worked for this Department of Government?

found sexual discrimination in both Departments, though the greatest percentage of complaints from both women and men appeared in the Defense Department.

State: Social Demography

> "Believe me, Ed. The savages in the labor movement [in Ethiopia] would not be receptive to Miss Palmer except perhaps to her natural endowments."
>
> *U.S. Ambassador Korry*[190]

The Department of State and particularly the Foreign Service, as our review of its organization revealed, has been largely an inhospitable arena for women. This exclusion of women from the prime focus of United States foreign policy-making may stem, in part, from the traditional association of men with diplomacy.

> The popular image of the Foreign Service, based partly on legend as well as historical fact, is that of a diplomatic corps comprising members of the upper classes from the Northeast with degrees from Ivy League colleges. The corps' distinctiveness is reinforced by a personnel system that is separate from the Civil Service, of which most federal employees are a part. . . . The Foreign Service has developed a distinctive subculture and mode of operation that have important ramifications for the State Department's role in foreign policy. The subculture reinforces elitism and promotes respect for tradition, precedent, and conformity above all else.[191]

As one "old hand," a woman, at the Department commented when asked about the position of women at State: "Tradition. The men haven't gotten used to women at State. It's a whole change for an institution that has been deeply rooted in tradition. Diplomats were representatives of a king. Women were always the courtesans in the background trying to influence men, not actors in their own right." As we saw in Chapter 1, the notion that only men can serve as diplomats for the king or government is, of course, linked to the cultural view that political involvement generally is an arena for men, and that women are neither knowledgeable nor interested in foreign affairs. Consequently, this subculture creates pressures to avoid rocking the boat, or expressing views that may be seen as challenges to the wisdom of one's superiors, and to avoid dress and behavior that would deviate from the norms of the group.[192] This tendency leads to the efforts to exclude women. A woman with many years of experience explained: "There is this buddy business. Men feel more comfortable among themselves with other men, especially late at night when they loosen their belts. Especially when working on something on a crash basis." Not so surprisingly, given the social values regarding women's knowledge of foreign affairs and the appropriateness of the field for women, and the organizational dimensions of the Department, many women at State reported having been victims of sex discrimination, and this situation does not seem to be improving. In fact, the number of formal discrimination complaints filed against the Department increased from 25 in 1983 to 32 in 1987.[193] In fiscal year 1988, 55 informal discrimination complaints were filed, though 31 were resolved through review, and in 1989, 75 informal complaints were filed, leading to 42 formal complaints. The most frequently cited issues in dispute were promotions and performance levels.[194]

Table 2-5 reflects the incidence of sex discrimination at State experienced by our interviewees. Thirty-one percent of women felt they had been discriminated against while working for the Department. Interestingly, appointees were slightly more likely to have experienced discrimination than careerists (33.3 percent versus 28.6 percent). The types of discriminatory practices reported covered a gamut of activities from being passed over for promotions or special assignments, to not being taken seriously. Many problems were the direct result of previous Department practices. For instance, the rule that all women had to resign from the Foreign Service when they got married was cited by a couple of our interviewees who were able to later return to work in the 1970s when the practice was stopped, in part as a result of a court order. One has to assume there were many more women who were not able to come back after the changes were made, and perhaps still others who postponed

Table 2-5. Sex discrimination in the State Department: Attitudes and experience

	Women		Men	
Experienced Discrimination[a]	31.3	career 28.6 appointees 33.3	0	career 0 appointees 0
Discrimination in U.S.[b]	4.6		4.4	
Discrimination in Government[b]	5.1		5.0	
Discrimination in State[b]	5.0		5.6	

[a] Responses indicate the percentage saying they had experienced discrimination on account of their sex since working for the State Department.

[b] Figures represent the average score in response to the following question: On a seven point scale where one represents severe discrimination and seven represents equal treatment, how would you rate the position of women in the United States? in the federal government? in the State Department?

marriage or never got married because of the Department rules. One of our women at State, for instance, had started her career in the Foreign Service in the 1940s but was forced out in the 1960s when she married. She explained:

> In 1971 things changed. The State Department finally admitted FSO women could be married. And women started getting equal treatment administratively. Before women FSOs were only entitled to a skimpy allowance of a secretary, because that is what a woman got. Same with housing. Then they allowed for reinstatement of women who hadn't resigned. But I didn't bother, I had a higher rank in the civil service.

Women with longer histories in the State Department also recalled early experiences when they were first in the Foreign Service, when efforts were made to limit their rotation or early training to the traditional women's fields at State, counselor affairs and administration. (See Ambassador Ridgway's interview in Chapter 3.) Typical is the quote from a woman in her sixties in response to whether she had ever faced discrimination (although often the older women did not recognize these practices as sex discrimination at the time).

> It has been difficult to get women into titled positions. Oddly enough, I don't think it was discrimination. I think it was chivalry. Particularly in the Foreign Service, men are very hesitant to ask women to do unpleasant things, except secretaries. But I don't think it was motivated by discrimination in the literal sense. It was merely just the price you paid.

In addition to the problems encountered in other male-dominated organizations, one of the difficulties unique to the State Department was also reflected in the interviews: the discriminatory behavior and attitudes of men in other nations. Because success in overseas assignments in key missions is so important to progress up through the ranks, the inhospitable (or perceived inhospitable) environment in other nations for women in positions of authority can be and has been a problem. One man, when asked to identify views that limit women's influence, talked about the issue used to keep women from foreign political posts, the cultural stereotypes of other nations.

> The attitudes of other countries toward women, although they are changing too. My colleagues, the ladies I speak to about it, say if they can be regarded as a third sex or something they can get by with work in the Middle East. Because that's the only way. If they are regarded as women, then men in those countries want to put them off somewhere. And they

can't be regarded as men, so they have to be regarded as sort of something else to be present in the discussion.

A woman commented, however, that being a woman in a foreign culture need not be a hindrance. She cited the case of a very attractive woman who several years ago was assigned to a political slot in Italy. While both the respondent and the men at the embassy had doubts whether this woman could work effectively in that Latin culture, they were surprised by her success. When the respondent asked the men at the embassy how the woman was doing, she was told, "Italian men ... are stunned by it. They don't like to say no to her, so she always gets an appointment with anybody. They all show off and they tell her things they wouldn't tell any of us." A woman specialist in Middle Eastern affairs discovered some of the same disparities. The men in the U.S. felt women would be ineffective abroad, while the foreign government officials themselves had no problem. "Working in the Middle East there are a lot of people who think a woman can inhibit policy. Some see women in the Middle East as a disaster. However I had more trouble with the British than the country people."

In general, however, women at State were upbeat about their status. When asked to evaluate the level of discrimination in their Department on a seven-point scale (with one as severe discrimination and seven as equal treatment), the women at State gave an average score of 5.0 (see Table 2-5). This was only slightly lower than their ranking for the government as a whole and better than the ranking they gave to the United States. However, it should be emphasized the women did not give the Department a 7 and a few were quick to point out the Department was not exactly a leading government agency in improving women's status. To quote, "Only when forced does State do better. So I'd say it was a three. Except when a Court tells them to do something, they wouldn't do it on their own." Moreover, the women at State were in general agreement with the proposition that things for women were improving (see Table 2-6).

Interestingly, when asked to evaluate the Reagan Administration, women in the State Department were both more divided and more negative than the men in the Department. Most women (61.5 percent) believed the status of women in the Department had improved during the Reagan Administration, though they tended to consider the improvement as a function of the general improvement in the status of women nationwide, rather than as a result of administration policies. However, a fairly sizable minority (23.1 percent) reported things had gotten worse, and 15.4 percent indicated there had been no change. In contrast, the men saw women's status as remaining the same or improving. Several of the women who saw a decrease focused on the decline from the Carter years in the numbers of women in the upper ranks of the Department. "I think the

Table 2-6. Position of women in the State Department

Position of women during the Reagan Administration[a]			Future of women in a new administration[b]		
	Women	Men		Women	Men
Increased	61.5	44.4	Improve	80.0	35.0
Remained the Same	15.4	50.0	Remain the Same	20.0	50.0
Decreased	23.1	5.6	Decline	0.0	0.0

[a] Figures represent the percentage indicating the position of women in the State Department had increased, decreased, or remained the same during the Reagan Administration.

[b] Figures represent the percentage indicating the influence/position of women in the State Department will improve, remain the same, or decline under a new administration.

progress of women is in a slow upsurge in the Foreign Service, but in the top echelons there are fewer. The Carter Administration made a deliberate effort to put women in." Another appointee emphasized the lack of women in the appointee positions as the critical variable indicating the decline in women's status:

> Decreased, but I'm not sure it's a function of the Reagan Administration. The number of women ambassadors is shockingly low, which reflects the lack of credibility of women. Not so far as the [Foreign] Service is concerned. But we've also got the highest number of political appointments at State, and those appointments are not going to women.

When asked to evaluate the prospects for women in a new administration, most women (80 percent) expected things would improve. (Of course, in the summer of 1988 our respondents did not know who would be the next President.) Men in the Department were more cautious in predicting improvements, but no one from either gender expected the status of women to decline. Most of those who predicted improvements, however, saw it more as a function of a long-term trend in the hiring practices of the Foreign Service. "The number of women brought into the Foreign Service is always increasing and those already in will be promoted into the more senior positions." Others saw the future as rosy because of improvements in societal views towards women. "I think women have already achieved a foundation. There is a consciousness of women, and women interested in jobs and in working." The few who hesitated about the future referred mostly to the fact that the process would be slow and the prejudices against women still deep. "Hope it will change. When you think about it, however, outside of intelligence, diplomacy is the last bastion of white male supremacy."

A final repercussion of social demography is the problem of sexual harassment. Just as societal stereotypes have led to the denigration of women's abilities and contributions, they have also created a climate in which women have become the targets of unacceptable behavior. A 1980 study of over 20,000 federal employees by the U.S. Merit Systems Protection Board discovered that 42 percent of female employees and 15 percent of male employees reported having been sexually harassed in the previous 24 months.[195] Similarly, a survey by *Government Executive Magazine* of 941 of the highest ranking women government executives reported that 40 percent felt they had been sexually harassed.[196]

Additionally, the hierarchical structure of organizations can contribute to the incidence of sexual harassment. In hierarchical organizations there are major power differentials between individuals resulting from their positions in the hierarchy. By giving some individuals authority over others, the organization creates a situation in which certain individuals have the opportunity to use the promise of rewards or the threat of punishments to obtain sexual gratification from their subordinates.[197] In February 1981, the State Department issued its first policy statement prohibiting sexual harassment, and establishing procedures for the filing of formal complaints.[198] Despite such policies, studies by others have found widespread sexual harassment in the State Department. Indeed, the largest proportion of women employees in any government agency, 52 percent, claimed to have experienced sexual harassment while working in the State Department.[199]

To summarize, women at State face some difficulties trying to influence foreign policy. While many of their problems can be traced to traditional stereotypes that limit women's progress in other male-dominated organizations, others are unique to the field of diplomacy and foreign affairs. Establishing credibility in a subject seen as an area of male expertise, while perhaps less of an issue at State than Defense (see below), presents some difficulties. Even with these limitations, however, we get a feeling that women may have a better chance to break into the higher ranks at State than at Defense. More and more women are coming out of school with expertise in international affairs, confident of their ability to succeed. With some of the more obvious barriers to their progress at State under attack in the Courts, one can look forward perhaps to a day when they will be as influential as men in positions of power in the Foreign Service.

DOD: Social Demography

> A warrior mentality saturates Killeen. Essentially, the conditioning and daily reinforcement of violent values [creates] . . . a social context of institutionalized violence.[200]

When we look at the social demography of the Department of Defense we see perhaps the last, great male arena of power, the arena of preparing for, and fighting in, war. As was discussed in the Introduction and Chapter 1, while questions about women's peacefulness and men's aggression have dominated feminist literature for several years, the general perception of the public (and indeed many feminists) is that war-mongering and war fighting are the preserves of men. Even civilian leaders approach international problems in a macho or militaristic spirit, as a result of their conditioning experiences within the Department. The emphasis is on toughness (associated with military deportment) as the deciding factor.[201]

> Attitudes have a major impact on the partnership role and full utilization of women in the Department of Defense. "Women cannot do man's work." "Women belong in the home." "Women are taking away men's jobs." These are all clichés that have impeded the progress of women in the goals of equal opportunity. ... Fears that moral standards would be lowered through close working relationships do not seem to be any more valid for the Services than in the civilian sector.[202]

As a result, this organizational ethos magnifies the impact of societal stereotypes, resulting in *greater* resistance to women. For example, one public opinion poll taken in 1990 found that the public strongly (72 percent men and 79 percent women) agreed that women should be allowed to serve in combat units if they want to.[203] This degree of acceptance has not yet been found in the defense hierarchy. As was discussed in Chapter 1, the problem of establishing credibility is particularly severe for women who are generally not seen to be knowledgeable about defense issues. As a result, in a study of 941 of the highest ranking women in the military, nearly 70 percent said their views were not as respected as men's.[204] The problem is further exacerbated by the importance of a military background, and the fact that most women civilian policy-makers do not have this credential. A woman in the naval weapons area outlined the problem:

> In the Navy the bigger problem is actually being a civilian. First, you're a civilian. That's the first problem you run into because you haven't had a command and you probably haven't been at sea. There is a very definite hierarchy of credibility within the Navy. And it's first the unrestricted line officers, below them are their own engineering duty officers and then you go down from there to civilians and then you get down to women. So it's partly being a civilian. So generally the problem in influencing is that you don't *appear* to have had direct experience, so you have to demonstrate acquired experience. You don't have weapons, you don't have a uniform, and that means you have to spend a lot of time listening and learning in order to acquire experience.

Another woman, also in Navy weapons, reiterated the point:

> The military themselves have discrimination against civilians, whether they're male or female, because most civilians have not been in operations. So there is that bias or perception that civilians don't know what they're talking about. Then when you put the women on top of that, it makes it even a little worse. DOD is a very macho world. You just don't have that many military women at the top officer, the admiral or general, level. We have laws that prevent females from serving in combat positions and that, in essence, is the hard core of the military. If the military stays male, women will always be less effective because they have not had to demonstrate to peers, to male peers, that they know what they are talking about because they have not been "under fire." Put it in quotes because there's a lot of men who have not been under fire either.

This problem is also recognized by some men who see their own military experience as an advantage. A man in intelligence commented when asked about any special traits he as a man brings to his job, "In my particular job I deal almost exclusively with military strategies. Because women are very lately in military jobs and combat in particular, men have an advantage."

As is clear from these quotes, the failure to let women serve in equal numbers and positions with men in the military presents a double burden for women civilians who try to influence United State's defense policy. The women, and men, who discussed this problem indicated that as a result of their lack of "surface" credibility, women had to prove themselves to their colleagues. One woman noted:

> I think being a woman partly limits my ability to influence Navy policy, particularly in the operations area, but it doesn't completely restrict it. It takes longer in terms of building rapport and establishing capabilities. You come with no certificates that say you know something and so you have to continually prove to each new guy who comes in every three years that you do in fact have some knowledge.

Credibility is not the only problem women face. One of the major results of the amplification of societal values in conjunction with the other organizational factors is the problem of sexual discrimination. As one might expect, given the still pervasive and negative views about women in the military and the more restricted organizational environment, discrimination has been and continues to be a pervasive problem. In 1984, 3,161 EEOC complaints were filed against the Defense Department. There were, however, variations among the services. While the Army had a complaint ratio (or complaint to number of personnel percentage) of 0.2, the Navy's was double that at 0.4.[205] This level of discrimination in the Navy was revealed in November 1991, when an 18-year-old lawsuit for sex discrimination was resolved. The class action suit was filed in 1973 against the Navy, claiming discrimination over hiring and promotions. In finding for the plaintiffs, Judge Harold Green further complained that "the government has sought to prolong this litigation by every means possible, both fair and foul."[206] Similarly in our study, women at the Defense Department were much more likely than those at the State Department to report having experienced sex discrimination. As Table 2-7 indicates, 68.8 percent of all the career women at Defense answered in the affirmative when asked if they had ever experienced sex discrimination.

Interestingly, all of the men in our sample who reported discrimination because of their sex (5.4 percent) were at Defense, suggesting perhaps the negative resistance of the men in that Department to efforts to improve the status of women. As with the women at State there were complaints about slow promotions or a failure to be moved up in rank. A woman at Defense, in response to the question on discrimination, for instance, answered, "Of course. Slow promotions, and not being used according to my job description." But as this quote implies, often the failure to promote is tied to a lack of respect for a woman's abilities. The following is a fairly typical description of the discriminatory experiences of women at Defense.

It is a matter of perception. And I think in my previous job there were some things which happened to me which would not have happened

Table 2-7. Sex discrimination in the Defense Department: Attitudes and experience

	Women		Men	
Experienced Discrimination[a]	56.0	career 68.8 appointees 33.3	11.1	career 6.3 appointees 50.0
Discrimination in U.S.[b]	4.2		4.4	
Discrimination in Government[b]	5.0		5.4	
Discrimination in Defense[b]	5.1		5.3	

[a] Response indicates the percentage saying they had experienced discrimination on account of their sex since working for the Defense Department.

[b] Figures represent the average score in response to the following question: On a seven point scale where one represents severe discrimination and seven represents equal treatment, how would you rate the position of women in the United States? in the federal government? in the Defense Department?

to a man. A number of small things people did to me and my branch that they would not have done if I were a man. They thought it was easier to reject my recommendations.

Others discussed experiences where their orders were challenged or senior colleagues refused to deal with a women. The slow effort to build credibility, moreover, was frequently seen as negated when they had to deal with men not ordinarily in their circle. One women's experience is probably typical. "If they know your expertise, they will listen to you. They will ask your advice. Often if you walk into a room of strangers, however, they merely will just assume you are a secretary."

Perceived or anticipated sexual discrimination by male foreign nationals, a problem at State, was also seen by several of the women at Defense as a problem. For instance, a woman told the following story. "Early on when I first joined the government, I was invited to participate in peacekeeping in the Sinai, and I later found out that there was a glitch. A guy put me out because he felt a woman should not be involved in Israelis versus Arabs." Another woman reported a similar problem with a man in her own Department, who used the supposed views of citizens of other countries to limit her progress.

> When I first started in this area, some stupid man got a hold of my boss and said, "Oh the Japanese won't deal with a woman." I had already been there several times and the ambassador and his deputy had asked me to come back because I was negotiating something for the Japanese they hadn't been able to get done. I had to overcome that silly stuff.

A woman at Defense also focused on the fact that discriminatory behavior more commonly comes from older men or those whose backgrounds did not involve working with women:

> A lot of our political appointees now, because of the restrictions on going to work for companies afterwards and ethics, and the "revolving door," tend to be retired people. Now retired people in their sixties, let's say, coming up through have not worked with many women in industry in responsible positions. They're not very much used to it. They tend not to take you seriously. That has occasionally been my experience. Again less so than with government careerists than with political appointees, who are particularly older men who never worked with women in career positions, their wives never worked. It is out of their frame of references and they are inclined not to take you as seriously.

Perhaps surprisingly, given these findings, the women at Defense rated the overall position of women at Defense as virtually identical to the women at State, (5.1 at Defense, 5.0 at State). (See Table 2-8.) Moreover, the women at Defense gave their Department higher ratings than they gave government as a whole, or especially the United States more generally.

The men at Defense, like their counterparts at State, were even more positive in rating women's status at all three levels. The high ratings at Defense may reflect the perception that the military is working hard at recruiting and promoting women. One woman SES working for the Navy, when asked to rate the status of women in the Department of Defense on the seven-point scale, commented:

> I think six. They're really trying so hard. They really are. What they're trying to do for women in the military is to increase their involvement in the operational Navy. It's a very, very hard problem and the Navy is working very hard on it. I don't agree with all the solutions they've come up with, but I really agree with the fact they are trying.

Alternatively, one woman argued that the difference between State and Defense was the lack of community in Defense.

> The few women that there are here have not represented any threat and have just gone about their business. I get the impression that State Department has in effect responded even more slowly than society in general, or certainly more slowly than some government agencies. In the seventies there was still some discrimination with promotion, but there was also the institutional discrimination in the sense of a small club of people, which the Foreign Service is, of very similar backgrounds, with very similar attitudes, most of which were anti-female. That never existed in Defense. It is not a club, they are civil servants. They're military officers,

Table 2-8. Position of women in the Defense Department

Position of women during the Reagan Administration[a]			Future of women under a new administration[b]		
	Women	Men		Women	Men
Increased	54.5	4.4	Improve	72.7	50.0
Remained the Same	36.4	38.9	Remains the Same	22.7	50.0
Decreased	9.1	16.7	Decline	4.5	0.0

[a] Figures represent the percentage indicating the position of women in the Defense Department had increased, decreased, or remained the same during the Reagan Administration.

[b] Figures represent the percentage indicating the influence/position of women in the Defense Department will improve, remain the same, or decline under a new administration.

they're scattered all over, they come in for tours here and there and they just are like a big corporation or something. So there wasn't on the one hand enough women to bitch, there was on the other hand an institution which was not as cohesive as the Foreign Service was, and so unicultural as the Foreign Service was. People around this building don't bother, they have no unity. Some possible answers are that State had rules and laws that were supposed to be nondiscriminatory. State always maintained that there was the Foreign Service, and if you got into it, you were promoted and treated equally and so forth. It was patently false, so there was a clear discrepancy between the image and the reality. In Defense, in the first place, in the military culture no such claims were ever made. Secondly in the civilian side of Defense women weren't there, so who was there to do a law suit? There wasn't, and there isn't to this day, any sort of community of women that think of themselves as "Women in Defense." In the first place, we're civil servants, whereas in State they're Foreign Service Officers. We have no cohesion. There is just not enough women to complain, and not enough to complain about.

Moreover, when asked to evaluate the progress of women during the Reagan years, women at Defense were perhaps more uniformly upbeat than the women at State. While slightly fewer women at Defense than at State thought women's status had increased (54.5 versus 61.5), fewer women at Defense thought things had gotten worse (see Tables 2-6 and 2-8). Few of those who saw improvement, however, attributed it to the Reagan Administration. In contrast, several respondents noted the improvement came in spite of Reagan. "Army tried to scale back women's roles when Reagan came in. However, Secretary [of Defense] Weinberger and Secretary [of Defense] Carlucci were very favorable toward women. And the Secretary of the Air Force was also favorable. There was lots of evolution, although military is not always a leader." Another woman working for the Navy echoed this last point: "I think what I've seen during the Reagan administration, what I've seen at the top is a lack of emphasis on those [affirmative action] goals that have affected the lower levels. So there is not as much attention given to attaining the goals we have."

Looking toward the future, women at Defense were only marginally less optimistic than women at State. Of the former, 72.7 percent expected to see improvements, in comparison with 80 percent of the latter (see Tables 2-6 and 2-8). Several other respondents noted the need for time, for the women hired in at the lower ranks to work themselves up to positions of authority. When asked if there were too few women in DOD, a male who ran the career program in Air Force made this point forcefully, perhaps tipping his hand as to his feelings about how the process was working to the detriment of men:

That's a complex question. If one were to look at the numbers, certainly I would say there are too few. It's an anomaly and a deplorable anomaly. In the nonpolitical realm it takes time for women or anyone to go up the chain. When we hired women, we didn't hire them at the senior ranks. They were all these college graduates. We have a massive recruiting effort now, we're looking for women and minorities. Smart people first but it takes time for the system to bring these people forward. The process is working and women are being promoted ahead of men—no I won't say that—smart people are being promoted. But I can't make somebody a super grade unless they've gone through the process. The process doesn't allow it. Women in the Air Force are approaching [GS] 14 and 15 level. My guess is it will take another generation, another 10 to 15 years.

Others indicated that the increasing number of women in the military would help recruitment of women to the Defense Department. Some thought the process would take much longer because women were less likely to have the required educational background. Others felt cultural stereotypes, starting with the youth, would have to be eliminated first. A woman in the Navy responded to a question regarding progress in the last four years, "Not in four years. I think what we're doing is undergoing a cultural change that starts with little girls and little boys playing soccer together. What's going to change are the attitudes of the kids who are in school together now and view each other as more equals. They'll make the change." A man at Defense expanded on the role of cultural conditioning:

Discrimination implies a cognitive awareness and a decision to discrimi- nate and I wonder if that is the same. Or are women carrying the stigma of their maturation process, or of not entering into the workplace in certain areas such as government? While I feel they are under-repre- sented in the country, in the government, in the Pentagon, I am not sure that it is positive discrimination, or conscious discrimination against them because of gender, but because of a host of social situations created over time which limit the number of women coming forward to compete.

Unlike the abovementioned alternatives, our discussion of societal values and organizational practices suggests that both traditional cultural prac- tices and active discrimination have limited the progress of women at Defense.

Similarly, the social demography within the Defense Department has contributed to a significant problem of sexual harassment. Sadly, sexual harassment has a long history in the military. During World War II when women began to enter the armed forces in large numbers, women were subjected to dirty jokes, slander campaigns, and obscene cartoons. There was:

> a whole gamut of sexual harassment that military women were subject to, which ranged from verbal abuse to outright propositioning and created at its least a hassle and at its worst a climate of hostility and fear. "You can't even go into the chow hall without running the gauntlet," complained a corporal. "You feel naked and you want to hide. It doesn't do any good to complain to your boss about it. He just shrugs it off as a joke. And, you can't complain to the women officers because they are powerless to do anything about it, besides they get the same hassle from the guys—sometimes worse."[207]

These same types of behavior have continued. Sexual harassment has become a major problem at Defense, particularly in the uniformed services. Research has found sexual harassment to be prevalent at the military academies.[208] Similarly, a 1990 report by the Defense Manpower Data Center indicated that 64 percent of women on active duty had been subject to "uninitiated and unwanted sexual attention."[209] Moreover, the report found women were reluctant to report the incidents because they feared reprisals or thought nothing would be done.[210] Similar studies by DACOWITS of military installations in Southern Europe and in the Pacific found widespread harassment. In particular, DACOWITS reported: "The Navy and the Marine Corps in the Pacific condone sexual harassment, discrimination, and 'morally repugnant behavior.'"[211] DACOWITS even concluded that DOD has done little to correct the problem. DOD's response "has not been overwhelming. ... They've just thrown up their hands and said there's nothing we can do about this."[212] Part of the problem is that:

> Frequently, the target of the complaint is a senior person in the chain of command, further inhibiting women from filing complaints. "The very people who should be exercising leadership are the ones committing harassment."[213]

> Military officials say it is difficult to assess the magnitude of the problem, yet concede they have made little effort to do so. None of the services—Army, Navy, Air Force and Marine Corps—keep comprehensive statistics on reports of sexual harassment and discrimination, or records of how the cases are resolved. [214]

In the spring of 1992, disclosure of the "Tailhook Incident" by Lt. Paula Coughlin focused public awareness on sexual harassment in the military. Lt. Coughlin had been the victim, along with at least 26 other women, of a vicious sexual attack by a group of male Navy aviators at their annual convention in September 1991.[215] Groped and partially disrobed by the pilots while trying to walk down a hall, Lt. Coughlin had reported her experience to the admiral for whom she was an aide. Foot-dragging by the investigating officers and stonewalling by the naval aviators convinced Coughlin that she had to tell her experience to the public. The resulting firestorm of outrage over the Navy's handling of the incident resulted in the resignation of the Secretary of the Navy and a congressional investigation.[216] The Chief of Naval Operations, Adm. Frank B. Kelso told a congressional committee, "Until Tailhook, we dealt too often with sexual harassment at the local level, one case at a time, rather than understanding it as a cultural issue that had to be addressed throughout the Navy. This incident has galvanized us to re-examine the whole treatment of women in uniform."[217] Several of those who testified at the hearing linked sexual harassment in the military to the exclusion of women from combat positions, arguing that until that policy is reversed women can never expect to be treated as equals.[218]

Women soldiers stationed in the Persian Gulf during Desert Storm also indicated sexual harassment was pervasive. One woman was quoted as describing the problem as follows: "There were hard stares and even harder hits. Some guys hadn't seen a woman in five months and they acted like animals. . . . They assumed we were [already] doing it."[219] More seriously, during Desert Storm at least 24 Army servicewomen were raped by fellow soldiers, a number of whom were superior officers.[220] There is also evidence that the problem of sexual harassment by members of the military is not restricted only to other service personnel. A study by Anson Shupe and William Stacey found that the military conditioning and daily reinforcement of violence plus the devaluation of women has spilled over into civilian life as well, leading to a much higher level of severity of family violence (battered wives and girlfriends) located around military bases.[221]

A male with responsibility in personnel matters reported that sexual harassment is not a problem limited to the military side of the Department, though the incidents he described were of a less serious nature:

> My overall comment, I do think there is a problem, even in the government, and I think this has to do with old men. There is sexual abuse—but not the kind you could ever pin down. I think harassment is everywhere—I don't mean the real kind you would do anything about—I mean the innuendos, the comments all done in jest and those kinds of things [done] with the nicest motives but having the most terrible effect. As part of the career program, people come to me and say "my boss reacts to me this way, what can I do?" And it's not a matter of putting the guy in jail. I honestly believe, in most of the cases I hear or know about, it isn't done maliciously. There is a generation who believes when a woman is attractive, they should pay her a compliment no matter what.

So they, even during the course of a business meeting, they might make a compliment not done maliciously, but it's done. It is a part of stereotypes those people have.

In sum, the atmosphere in the Department of Defense makes it very difficult for women to have influence. The macho nature of the policy area and the reliance on military expertise and experience hinder the credibility of women who do make it into decision-making positions dealing with military-defense questions. Under such circumstances, the constant refrain from women at Defense about the need to prove themselves becomes even more understandable. (Those who are restricted to traditional concerns, for instance, personnel and family, report few or no problems with establishing their credibility.) While the women who have made it into the key decision-making positions in the Department believe they personally have been able to overcome the doubts about their ability, at least among their immediate colleagues, the future for women in the Department is questionable at best. On the plus side, more women today have acquired a military background and more women have been recruited into the civilian ranks. These trends will increase the number and credibility of women in the Defense Department. However, on the minus side, women still face restricted opportunities in the military, especially the exclusion from combat. Thus the perception (by the public, the military brass, and the ranking members of Department of Defense), that the military-defense area is one where women lack the credentials to *really* know what they are talking about, can be expected to continue for sometime.

Conclusion

Our review of the Department of State and the Department of Defense generally confirms our hypothesis that both agencies have an ethos that tends to restrict women's influence on the foreign policy process. Women in both Departments have historically been nearly or virtually excluded from positions of authority. While the situation for women is improving, they still tend to be negatively impacted by the ecological context and internal topography of both Departments, which tend to place women far from the center of policy-making power. Likewise, the social demography of both State and Defense tends to denigrate or dismiss the women's knowledge of foreign and military affairs.

The ecological context, or organization, of both Departments also undermines women's positions. As they are extremely hierarchical structures, women have found it difficult to break into the decision-making ranks at State and Defense. Moreover, women who do find themselves in higher-ranking positions are often segregated by the internal topography of both Departments to areas with limited impact on foreign policy, for instance, personnel and legal services in Defense and consular and administrative affairs in State.

Lastly, we found the social demography or the ability of women to "fit in" to each Department is severely hampered by traditional views of women's knowledge and training in foreign and military affairs. In the State Department, women reported that traditional stereotypes about women in other countries and our own served to hamper the ability of women in positions of authority. In Defense, the difficulty of establishing credibility is an especially critical problem.

In this rather hostile setting women are not without power. Many of our respondents rated their own influence rather highly. However, relative to men, women are few in number, restricted in opportunity, and diminished in terms of their contributions. Prospects for change are on the horizon. More women than ever before can be found in the civil service ranks below the SES and SFS level. The next generation of women in the two Departments will be a larger class and may enter perhaps more welcoming climates. However, the impact of these societal and organizational factors can be ameliorated or reinforced by the individual factors, which are the subject of the next chapter.

Interview
ALISON PALMER
Tireless Foe of Sex Discrimination

Alison Palmer spent much of her professional career in the State Department working to eradicate the legacy of years of discrimination against women. The primary litigant in several major legal actions against the State Department, Ms. Palmer can take much credit for the improvements seen in the last two decades in the way women are treated at State.

Her own career in the Department is replete with examples of the discrimination faced by women. Hired as secretary even though she had a degree from Brown University, she soon took and passed the written exam for the Foreign Service. Her experience with the oral exam, however, suggests why women have trouble with it.

The oral exam is supposed to be broad-ranging. It's supposed to give you the chance to express your personality. The written exam takes care of all the factual stuff. I think the first question to me in the oral exam was "what states does the Suwannee River flow through?" And there was another question, "What was the treaty of Ghent?" Now that's a tricky question, because there were three Treaties of Ghent. ... I think the obvious intent of these questions was to make me fail the oral.

Well, I went overseas as a secretary, which I've always been grateful for because I think it's good to know how the other half lives, so to speak, and I really enjoyed Africa very much. I took the written exam again overseas, and passed it again, and came back and passed the oral exam. I think they did ask me some much more reasonable questions, you know, something that we could talk about. But also, I think that I had proven myself by serving in a hardship post. I was the first woman to finish a tour of duty in Ghana at that time. Others had left. In fact, I replaced a young man who had been out there as a secretary. He asked to be transferred after a year; he couldn't stand it.

I passed the oral exam in 1958 and I was still in what was called the Staff Corps. They wanted to send me overseas for another two years in the Staff Corps—you have no way of knowing when you are going to be appointed as a Foreign Service Officer in the Foreign Service, they have a register. I said "But suppose they reach my name on the register when I am overseas? What happens then?" They said "Oh, they could just convert you into a Foreign Service Officer." I found out years later that they have never in their lives done that and they wouldn't have done it, so it was really a very careless and casual bit of advice given me by the personnel office. But anyway, I said that I did not want to go overseas, I wanted to stay in Washington. So they assigned me as a Personnel Officer in the State Department and I was waiting for my name to come up in the register. They usually appoint a class of about 30 people at a time for a two- or three-month officer training course. I would drop in the board of examiners office to see how my name was getting along on the register, and three classes were appointed after a period of about nine months and my name hadn't been called. So I went in and asked, and they said "Oh! A couple of months ago we notified your supervisor that you would be appointed as a Foreign Service Officer, and he said that he didn't want to lose you, and that we should take your name off the list until you finished your staff employee assignment in a year and a half." I have all the documents about it. I was outraged. I know they would never have done that to a man. For a man, they would have office parties—Good bye—Good Luck! Congratulations, well done, we will be watching your career. So I just stomped my feet and said "Put my name at the top of the list so I get into the next class." I have a little memo that was written to my supervisor saying that Miss Palmer has been appointed "ex-quota" off the list, to the next class.

> Eventually assigned to the Belgian Congo, Ms. Palmer had barely arrived when the revolution broke out. Her bravery and cool head in this difficult setting resulted in her becoming a "media darling." But her experiences did not help her career at the State Department. Assigned to a non-job, she was forced to play a high-stakes game of criticizing her boss (a political appointee) for not giving her any work to do, before she was given a real assignment. Again her performance in the field was outstanding, and she was assigned to a year of African Studies at Boston University. Expecting her next position to be as a political officer in an African country, Ms. Palmer encountered yet another round of discrimination.

I went to Boston University, which I was very happy about because I love Boston. Then the trouble started. I went through Washington on my way to Boston and my career counselor told me that I no longer had to worry about the fact that I was a woman in the service, I had proven myself, I was fully accepted, as was shown by my being accepted in training. They used to say that they wouldn't give training to women because women are always leaving to get married. My answer to that was "Have you forgotten the two men who went through two years of Arabic language training, very expensive, full salary, all that, and then quit the day they graduated to go work for an oil company?" Talk about a double standard! . . . After I finished Boston University, I was [to be] assigned as political officer at Dar Es Salaam, Tanzania, which was ideal, because the African Liberation Committee had its headquarters there. Tanzania itself is a very interesting country, because of the attitude toward socialism and so forth. . . . So I took some Swahili language tapes with me up to Boston University to start working on the language, even though language was not a requirement for that particular position. Then I found out through the grapevine that my assignment had been canceled. So I called my counselor who said, "I'm very sorry, but the Ambassador said that he didn't want a woman officer." That was the first time somebody had in so many words said "it." I said, "Well, why didn't you tell me about it?" and they said, "Don't worry, Alison, it will never happen again; we'll take care you; you can be the political officer in Uganda." Well, that's not as good an assignment, but, you know, it's still in East Africa and is an interesting post. So I said, "If anything happens again, all hell is going to break loose." Then they called me back and said, "The Ambassador there doesn't want you because you are a woman." At that time the Assistant Secretary for African Affairs was a political appointee named G. Mennon Williams, as in Mennon Shaving Cream, but a very good man, very good man. He wrote a letter to the Ambassador to Ethiopia and he said nice things about me, like, "Miss Palmer is an outstanding Africanist" (I don't know how they knew that) and "she has been turned down twice by our Ambassadors to two other Africa posts who thought it was unsuitable to have a woman (this was just *asking* for trouble), but we hope very much that you will accept her." Well, in case anybody had forgotten, authority for making assignments rests with the Secretary of State, who delegates it down to various levels, not with ambassadors. But Ambassador Ed Korry, who had been senior Associated Press correspondent in Europe at some point or other, was a political appointee, and I don't know what his credentials were. But anyway, he wrote back and he said that "the savages in Ethiopia would not be receptive to a woman, except maybe to her form." I said, "I'll call you back."

It was a cold winter's night, I think it was January 1966, and I was living in a funny little apartment where the heat was great when it was warm outside, and the heat turned off when it was cold outside. So it was real cold, I couldn't sleep, and I walked up and down. It was too cold to sit down. I think I was even wearing mittens and a ski cap as well as whatever else. I couldn't figure out what to do. I think that what I was doing was theology, although I wouldn't have known that at the time, trying to figure out: "Why is this wrong?" Obviously it was wrong because I was a capable Africanist and the State Department had assigned me to these places, and it was stupid to let an ambassador turn me down because of sex discrimination. But it was also wrong in a broader sense that the ambassadors were putting me in a group instead of treating me with respect as an individual. I realize this sounds a little pompous, but this is how it went through my mind. . . . So, I was scared to proceed. I was so ignorant that I thought: "Gee, if I write a letter, and say that these ambassadors are discriminating against me, is that libel? Or if I say it, is that slander? Can they sue me? Could I end up in jail?" I didn't know, I didn't have any knowledge of the legal situation involved. I certainly thought it was very possible that I could get fired from the State Department, and I knew what that would mean. But on the other hand, I felt that if I didn't proceed, my only reason for not going was this fear, and for the rest of my life, whenever I thought about this (which would be a thousand times a day, depending), I would know myself to have been a coward. I didn't have any real sense that I was doing this for all women Foreign Service Officers, for all womankind, or for the Constitution or the Bill of Rights, or to better the State Department, although I think the State Department is better for it. But I just felt that I had to proceed. My alternative would have been to say, "Oh, the heck with it, they want me to be a consular officer or personnel officer, I can have a perfectly legitimate career there and still enjoy being in the Foreign Service." But I said, "No! I've chosen to be a Foreign Service Officer, chosen to be a political officer, chosen to be an Africanist, the State Department has affirmed all these; how am I going to let them get away with this?" I said, "I am going to fight this to the Supreme Court (which I actually did), I'll fight it as long as I live, and the State Department will never hear the end of it" (which is also true).

> The resolution of her case took several years and involved both an EEO complaint and a lawsuit. When she won and received her settlement, she used the funds to lay the groundwork for a larger class-action suit against the Department. The new suit alleged a pattern of sex discrimination existed at State. The result of this second action led eventually to a major judgment against the Department. Ms. Palmer's rationale for the second action reveals her courage and the sacrifices it has entailed.

Obviously I brought the first one for myself, although when we filed the first lawsuit in 1972 we included a lot of statistics and a lot of testimony about the status of women generally, just to strengthen my case. But all during this time, women were coming to me telling me these horrendous stories. I sensed obviously something needed to be done, and obviously the State Department was never going to do it; they could not see this at all. I was the only one who in a certain sense had already burned her bridges. I liked to hope that maybe I could have had a career after all, even without the class action, but I don't really think I could have. I was already a leper, if you will. So, I guess you could say, I was "called" to do it. (I was ordained an Episcopal priest in 1975.) I was the person with the knowledge and the ability. What would have been nice, this thing really bothered me a lot, was to get some financial support from women FSOs. In the entire 14 years, the total sum of money contributed by anyone other than myself was less than $20,000, and of that I think a couple of thousand came from the Thomas Legal Defense Fund. This case was involving at least 500 women Foreign Service Officers, and they get good salaries. Many of them are single, many of them overseas get housing allowances. If any of them had contributed even ten dollars a week, that adds up to a lot from several hundred people over the years. I really feel that that was not an unreasonable request to make. . . . We did a couple of mailings, asking for money, and decided that it really wasn't worth the time or the effort with the response. I don't know what the reason was, why they didn't contribute. . . . I must say I've often thought about what would have happened if I hadn't started the class action lawsuit, if I had just gotten my special promotion out of the first AA complaint. Granted, there would have been plenty of senior people in the State Department who never would have forgiven me, but I might have outlasted them, if I had been quiet and good and worked very hard and been the nice, good, capable Foreign Service Officer, which I was supposed to be. (At one point the State Department testified that I was in the category which they classified as "walks on water." Very useful.) What happens when you start being a troublemaker is that they start saying, "Well, she just couldn't get promoted so she's just complaining, whining, you know." So it was nice to have all of these little goodies along the way, saying that whatever else I was, I was a very capable officer.

Certainly the class action turned out to be a nightmare for the law firm and me. I asked the head of the law firm right at the beginning, to give me an estimate of how long it would take and how much it would cost. He said it would probably take about a year and cost about $10,000. Where are we now? We are just about starting the sixteenth year, as of February 1992, and no end in sight. I forget how many millions of dollars of legal fees the U.S. government paid to the law firm, but it's a lot. It took us three years to get certified as a class action; normally that is quite a routine matter. We had seven or eight women Foreign Service Officers, plus the Women's Action Organization, saying that they were a party to this lawsuit, but it took three years to get a class certification. . . . We didn't go to trial until 1985. We lost and had to go to the Court of Appeals and come back again, and so on and so forth. We've been up to the Supreme Court on some side issues from time to time, so it's been a real nightmare.

> Neither suit eliminated sex discrimination at the State Department, and neither completely eliminated the legacy of discrimination from Ms. Palmer's career.

In the first case, I had gotten a special promotion, but it was about a year late. We asked to have it back-dated and they didn't, so I had to go to court to get it back-dated, which just seemed like an awful waste of time and money. We had also asked that I be given some kind of priority in assignments, to make up for all of this. We knew that my career had been damaged by all of this conflict, and we wanted some kind of special assignment to compensate for it. We didn't get that, that was a disappointment. In the class action, I would like very much to have gotten some kind of compensation for people like myself, the women who had left the Foreign Service for whatever reason, presumably because their careers were just not going anywhere because of discrimination. It would have been nice to get back pay or a chance of being reappointed. We just couldn't get enough material together, so we had to let it go. It is too bad, because they had been damaged. The only thing we got for women who had left the service was the chance for them to get Superior Honor Awards (one of the top awards in the service) by submitting evidence that they had done outstanding work while they were in the service, but had not received recognition because of sex discrimination. One of my lawyers suggested that I deserved such an award for my contribution to equal employment opportunity at State, and State agreed, although at first they thought we were joking. Of course, State often devotes whole sections of the employee newsletter to praising employees who have worked for equal employment, but somehow State had never thought of me as a candidate for an award. The following is the text of the award I received:

> For outstanding service to the Department of State in the furtherance of Equal Employment Opportunity objectives and as an agent of change in the Foreign Service environment. During the years 1975 through 1981, you showed exceptional initiative, leadership, and moral courage in pursuing equal treatment for all employees. Your efforts heightened awareness at the Department of the need to examine and, where necessary, challenge existing practices and perceptions which limited opportunities for women. Your personal and professional efforts in advancing the goal of equality of opportunity for men and women are in the finest tradition of the Foreign Service.

As far as the remedies for women in the service, we are getting them. They are getting special priority assignments and so forth. [The lawyers] are having a lot of trouble with the women, God bless them, because [the women] are letting the State Department talk them out of it. ... We try and talk to them. We send out letters to the women who are in the class saying, "for heaven sakes, if you have any question, any doubt, any problem, or any obstacle, call the lawyers. It's free, call collect, PLEASE let us help you!" I think it is probably the old fear about being seen as a troublemaker. You are never sure what is going to be said about you in the corridors, and they may feel that if they argue with their career counselor, he is going to go around and say, "She really was awfully difficult when we talked about that assignment." That's enough to do you in.

> From Ms. Palmer's perspective, the culture at the State Department
> helps to explain why she believes discrimination at the Department
> is worse than elsewhere.

Obviously, there is discrimination against women in every field, but I think it is worse in the Foreign Service for several reasons. One reason is that we are a monopoly employer. If you run into trouble as a professor at one university, at least theoretically it might be better some place else, you have a theoretical possibility of moving to try to find a better situation. You can't go any place else to be a Foreign Service Officer. We used to joke about this sometimes, that we would open up our own State Department in a tent across the street: "Foreign policy made while you wait; wars declared; treaties signed." Bitter sarcasm, but there is no place to go as a Foreign Service Officer. There is no competition. So I think in that sense, they are less subject to influence. Also, I think they tend to be a little bit behind the times, simply because of being overseas. ... Maybe the Foreign Service attracts somewhat conservative people. Certainly the whole business about "X percentage of our career ambassadors are from Princeton, Yale, and Harvard," that leads to a conservative mind-set.

> A staunch feminist, Ms. Palmer's courageous sacrifices for other
> women have not always been recognized by those who have benefited
> from her efforts on their behalf.

What I think is very interesting, this last lawsuit, the one we've just won and gotten all these goodies for over 200 women FSOs, not a single woman has said "thank you" to me in any way, shape, or form, which I find quite amazing. In 1983, when we had the out-of-court settlement on recruitment, the Department was required to appoint 75 women as Foreign Service Officers, who had been turned down because of discrimination. These were women who wanted to be Foreign Service Officers, and had gone through the whole laborious process, some of them had gone through it two or three times. When they got to be Foreign Service Officers, only one of them has ever written to say, "thank you." I don't know why this is, it may be that they don't know I exist, although heaven knows I've been quoted enough in the papers from time to time. I have spent thousands and thousands of hours on this lawsuit, and obviously lots and lots of money (in 1990 I finally received a check for over $225,000 as a refund for the money I had spent from 1976 onwards), not to mention the emotional ups and downs. I don't know whether they are not aware of it, or they just say, "what the heck." It amazes me to say the least. If I had wanted to be an officer and couldn't and then somebody did something so I could, I think I would say, "thank you."

> There were times, however, when Ms. Palmer did find emotional rewards and occasionally there was an opportunity to "pay back" those who damaged her career.

The day that I filed the class action lawsuit in 1976, at the State Department noontime press briefing a reporter had heard about it, and asked whoever was the press spokesman at the moment about the suit . . . and he didn't know [about it]. He didn't know, and he didn't like the fact that he didn't know. So he went back upstairs and spoke to the Director General, who spoke to the Under Secretary for Administration, Larry Eagleburger. He called in the Federal Women's Program Coordinator for State, a woman named Georgiana Prince, and asked her if she knew anything about this class action. She said that, well, she had talked to me from time to time, she knew I was thinking about it. She had no knowledge of when or if it would be filed. Eagleburger was furious; he was livid, because he knew me. . . . He said, "I don't care what it takes, we are going to *GET* Alison, we are going to *GET* Alison, I don't care how we do it, we are going to get her!" Georgiana testified to that at the trial. In 1989, when we finally got this consent decree and remedial order and all that good stuff, and there were press reports about that, I sent a copy to Eagleburger who was now back as, of all things, Deputy Secretary of State. I told him about the testimony, because I don't think he knew that Georgiana had testified to this, and I just quoted this business about "We are going to get Alison" and then I said, "I am enclosing the report of the outcome of the lawsuit that was filed in 1976. As far as I know you didn't 'get' me." He never replied to this letter.

Interview
EVELYN P. FOOTE
*Advocate of Equality in the
Military*

Brigadier General Evelyn Foote retired from the Army in 1989 from the position of Commanding General of Fort Belvoir. Her career spanned the transformation of women's role in the military, from being an auxiliary one into being regular military. Though she entered the military to escape limitations upon careers for women, Brig. Gen. Foote also experienced the negative effects of the organizational culture of the Defense Department upon women.

I joined the military because I was frustrated by the blocks to progression in the civilian sector. I graduated from high school one week after my seventeenth birthday, and decided I was too young to go to college. So I worked in Washington, D.C. for a year with the FBI and then went for two years of college. I then had to take another year out to earn more money, went back to the FBI, got another leave to go back to college and completed my degree in 1953. After working for a year as a grocery store clerk in Washington, I went back to the Federal Bureau of Investigation. It was a very good experience—I would say that—very interesting, but it didn't take me too long to realize that at about the grade four level, grade five at best, a women capped out in the Bureau. In those years, the late 1940s and early 1950s, women were not given the opportunity to be FBI agents. I think my highest horizon point was probably being supervisor of the typing pool, which didn't thrill me. So I left in 1955 and took a job as a copy girl on the *Washington Daily News*, a Scripts-Howard tabloid which is no longer published. When we were not running copy, we were supposed to be writing byline stories in order to be given a chance on the staff. I actually had about 27 byline stories and was being considered for the staff, when I got wooed away to be the Director of Public Relations for Gray Line Sightseeing in Washington. That was my big mistake. I really was not built to be a "huckster," selling a commercial product. So I quit. I went to work for Blue Cross/Blue Shield of Washington, but again found out quickly that I could rise to be the clerical supervisor of the enrollment department, which was the sales department, and could manage the business appointments and tasks of 18 sales representatives, all male, but could be neither a sales person nor the manager of that department. That was all men's work. There was just something very, very dissatisfying about a self-limited horizon. It was about that time I met my first woman Army Officer at a reception, and told her that I was actively looking for information about working for the government overseas, either with the State Department or with the U.S. Information Agency. The officer said she would get the information for me about Army civilian opportunities abroad. In the literature she sent, she slipped in a book on the program for women officers. Six months later, I was raising my right hand, saying "I do" to an appointment as an Army officer. You can't lose anything for two years: good experience, good change of pace. At least, although it was in the Women's Army Corps, my pay would be the same as a male lieutenant from day one, although the assignment opportunities were not quite so equal. So I decided two years would be a good period of time to think out the future and get some leadership experience, fully planning to come off active duty at the end of two years. Of course the two became ten, became 20, became almost 30, and suddenly it was a career.

After basic training, I was assigned duty as a platoon leader at the Women's Army Corps Training Center. I really enjoyed working with people; teaching, mentoring, taking young women who came in from civilian life, so naive about what the U.S. Army is, because they had nothing that would give them a frame of reference for what it would be, as most men did, what with Dad telling them their World War II experiences. Not only did I enjoy it, but I apparently had a knack for it. I went from the platoon leader position to recruiting in the Pacific Northwest—Oregon, Washington, Northern Idaho—for three years. I was recruiting women for the Army officer programs. After this tour, I went back to Fort Belvoir, Virginia, where I commanded a female company for two years. I came there as a Captain in 1964 and stayed to 1966, then returned in 1988 as the Commanding General of Fort Belvoir, a position that would have been totally impossible prior to 1967.

When I came on active duty, the highest rank that a women could achieve in the normal course of events was Lieutenant Colonel (LTC) in the Army or the comparable rank of Commander in the Navy. This was by law. The only women who were promoted to the rank of colonel were the directors of the Women's Army Corps, the women in the Navy, the women in the Air Force, the women in the Marines, all "gender specific eagles." We only had one women's battalion in the Army that a woman could command. You might have 15 LTCs, but only one at a time could command that unit. As you can see, command as a LTC was rare for a woman. But all of this began changing in November, 1967, when Lyndon Johnson signed into law Public Law 90-130, which removed the artificial ceilings on grade and on the number of women who could serve within the regular forces of any of the service components. There had been intensive, behind-the-scenes work on the part of the directors [of the women's branches] for a period of about ten years to get the U.S. law changed. Theoretically at least, PL 90-130 made it possible for a woman to become a general or an admiral, although this didn't happen in a hurry. Neither did we get a lot of colonels in a hurry. It took a while. We had to "grow" them, because we had so few women serving in the officer ranks at that time.

I was in Vietnam in 1967. I went over ostensibly to be a staff officer with the U.S. Army Support Command in Saigon. En route to Vietnam, I was promoted to the rank of Major. So, when I arrived overseas, I had been promoted out of that job and into duty with U.S. Army Public Affairs at U.S. Army Vietnam Headquarters. Apparently, somebody had found out about my limited newspaper experience. I was working with the more than 600 accredited correspondents who were in country to report that war. It was fascinating. I can't think of a place in this world I'd rather have been than with the Public Affairs people. While other women officers were not permitted to travel much throughout Vietnam, I was out with both Corps Tactical Headquarters and visited every Army division and separate brigade as part of my job. Yes, it was quite a year.

I had almost 30 years of service (February 1960 to September 1989) when I retired. These were three decades of tremendous change in how women within the Army were trained, assigned, and utilized. From a very constrained utilization, when I came in to the Women's Army Corps (one of the very few ways women officers could enter the Army in 1960). The disestablishment of the Corps in October 1978, and the integration of Women's Army Corps members into the other branches of the Army for training, assignment, and career progression was a profound change. I went from the Women's Army Corps to the Military Police Corps. While I knew absolutely nothing about the Military Police, I selected this Corps because I knew that at least 50, perhaps 60, percent of the women would go into the Adjutant General Corps. That Corps, which is oriented on personnel and administration, could not possibly give this sudden deluge of women assignments which were really good assignments. It took women in the Adjutant General Corps considerable time to achieve training and jobs equal to men in the Corps. So I picked a Corps atypical to women—the MP Corps—and never regretted it. I guess you might say I entered a new world, coming from 18 years of having been managed by gender, and suddenly being pitched head first into a branch in which I had no training or experience. This happened when I was a Lieutenant

Colonel: most of my fellow MP officers of that grade had had 18 or 19 years of being developed in that corps. It was very interesting. . . .

> After her tour in Vietnam, Brig. Gen. Foote returned to the United States, where her assignments included the Military Personnel Center, Personnel Staff Officer at Fort McPherson, Commander of the Second Training Battalion at Fort McClellan, and faculty member at the U.S. Army War College. She then went abroad for her only Military Police assignment.

I had a truly great command tour! No MP schooling, no MP experience, no bad habits as a MP Commander to unlearn: the circumstances were ideal for me. I commanded the 42nd Military Police Group. Its mission was to execute the military customs program for the U.S. European command. This was a two-year command tour; my third year in Germany, I was in a holding pattern of sorts, waiting to be promoted to the rank of brigadier general. For ten months, I was assigned with the 32nd Army Air Defense Command headquartered out of Darmstadt. I was the personal assistant to the commanding general, working for him primarily in personnel matters. I then returned to the United States in May 1986, to be the Deputy Inspector General for Inspections at the Department of Army. I had the worldwide Army Inspection Program responsibility, as well as oversight for the intelligence oversight program and the nuclear and chemical inspection responsibility. This was a two-year assignment. I then was selected to command Fort Belvoir, with its 15,000 people and its then 72 major tenant activities. It was a wonderful assignment, and I did a lot of interfacing with Congress and the state or county governments of Virginia. I have no complaints about the types of assignments the Army gave me, none at all. I consider myself very lucky. I had to retire: mandatory age caught up with me and I retired just before my sixtieth birthday.

> Particularly at the beginning of her career, Brig. Gen. Foote was confronted with the organizational limitations imposed upon women, and as a result, became committed to improving the status of women within the Defense Department.

Throughout my entire career, I worked to change those ignorant policies which limited the utilization of women. I worked extensively in personnel policy change; personnel management change; in bringing women into the ROTC program, the Reserves, and National Guard; in eliminating this structure known as the Women's Army Corps, and integrating women into the Army mainstream, serving with the men in previously all-male units. Most of the men in the Army had little experience in being assigned with, or working with, the women of the Army. With the elimination of the draft and the greatly increased utilization of women, things changed. Women were being assigned across the board to all of the Army's organizations, except the infantry and the armor, and in very limited ways into the field artillery. In field artillery today, women don't have a snowball's chance in hell of ever competing with the men. They cannot work in the cannon field artillery, which is the very heart of that combat arms branch. They can't be assigned to Lance or Multiple Launch Rocket System units. It's all very frustrating. The Army has assigned many women right from West Point to Field Artillery, knowing full well that their career opportunities were miserable. These fine officers leave the Army early, and our sizable investment in educating them goes down the tube, leaving them bitterly disappointed and disillusioned. I think it's sheer hypocrisy to let women join a dead-end program, to let them get a toe in the door, then give them no real chance to perform and advance. So if there is one thing that I have railed against, it's the artificial constraints on utilization of people based on gender; the combat exclusion policy, which has no rhyme or reason. I think men and women should be allowed to compete for any job that they have a capability for, a desire for, and an aptitude for. They must be able to do everything that is required within that job. To keep women soldiers from aspiring to have some operational experience makes no sense. The woman who trains the male Air Force jet pilot, who cannot herself be a jet pilot for the Air Force in the operational sense, is a good example. We have aircraft carriers out in the ocean that have 6,000 people aboard, and it is probably one of the most comfortable environments in which to live, but a woman cannot be there because serving on a carrier is defined as "combat." As long as women are operationally excluded, they will never acquire the experience that leads to their acquiring rank of more than one star. Unless they get the operational experience, they will never be in a position to have a significant impact on national defense policy. It's about time women did begin to impact national defense policy in a meaningful, consistent way. After all, women in America represent more than half of our population.

If men continue to have access to areas where women are not permitted to serve, then the men, by the very fact of the exclusion of the women, view them as being less qualified than they. The women absolutely hate combat exclusion, because it is an artificial barrier. . . . The women who serve the combat forces forward are not given credit for being in combat. They *are* in combat, and if they are attacked, they will attack back. These women will use their weapons because they have been trained to. I love the body bag question: "Are you ready for your daughter to come home in a body bag?" I said, "No, I'm not ready for either my son or my daughter to come home in a body bag." The whole theater is a combat zone, and some women in the rear area and some men in the rear area will be killed. Some women and men serving forward will also become combat casualties. These are the 1990s and the battlefield is a highly fluid battlefield. Yet much of our thinking, and many of these exclusionary policies, are predicated upon World War II battlefield mentality: fronts and rears, boundaries and brigades. I'd like for somebody to tell me where the front and the rear were in Vietnam. Seems to me it was 360° around any man or woman who was over there. There are no safe zones, front or rear.

Military women want no artificial barriers. The enlisted women and the officers may have different attitudes toward combat situation. Both enlisted and officer groups, however, hate career limitations based only on grades. Don't get me wrong, women officers are not jumping up and down to be in the infantry, but they are very much aware of the fact that as officers, if they are excluded from the operational arena, then their career horizons are often limited. Having said that, I'll now say I haven't met many women officers who want to be in the Infantry or Armor. Those women who do wish to compete in Infantry or Armor shouldn't be denied that opportunity solely because they are women. If they can meet the same standards the men meet, they should be given the chance. If not, the women shouldn't be there. A single standard of performance, strength and endurance is the key. For Pete's sake, you don't put every man in the infantry; a lot of those guys couldn't perform all the tasks either. So, match people's capabilities with their aptitudes. . . . The woman officer, I think, intellectualizes the exclusions much more than the enlisted woman. They don't want to be put down.

> The organizational culture in the Defense Department, in particular, includes a masculine gender ethos which contributes significantly to the issue of sexual harassment. However, Brig. Gen. Foote also sees within the Defense Department significant opportunities and prospects for change.

We're always studying the problem of sexual harassment in the armed forces. Every year, there are more studies on sexual harassment. People ask me "have you ever been sexually harassed?" I tell them, "sure." I took care of the problem. But sometimes, the problem is so bad that it takes more than the individual acting; it takes the leadership to act. In my experience, I have found that where there are significant problems with sexual harassment, or discrimination, or racial discrimination, the problem begins with the leadership of an organization. If the leadership permits it, it will be. If the leadership is against it, it will not be. There will be a much more enlightened, open environment. So far as policies about females, I think we have gone downhill with Presidents Reagan and Bush.

These are the years when we suddenly find the armed forces putting the brakes on the number of women entering. The present combat exclusion rules are an insidiously effective way to limit where women will be assigned. The "good old boys" made this happen. Carter was very much for advancing women in the military and increasing their numbers significantly. Reagan was no friend of women in the military, and I don't see Mr. Bush in that light either. I think he's too busy with other things to worry about women in the military or to even realize how many of us were over in the Middle East.

I think the policies concerning how women will be utilized is a mixed bag. The Defense Department speaks a good "there will be no discrimination" game, but let's face it, the old boy network is in place and working well. The current generation of leaders is not the one which is going to turn the corner. The ones who are going to turn the corner are the ones who have been trained since the early seventies, and are being trained right now, to a far more equal world, to a world that is far more blind to gender. The senior leaders we have here now are still the men who graduated from West Point about 1960–1965; many served in Vietnam. Wait until we get to the leadership that never went to Vietnam. Those leaders who trained with women from day one are the ones who are going to make the biggest difference in the years ahead. I think it is these leaders coming who are going to knock out the combat exclusion policies. I also think as we increase the number of women who are graduates of service academies and the ROTC, they're not going to put up with artificial restrictions. They are going to stand up and be much more vocal than some of them have been willing to be in the past.

We have women who, when push came to shove, took the Armed Forces to court. Women who said "I will not willingly leave the Army just because I'm pregnant, that violates my rights. I have a right to stay and to work within the Armed Forces and to have a family too," to the women who took the Armed Forces to court because they could not declare their husbands as their dependents, although it was automatic for a man to have his wife declared his dependent and to get the allowances accordingly. Only in recent years have women entered the Armed Force in great numbers, entered this last male "tree house in the sky." For years military service has been a man's domain. The presence of women who are as competent and productive as a man is a devastating blow to the psyche of a lot of men who thought only men could be soldiers. It is a real blow to the ego of many males that women are doing so well in the military.

There will be no turning back. Statistics, the demographics alone, will not permit that to happen. In fact, many men and many in the leadership realm will tell you that if it had not been for the quality women who came into the forces during the early years of the all-volunteer force, the whole project would have fallen flat on its face. The women *made* the all-volunteer force succeed and they were the quality cut of the all-volunteer forces in the early years. Many of the men agree: exclusionary rules have got to go, combat exclusion has got to go. Many male commanders will tell you, "I ignore the regulations; I've assigned women to command units where women are not supposed to be because they are the best I have, but don't tell on me."

I would not exchange my experience for anything. I think there is no greater calling in the world than professions such as teaching or the military or public service of any type. The man or woman who has that true call and love is a very fortunate person.

Addendum, March 1992: Congress wrote into the 1992 Defense Appropriations Act its approval for qualified women pilots to train in combat aircraft and be utilized as combat pilots. The Department of Defense has done nothing yet to put into effect this new "will of Congress." DOD is waiting for the results of the "study" of a Presidential Committee tasked to recommend by November 1992 how and where Armed Forces women should be assigned. The Commission is heavily weighted with very conservative people who do not want to remove combat exclusions from the assignment of women.

The beat goes on. . . .

3

Individual Factors:
Attitudes, Attributes, and Obstacles

For women, managerial achievement is radical and deviant behavior.
Carolyn R. Dexter[1]

Indisputably the formulation and conduct of American diplomacy remains male-dominated and male-oriented. Throughout the nation's existence, United States foreign policy has been the domain of white Anglo-Saxon, Protestant males.
Edward P. Crapol[2]

Given the societal and organizational barriers to women's careers as exemplified in the quotes above and the earlier chapters, one is forced to question how it was possible for women to break into the circle of foreign policy decision-makers. More specifically, how were the women in our study able to surmount the insurmountable barriers that have prevented so many other women from assuming positions of influence? What special personal characteristics do they possess that made their ascension possible? How do their individual attitudes and attributes provide assistance or obstacles to career development?

Women's Career Development: Theoretical Foundations

The existence of widely different attitudes or orientations to work between the sexes is assumed both popularly and by psychologists and sociologists of work. The causes for such differences are perceived in nature, in childhood socialization, or in the family situation. It is widely assumed that there exist persistent differences between the meaning of work for men and for women, between the degree of their active or passive attitude to the work situation, and between the level of their interest in advancement and their commitment to the occupational or employment role.
Judith Buber Agassi[3]

The scholarly community has only recently begun to evaluate the career development paths of women. Early theorizing on why people chose certain occupations, or what factors affected progress on the job, focused almost exclusively on the careers of men.[4] Any prior research that focused on women, moreover, tended to be poorly constructed and biased by the view that a woman's "natural" position in life was to be a mother and wife.[5] Often the possibility that a woman would choose any other career was seen as evidence that she had some psychological problem, or that she was not a *real* woman.[6]

More recently, in large part because of the massive influx of women into the work force (57.3 percent of all women worked in 1990, up from 30.5 percent in 1960), theorists have begun to direct their attention specifically to women.[7] Initially the work in the early 1970s merely modified existing theories of male career development, adding marriage and children to the list of variables one had to consider in plotting the occupational progression of women.[8] Later scholars rejected the "add on variables" approach to explaining women's careers. Barbara Gutek and Laurie Larwood were among those calling for a new theory of career development focusing on women.[9] They argued: "There are nevertheless many elements specific to women's experience which the male model does not easily accommodate."[10] Among the variables which they thought should be included were "career preparation, the opportunities available in the society, the influence of marriage, pregnancy and children, and timing and age."[11] With respect to the first, the initial issue concerns whether a woman even planned on having a career outside of the home. If she did not, her preparation in all probability will be inadequate if she later decides to work.[12] The variable of opportunities available refers to the very real discrimination against women entering certain professions or jobs. Medicine, law, university professor, business management, bartender, steel worker, miner, and, as we saw in the last chapter, even soldier and diplomat are all examples of careers that have until very recently been closed to women. Certainly a young woman in the 1930s, 1940s, or even the 1950s and 1960s, might have quite realistically considered opportunities in these and many other fields not viable options when planning a career.[13] Additionally, marriage, pregnancy, and children are obvious variables to include in a theory of women's career development. In our society, even in the last decade of the twentieth century, it is still the woman who is expected to neglect her job or forgo one altogether for the sake of her husband and family. Theories of men's careers may one day have to be rewritten to take these factors into account, but today *most* men's work lives are unchanged by marriage or children.[14] Timing and age highlight the fact that traditional (read male) career patterns are based on uninterrupted progression. Women, who often start their careers late in life or who drop out to raise young children, may have, as a result, very different patterns of progress on the job from men.[15]

Gary Powell, building on Gutek and Larwood's work and current research on women and men's careers, proposed a theory of career development that could apply to women and men.[16] As discussed earlier, his
model had six sets of variables: societal factors; personal factors; actions
of individuals; family factors; organizational factors; and decisions by
organizations. The first, societal factors, takes into account Gutek and
Larwood's notion of opportunities plus other societal variables including
norms about men and women's roles in society and the workplace.[17]
Personal factors encompasses Gutek and Larwood's notion of preparation
and includes the further variables of family background, socialization
experiences, past work experiences, demographic factors, needs and abilities, and career attitudes.[18] The third variable set focuses on the actions
of individuals, whether they set goals, plan their careers and employ
tactics necessary to get ahead.[19] The fourth group, family factors, includes
marital status, and presence and age of children. The last two variable
clusters incorporate the past and current practices of business or government organizations that structure a person's career.[20] Since organizational
factors and decisions of organizations have already been discussed in
Chapter 2, the remaining four sets of variables will provide the focus of
this chapter.

Societal Factors

Powell included several items in this category: societal norms, legal
factors, sex segregation of occupations, and government programs.[21] The
first of these we have reviewed at some length in Chapter 1. As we discovered, Western society has generally dismissed the advisability of careers
for women outside the home until the last two or three decades. Young
women growing up in the 1920s through the 1950s would have been
encouraged to prepare for marriage and a family, but not for work. If a
young woman wished to hold a job before marriage that might be acceptable, but pursuing a lifetime's career in a professional field was not seen
as appropriate by mainstream society. Attitudes on the question of work
for women began to change in the decades after World War II.

One of the primary factors producing this alteration in societal norms
was the increased involvement of women in jobs outside the home. While
public and governmental pressures to return to the home were pervasive
after the war, many women who had obtained a job to support the war
effort found they liked working and stayed on in the marketplace.[22] Others
joined them in the 1950s as "women's occupations" (teaching, clerical,
and service) burgeoned.[23] The 1960s saw the rapid proliferation of jobs for
women as the professions reliant upon women workers continued to

offer attractive wages. The percentage of women working outside the home rose from 37.7 percent to 43.3 percent in the decade between 1960 and 1970. The 1970s and 1980s also witnessed an increase in employment of women of almost ten percent from 1970 to 1980 with an additional six percent in the 1990s, resulting in 57.3 percent of all women working or looking for work by 1990.[24] The primary reasons for these latter increases were economic and political. The 1970s and early 1980s were a time of rapid inflation. The single wage earner's salary, as a direct result, failed to keep pace with expenses. Many women were forced to take jobs outside the home in order that basic family needs might be met. Politically, the Women's Movement had helped to open up many careers and career opportunities for women. Young women especially, but not exclusively, were able to take advantage of the altered climate in the marketplace.

The changed work climate, as predicted, produced an alteration in attitudes toward women working. While few accepted the idea of an employed married woman in the 1930s, by 1989, 44 percent of a national sample (57 percent of those aged sixteen to twenty-nine) agreed that society looks *down* on women who do not hold paid jobs.[25] Most women also reported valuing their jobs, although, as we saw in Chapter 1 society still expects women to place family demands ahead of career. Other societal views that limited women's professional opportunities, for instance the notion that women are ill-suited to manage others, have also declined over time, perhaps influencing the career choices of younger women, although, as we also saw in Chapter 1, many societal views still limit women's career horizons, including stereotypes concerning women's mathematical abilities, and military and foreign policy skills.

Thus, in Gutek and Larwood's terminology, the career opportunities available in society for women until recently have been fairly limited, and women's career development has been shaped accordingly. Women reaching adulthood before 1960 would not have been expected to prepare for, or to have, a career. Young women in the post-Women's Movement era would have increasingly anticipated just the opposite and would have been encouraged to plan on a career. Thus we might expect some differences between the career patterns of the women in our sample depending on their age.

Changes in the legal protections afforded women who desired a career, Powell's second societal factor, have also rapidly advanced in the last three decades, beginning in the 1960s with a call for equal employment opportunities. This demand was enacted into law in 1963 with the Equal Pay Act and 1964 with the passage of the Civil Rights Act which prohibited discrimination against women in the terms and conditions of employment. However, equal education opportunities, the prerequisites for equal professional opportunities, did not become law until Title IX was added to the Educational Amendments Act of 1972. Again, these changes in legal factors would be most likely to benefit women who were under the age of forty when our survey was conducted in 1988. Older women, in all probability, would have experienced discrimination in employment and education when they attempted to pursue careers.

Moreover as we saw in Chapter 2, legal prohibition against employment discrimination, in the marketplace or the federal government generally, did not necessarily mean the end of unequitable and unequal treatment of women in the State and Defense Departments. Indeed, lawsuits against both Departments, alleging discrimination in all aspects of employment, began only in the 1970s, taking until the 1980s and 1990s before some of the more subtle forms of discrimination were successfully challenged in the courts. Legal discrimination, of course, still is widespread at the Defense Department, where the argument of national defense is used to keep women from serving in critical military, especially combat, positions.

Powell's third societal factor, sex segregation of occupations, is a persistent problem for women planning to work outside the home. As we just noted and discussed in detail in Chapters 1 and 2, women are still prohibited from serving in combat and restrictions on the employment of married women by the State Department limited the Foreign Service option for most women until recently. Young women who contemplated employment outside the home in years past would have probably focused their attention on a few "women mostly" careers. Those fields considered appropriate for women wishing to work largely involved service to others: clerical, secretarial, nursing, and teaching. Most guidance counselors or career placement officers would have probably been reluctant, if not opposed, to suggesting alternative careers to their young women advisees. It has taken the Women's Movement and the *legal* abolition of sex discrimination in employment and education before our society has even begun to consider women for fields traditionally populated by men. The rapid proliferation of women entering the fields of law, sports, and medicine, however, often obscures the persistent sex segregation in the market place. Most nurses, elementary school teachers, secretaries, and clerical workers are women, and most construction workers, medical doctors, and lawyers are still men.[26] The chosen career of our interviewees, management, is also considered a traditionally male field. Indeed, as late as 1989 only 39.8 percent of all executive, administrative, and managerial jobs were held by women (while women were 45 percent of all employed persons).[27] Moreover, women managers tend to be concentrated in the traditional female fields of education, health, and personnel. Women planning careers in an earlier era would have discovered few women managers or decision-makers, especially in the areas of defense and foreign policy, who could have served as career role models.

Powell's last societal factor, governmental programs, presents some interesting considerations. As we saw in Chapter 2, both the government agencies we are examining, the State and Defense Departments, were highly discriminatory against women in the past. Yet it is likely that government generally, and possibly even the two Departments, were more equitable in their treatment of women than was private industry. This would have been particularly true in the era before the Civil Rights Act of 1964 when discrimination against women by businesses was widespread. Women contemplating careers before 1964 might, therefore, have found the government an attractive opportunity relative to their other choices.

Influence of Societal Factors on the Career Patterns at State and Defense

Though we did not ask the women and men in our sample to specifically assess the influence of each of these individual societal factors on their own career choice or career development, the impact of the factors was evident in many of the descriptions of our interviewees' career paths. Social attitudes on the inappropriateness of work for women was particularly reflected in the career histories of our older women. They reported choices where they did not so much plan a career as "fall into one." Note the following answer from a high ranking woman at the State Department as to why she chose a career in government:

> World War II was going on and I wanted to do something, but I didn't think my temper was suited to the military. Someone mentioned the Foreign Service and I thought that it would be very interesting to try for two or three years. I started off as a senior clerk and secretary and 43 years later I'm still here.

Legal considerations also loom large, again especially for women hired before 1964. As anticipated, for many of them government employers were less discriminatory than private industry. As one interviewee noted in explaining her choice of a government job over one in industry, "Government never offered the same salaries as business, but the criteria [used to determine] whether you start at grade five or seven depends on degree and grades, not on whether you are a man or woman, black or white, pink or green. It doesn't matter. It doesn't come into play." (Also see the interviews with Evelyn P. Foote and Rozanne L. Ridgway in this regard.)

Sex segregation of occupations was also mirrored in some of the interviews, again especially among the women over sixty. As the quote above suggests several of them were initially hired at the State Department in clerical positions, and had to overcome the view that women could only serve in that capacity. One of our interviewees, for instance, was among the hundreds of women fired by the State Department for "moral turpitude" (her words) when she married in the 1950s. Correspondingly, the particular difficulties of choosing a career where women are not naturally found (foreign policy) more generally was revealed in the interviews and has been discussed in Chapter 2. It was also exemplified in the profile of Mary Olmsted. As outlined in Chapter 1, most of the women indicated they were aware of the widespread public view that women do not know as much about foreign affairs as men. Why this stereotype did not prevent our women from entering the field is a puzzle. Perhaps because most of them reject this stereotype as it relates to their own personal knowledge, they simply did not consider it a limiting condition in pursuing their own careers.

Personal Factors

Most early theories of career choice and development relied heavily on the attributes of the individual. A person's education, experience, needs, abilities, family background and upbringing were generally found to be strong determinants of the kind of job a person chose and how successful they were in their career. Even today, one's education obviously largely determines one's career preparation and by extension career choice and career success. Studies have shown that women who are college graduates are more likely to have uninterrupted careers than those without a college degree.[28] Education level is also associated with progress up the career ladder.[29] Indeed, education might be more important for a woman than a man in achieving career success. Thomas R. Dye and Julie Strickland, for instance, found that women in positions of institutional leadership in the U.S. tended to be better educated than a similarly situated group of men.[30] Additionally, choice of major or field of study can influence one's occupation and future success on the job. Women, because they are repeatedly told by teachers and society that they possess less mathematical and analytical ability than men, have (with the support of their guidance counselors) stayed away from those areas of study and related careers.[31] Research has also shown that the more a young woman clings to traditional views about women's roles, the more likely she is to avoid preparation for entrance into "male" careers.[32] Because stereotypes about women's ability have only recently shown any signs of decline, we would expect older women to be more likely to hold these traditional views about career choice.

Age generally is an important predictor of women's career patterns. Not only are older women more likely to hold traditional views about appropriate careers for women, they are also less likely to be as educated as older males simply because they were not expected to prepare for a career outside the home. Both factors contributed to our expectation that fewer older women than older men would be found in positions of authority at State and Defense. Research on careers has also discovered that career progress is very much determined by first jobs held, with each succeeding job helping to influence subsequent positions, although this is more true for men than women.[33] Thus even if some women did go to work in the Departments of State and Defense before the 1970s, the discriminatory behavior of both institutions during that era means we should anticipate few women would have had as their first assignment a position of authority in either Department. Thus, their progress up the career ladder would be severely limited, meaning we would find few older women in our sample. Larwood and Gattiker made similar predictions about older and young women workers.[34] They hypothesized a "dual development" model of careers. Older women, they reasoned, because of societal and institutional barriers would be likely to have obtained only the career success of the younger women. Older men, it was expected, would be further up the career hierarchy because they would not have encountered the difficulties the women did in climbing the organizational ladder. Younger men and younger women, on the other hand, would be expected to experience similar career paths, given the changed climate regarding women working. The results of Larwood and Gattiker's research into the careers of 215 successful business persons in 17 major firms substantiated their expectations.[35] Thus, we should expect to discover some age disparities between the men and women in our sample.

Family background and upbringing are also important determinants of career choice. Socialization to traditional or nontraditional views of women's capabilities and possibilities begins in the home. Research shows that how one is raised, and in particular whether parents encourage a young woman to succeed and to obtain an education equal to her brothers or other young men, are powerful predictors of career choice and career success.[36] Schools, teachers and professors, peers and the mass media also influence young women with regard to whether they will seek employment, and if so, in what field.[37] An individual exposed to all these influences develops certain career attitudes, needs and abilities that, in turn, will directly influence career choice.

All of the persons in our sample are highly motivated individuals or they would not have achieved the success they did, but their backgrounds before joining government are not necessarily the same. We might anticipate women to have joined the State and Defense Departments with different personal histories and characteristics from their male contemporaries, given the likely divergence in the socialization experiences of the two groups. It is possible that an examination of some of these family and personal background factors of the men and women in our sample will help reveal these disparities and, therefore, help us to understand better the career choices of our women.

The Influence of Personal Factors on the Career Patterns at State and Defense

Table 3–1 reports some of the basic demographic information on our sample. One of the first things to note is the younger age of the women compared to the men in similar positions. Over half the men were over fifty years of age, while only a third of the women were this old. These results fit our expectations and the findings of Dye and Strickland with regards to women in leadership positions in the U.S. more generally.[38] Part of the explanation for the difference can be found in the cultural stereotypes mentioned earlier. Many older women, unlike older men, would not have prepared for or pursued a career. Thus, many more older men will be found in both Departments as women of this age group would have chosen not to work outside the home. Also contributing to the age discrepancy are the past practices in State and Defense that until recently kept most women out of the Departments or restricted them to clerical or other limited positions. Moreover, before 1970 the State Department regularly fired women who married and thus many young women in an earlier era saw their careers end before they were thirty.

The figures in Table 3–2 also suggest some rather interesting differences in the educational background of the two genders. In contrast to the research of Dye and Strickland on men and women in leadership positions generally in the U.S., the data in the table indicates that the men in our sample were generally better educated than the women.[39] Over one-third of the men, but only one-fifth of the women, have an advanced degree beyond a Masters. This difference persisted even when we controlled for age. Two-thirds of the men under forty have a Ph.D., M.D., or law degree, while only ten percent of the women under forty have an advanced degree. The same pattern held for men and women in all the other age groups as well. This educational "gap" may reflect a legacy of

Table 3-1.   Age distribution of all women and men (%)

	60 or older	51–60	41–50	40 or under
Men	18.4	36.8	36.8	7.9
Women	7.5	25.0	42.2	25.0

Table 3-2. Highest degree of all women and men (%)

	High School	Bachelors	Masters	PhD/MD/Law Degree
Men	0.0	26.3	36.8	36.8
Women	2.4	29.3	48.8	19.5

societal views that encouraged men, but not women, to pursue all the education needed to prepare for, and advance in, their careers. One would expect that as this societal view changes, and younger women are socialized to prepare for a lifetime career, they would obtain education levels equal to those of men. A sample of men and women in the governmental levels below the Senior Executive and Senior Foreign Service might reflect this. However, another explanation for the educational gap may be found in the difficulty women face in obtaining advanced degrees. For one thing, women have been less likely to receive fellowships for graduate study, making advanced education more difficult. Additionally, since many of the people in our sample reported they worked on their advanced degrees while employed by the government, women would have been less likely to have had this opportunity since their employment histories tended to be shorter. Furthermore, women with family responsibilities may find combining work with school harder to do than men who are not expected to raise the children or prepare dinner. If the latter is true, the educational deficiencies of women may continue to persist for several generations. Regardless of the source of the gap, women may well be disadvantaged relative to men in their efforts to progress up the career ladder by their weaker educational background.

Additional educational differences are also indicated in two other tables. In Table 3–3 we see the women in our sample were not only less likely to have an advanced degree, but they were also less likely to have obtained their highest degree from an Ivy League school. Almost half the

Table 3-3. School attended for highest degree for all men and women (%)

	Ivy League	Seven Sisters	Other Liberal Arts College	State University/ College
Men	47.4	0	21.1	31.6
Women	20	7.5	55	17.5

men attended an Ivy League institution, but only a fifth of the women did so. The difference, no doubt, is a reflection of the previous discriminatory and all-male practices of these institutions, practices that were legal until Title IX. One might expect that lack of an education from a prestigious school could be a drawback, or could have been a drawback, for women. Interestingly, the propensity to have an Ivy League education was more pronounced at State, which reflects its northeast elite image. There has been a recent governmental concern about the extent of Ivy League representation within the Foreign Service and the degree to which it produces a diplomatic corps unrepresentative of American society. Indeed, our findings parallel those of a congressionally requested study, which reported that 41 percent of the SFS had attended Ivy League schools.[40] Thus, women's lack of an Ivy League degree becomes more critical in a culture dominated by such degrees. At least in our study, the disparity between women and men was not too severe for career officials at State, with 42.9 percent of the women and 46.7 percent of the men reporting an Ivy League education. However, the contrast seemed quite pronounced for political appointees. While at State overall, 26.7 percent of the women and 50 percent of the men attended an Ivy League institutions, the figures for appointees were 12.5 percent and 60 percent, respectively, for women and men. At Defense 11.1 percent of appointee women, 100 percent of appointee men, 37.5 percent of career men and 18.8 percent of career women indicated they had a degree from a prestigious school. The greater disparity for appointees may reflect the fact that they tended to be older than careerists, and thus more likely to have received their degree before Title IX, and before the elimination of sex discrimination by the Ivy League universities.

Another educational handicap for women was the lack of scientific or mathematical training, perhaps due to stereotypes about women's abilities in these fields. Several of the men we interviewed in very technical offices reported that they had few women working in their area and did not expect that to change as long as women shied away from studying in these fields. This is particularly a problem for women at the Defense Department, where many of the positions require a technical degree at entry level. As shown in Table 3–4, 21 percent of the men and 12.5 percent of the women reported a degree in math or science. These people were virtually all concentrated in the Defense Department, as no women at State and only five percent of the men in that Department had a technical or scientific highest degree. In Defense, only half as many women as men (20 percent and 38.9 percent, respectively) had training in math, computers, science or a related field. Women were particularly absent in the sciences with 22.2 percent of the men but only four percent of the women listing science or engineering as the major of their highest degree.

Table 3-4.   Major of highest degree (%)

Major	Women	Men
Political Science/International Relations/Public Administration	52.5	39.5
Math/Accounting/Computers	10.0	7.9
Humanities	10.0	10.5
Law/Other Social Science	20.0	23.7
Science/Engineering/Medicine	2.5	13.1
Business	5.0	5.3

Gender stereotypes thus appear to have limited women's educational attainment in ways that may hinder their selection to positions and their advancement in both Departments, especially Defense.

One additional interesting aspect of the data is the higher proportion of women with degrees in government, political science, or public administration. This was most true for the youngest cohort among whom 80 percent of the women but none of the men had their highest degree in this area. That many of the women pursued degrees in these traditionally male fields indicates that at a young age they showed interest in nontraditional careers, and began to prepare for jobs in the government. The burgeoning number of women obtaining degrees in political science (27 percent of all Political Science Ph.Ds in 1987 were women, up from eight percent in 1949), suggests we may see even more women in government positions in the years to come.[41]

We also know something of the immediate occupational background of our sample, since we asked respondents whether their previous job was in government and if it involved foreign affairs. Not surprisingly, virtually all the women and men in our sample had moved to their current jobs from another government position. Only a handful, mostly appointees, had come from private practice or industry, and their stories are interesting examples of how men and women might transfer from the outside to the inside of government. The following account from a young man probably is typical:

> I always wanted to be in government. I originally came to Washington to go to the Foreign Service School at Georgetown with the idea of going into the State Department. After college, I did other things [military]. Eventually, I went to law school. I went into government after law school as a lawyer. Some of the things I did earlier [at other governmental agencies] led me to be asked to come to the State Department when the Reagan Administration came in. At the time I was practicing law and I didn't like it. I was glad to come back to government. The man I worked

for at [the other agency] came over to State with the new administration. He recruited me.

An older woman appointee told a similar story, but one in which her status as a Navy wife and her husband's connections also play a role:

> I worked for an admiral at the Naval Academy setting up a program for families. . . . Then I went on my merry way continuing my work [outside government]. Then the office I am currently in was set up by my boss, and he asked this particular admiral for names of people whom he would recommend for the job. And he [the admiral] recommended me and that's how I got the job. [It was a] matter of timing and being available and who knew you when. Although my boss had interviewed a number of people, he was interested in two things; people with prior Navy experience, either a spouse or prior Navy, and someone with a professional background. I was one of the names that surfaced. That's how it happened. So I did not pursue [this job]; had not even heard about it; and wouldn't have heard about it, had the admiral not called my husband [a Navy officer] and asked "is your wife interested in this job?"

With regard to whether their prior position involved foreign policy, most of our respondents said yes, although more men than women reported that it did. This difference, however, was true only of the older cohorts of women and men. Men and women under forty were equally likely to have had another foreign policy position. Younger women were thus more likely to have been educated for a field in government and foreign policy and to have had consistent career path in that field. This is exactly what we would have anticipated. Cultural stereotypes and the practices of the Departments would have had their greatest impact on the older women. Younger women were more likely to have expected and prepared for careers that in the past would have been considered male professions.

We also asked respondents why they chose government work, and their answers were often rich in interesting detail about the influence of family, personal background, career goals, and motivations. Tables 3–5 and 3–6 report some general categories of responses for women and men overall and for different subgroups. Coding from the open-ended question (multiple responses were possible), we identified six distinct background experiences and five reasons or motivations that best captured the most common themes. Looking first at the experiences, we found several notable differences between the women and men. The former were considerably more likely to have mentioned a political experience, although the difference could be partially attributable to the greater number of women appointees in our sample. This group included several women who had

Table 3-5. Factors mentioned as reasons/motives for choosing a career in government: All men and women[a]

	All Men (%)	All Women (%)
Political experience	2.6	14.6
Military experience	36.8	7.3
College experience	39.5	41.5
Industry experience	15.8	19.5
Government (including internship) experience	18.4	41.5
Educational experience	71.1	53.7
Service to country reason	36.8	24.4
Opportunity reason	18.4	34.1
Interest in government/politics/area reason	63.2	75.6
"Fell into it" reason	10.5	33.0
Family reason	18.4	31.7

[a] Figures represent the coded responses to the following question: "One of the things we are most interested in is why people come to be involved in government. What made you pursue a career in this area?"

worked in Ronald Reagan's campaigns for Governor of California and/or President and were subsequently rewarded with a position in Washington. Women were also more likely to have mentioned a previous governmental experience. Several of them, for instance, recalled internships in government agencies while in college or graduate school. Some of the women also had held positions in other agencies before coming to State or Defense.

For men, often the key event in their lives that brought them into government was a stint in the military. This was particularly true for the men serving in intelligence in both the State and Defense Departments. Typical of this group is the following brief answer from a man at the Pentagon regarding his choice of career. "[I] joined the Navy during Vietnam. When I got out of the Navy—[I] was in intelligence during Vietnam—I went into the civilian-end of intelligence. Been in it [at the Pentagon] since 1971." Interestingly, the gap between women and men in military experience was most notable for the younger cohorts, although the oldest (over sixty) cohort also showed a large difference. This may have been an artifact of our sample, or it may reflect the large number of men who were recruited into government service after World War II and the Vietnam conflict.

There was also some indication that men's educational experiences were more likely than women's to lead to a position in government. If we exclude the political appointees and look only at the career government

Table 3-6.   Factors mentioned as reasons/motives for choosing a career in government by age[a]

		60 or older	51–60	41–50	40 or under
Political experience	Men	0.0	0.0	7.1	0.0
	Women	0.0	10.0	17.6	20.0
Military experience	Men	57.1	21.4	35.7	66.7
	Women	33.3	20.0	35.7	66.7
College experience	Men	14.3	50.0	42.9	33.3
	Women	33.3	50.0	47.1	30.0
Industry experience	Men	28.6	14.3	14.3	0.0
	Women	33.3	20.0	17.6	20.0
Government (including internship) experience	Men	0.0	21.4	14.3	66.7
	Women	33.3	50.0	41.2	20.0
Educational experience	Men	57.1	78.6	71.4	66.7
	Women	0.0	70.0	58.8	40.0
Service to country reason	Men	42.9	28.6	50.0	0.0
	Women	33.3	10.0	29.4	30.0
Opportunity reason	Men	14.3	21.4	21.4	0.0
	Women	33.3	20.0	47.1	30.0
Interest in government/politics/ area reason	Men	85.7	71.4	50.0	33.3
	Women	100.0	90.0	70.6	70.0
"Fell into it" reason	Men	0.0	14.3	14.3	0.0
	Women	33.3	30.0	23.5	0.0
Family reason	Men	28.6	14.3	14.3	33.3
	Women	0.0	30.0	5.9	80.0

[a] Responses based on the same question as in Table 3-5.

officials, 80.6 percent of the men but only 47.8 percent of the women referred to an educational event in describing their path to a job at State of Defense. Often the experience discussed was the advice or intervention of a professor. Most of those who said their education was important noted the value of their degree or the field of their degree. As we have indicated already, women were less likely than men to have an advanced degree, or one from prestigious Ivy League school, or one in a technical field. For many of the male respondents, and for those fewer women who answered that educational experiences were important in getting them into government, their degree, or what institution it was from, was often the factor mentioned. This was particularly true of the men and the many fewer women who were in technical fields at Defense.

Interestingly, in the related area of college experience, men and women showed fewer differences. This was largely due to the fact that for both groups decisions on careers or interviews for first jobs were made during college. Several men and a few women noted the key role played by professors or other academic mentors in helping them decide on a government career. The following experience from a woman at State was probably rare but does suggest the importance of mentors:

> [It was a] series of accidents I suppose. We like to think we're masters of our fate but most of us aren't. I was in London and got interested in foreign policy. I came back to the U.S. and took a job as a researcher for television news doing documentaries. But a professor of mine at _____ turned out to be what they call a spotter for the CIA and [he] put them in touch with me. [I] worked [several] years in the CIA as an analyst.

Shifting from experiences to reasons for joining government, the overall figures show no statistically significant differences in the motives given by the women and men. With regard to the first reason, service to country, men were somewhat more likely to cite this as a reason than women. It is possible the military background of the men was a factor in this regard. However, among the youngest group, it was the women who were more likely than the men to give this as a reason, and none of the women in this age bracket had had a military background. Along these lines, Perry and Wise have suggested that public service as a motivational base for government employment needs to be researched more carefully.[42] Our data indicate sex and age might both be factors to consider in exploring how this motivation works.

Turning to the other motives, we discovered a notable difference between men and women with regard to opportunity reasons. When we looked at career officials especially, we found the women were much more likely than men to mention opportunities for advancement (43.5 percent versus 19.4 percent). This was particularly true for the women at the Defense Department, 56.3 percent of whom mentioned opportunities as a factor, and for women forty to fifty years old (47.1 percent of whom cited this motive). An examination of their answers reflected a point we made earlier: for many of our interviewees, when they were starting their careers, the government was a more equitable employer than private industry. For women wishing a career with possible advancement and equal pay, the only place to go was Washington. The following is a fairly typical scenario:

In 1962 I graduated from [college]. Equal pay for women was unheard of in industry. The government was the only employer offering equal salary for [equal] accomplishments. I had no idea what area I was getting into, [as] they don't teach weapons in school. But that was the primary reason I came to work for the government. I was very naive, and when I was in an interview with [a private company], I was shocked when the statement was made to me, "For a woman we'll pay. ... " I'll never forget those words. They violated every sense of fairness I had. So I said a few four-letter words and stalked out of the interview. What did I know? I was just a poor little naive girl in [the South]. I'd never been out in the big world. The recruiter had no hesitation to put it into those words.

A woman who graduated in the 1950s recounted a related experience:

Frankly, when I got out of college in 1956, I was a political science major, the first thing I was asked on all of those interviews (where I was going to go out and save the world) was how fast can you type. Since I don't type very fast, I joined the Air Force, because at least I found there I didn't have to type, and I got paid the same as the men got paid. In 1956 that was one of the few places that was true.

Similarly, a woman whose career began in the 1940s pointed out what to us seems a limited opportunity, but given the times was the best a woman desiring a career and travel could expect:

When I got out of school, my greatest ambition and desire was to travel abroad. You couldn't because the war [World War II] was on. The State Department was the only department hiring women with a political science background. The only department hiring women for overseas, and then [only] in a clerical capacity. [Women] couldn't get a professional job, so I joined State in 1945, right out of graduate school. [I] went to Moscow because there was a vacancy.

What is clear in all three of these quotes was the *relative* advantage of a career in the government or the military over a job in industry. Theoretically, things have changed now and women have greater opportunities in the private realm, although one of the three women quoted above doubted that it really was better for women in business today. "Do you think it is really different now? It's just not as overt. Talk to some of the ladies in industry." In terms of understanding women's career paths, what is clear is how critical opportunities were and are for women who wish to work outside the home. For a significant proportion of our sample, one of the key reasons they are working for the government was it was the only arena in which they could expect to receive equal, or somewhat equal, treatment with men. What is interesting about these quotes, also, is that these women who were seeking jobs in the 1940s, 1950s, and 1960s displayed a consciousness about discrimination long before the Women's Movement. Their experiences, no doubt, were typical of those encountered by other women of their generations and help us to understand why we eventually had a Women's Movement which had as its primary goal equality in the marketplace. Moreover, their responses may indicate another reason why they were not daunted by the societal views regarding the abilities of women in foreign policy. Based on the actions of potential employers, government recruiters and private employers, the former seemed to be acting as if women were qualified for positions of some authority. Potential business employers, however, seemed much less willing to grant that women seeking jobs with them could ever succeed in the corporate world. A natural conclusion that might have been drawn, by the women whose experiences we have recounted and their contemporaries, was that women had more ability relative to government work than business.

Turning to the other motivations or reasons for joining government, Table 3–5 also suggests women were more likely than men to indicate an interest in politics or foreign affairs as a factor in their choice of career (75.6 percent to 63.2 percent). Among career men and women, 78.3 percent of women but only 61.3 percent of men mentioned this variable (data not reported in the table). This dovetails with our earlier finding concerning the larger proportion of women in our sample with educational backgrounds in government-related fields. For example, a young woman in a high-ranking position in the State Department crafted her career around her love of politics. "I came from politics and I came to [Washington] D.C. to work in politics. I spent eight years on Capitol Hill before I went to the White House. I sought to pursue a career in politics, not necessarily government."

The next to last reason in Table 3–6 reflects the reality of career choice for many people. They do not so much plan a career as "fall into one." Women, not surprisingly, were somewhat more likely to mention this aspect of their career history. This was particularly true for the older cohorts of women who would have been raised in an era when careers for women were atypical or short-lived, existing only before marriage and children came along. Indeed, among our younger group of women, those under forty, no one said they "fell into their career," whereas one-third of the women over fifty-nine mentioned an unplanned career path. An older woman at State recounted a familiar career choice, an innate interest in the field but no real plan to join the Foreign Service.

I wasn't looking for government work. I was going to teach and I suddenly realized I wasn't going to enjoy teaching. I was in my undergraduate days [and] I became aware of something called the Foreign Service. It seemed people in it were doing interesting things. I began to realize that the thing they called the Foreign Service was the thing textbooks were calling diplomats. So I just applied for it in the way college students apply for something without a lifetime career [goal].

For the youngest cohort of women the critical factor was often family-connected. Two types of general reasons made up this category. The first was typical of the reasons given by both men and women; a parent or relative encouraged a person to follow a certain career path. The following two comments, the first from a man, the second from a woman, reflect this type of influence.

> My father, who will be sixty-five this summer, has no pension. I was dating and subsequently married a government employee who told me all about the wonderful things about a government pension and being a government employee. ... I had been approached about coming into government by the Assistant Secretary of _____ at an alumni meeting. I thought about it. I was working as a consultant to government and it looked like a pretty good deal. I subsequently found after getting in government that I liked it.

> My family had an impact on me. My father is a professor. My sister went through Georgetown University School of Foreign Service. Both of them made me politically aware and conscious. I myself went through George-town School of Foreign Service. So, at a younger age, relatively speaking, I made a conscious decision to pursue that course. Family and academics drove me into this area.

Interestingly, none of the oldest group of women mentioned this kind of influence, perhaps because families of their generation were not support-ive of daughters' careers, especially when they might involve travel abroad or the military.

A second family reason can also be found in the responses of women, again especially young women. This was the need to accommodate one's career to the career of a husband. Several women recounted how they took their job in government so they could either be near their husband, or put him through school.

> I was hired by the Navy right out of college and that happened because I'd gotten married at the end of college. My husband and I were both looking for a job and the Navy offered us both a job.

> My husband decided to come back to law school and get a Masters in taxation. So we came [to Washington] and I began applying for jobs. This

was the first job I got, which was good because he wasn't working and neither was I.

While this rationale may be increasingly typical in an era of dual-career marriages, as we have discovered, women at State who married before 1970 would have automatically lost their jobs in the Foreign Service. Accommodating the dual career couple is indeed a modern-day phenomenon.

Actions By Individuals

The preceding review of the reasons given for government employment focused primarily on career choice; it told us little about how people managed to move up the career ladder to their present positions. In examining this process, Powell reminded us that actions taken by the individual are also important. He described three key personal actions: goal setting, career planning, and career tactics.[43] Goal setting involves deciding upon the career and policy agendas one will aim to obtain. Powell explained that women might be expected to have less success in setting goals than men because of lower self-esteem and external support.[44] Closely related to goal setting is career planning. As we have already seen, women tend to evidence less career planning than men, often "falling into" a position rather than deciding upon a profession and taking the necessary steps to attain it. Career tactics include all the strategies one can adopt to get ahead; most importantly, becoming informed about one's profession and workplace.[45] Often the easiest way to accomplish this is to acquire a role model or a mentor, and/or join an informal network at one's place of employment.

A role model is an individual chosen because he or she possesses the skills or qualities that a person wishes to emulate. The person then "mimics the behavior that evokes desired outcomes or accomplishments."[46] This is in essence a passive leadership technique. Mentoring, in contrast, is an active process, by which a person "leads, guides, and advises someone more junior in experience toward career accomplishments."[47] The importance of mentoring opportunities has been a significant topic of discussion in the area of career development for the past 20 years, particularly in the fields of academia and business. In many instances, it has been stressed that having a mentor has been one of the more critical variables in terms of advancement through the profession. "Much anecdotal evidence and research suggests that in academe, as in the business world, success often depends not only on what you know but whom you know—not only on hard work, but also on encouragement, guidance, support and advocacy from those who are already established in the system."[48] Similarly, Gary Powell noted that most corporate presidents, who have predominantly been male, have had mentors who were critical to their success.[49] It is through the mentoring process that the standards for professional behavior are handed down:

> Mentoring includes teaching protégés how to make decisions, guiding, advising, helping to fit events into the broad picture, serving as an advocate, role modeling, giving constructive feedback, motivating, and protecting. Mentors are critically important for helping men and women climb career ladders.[50]

Similarly, Anderson and Ramey have described five different roles of mentors; educator, sponsor, coach, counselor, and confronter. The educator mentor shares knowledge it would take years to acquire. The sponsor mentor widens the exposure of the protégé and guides, develops, polishes, and fine-tunes his or her skills and talents. The coach mentor uses face-to-face leadership while also providing data to the protégé. While the mentor as counselor advises and encourages problem-solving, the mentor as confronter clearly identifies alternatives and consequences to the protégé and tries to resolve aberrant performance behaviors.[51]

In a 1985 article, "What to do about toxic mentors," Kay Darling identified four basic mentor types: (1) the traditional mentor; (2) the step-ahead mentor; (3) the co-mentor; and (4) the spouse mentor.[52] The traditional mentor is described as one who gives wise counsel. The step-ahead mentor is seen as paving the way or giving valuable guidance to the protégé, while the co-mentor is engaged in a reciprocal relationship with their mentee. The spouse mentor obviously performs a special type of co-mentoring which can be one-way or reciprocal.

Research has shown that the tactic of having a mentor is more available to, and more utilized by, men.[53] As a consequence, the mentoring system has tended to bolster the professional development of men, but to deny the same help to women. The causes of this disparity are numerous. The lack of women in leadership positions within organizations has an obvious impact upon women, in that they are faced with a lack of female role models and potential female mentors. Women seeking mentors thus must consider the possibility of a male mentor. As one study found, not only do men have more access to mentoring than women, since men more often mentor men, but among women who have a mentor, women are just as likely to have male mentors as female mentors.[54] However, obtaining a male mentor is particularly difficult for women. As studies have found, "Members of professional peer systems tend to choose persons most like themselves as protégés—but to overlook (or actively exclude) newcomers who are 'different'. ... Indeed, these systems have tended to function as 'old boys' networks' in which male mentors guide and foster male mentees."[55] Thus mentoring opportunities are clearly limited for women in fields like foreign policy, where the leaders have predominantly been male. In fact, in such arenas, the lack of mentoring creates a double bind for women. Because they are in fields in which women have been excluded, they already have "outsider" status, and thus they are even more likely to need the contacts and the informal knowledge about how the system works that a mentor can provide. Additionally, being seen as the newcomers and kept outside the "inner circle" can also be personally damaging to women and their self-confidence. As the Project on the Status of Women concluded: being a protégé of a senior person can have a special significance for many women, "who enter some professional areas with some conflict between the desire for accomplishment and limited preconceptions about what a woman should—or can—do. Women often don't receive the same support for professional achievement as men do, and encouragement from others can be especially influential."[56]

Thus women are faced with a paucity of potential female mentors and with the reluctance of men to serve as mentors for women. The preference of mentors to choose a mentee most like themselves is particularly heightened in terms of gender differences. Many men hesitate to mentor women, either because they are not used to working with women and are not comfortable with women colleagues, but additionally also because they fear rumors of sexual involvement:

> Simultaneously, women's "overvisibility" may lead senior persons to avoid the risk of choosing a woman as a protégé. Often, in settings where women are new or few, they tend to stand out because of their very difference. While a male protégé may fail without anyone's noticing, "a woman's mistakes are often loudly broadcast;" consequently, to protect their own reputations, men may "maintain higher standards for female protégés than for male protégés," or exclude women altogether.[57]

In addition to facing the structural barriers to obtaining a mentor, many women exclude themselves from the opportunity of having a mentor. "Some women may be unaware of how the protégé system works. They may be more hesitant than men about 'exploiting' personal ties for professional gains and more concerned about the potential confusion of personal and professional relationships."[58] Even in instances in which there are women in leadership positions, these senior women may not have the status to be effective mentors, or they may not have developed a working relationship with the "powers that be" that would enable them to provide assistance to others. As a result, some junior women are skeptical of the less famous women in senior positions: "Could they really be as good as the men? Were these women still appealing to men? I feared they were not, and for that reason I feared even more being identified with them. Moreover, I did not need to take such women as role models to assure myself that women could think."[59]

Correspondingly, some senior women are not interested in fostering mentoring relationships with junior women:

> Some senior women (although their number is declining), may still iden-
> tify more readily with their male peers than with women lower down on
> the academic ladder. Likely to have been mentored by men and to view
> the institution from a male perspective, they may see themselves as
> "better than most women," and as proof that academe is a meritocracy
> where differential treatment by sex does not exist.[60]

This tendency has been referred to as the "queen bee syndrome." "The queen bee syndrome has been suggested as a way of identifying women who are successful in spheres that typically exclude women. These women have 'made it' in the professional world, and they do not choose to help other women or men to succeed."[61] Berenice Fisher has admitted to this type of perspective. "My earlier career struggle seemed male identi-fied. I knew that some of the attention I enjoyed, in both senses of the word, stemmed from my status as a 'special woman,' and that if many women had pursued the same path I would not have been so special."[62] Though some women may resist the practice of mentoring out of a desire to protect their own "privileged" position, other senior women who have made it have a distrust of the whole concept of mentoring as such. Again, Berenice Fisher frankly acknowledged her initial rejection of mentors.

> The first time I heard the claim that we, as women, needed female role
> models to make our way through the world, I felt angry. This was the
> early nineteen seventies, and I had struggled long and hard to make
> myself an independent woman. That effort has been a lonely one, in a
> environment that offered little support. Now, with a burgeoning move-
> ment demanding justice and equality for women, many people, including
> some feminists, argued the need for role models as well. Secretly, I felt
> a certain contempt: what we need is guts, not role models![63]

Though Fisher finally recognized that people desiring role models were trying to seek validation from others in order to deal with the problem of loneliness, which was the result of a social system that systematically isolates women from potential sources of support, she argued that such advocacy of role models perpetuates the logic of domination.[64] "While feminists indict political authority as leading to domination, we accept the social authority of role models and heroes as naturally benevolent."[65] Her article entitled "Wandering in the Wilderness" reemphasized the fact that women desiring progress or seeking to break into male-dominated fields in a male-dominated society have a special burden. "Since patriarchy assigns us the job of sustaining traditional culture, through rearing children and taking care of many other people, any changes that strain this social web—including even our own rebellion against it—threaten to tear us apart."[66] This burden thus makes women feel even more alone and may lead to a search for role models, or others who have been able to survive.

> Thus, the loneliness of women trying to create new kinds of lives or a new kind of society is not merely psychological or even sociological. It is historical and ultimately, perhaps, existential. It is the loneliness of not knowing where our efforts to change social relationships will take us and whether, in the end, the struggle will be worth the cost.[67]

Though there may be benefits for women in the pursuit of role models or mentors, other studies caution that there can be disadvantages to these relationships which fall disproportionately upon women, both upon those who serve as mentors and upon mentees. Ronnie Braun described three negative results of a situation in which mentoring does not work out: (1) the protégé can become overly dependent, or conversely the mentor may become condescending and domineering; (2) the results of a sexual mentoring relationship may make the protégé feel she cannot fulfill her talents without him; and finally (3) the overall reality dawns that a mentor can know what is good for you for only so long.[68] Mentoring can have particularly negative consequences if the mentor has a destructive personality, or declines in power. The whole issue of dependence or overdependence can have negative consequences for both the mentee and the mentor.

> There is also a danger of some women protégés transferring their own dependency needs into the mentoring/protégé relationship. The conscious or unconscious wish to be taken care of by others impacts both the protégé and the mentor by endangering the effectiveness of each. This behavior has been described as the "Cinderella complex" and is defined as personal and psychological dependency, a network of largely repressed attitudes and fears that keep women retreating from the full use of their minds and creativity.[69]

Fisher further detailed another set of negative consequences which may befall those who serve as mentors: "I think that many women who are attracted to the notion of role models envision a historical progression in which women who have themselves found role models then act as role models for women who come after them. Such a progression, combining both nurturance and justice, feels particularly right."[70] However, she concluded that this is mistaken. The mentor must face the costs entailed in taking responsibility, or care of, the mentee. It can be a demanding relationship.

> By sharing these home truths, . . . we do reveal aspects of ourselves with which we may be uncomfortable. We make ourselves vulnerable. We allow ourselves and others to question the process by which we have done what we have done, not merely to accept it as a final truth but to open it up to reinterpretation and re-creation as well. This sort of interaction with other women requires self-revelation in the best sense.[71]

As a result, many women have relied less on a strict mentoring relationship and have instead frequently built informal networks, where participants share professional experiences, sound out approaches for handling difficult situations and work out advancement strategies. However, for these to be effective, women must be prepared to assume the additional tasks that a mentor would have performed, such as the sponsoring activities of self-promotion. Women must be prepared to publicize themselves:

> Women have been socialized to believe that it is somehow unladylike to call attention to one's self or to one's achievements in any overt way. One must wait to be noticed, to be recognized, to be asked. They seem to believe that if they are "good little girls" and do what they are told and perform exceptionally well, they will be recognized and rewarded. Well, that's a nice fairy tale that has little to do with the realities of organizational life.[72]

Where women can establish these networks, they can serve as a source of information about the workplace. This information becomes the basis for making correct career moves, including deciding who would make a good mentor. Unfortunately, these networks are often gendered. This is reflected in the most common terminology used to describe them, the "old boys' club." As the phrase makes clear, women are generally excluded from this inner circle of the most important persons in the workplace, with often disastrous consequences. Women, we are told, because they are left out often do not know what is happening, who is getting a promotion, where the new positions are being created, and who is going to be fired. Excluded from the "old boy network," women often attempt to form their own "old girl network." Such women-centered groups are possible and useful, however, only where there are enough women in positions of influence or power to have access to the valued insider information. At Defense and State throughout most of their respective histories, the number of women and their locus of influence have been so limited as to make an "old girl network," at best, weak. Thus, the career-enhancing strategies of joining a network or obtaining a woman mentor have been restricted. Only women who have recently been admitted to the Departments can reasonably expect to have the wherewithal to use the former effectively.

Influence of Actions by Individuals on Careers at State and Defense

Our research has provided preliminary data that gives us some insight into how the women (and men) in our sample made it to the top of the foreign policy establishment. Specifically, we queried respondents about their policy goals and policy accomplishments in their current positions and the tactics used to obtain their present job. We shall leave the discussion of their responses to the first two of these to Chapter 6, where we shall look more explicitly at the management styles of men and women. Our inquiry into tactics used to get ahead was focused upon one question: whether respondents had sought or been asked to take their current position. There are several reasons to expect the women in our sample to respond differently from the men to this question. First, women are generally thought to be less aggressive than men. Whether this is a product of socialization or genetic or hormonal factors is, as noted in the Introduction, a matter of intense debate.[73] Second, it has been argued that women are less likely than men to evaluate their own success as a result of their intelligence and abilities.[74] Although recent research suggests this is not always true, there is reason to expect that successful women might underestimate their own role in achieving their positions and therefore be less willing to take further action to move their careers forward.[75] Third, prior research has found that women underestimate their worth and as a result ask for, or settle for, lower salaries.[76]

Table 3–7 gives a breakdown in the percentage of men and women in different categories who reported that they sought their current position or were asked to take the job. While none of the relationships were statistically significant, they were consistent. Women, regardless of subcategory, were always less likely to have actively sought their current position. Overall nearly half the men but only one-quarter of the women undertook a proactive effort. Older women were particularly unlikely to have sought an advancement; none of them reported that they initiated the efforts that led to their current position. Political appointees were also unlikely to say they sought out their present job, especially the women. Perhaps an extreme case of those who waited to be asked was the women

Table 3-7.   Percentage of respondents who sought or were asked to take current position[a]

		% Sought	% Asked	% Other (volunteered)
Overall	Men	47.4	47.4	5.3
	Women	26.8	56.1	17.1
Career Officials	Men	51.6	41.9	6.5
	Women	39.1	39.1	21.7
Political Appointees	Men	28.6	71.4	0.0
	Women	11.1	77.8	11.1
Age: Over 60	Men	42.9	57.1	0.0
	Women	0.0	66.7	33.3
50–59	Men	42.9	50.0	7.1
	Women	20.0	80.0	0.0
40–49	Men	50.0	42.9	7.1
	Women	47.1	29.4	23.5
Under 40	Men	66.7	33.3	0.0
	Women	10.0	70.0	20.0

[a] Responses based on the following question: Did you actively seek the position or did someone ask you to take the position?

quoted earlier in the chapter who "did not pursue [the job], had not heard about it, and wouldn't have heard about it had the admiral not called my husband." More common, especially for the career women, was a pattern whereby they were aware of the position that was the next step and while they may not have asked for it, they did try to work hard so as to be recognized and therefore asked to take it.

This reluctance to seek out a promotion may also be the result of discouragement on the part of women who have already had to struggle to overcome so many barriers to their careers. Perhaps they no longer have the energy left to advance their careers, or perhaps their decision to stay in their present job is a tactic: to refrain from seeking a promotion you fear you will not get in order to avoid the resulting disappointment. In her congressional testimony, Mary Lee Garrison, a Co-President of the State Department chapter of the Women's Action Organization, described the resentment felt by career Foreign Service Officers at the suggestion by Charles Untermeyer, the White House Personnel Director, that the Administration was recruiting female political appointees for State in order to supplement the Department's affirmative action program.

It very much affects morale and cheapens the accomplishments of those women and minorities who have worked darn hard to get to those levels. It tars everyone who has any appearance of being a women or minority candidate with a brush of incompetence, and even more tragically, it presents to young people ... a very warped picture. For those who are ambitious and interested in achieving ambassadorial rank, it becomes very obvious ... that the way to do that is not through the career Foreign Service, but rather ... become active in politics, ... and you will be rewarded ... with an ambassadorship.[77]

As Garrison suggested, younger officers may not be as reluctant to pursue career advancement. However, younger career women in our sample were generally more unwilling than the young men to seek out and ask for a promotion. Although, as the profile of Michele Markoff also indicates, many of them were not adverse to pursuing alternative, more risky, career paths (see the profile at the end of the chapter). Thus, perhaps the reluctance of women to take appropriate and aggressive career tactics may cease to exist in the younger generations among whom both women and men are expected to have careers.

Several of our respondents also volunteered comments about the relative availability and use of mentoring or networking opportunities or strategies. With respect to mentoring, many of the older women mentioned the lack of mentors for them because of the absence of women in management positions in both Departments when they entered government. A senior woman at State explained, "There were so few women around. I'm just trying to remember when I first met a senior woman Foreign Service Officer. There just weren't enough of them around." Those women who did mention that they had a mentor were often the younger women. However, one older woman who had been in the military noted that other women had functioned as mentors for her.

I had senior women who, from the time I was a First Lieutenant on, were serving as mentors. Some very special mentors. ... Where I would go and talk to them. They treated me as a professional and not as a woman. I was simply an officer who happened to be a woman, not a woman who happened to be an officer, and there's a difference.

Because of the absence of senior women who could act as mentors, those who had mentors often had male mentors. One woman appointee in particular gave her husband credit for being her mentor, thus following the spouse mentor model noted by Darling. Others were fortunate to have male mentors at work. Although, as one noted, she was forced to rely on men because she had no female colleagues who could serve in this capacity. "One of my greatest regrets was the absence of a woman mentor.

I think there simply weren't very many women when I was young. I've had lots of male mentors. I've never had a female mentor." The helpfulness of the male mentors, however, is an open question. One woman, for instance, cited a man as a mentor merely because he "treated me normally, treated me the way I treated my staff, and that was so unusual then, I always thought fondly of him." This description suggests how minimal the help from a male mentor might be, as a mentor should do more than treat you "normally." Indeed those who had good mentors could be very specific about the help they received. One woman who had several such good mentors commented:

> So I had men and women that I felt very comfortable going to, to discuss careers and experiences, and how to handle this or that. It's not necessary to have a mentor but I think it is a great help in creating you. If you've got a good mentor ... they can be worth their weight in gold, because they give you the proper perspective and balance. It's easy, if you try to hack it through your way alone, to come out with perhaps a little bit of a distortion in what really is of value in what you are doing.

Given the importance of mentors for women, it is not surprising that both those women who had been mentored, and those who had not been so lucky, often serve as mentors to the younger women coming up through the ranks. A woman who had not been mentored her self commented:

> Now on the other side of the coin [because I didn't have a mentor], I feel it is extremely important to be a mentor. I have lots of younger women, and some of them who are not so young, that I have tried to help along the way. I have found doing that to be both a pleasure and, in some sense, an obligation.

The type of advice given covered a wide range of topics. One woman recalled her first and subsequent advice to mentees:

> The first person who ever came to me was a gal who wanted to know if she should wear pants to a meeting as opposed to a dress. She simply came to me because I was older and I was there. But most of it is essentially job counseling, people who are either unhappy with their current jobs or who are simply without a job at the moment, coming out of college, or something. How do they go look for a job? Who do they talk to? What do they do? It is getting to the point I'm mentoring daughters of men I have known in the business. Every year, I get three or four of them in here who want to know, "what is the world like out there?" and "how do I go about this?"

This woman clearly feels an obligation to serve as a traditional mentor. The burden on her time, because she is one of a few, comes through in her comments. Others who mentored also noted the heavy time responsibilities involved in mentoring. Perhaps because of this, some of our interviewees who had wanted to work with, or get the support of other women, sometimes encountered the kind of resistance implied by the queen bee syndrome. The most common reference was to the competition between women: "I think one of the greatest tragedies in my experience is that women, rather than compete with men, will be moved into the trap of choosing the only other woman in the entire organization and competing with her. They get nasty about it." Another woman contrasted the help men give each other with the experience of women. "Sometimes women are more of a problem, it's funny. There is no networking, no old girl network. It is more cutthroat between women. Maybe because there are fewer women. People don't help people get ahead like men do. Strange."

These were not the typical descriptions of the relationships between women. However, the absence of women mentors and the absence of an "old girl network" were an oft-noted refrain, sometimes tied to the person's own lack of advancement.

> It took me almost twice as long as my colleagues to attain the same level they attained. I had to work harder, to prove myself. Part of it is the "old boy network." They are very comfortable with the people they know and to some of them women are unknown factors. We don't have an "old girl network" at DOD.

Thus, to make it up the career ladder at State or Defense it helps to have a mentor. Only some of our women interviewees have had the support of either a mentor or a network that would have been more readily available to their male colleagues. The dedication of the women we interviewed to providing such support to younger women, however, possibly means the next generation of women in the foreign policy process will not have to struggle alone, or work so hard, to make it to the top of their chosen profession.

Family and Personal Appearance Factors

As Gary Powell and Gutek and Larwood argued in examining the careers of women, emphasis should be placed on the variables of marriage, pregnancy and children, since these factors determine that women's career patterns will be significantly different from those of men.[78] In accepting this rationale, we are going to discuss the personal and family characteristics of women policy-makers, emphasizing those of marriage and children. We shall also mention a factor not discussed by Powell, personal appearance.

The frequency of marriage among professionals is a variable which operates differently for women and men. As studies by Dye and Strickland, Valdez and Gutek, and others have found, professional women tend, more than men, to be single, widowed, divorced, or separated.[79] Similarly a survey of 1500 women and men who had received MBA's from the University of Texas over a 60 year period found that women were more likely than men to be single, or divorced, or to have married several times: in particular, 52 percent of the women, but only 17 percent of the men, were single.[80] A 1982 survey of female senior executives found that 52 percent had never married or were widowed, separated, or divorced, while a similar study of male senior executives in 1979 found that only five percent of the men were unmarried.[81]

As Valdez and Gutek concluded, these statistics are especially noteworthy considering the fact that a larger proportion of managerial workers are in the thirty-six to forty-five year age category, which has the highest proportion of married women of any of the age groups.[82] The primary explanation for this phenomenon centers around the conclusion that, due to job discrimination and the competing requirements of household responsibilities, careers are ultimately more demanding for women. This becomes particularly true as one moves into careers which are highly taxing in terms of time and commitment. Under such circumstances, for many women, careers and marriage are not compatible. According to the "role conflict theory," one way of dealing with the strain experienced by those with ambitious careers plus competing home demands is by the "elimination of roles."[83] Thus those concentrating on a career may forego marriage. In a study of state bureaucrats by Kelly and Guy, this was exactly the pattern they found. In all the states examined, women were much more likely to be living alone, never married or divorced, and living without dependents. Traditional sex roles did not interfere because, for women, they had been abandoned. Apparently, the way women in demanding careers reconciled conflicting demands of work and home was to forsake one role for the other. Attempting to combine both relegates women to the lower ranks in the hierarchy where the job does not consume as much time or energy. As Kelly and Guy concluded, "Only when women are not seriously burdened by family obligations will they move into elite positions."[84]

The same logic or explanation is also applied to the variable of having children: as the level of commitment and preparation required for a job rises, there is a general increase in the proportion of childless women and a corresponding decrease in the proportion of women with three or more children.[85] As the studies of senior executives discovered, 61 percent of the women had no children, while this was true for only three percent of the men.[86] Subsidiarily, Valdez and Gutek anticipated that women professionals and managers would have fewer children than those in lower-status jobs, and the results of their study provided support for this hypothesis.[87] The impact of having children is especially significant for women, since women have traditionally had the primary responsibility for child care and housekeeping, and unfortunately these demands do not decrease merely because a woman is employed outside of the home.

> Moreover, because women bear the primary responsibility for child care, their work and family demands are simultaneous, whereas those experienced by men are more typically sequential.... Not only are the demands of the family allowed to intrude into work role more than vice versa for women, but given situations requiring a choice between the two roles, the family will often take priority.[88]

In addition, it has been found that "employers or superiors view marriage and children as a burden or hindrance for a woman's career, while they regard them as assets for a man's career."[89] As a result, marriage and children can have a negative impact on a woman's career, perhaps by lowering her career commitment, or by steering her into a more traditional career thus reducing her career attainment.

Another personal factor which has been mentioned as having an impact upon career opportunities is physical appearance. Attractiveness can serve as an asset or a detriment. It can be a benefit to the extent to which it correlates with gender stereotypes. Applicants for a job who look nice have an advantage in seeking positions which are appropriate for their own sex. However, attractiveness can be a disadvantage when seeking jobs that have been traditionally reserved for the opposite sex. An overly attractive appearance would tend, therefore, to be a detriment for women seeking male-dominated jobs.[90] Thus, several personal and family factors, including marriage, children, and physical attractiveness are hypothesized to affect the careers of women in management positions.

Influence of Family Factors on Careers at State and Defense

The women managers at the State and Defense Departments fit the expected pattern with regard to marriage and children fairly well (see Table 3–8). Whereas nearly all the men (89.5 percent) were married, only 61 percent of the women were currently married. Similarly, 89.5 percent of the men had children, but barely half (53.7 percent) of the women did.

Table 3-8.   Marital and parental status of women and men in the foreign policy arena

	Overall		Appointees		Careerists	
	Men	Women	Men	Women	Men	Women
Percent currently married	89.5	61.0	100.0	44.4	87.1	73.9
Percent with children	89.5	53.7	100.0	38.9	87.1	65.2

Women also had significantly smaller families. Half the men had more than two children, but only 32 percent of the women with children had more than two, though this result may be an artifact of the younger age of the women. Perhaps for the same reasons, among persons who had children, women were more likely to have younger children. None of the men, but a quarter of the women (23.4 percent) had a child under the age of six. No notable distinctions characterized or differentiated the two Departments with regard to any of those variables.

As suggested by the previously noted research, the women in our sample seemed to be avoiding or delaying marriage and a family, and if they had a family it tended to be smaller. This was particularly true for the political appointees. While all the males in these positions were married, less than half of the women were presently married. One appointee explained her decision not to marry as follows:

> I hope we could get to the stage where there is no peer pressure either way. I spent years thinking that, of course, I want marriage and children, as everybody does, but always someplace off in the future, never right now. And then I spent years thinking that there must be something wrong with me because I didn't want marriage and children. And if the Women's Movement meant anything to me personally, it was realizing that there is nothing wrong with not wanting to have a family, or to consider a career.

The figures for career civil servants in both Departments, while still suggesting women were delaying or avoiding marriage, were more nearly equal as 87.1 percent of the men and 73.9 percent of the women were married. The figures for children were also more skewed for appointees, with all the men but barely a third of the women having children. The percentage of career men and women with children were 87.1 percent and 65.2 percent respectively. The differences between men and women appointees regarding the number and ages of children were not statistically significant, but they did show women with smaller and younger families. Again this might be the result of the younger age of the women appointees or the result of a deliberate decision to limit family size or to delay the start of a family.

Not surprisingly, when we asked our interviewees whether they found it difficult to combine a career with parenthood, women were significantly more likely to say yes. More than half the women (54.5 percent) who had families, but only a quarter of the men (27.3 percent) answered in the affirmative. Among career women and men the problems seemed to be greater, with two-thirds of the women (66.7 percent) and almost a third of the men (30.8 percent) citing problems. Only 28.6 percent of the women appointees and a minuscule 14.3 percent of the men appointees indicated role conflict. One might speculate that appointees, because of their greater earning power or less structured career path, had been able to more easily manage the two careers of professional and parent. One appointee at Defense, for instance, replied that she had no conflict because her children were grown. Another indicated she had been able to have a family because she could afford live-in help. For those appointees and career women with young children at home, the range of problems associated with raising children and being in a high-powered career were familiar ones; lack of good child care, no free time, conflict between demands of the job and demands of parenting, having to travel, and guilt. One women described her experiences as a young mother as follows:

> I was one of a very few working mothers, many said it was a mistake. I was able to accomplish what I did by trying to be a superwoman. I worked 22 hours a day. The workload was backbreaking. I went through [my] twenties and thirties feeling exhausted. I went to the doctor for vitamin and iron shots because I never had any energy. I stayed in a job nine years, which was not the best career move, but it didn't require overtime or travel.

One high-level appointee described a similar role choice:

> I made a career choice: the child and the family, versus the career issue. My beliefs are that children should spend time with their parents, and that that's more important than money. If a person finds that his or her career is so fulfilling, or can only be fulfilling if he does it 14 hours a day, he shouldn't also try to raise children. When my children came along, I was doing very well in the Defense Department, and could have done much better. I made a conscious career decision not to do so, to try to keep my working hours to 50 hours a week and to minimize my travel. I made a conscious choice to spend time with my children. I've been very happy with that choice. I never had any doubts about making it, but I find myself resenting that I had to make it. I think it is unrealistic to

think you can do both. I've never seen anybody, male or female, do both well. I mean I do my job well, but I'm not at as high a level as I could be if I did it more hours a week. I know women who have chosen the career over the children and, in my opinion, their children aren't as well off as mine are. A few, a few young ones say they are going to make it, but most of them don't in the end. It's just too tempting. I mean if you can see a big job within your grasp you are obviously not going to throw it over-board, unless you're very highly motivated as a parent and unless you have certain beliefs about the importance of parenting.

The double burden of work and family is reflected in this quote from a woman at Defense;

Becoming a parent put a strain I didn't have before, involving whole issues of logistics, supply, and security. Children presented different kinds of requirements. I was torn between the job and home in terms of time and energy. I was dedicated at home and on the job, but it was difficult to do both.

A single mother's response is even more poignant in describing the trade-offs she had to make:

[I] hired women housekeepers because I was a single parent since he was four years old. I was like most male executives, I had no idea what was happening to my kid. Someone else was taking care of him. It wasn't until the last couple of years, before I started to pay attention to him. My career had gotten down to earth, I'd gone as far as I was going. I had an awful lot of male friends whose kids had disappeared and they were sorry they had never seen them.

Interestingly several of the younger men reported some problems com-bining roles too. One man at Defense responded:

Time. Extremely difficult. Need two of me, or 30-hour day. I don't feel I have enough time with children. Most stressful aspect of my life is the competition between my career and my kids, and resolving that conflict. [I'm] always compromising—painful no matter which one gets the short end of the stick.

An older man, however, was frankly surprised by the question regarding problems combining career and parenthood. He replied, "No. But I don't know how to answer that question as a man. That's sort of a strange question to ask. I'm supposed to do that [pursue career]." One might expect this attitude to influence this man's view of women colleagues who do work and have children. Indeed several of the women in other parts of the interview noted that they encountered colleagues and bosses who indicated that the women either could not manage a career and parenting or should not attempt to combine both.

Besides parenting conflicts, another personal issue for several of the women we interviewed was the problem of looks, or more specifically the problem of dealing with the stereotype that good-looking women cannot be smart or competent. The problem was laid out by an appointee at State in response to a question asking if there were any views about women that limited women's influence in policy making;

> Well, there is a very profound one. The public thinks you have to be ugly or look like a spinster to be taken seriously. Not that I am pretty anymore, but when I was a young woman I was, I had a certain drama in my looks. Being well dressed, which I usually am, I tend to watch my hairdo, I wear nice jewelry and so on. The public thinks she looks nice, she looks like the [job title]. They think that, therefore, it means you don't have any brains. Unless you look [unattractive] you can't be bright, and I resent that very much, for I think a woman should be physically attractive and men should whistle at her when she walks down the street, but she should also be bright. She doesn't have to be a bimbo. You know I have seen beautiful women not taken seriously because they were beautiful. I do think it's hard. You know people believe that it is a disadvantage in this life to not be beautiful, but the disadvantage in this life is to be beautiful, or to be glamorous, anything like that. Very bad, and other women resent it as well as the men.

The problem with being attractive was linked by several or our respondents with having to travel on business with male colleagues or bosses. One woman made this connection, recalling how a colleague had told her "My wife certainly wouldn't let me travel with someone who looked like you." She replied, "I'll be happy to assure her she has nothing to worry about." Her answer indicates one way with which this issue can be dealt. For women of an earlier generation, an alternative strategy might have been to have attempted to hide or cover up their looks by adopting nonflattering styles. A woman at Defense commented on her problem with being attractive by noting:

> I find a lot of women out in the field or in government here in Washington who were the pioneers. You can almost always tell them because there are certain mannerisms or ways of dressing, particularly in the military, of the people who have had to tear down the barriers for other women. There is a big difference in some of the younger women in the military, their haircuts are very feminine, where at one time if you were in the military, you wore a certain haircut.

While women entering the Departments today may not have to adopt a gender-neutral style, our examination of appearance and family factors reveals the limitations under which women in management positions in government continue to labor. These additional burdens on women attempting to develop careers in already hostile environments suggest yet another set of variables which can help to explain the limited number of women in the high level positions in the State and Defense Departments.

Conclusion

Our review of the background and motivations of the women on the inside of the foreign policy process has revealed some interesting differences with the men on the inside. As anticipated, there is a legacy of societal views on the career paths of women, especially older women. Specifically, they were more likely to have fallen into a career, and to have faced discrimination by business in seeking their first job. The personal background of our women also suggest that they are academically less prepared than men, especially for technical jobs. Whether this reflects societal influence, discrimination or personal attributes is uncertain, but the result is a probable negative impact on women's careers. The factors mentioned by the women and men in our sample as reasons or motivations for pursuing a career in government also indicate some of the ways society directly or indirectly influences careers. Men's experience in the military, the prodding of professors and family, in addition to the other differences, suggest men's paths into government diverge in some notable ways from those of the women in our sample.

Social pressures on women or differences in internal motivations are also indicated in the limited evidence concerning women's less aggressive behavior in seeking promotions. More definitive evidence, that in our culture women have a difficult time managing a career, is indicated by the sizable number of women in our study who have delayed or avoided marriage and children to pursue demanding careers.

Many of the differences we found in the background of the men and women at the State and Defense Departments were sharper for the older generations. The greater similarities between the sexes in the younger cohorts lead us to expect fewer differences among women and men already in the career funnel at both Departments. Additionally, this narrowing of difference suggests that those discrepancies we found are more the result of historically diminishing societal factors than of any innate, gender-linked, unique qualities of women and men. If our supposition in this is true, we should not expect to find the women at State and Defense to diverge too markedly from men in the Departments in how they think or how they behave. Section II will explore this possibility.

Interview
ROZANNE L. RIDGWAY
The Mentored Outsider

Rozanne L. Ridgway was one of the highest ranking women at the State Department in both the Carter and Reagan Administrations, serving, respectively, as Counselor of the Department from 1980 to 1981 and Assistant Secretary of State for European and Canadian Affairs from 1985 to 1989. Currently she is President of the Atlantic Council. She is a frequent commentator on developments in the former Eastern Bloc countries, appearing on such television news shows as the *MacNeil/Lehrer Newshour* and the *Crier Report.* Ambassador Ridgway began her career at State in 1957 as a career foreign service officer. Her decision to enter the diplomatic arena in many ways exemplifies the decision process of the other women from her generation at State.

I did not go away to college. ... I went to a grade school across the street from my house, I went to high school six blocks away, and I went to a university across the street in the other direction from the grade school. I loved history, and I went to the university with everybody in the neighborhood assuming I would end up at that university teaching. You go along with that kind of thinking. I guess that's what I thought I was going to do. I wasn't excited about it, but if that's what you're supposed to do, then that's what you do. However, two things happened in succession. In 1953 or 1954, *Life Magazine* did a story on ten women with interesting professions. One of those women was Patricia Byrne, now recently retired, who at the time was a career Foreign Service Officer and a Vice Consul. She was a graduate in History from Beloit College, which was very much like the school that I was in, Hamline University. So I became aware of something called "The Foreign Service" as a career. The next thing that happened was that in the spring of 1956, maybe late winter in 1955, a Foreign Service Officer on home leave in St. Paul gave a talk to a class I was in about careers in the Foreign Service. He had some application forms and so I filled in the application forms for the Foreign Service examination for the summer of 1956. I did not expect to pass it. In fact, however, I passed it, to be sure with a miserably low score to the great embarrassment of the family. I said "you don't understand this examination, passing it at age twenty is passing it at age twenty. I'm not going to knock it."

Now a couple of things happened along the way that may not represent the experience of other women. Employers came to campus to interview people and I did two interviews. One, as I recall, was General Electric from Cincinnati, interviewing for technical editors. You know from your work in the field that these were the jobs for the ladies in the late 1950s, . . . editorial assistant, technical editor. I interviewed for technical editor. They weren't impressed with me, and I didn't get any job offers. I was probably going to end up writing instructions that got stuck inside of a Mixmaster. The other recruiter was with the telephone company. Today, by the way, I'm on the Board of Bell Atlantic. The telephone company representatives came and they certainly did want to interview women. They showed me their organization and their pay scale. The salary numbers were the ridiculously low numbers of the 1950s. You'd start out as a customer representative and that was fine. But, in all innocence, I was just simply not raised with any sense of there being things that I couldn't do. So when they put this chart in front of me and said, "Here's the customer representative and here's the department of customer services, and if you perform well you get a five dollar raise every six months," I said to myself, well I'm certainly going to perform well, so I asked, as I looked at this great organization chart, "How long did it take to get from the bottom to the top?" They said "Oh, women don't do those jobs up there, but we can offer you this great career where you might end up supervising 12 or 24 customer representatives." I mean they just frankly said that women don't go across this line to senior management. Thank you very much, but no thank you. So I joined the Foreign Service.

> Once at the State Department, Ambassador Ridgway was faced with two problems. First, and most obvious to her, was the difference in her background compared to the other members of the entering class of new Foreign Service Officers. Second, and much less recognized by Ambassador Ridgway, was her sex. As she tells the story, her ability to work hard, her strength of character, and some very special mentors helped her overcome both problems.

So off I went into the Foreign Service in June of 1957, about nine days after I graduated, and really wet behind the ears. I was asked if I wished to be assigned overseas or if I wished to be assigned in Washington. Some instinct told me that going overseas was too big a jump. I did not have a foreign language that would pass muster. Mostly, I had never lived away from home and here I was going from this neighborhood-bounded life of a close-knit family, my whole life had been within the confines of six blocks. So I said, no, I would take the Washington assignment first. I did. I served in Washington from 1957 to 1959 in a job as an information specialist. But I had a different kind of a background. I suppose instinctively, looking back at it now, people in sociology would say it was a pretty wise, survivor's kind of background, but it didn't go over well in the first part of my Foreign Service career. I got down here and there was a reception for the entering class, for our class, at the Foreign Service Club. I walked in and everyone was drinking either manhattans or martinis and talking about David Reisman and the *Lonely Crowd* and Samuelson economics and all that stuff. Well, my university did not use a Samuelson economics textbook. I did not do Sociology. I did not like David Reisman and I didn't drink manhattans or martinis. I didn't want to have a drink that night. I probably had a manhattan or something, but in any case, I looked around and I said to myself, and I said to my parents when I wrote after that evening, "either I'm going to make it or they're going to make it, but I'm not in a group of the same kind of people that I am, and both types can't make it." When I graduated from that basic introductory course, which in those days was 16 weeks long, and I've seen my file since, I was listed in the third quartile of the class with an "unlikely prospect" of success in the Foreign Service. For reasons you and I both know, there are different kinds of standards out there.

So the first job I got was not even in the State Department building. It was on Nineteenth and K Streets which is about a mile away from the State Department. It was the least valued of any assignment that anybody got. I was answering public correspondence at the International Educational Exchange Service. To this day I can give you the opening paragraph on that letter. . . . I had a wonderful boss, a wonderful boss. People talk about women and the influence of women on their lives. Her name was Gertrude Cameron, rest her soul. She was interested in my professional development, although she didn't tell me that. I've heard stories from other women who have had disastrous experiences with women supervisors. I got into my first job as a result of this rotten ranking from my first training course and here I was, working for a woman who was testing me every day. . . . I was diffident, the word everybody used about me was "diffident." I was shy. I had a sense of not fitting in because of the training group. I had a lot of confidence about doing my best and learning, but those were qualities, as you can imagine when you read the literature, that women are not supposed to have. But I had the kind of boss who tried to draw me out of it. She ranked me in the middle of my class on my annual evaluations. They were not competitive gradings at all, but efficiency reports in those days were longer. They were not subject to legal suit, and so you learned also from your own annual evaluations.

My next assignment was in Manila from 1959 to 1961, still on the "fringes" of the Foreign Service as a Third Assistant Personnel Officer. . . . As you can imagine, my bosses, the Second Assistant Personnel Officer and the First Personnel Officer were women. The administrative section of the embassy was all full of women. The Disbursing Officer, the Budget Officer, . . . that's where the women were. I went out to Manila under what was called the junior officer rotational program. However, before I arrived in Manila, the men at the embassy met and decided that, as I was the first woman to come out in a long, long time on the junior officer rotational program, they were going to stop the rotation program, and they did. I arrived expecting to be a personnel officer one year, and then to move into other sections of the embassy on a rotational assignment for the second year, but instead there was no rotation for me. So I stayed two years in personnel, once again with women who wanted to help, who were very supportive. I was twenty-four, twenty-five when I went out, these women were in their mid-forties. They had not come into the Foreign Service as I had as a Foreign Service Officer who had passed a competitive examination. They had been in the Foreign Service secretarial corps, and had gradually worked their way up the administrative side. People would say that, by definition, they should have been mean to me, they should have been jealous, they should have been almost conspiratorial in designing failure. They were none of those things. They were a support group. They took me places, they included me in things and they helped me learn. At the end of the first year, I moved up to be the Second Personnel Officer. I learned things about people out there I could not have learned with the background that I came from.

I left the Philippines in November of 1961. I went out to Palermo in July of 1962 as a Vice Consul. Once again, not Rome, once again, not mainstream. I issued immigration visas. I issued tourist visas. There was about an even mix of men and women senior officers there, but again, an atmosphere of training. I didn't run into the jealousy and conspiracies that people tell me about. In the meantime, I got for the first time the real foreign setting where I had to live in a foreign language. I loved it. . . . In the spring of 1964 when that assignment was up, my efficiency reports had been good, but they were in noncompetitive areas. I got fine efficiency reports as a personnel officer. I got fine efficiency reports and evaluations as a vice consul, but you know, where was it at? The Foreign Service inspectors had come through Palermo and I said "Look, I would like very much to be doing political work," and I guess I pressed them or something. Anyhow, in the spring of 1964 I was assigned to The Hague as a number two political officer in the political section of our embassy there.

Ambassador Ridgway never made it to The Hague, but she did get another assignment that channeled her career in a positive direction.

I was assigned to the Department of State in Washington in the Office of NATO Political Affairs as a political officer. It was a major career break for me. I went to work for a man named George Vest, who to this day tells me he selected my file from out of 12. It was the only woman's and this was not when the Department was pressing everybody to pick a woman. I joined a staff of approximately 25 people. Over the course of time, at least, 21 of those people reached ambassadorial rank, assistant secretary rank, Deputy National Security Advisor, you name it. It was the most talented group of people I ever was a part of until my last assignment. . . . I was asked to contribute to a document which was to be sent to all our embassies in Europe. So I wrote my little paragraph and handed it in. The head of the office called me in and said "You know Roz, I appreciate the effort, but this is not how we write." I was kind of stunned. . . . He went on to tell me how to write for embassies and policy people. The assumption was the audience had the facts, they wanted analysis, they wanted insight, they wanted opinion, they wanted a little bit of prediction. . . . I found this the most interesting kind of writing. . . . I had three years of that kind of experience, and that quality of leadership. I was certified, as you can imagine, by that group. Those who talk about networking and the "old boys' club," well I was certified by the "old boys' club." As the other officers moved through the ranks and became part of the new "old boys' club," there I was.

After serving as the second-ranking political officer in the Oslo Embassy, Ambassador Ridgway's next assignment seemed to take her off her career path. However, it turned out to be a very fortuitous move. Appointed as the Ecuador Desk Officer, she became the State Department's expert on fisheries wars. The region was a "historical teapot boiling away, and the lid blew off the teapot." The result was known as the Tuna Wars. Promoted to Deputy Director for Policy Planning for Latin America, Ambassador Ridgway soon found herself writing for President Nixon "because the war just took off and threatened our whole relationship with Latin America."

After all this excitement, Ambassador Ridgway was disappointed when the State Department wanted her to be Director of the A–100 course for the entering class of Foreign Service Officers, a "dead end position." She was rescued, however, by a former colleague who made her his Deputy Chief of Mission (DCM) at the new American Embassy in the Bahamas. When this assignment was up, she asked for and was sent to the Senior Seminar for Foreign Service Officers, one of the most junior diplomats to receive such a assignment. While in the Seminar,

> the Undersecretary of Management requested she take a position helping out in Oceans and Fisheries until a replacement for the Ambassador in the area could be found. She refused. Instead, she asked to be the replacement. Her persistence paid off. She left the Senior Seminar and was named Deputy Assistant Secretary for Oceans and Fisheries in 1975 and Ambassador for Oceans and Fisheries in 1976. Her insistence on being considered seriously surfaced again in 1977. Offered an unnamed embassy in an out-of-the-way location, she balked.

Now I'm not going to give you the name of the embassy I was offered, but I was offered an embassy in the spring of 1977 and I said "yes." I went home and thought about it, talked with a friend of mine and got angry after the discussions. My whole career had been bounced around on the edges, Philippines, Palermo. I was never in the middle of anything except for my one little NATO job. Palermo was an island, Manila was an island, the Bahamas were islands, and here they were, about to send me to another island. I take some pride in being the originator of the phrase about sending women to hyphenated islands. So my friend and I went out and got a bottle of Gallo burgundy and we sat down, and we talked and we got out the atlas. We started down an alphabetical list and stopped at _____. I went back to the Department the next morning and I said I don't want to go to "X" I want to go to "Y." I was in Finland until 1980. I had a wonderful time and with the flow of learning continuing, it was just marvelous.

> As these experiences makes clear, Ambassador Ridgway's career was not free of difficulties, but her willingness to work hard at any assignment she was given propelled her career forward. In describing her march up the ladder, she focused on the help she received, not on the problems.

I often wonder whether, because I came out of the fifties, educated to accept prejudice, I didn't know bad things when they were happening to me, or whether, as I look at the way I was raised and everything else, was it good fortune? Maybe the world then was nicer than people said it was. I never ran into anybody who seemed to want to stop my career. I never ran into anybody who wanted to set me up for failure. I ran into people who were helping me along. Was I being discriminated against at the time? Sure I was, when you look at that string of first assignments. The diffident twenty-one-year-old-girl being marked down for youth and for diffidence, and for not playing the classroom game of jumping up and asking questions and that kind of thing. But I was also twenty-one. I mean, why would you believe, when you see a young woman from this background, at age twenty-one, venturing out on her first foray from home without a foreign language, why would you believe that she had the qualifications to survive and succeed in the foreign policy business? Wouldn't you sort of pass her off to the side as not likely to make it? Yet I wasn't harmed by any assignment. So, in the early 1970s when you started getting lawsuits from the women in the Department, when you started getting angry meetings and people shouting, I was never a part of it. I simply couldn't respond to it and to this day I cannot respond to it. . . . As far as marching for quotas, marching for lawsuits, the unfortunate women of the Department went one way and I didn't follow them.

> Ambassador Ridgway's only damaging experience with discrimina-
> tion, from her perspective, came in 1980 when she was appointed
> Counselor of the Department by President Carter. In that job she
> spent "the most wretched year of my entire career." A position of
> importance was transformed into one of little influence. Moreover, as
> a former Carter appointee, although she was a career diplomat, her
> prospects in the Reagan Administration were dim. Fortunately, her
> experiences with the fisheries issues led once again to a senior ap-
> pointment when this topic threatened U.S.-Canadian relations. After
> helping iron out a difficult problem, she was appointed Ambassador
> to East Germany. In this office, she came to the attention of Secretary
> of State George Shultz, who appointed her Assistant Secretary of State
> for European and Canadian Affairs, where she served as a key advisor
> to the Secretary of State and manager of 5000 people with a
> $300,000,000 budget.
> As is clear from this brief summary of Ambassador Ridgway's career,
> she was blessed with good mentors at nearly every stage in her career.
> Not surprisingly, she feels a sense of obligation to continue the tradi-
> tion of helping other with their careers. Indeed, Ambassador Ridgway
> attributes her own success in part to her ability to attract and lead
> young staffers.

I have tried to contribute where I could, in the model of the people I had in my life, the Mrs. Camerons and the John Hugh Crimmins, and the George Vests and the David Poppers, in terms of taking the time to help people to write and taking time to give people an opportunity to present themselves. I have spent a lot of time helping people learn how to write, how to present themselves. It sometimes gets to be a joke. I don't pay attention exclusively to the women. . . . While at State, when papers would cross my desk, I would not turn to the name of the senior officer who signed it, but I would turn to the last page, to the name of the person who wrote it. If there was something wrong with it, I would call directly to that person and invite them to come up and discuss it, or insist that they be included in any meeting reviewing whether what was proposed was a smart thing to do or not. I would get those junior people to my office and try to take more time with them, explaining what I was doing and why I was doing it. I always hope that I can educate and help. . . .

I work hard and I'm bright enough to be able to understand new problems, and if I don't, I put the time into understanding them. I guess I'm not afraid to say I don't know, and I'm not afraid to surround myself with people who are incredibly bright, probably far brighter than I am. I love it. I learn from them and maybe my major contribution has been, in fact, not the substance of foreign policy but that I've jumped all over. I'm not really an expert in anything, but I know how to organize, to free talent. Maybe that's what I do best, to lead and to inspire and encourage and applaud and work hard to see people get their rewards and move on to new challenges. . . .

There are points along my career I did absolutely the wrong thing. You don't say no to an Undersecretary of State and you don't walk away from a political assignment, but I just sort of enjoyed myself and let happen what happened and I didn't pay any attention to career management. The lesson of my career, besides the assistance of colleagues along the way, is that you precisely don't try to manage it. You seek out positions that may be interesting and you do your very best in meeting the responsibilities that go with those positions. In sum, there's no substitute for hard, careful work, and it is the result of that work that makes others willing to help.

> Ambassador Ridgway's successful trip from the Midwest to the top of the State Department is testimony to her ability to work hard. Moreover, as we shall see in our next profile, while her background and career management style may be atypical, Ambassador Ridgway's experience with mentors is not.

Interview
AVIS T. BOHLEN
An Insider's Career Path

In January of 1991, Avis T. Bohlen was serving as Deputy Assistant Secretary of State for European and Canadian Affairs, a position which involved responsibility for NATO, political-military affairs and arms control issues. Her career had begun in the Arms Control and Disarmament Agency, where she was a member of the U.S. delegation to the Mutual and Balanced Force Reductions Talks in Vienna. Ms. Bohlen entered the State Department in mid-career at a middle level position as a Political Military Officer in the Office of the Soviet Union. From this initial position, she held a series of increasingly important jobs involving arms control issues, including Chief of the Strategic Affairs and Arms Control Section in the Office of NATO Affairs, Executive Director of the United States Delegation to the U.S.-Soviet Nuclear and Space Arms Talks in Geneva, and Director of the Office of Western European Affairs. Unlike Ambassador Ridgway, Ms. Bohlen's background led her almost naturally to the field of foreign service. Her father was a Foreign Service Officer and, as she explained her choice of career, "I didn't start out my working life doing this, but I was born into it."

With her father in the Foreign Service, Bohlen grew up around the world, spending time in Washington, D.C., France, the Soviet Union, and the Philippines. Her education was also more typical of the Foreign Service cadre, B.A. at Radcliffe College, M.A. at Columbia University, and study abroad in Paris. Moreover, since she entered the State Department at a much later date than Ridgway in the 1970s, Ms. Bohlen has profited more directly from the State Department's recent efforts to improve the status of women in the Department.

Certainly at some moments in my career I have benefited from being a woman. My present position as Deputy Assistant Secretary and the mid-level entry were cases where people were, all other things being equal, glad to hire me because I was a woman. Whether I would have advanced more rapidly if I were a man, I don't know. . . .

In some areas women do, at least initially, have a harder time at State. This can be especially true in interagency meetings and relationships. Sometimes there is a tendency to discount what women say, though that's certainly not universal. This can make it harder for women to be taken as seriously as men, at least at the outset. But over time, if you prove your competence and expertise, then your judgment is valued and you are respected as a professional. . . .

Where unconscious prejudice can creep in, without men being aware of it, is that many men feel more comfortable working with other men. That's changing because there are more younger women coming in all the time. Also many men have made a conscious effort to overcome this feeling, and it can be overcome. But at the same time, women are often passed over for senior jobs because people at top levels want a team they feel totally confident in and at ease with, without being in any way aware that this may work against women. A policy decision was made early on in the Baker administration that every bureau in the State Department should have a woman as a Deputy Assistant Secretary. Allegedly the reason for this was that a senior official asked how many of the proposed candidates for Deputy Assistant Secretary were women and how many were minorities. Out of a hundred candidates there were, I think, three women and one black. Since the Foreign Service also faced a class action suit, the State Department decided to institute a policy of at least one woman per Bureau. As one of the beneficiaries of this policy, I felt very ambiguous about it. I'm in a job that I think I could have reached on my own steam—not this year perhaps, but a few years down the road. I felt that people might believe that I was only here because I was a woman. But after being here a little while, and after thinking about the pattern of women being passed over all the time, it may be that you need strong policy guidelines imposed from the top. Is it credible that there were only three qualified women for the 100 senior jobs? But it is very complex. . . .

The class action suit has been very damaging for women in the Foreign Service. The court ordered corrective action has, in effect, allowed every woman who was part of that class action suit to virtually name her job. In addition, priority has been given to naming women as Consul Generals. You now have an absurd situation where of about 15 such jobs that came open this year, some two thirds were given to women. This creates new distortions and new problems. I have a lot of male colleagues who have been very badly and unfairly disadvantaged by this. It's a question of two wrongs not making a right. It seems to me incredible that the courts should get into saying in such detail what remedial action has to be taken.

Like Ambassador Ridgway, Ms. Bohlen has benefited from having a mentor. Indeed, she cites Ambassador Ridgway as *her* mentor.

I think the role model is important—just the idea that a woman can, especially in such areas as arms control, be a senior level official with some influence on policy.

Thus a common thread runs through the seemingly quite different career paths of Ambassador Ridgway and Ms. Bohlen. One was an outsider who had to continuously work to be taken seriously, and the other an insider almost from the beginning. One confronted a Department that put barriers in the paths of all but the most persevering of women, while the other found her career assisted by a Department forced to pay a penance for past discriminatory practices. Yet both have benefited from the support of strong mentors, and both continue the tradition of helping those below them on the organizational charts.

Interview
MICHELE GEORGE
MARKOFF
A Risk-Taking Career Path

Michele Markoff has spent the majority of her career involved with arms control matters. Beginning her career with the Arms Control and Disarmament Agency (ACDA) as a Foreign Affairs Officer, she rose quickly, moving to the Department of State where ultimately she became Executive Secretary (i.e., Director) of the U.S. Negotiating Group on Strategic Offensive Arms. In that position, she managed and coordinated the U.S. negotiating team's effort to achieve the long-range strategic nuclear arms agreement (START) with the former Soviet Union. After a hiatus as a private consultant, she returned to government with the Bush Administration. Currently she is Senior Policy Advisor as well as Director of the Policy Planning Group at the ACDA. In this capacity, she advises the Director of ACDA on all aspects of arms control policy and directs the Agency's mid- to long-range planning efforts.

The unique impact of individual factors can be seen in Ms. Markoff's career. In contrast to Ambassador Ridgway, who saw her background as an obstacle to a foreign service career, Ms. Markoff's cultural heritage was singularly conducive to a career in foreign policy.

The general thrust of my academic, and ultimately, career interests, was evident at an early age. Of White Russian descent, from a family that had spent many years in Manchuria after escaping the Russian Revolution, exposure to exotic languages and lively interest in foreign affairs was the norm at home, rather than the exception. As an American with such a diverse cultural background, I remember my earliest preoccupation was trying to understand the roots of the Cold War and the historical political antipathies that divided the United States, the Soviet Union, and China. That interest continued and was reflected in the academic choices I made. In 1969, I was chosen as the first U.S. high school exchange student to the Soviet Union. Ironically, because of Soviet reticence to send their children to the West, I understand that I was also the last high school exchange student until just the past few years. As part of my undergraduate college experience, I was fortunate to have been able to attend the Chinese University of Hong Kong, which enabled me to develop an in-depth perspective on China at a time (the early 1970s) when still very little was known.

My first exposure to Washington came in 1973 when I was chosen to be an intern with the Carnegie Endowment for International Peace. It was an exciting time to be in Washington, and I was working with talented and committed people with impeccable foreign policy credentials. When I had to return to the Pacific Northwest to finish my undergraduate degree (at Reed College), I was hooked on Washington and the desire to be involved somehow in public policy.

Nonetheless, I did not return to Washington until seven years later. My short experience there had made it clear how few women played important roles in the foreign policy-making establishment, and that was what I was interested in—contributing to the formulation of foreign policy. My strategy to overcome this potential obstacle was to acquire sufficient academic credentials such that no one would ever question my qualifications to fill the jobs I aspired to. So I quickly concluded my undergraduate work and went on to Yale where I stayed for six years.

While I enjoyed much of my experience at Yale, my aspirations and interests remained focused on issues relevant to public policy. Although I did well, that orientation was somewhat incongruous in a department (political science) known for its skill in training theorists and teachers. I concluded two degrees, one in International Relations, the other in Political Science, but regretfully never finished my dissertation. Academically, although I wanted to use my knowledge of the Soviet Union and China, I did not want to be cast as a Kremlinologist or a China watcher per se. Rather, I sought to employ my understanding of the Russian and Chinese culture and politics as a prism or lens through which I could shed analytical light on more generic issues related to defense and foreign policy. Ultimately, I focused on decision theory, applying it to alternative ways of viewing arms race behavior, in particular looking comparatively at the acquisition of strategic nuclear weapons by the United States and the Soviet Union. This focus led naturally to an interest in arms control.

I entered the U.S. government in the winter of 1981 when I was hired into the U.S. Arms Control and Disarmament Agency (ACDA) by former Yale professor Eugene Rostow who had been appointed Director of ACDA by President Reagan. As a Foreign Affairs Officer in the Strategic Programs Bureau, my duties were primarily to support the then new negotiations on Intermediate-Range Nuclear Forces (INF) and the new Strategic Arms Reduction Talks (START), both of which were being conducted in Geneva, Switzerland. Then as now arms control work usually means a regular commute overseas for those involved in what often are protracted and difficult negotiations. Although the work was exciting, it meant exceedingly long hours, and an environment in which I was frequently the only female expert on the delegation—although I am pleased to say that now there is quite a significant number of young, highly trained, women involved in this work.

Less than two years into my tenure at ACDA, I was offered a promotion to a civil service job in the State Department's Bureau of Political-Military Affairs, Office of Strategic Nuclear Policy. In that capacity, I continued my job of supporting U.S. efforts in the START Talks both in Washington and in Geneva. That job afforded me both unusual freedom of action and visibility. By the summer of 1985, former Senator John Tower, who was then head of the START talks, had invited me to be his special assistant, a relatively senior and prized job. I accepted the job, and with it, a regular commute to Geneva.

When Senator Tower resigned in the spring of 1986, I was promoted by his successor, Ambassador Ronald Lehman, to Executive Secretary (i.e., Executive Director) of the START Delegation, responsible for the management and coordination of all U.S. Delegation activities. That activity was interrupted briefly in December when Senator Tower, appointed by President Reagan to investigate the Iran-Contra Affair, asked me to join the investigative staff of the Presidential Commission on Iran-Contra (the Tower Commission).

> In 1987, Ms. Markoff resigned from the State Department to become a Senior Associate at former Senator Tower's consulting firm, John Tower Associates. During which time, she also served as a consultant to the President's Foreign Intelligence Advisory Board, and the Tower Commission on Iran-Contra, and became actively engaged in the 1988 campaign to elect Vice-President Bush to the Presidency.

My true initiation to Washington came following the election of President Bush. In early December, the President nominated Senator Tower as his choice to become Secretary of Defense. Within days, we had closed the consulting firm and moved to the Pentagon to begin pulling together the Defense Transition Team and to prepare the Senator for his confirmation hearings. The rest is a sad and all too sleazy chapter in the history of this nation's way of conducting its political business. I can only say that John Tower was an extraordinary man of great vision and capability. Moreover, he was one of all too few men of his power to genuinely respect and promote professional women to senior positions. I can say with confidence that all of us who ever worked with him will miss him terribly.

When Senator Tower's nomination was rejected on March 7th, 1989, and he was unceremoniously escorted out of the Pentagon, several of us remained, with some hope still of serving the Bush Presidency. However, failure in Washington, even if unjust, is never rewarded. With a new team coming into the Department of Defense, it quickly became clear that those remaining who had been closely associated with Tower were simply an embarrassment, regardless of talent or credentials.

> As is clear from the above narrative, Ms. Markoff's career path was radically different from Ambassador Ridgway's and Avis Bohlen's. In contrast to their strategy of working their way up within the bureaucracy, Ms. Markoff followed a riskier strategy of shifting between career government and political positions by leaving government in order to reposition herself. However, similarly to Ambassador Ridgway, Ms. Markoff attributes her success both to personal qualities and to the critical influence of a mentor.

I believe that I have been valued by each of my superiors for some basic and important skills. I tend to be prescient about understanding what Washington calls the "big picture," that is, looking at the future creatively, seeing how the pieces fit together, forecasting what sorts of policies might be called for, and planning appropriate initiatives to achieve the desired outcome. However, depth of analytical understanding is not enough. There are a vast number of smart and knowledgeable people in Washington. Because people communicate on paper in this town, you need to command a certain grace in putting your ideas into words that helps superiors communicate very difficult ideas easily, and with a spin or elegance that helps gain them credence. Lastly, I learned (the hard way) two good lessons early in my career that academe does not really concern itself with: mission and deadline. The first means that if your boss needs or wants something done, and there may be a reticent or even hostile bureaucracy in his or her way, you play linebacker—you just get it done. The second means that if you write something, no matter how brilliant, but it is too late to effect a policy issue of importance, you have failed.

Just like success in any profession, there is a healthy dose of luck, of being in the right place at the right time, and of course, particularly in Washington, whom you know is very important. And, to take advantage of those situations, I think it helps if you stand out, such as having a unique expertise at the right moment. For years, simply being female in this profession made one stand out, although all too often it would be a handicap. It is frequently important to be able to be perceived simply as one of a very effective team, since rarely in government do you accomplish anything important without the help and support of your colleagues.

Nevertheless, it is important to have instances when you can shine. This means, as a woman, you have got to speak up and not be intimidated by your wordy colleagues. That is often difficult if you are a junior officer. But having the courage to speak up is important, even if you insert your foot into your mouth every now and again.

This brings up the issue of risk-taking. Most of the successful men in Washington that I have observed have been risk-takers somewhere along the way. The conventional wisdom is that it is more difficult for women to abandon the safety net. I frankly do not know if this perception is accurate, but if it is so, it is self-limiting. Changing jobs every few years both gives you a broader set of credentials and tends to get you promoted faster. Working your way up through the career services like the Foreign Service, I believe, is still very difficult if you look at the numbers promoted.

My personal observation of Washington is that the greater the risks you take, the greater the possible rewards. For a woman to have a central role in a successful political campaign can often be the key that opens the glass ceiling. While you must have talent and intelligence to have staying power, what is valued and rewarded is the risk you take working on the campaign, the time you put in, and the loyalty that effort represents. Nonetheless, you have to be prepared to live with the consequences of that risk: the downside is you can lose. The most vivid illustration of that is my own experience with the Tower confirmation process.

That brings up the role of mentors. It is extremely important to have someone recognize your value and bring you along. Almost invariably, successful men in foreign policy have had a powerful mentor at some time during their career. Unfortunately, I believe it is much more difficult for women to find a mentor. Not only does foreign policy remain a traditionally male bastion still, but more pragmatically, men of stature who take on talented females in that role are often painted with the allegations of impropriety, no matter how false the perception. However, if you do find a mentor, there comes a time when you have to let go and stand on your own laurels, or risk being perceived as the consummate staff officer in perpetuity. In the final analysis, there is no easy way up.

I was exceedingly lucky to have survived professionally the events surrounding the Tower confirmation process. Courageous friends and colleagues stood by me and continued to believe in the value of my contributions to this arcane world of arms control policy. It was through their efforts that I returned to the Arms Control and Disarmament Agency, where I began my career, to direct the Policy Planning Group.

> Ms. Markoff's career path stands in sharp contrast to Ambassador Ridgway's and Ms. Bohlen's. Yet there is a common theme; mentors are important. Without them, perhaps none of our Insiders would have made it as far in their professions as they have. For women to successfully penetrate the glass ceiling in greater numbers, they will need both mentors and a foreign policy environment more embracing of women in the profession.

II

The Influence of Women
in the Foreign Policy Process

In Section I, we explored those factors that condition and shape the women at the top of the foreign policy establishment. We saw how the values and mores of our society have restricted the involvement of women in foreign affairs. More specifically, the cultural view that politics, especially foreign policy, is the preserve of men has made it difficult for women to break into the institutions that determine our nation's relations with other nation-states. While this view has been challenged recently by the Women's Movement and groups like the Women's Foreign Policy Council, it is still true that national opinion tends to discredit the possibility that women could be as effective leaders as men in this arena. Moreover, the public is also still somewhat reluctant to have women actively involved outside the home. For society, work for a married woman is acceptable, but the family and spouse should come first. Our examination of the State and Defense Departments also discovered that historically inhospitable environments confronted women who attempted to contradict societal views and assume leadership positions in foreign affairs. The widespread reports of continuing discrimination indicated that recent court cases have not yet eradicated the legacy of the institutional barriers facing women who attempt to enter these male bastions.

The backgrounds of our women Insiders revealed something of how they were able to overcome these cultural and organizational barriers. Often entering the field of international affairs by chance, or because other avenues of employment were even more discriminatory, the women in our study indicated little initial awareness of the problems they might encounter on the inside of the foreign policy establishment, although many sacrificed marriage or family or both to make it in the male-dominated environment.

In the next three chapters, we turn to an examination of the question of whether the barriers the women faced and their theoretically different socialization experiences have had an impact on how the women on the inside conduct foreign affairs. We shall look at three aspects of this question. First, we shall explore the extent to which the men and women in our study have dissimilar views with regard to foreign issues and goals. Second, we shall discuss whether women and men in the two Departments characterize the foreign policy decision-making process in the same way. Third, we shall investigate whether women manage their agencies and bureaus differently from men. We anticipate that the three factors discussed in Section I, societal, organizational, and individual, will continue to influence the attitudes and style of the women on the inside both directly and indirectly.

In examining these three sets of questions, we shall be returning to the debate presented in the Introduction, that between the maximizer feminists, who believe women are unlike men, and minimizer feminists, who think there are few differences between the sexes, or at least none that will remain once full equality is achieved. With regard to our focus in Section II, these two schools of feminist thought would expect quite divergent findings. The maximizers would predict that women would have distinctive, more peaceful, issue stands than their male counterparts; women would characterize the policy process in a fashion different from men; and women would manage those who work for them in ways distinguishable from their male colleagues. Minimizers, in contrast, would hypothesize that few differences would exist between the men and women in our sample in any of these dimensions. Alternatively, some minimizers might speculate that only a few dissimilarities would persist as temporary legacies of the discriminatory treatment and differential socialization of the women in our sample, but that these differences would be less noticeable than those found among men and women on the outside of the diplomatic arena where more traditional views about women's roles would hold sway.

What we discover in the next three chapters will thus be of direct interest to the maximizer-minimizer debate. To the extent that we find differences between men and women, we shall be bolstering the position of the maximizers. If we discover only minimal disparities, or ones that are not consistent for all men and women, we shall be adding support to the argument of the minimizers. Whatever our results, the debate will not be resolved, but hopefully its parameters relative to women in foreign policy will be more clearly outlined. We begin our examination with a look at the foreign policy beliefs of the women and men in our study.

4

Gender Gap in Foreign Policy Beliefs?

A polyphonic chorus of female voices whose disparate melodies are discernable sounds in the land. Among the voices are latter day Antigones ("Hell no, I won't let *him* go"), traditional women ("I don't want to be unprotected and men are equipped to do the protection"), the home-front bellicist ("go man, go and die for our country"), the civicly incapacitated ("I don't rightly know"), women warriors ("I'm prepared to fight, I'd like to kick a little ass"), and women peacemakers ("Peace is a women's way").

Jean Bethke Elshtain[1]

As Elshtain suggests, among the general populace there is not necessarily a single "women's opinion" on the issues of foreign affairs, nor are women united in a common desire to participate in the foreign policy arena. But what about the women on the inside, within the foreign policy process? Do their views have a common pattern? More critically, are their foreign policy values and goals different from, or similar to, those of the men in their Departments? Obviously, this question is an important one in determining whether having more women in the foreign policy establishment will influence the outcome of future diplomatic negotiations.

Gender Gap: Public and Elite Views

In recent years, a great deal of attention has been focused on the gender gap in electoral behavior. . . . In seeking to explain it, researchers stumbled on an even more interesting gender gap, a gap between men and women in policy preferences. Various explanations for the gap in policy preferences have been offered: men and women are socialized differently, or, feminist consciousness has altered opinions. Most such explanations share an underlying theme: the idea that, for whatever reason, women have different values and priorities than men. In effect, it is argued that there is a distinctive woman's perspective that shapes how women view politics.

Pamela Johnston Conover[2]

Our expectations regarding men and women's policy views are shaped by three often conflicting bodies of data. A first source of information is the theoretical and philosophic literature on women and peace. The second draws on studies of citizens or public opinion; and the third relies on research conducted using responses from elites. Turning first to the theoretical literature, as we saw previously, there are a number of authors from the maximizer school of feminists who argue that women are more peaceful than men. Indeed, many modern feminists take this position.[3] Borrowing heavily from the work of Chodorow and Gilligan, most of these theorists posit that women's training as mothers, or as daughters of mothers, gives rise to maternal thinking or an ethic of care.[4] Ruddick, for instance, reasons:

> There is a real basis for the conventional association of women with peace. Women are daughters who learn from their mothers the activity of preservative love and the maternal thinking that arises from it. These "lessons from her mother's house" can shape a daughter's intellectual and emotional life even if she rejects the activity, its thinking, or, for that matter, the mother herself. Preservative love is opposed in its fundamental values to military strategy. . . . Moreover, whether or not they either intend to become mothers or identify with maternal work, young women exhibit a way of thinking that is opposed to warlike abstraction.[5]

Maternal thinking, Ruddick posits, is not compatible with military practices. Mothers want to preserve life not destroy it. It is, however, consistent with pacifism. All that needs to be done is to infuse maternal thinking with feminist politics to make it a potent and powerful force against war.[6]

> When maternal thinking takes upon itself the critical perspective of a feminist standpoint, it reveals a contradiction between mothering and war. Mothering begins at birth and provides life; military thinking justifies organized, deliberate deaths. . . . Mothers protect children who are at risk; the military risks the children others protect![7]

Pamela Johnston Conover and others have argued a logic of care or maternal thinking should give rise to different issue stances by women and men.[8] Specifically with reference to questions of foreign policy, women should be more supportive of peace initiatives and more opposed to the use of force than men.

Other feminists have criticized Ruddick and those who posit women will have more peaceful views, noting there is little support for a special ethic of care among women.[9] Jean Bethke Elshtain in her work *Women and War* and Antonia Fraser in *The Warrior Queens* both argue, further, that there are numerous examples from ancient and modern times demonstrating that women have played an important role in war as either supportive mothers and wives, or actual combatants.[10] The cultural conception of women's naturally peaceful nature, Elshtain posits, is a recent phenomenon.[11] The theoretical literature, therefore, follows two strands; some women taking the position that women are "naturally" or culturally conditioned to be more peaceful, with others rejecting this view as unsubstantiated by the data or the historical record.

The results from public opinion research on average citizens also contains data that could support either a hypothesis that women hold different political views, or one that predicts women will be similar to men in their attitudes toward foreign policy concerns. The preponderance of research, however, favors the first of these predictions.

Expectations regarding dissimilarities in issue stands of women and men is one part of a larger debate concerning the existence of a gender gap. The idea of a gender gap encompasses three dimensions: women and men vote for different candidates for public office; women and men give unequal support to the two major political parties; and women and men take opposing positions on important public issues.[12] Research on the gender gap was given impetus by the outcome of the 1980 presidential election when women were significantly less likely than men to vote for Ronald Reagan.[13] The eight-to-ten-point disparity (depending on the poll) between men's and women's support for Reagan was quickly labeled the gender gap.[14] Subsequent elections have reported a continuation of the gap in voting behavior, with women tilting heavily toward Democratic congressional and gubernatorial candidates, thus forestalling the Republican realignment.[15] In 1988, however, at least one survey organization found that the gap had diminished to four points in the presidential election.[16] Moreover, a plurality of women (not only men) supported Reagan in 1984[17] and Bush in 1988.[18] Along with a slightly greater preference than men for voting for Democratic candidates, women in the 1980s also showed a greater tendency than men to identify with the Democratic party.[19]

Many of the commentators on the electoral gender gap have sought an explanation for it in the different political views of men and women.[20] Some have attributed it to the more conservative positions of the Republican presidential candidates on women's issues. However, most of the data gathered suggests that men and women do not take too dramatically different views on women's rights issues.[21] Moreover, there are only limited figures to suggest that gender issues are motivating the voting behavior of women.[22] Social issues more generally, however, do reveal a growing disparity in the views of men and women,[23] and some researchers believe this issue gender gap contributes to the electoral gender gap.[24]

However, the area of greatest issue dissimilarity between men and women, and the one many believe is most responsible for the voting behavior differences, at least in 1980 and 1984, is the topic of most interest to us, foreign policy. More specifically, many commentators believe it was the war-mongering position of Reagan that resulted in the greater reluctance of women to vote for his candidacy, especially in 1980.[25] Kathleen A. Frankovic in her analysis of the 1980 gender gap writes:

> Women are more likely than men to fear Reagan might get the country into war. Controls for this question *consistently* reduce the "gender gap" to levels that approach, even if they do not always reach, statistical insignificance. . . . In the 1980 election, the difference in the way men and women cast their ballots could be entirely eliminated by controlling for the willingness to be more aggressive in foreign policy even at the risk of war.[26]

Election results from 1988 also found it was the strong defense policies of Bush that attracted voters to his camp, while domestic concerns were of more interest to the Dukakis voters.[27]

Closer examination of the gender gap in foreign policy beliefs among men and women reveal that there are several different dimensions of this gap. Conflicting data emerges on just how disparate are men's and women's foreign policy beliefs, depending upon which of these dimensions we examine. The area showing the most consistent divergence in the positions of men and women concerns questions dealing with the use of force. Both with respect to domestic use of force (for instance, gun control and capital punishment) and international use of force (for instance, defense and troop levels abroad) women tend to be, on average, consistently less willing to support force policies. Tom Smith, for instance, in an examination of the results from several early public opinion polls, found an average nine percentage point gap between men and women concerning the use of force in domestic and international relations.[28] Shapiro and Mahajan, in a more comprehensive study (which combined all "use of force" questions from hundreds of public opinion surveys, taken by a variety of polling organizations from 1952 through 1982), reported an average eight percentage point gap.[29] Interestingly, this gap was narrower for issues in which the use-of-force question was ambiguous (for instance, the space program and this country's activity level in foreign affairs).[30] Moreover, when Shapiro and Mahajan divided the questions into domestic and foreign use of force, the disparity between men and women's views was greater on average in the former (nine percentage points) than in the latter (6.2 percentage points), with men generally supporting the more "violent" option.[31] However, compared to all other issue areas, the two force dimensions still had the largest gender gap.[32] Interestingly, and perhaps contrary to expectation, Shapiro and Mahajan found the gap between men and women on foreign use-of-force questions had declined from 1964 to 1983, although they attributed this to a change in the nature of the questions asked.[33] Fite and his colleagues reported no such decline, and indeed found evidence of stabilization or increasing disparity.[34] More recent public opinion polls have also found a gap in men's and women's opinions regarding the use of force.[35]

Still other researchers have reached similar conclusions when they examined men's and women's support for various international conflicts involving, or potentially involving, U.S. troops abroad. Baxter and Lansing, for instance, reported that surveys asking men and women's views on World War II, the Korean Conflict, and the Vietnam War consistently found women to be more likely than men to have seen these conflicts as mistakes, and to have opposed them earlier and more strongly than men.[36] Benson, in an examination of surveys taken in the early 1980s found women were more reluctant than men to support using U.S. troops in a variety of potential international conflicts. For instance, in a 1981 poll, 55 percent of men favored the use of U.S. troops if the Soviets invaded West Berlin, only 38 percent of the women supported military action in this hypothetical situation.[37] The public's evaluations of the war in the Persian Gulf in 1991 are typical of the gender gap in foreign conflicts. In December of 1990, women's opposition to the war was labeled the "gender gulf" with polls showing women 25 percent less likely to favor going to war. Commentators cited this gap between women and men as evidence of women's greater peacefulness.[38] When the war began in January 1991, polls reported that fewer women than men (68 percent versus 84 percent) approved of the United States having gone to war with Iraq.[39] Similarly, more men than women believed that the war was likely to be worth the cost (69 percent versus 48 percent), and that military air strikes should target all areas, even where civilians might get killed (57 percent versus 34 percent).[40] Throughout the course of the war, in a series of polls, women were, on average, 14 percent points less likely than men to think the United States did not make a mistake in sending troops into Saudi Arabia.[41] Similarly, women were, on average, 13 percent less likely than men to agree that the United States should take all action necessary, including the use of military force, to make sure Iraq withdrew its forces from Kuwait.[42]

Connected to women's greater opposition to war have been findings reporting that women are more likely than men to fear war, or to estimate a higher probability of one occurring. Frankovic reported a 19 percentage point gap between men and women in predicting the probability of war in 1982.[43] In polls taken in the early 1980s, women were, generally, more likely than men to estimate that Reagan might get the country into a war.[44] Indeed, throughout the decade women's greater fear of nuclear war was revealed in numerous public opinion surveys.[45] Research by Gwartney-

Gibbs and Lach on college students also found the women in their sample to be more pessimistic than young men about nuclear war.[46] Not only did women estimate the probability of nuclear war as more likely than men did, but they were also more doubtful about the U.S. surviving such a war.[47] The Daniel Yankelovich Group reported similar concerns among a national sample of women who were more worried than men about a wider range of threats to national security, including terrorist threats, tensions in the Persian Gulf and the Arab-Israeli conflict.[48]

While the data on use of force and fear of war indicated a rather consistent pattern of gender differences, research more generally on foreign policy attitudes has not always found a gender gap. Bardes and Oldendick, for instance, found no disparity between men and women in their positions on five dimensions of foreign policy beliefs: military strategies for preserving world order, involvement of the U.S. in world affairs; world problem priorities and solutions; support for détente; and support for the United Nations.[49] Wirls also questioned the existence of a gender gap, arguing that both men and women grew more conservative during the 1970s and 1980s, with men just moving in that direction sooner than women. "Across all areas—force, compassion, and risk—both men and women moved away from more liberal values of the early 1970s."[50] On the other hand, Fite and his co-authors found evidence of a gender gap on a whole series of foreign policy dimensions, but they noted, "The magnitude of these differences, however, is generally modest. Only for the use-of-troops questions are these differences substantial."[51]

A number of hypotheses have been proposed to explain the gender gap among the public. Some argue for innate biological differences and/or motherhood, others posit the discrepancies in the background of men and women as the basis for the gap. Pamela Johnston Conover, following the logic of Ruddick, hypothesized that feminism is the necessary determinant to mobilize any latent gender differences. She posits, "Thus, becoming a feminist helps women 'recover' their basic values which, in turn, shape their sense of political consciousness, and ultimately their preferences on political issues."[52] Another explanation, offered by Gwartney-Gibbs and Lach to explain their finding of women's greater pessimism concerning the possibility of nuclear war, focused on women's lack of power. To quote, "We speculate that structural and situational powerlessness experienced by women in everyday social and political life may teach them that they are powerless to effect change."[53] By extension, not feeling powerful about foreign affairs may lead to a different set of opinions not only about the possibility of war but concerning interactions with other nation-states more generally.

Several efforts to test these competing hypotheses have been made. Mark Jensen explored the possibility that sex role orientations would explain the disparity. He found that femininity (identification with traditional feminine traits) was correlated with support for the use of military restraint and nonsupport for nuclear weapons, although the results were weak.[54] Fite, Genest and Wilcox examined the effect of motherhood and found no influence. Controls for a variety of demographic factors also did little to diminish the gap. Partisan and ideological differences between men and women, however, did appear to contribute to the disparity in the political views of the two sexes, but controlling for these factors did not completely eliminate the discrepancy between men's and women's foreign policy views.[55] Conover's tests on the impact of feminism were more dramatic. She found that *only* feminist women, not non-feminist women, had different policy orientations from men.[56] She concluded, "Thus, in most cases, the sizable gender gap on foreign policy issues appears to be due to the antiwar, anti-involvement positions adopted by feminists."[57] Elizabeth Adell Cook and Clyde Wilcox have challenged Conover's results. They found feminist women and feminist *men* to both be more liberal on foreign policy issues. Moreover, even after controlling for demographic variables (race, education, income, partisanship, age), a modest discrepancy persisted in the foreign policy views regarding détente, involvement in Central America, and isolationism, between feminist men and women and between men and women in other groups (potential feminists and nonfeminists) as well.[58] Fite and his co-authors, also, doubt the power of feminism as an explanation for the gender gap, given that feminist men are also more liberal on foreign policy issues.[59]

Examination of Gwartney-Gibbs' and Lach's hypothesis on powerlessness has not been undertaken. We do, however, have some suggestive evidence on the level of information about foreign affairs, a possible correlate of power, among men and women. More concretely, it might be hypothesized that a lack of power in foreign affairs would produce a lack of interest in, and therefore, knowledge about the issues which, in turn, could possibly result in women taking different policy stands than men. The research of Shapiro and Mahajan allow us to indirectly test this hypothesis. They found that over the last few decades women have become increasingly less likely to say "don't know" in response to policy questions asked in surveys. The one exception to this finding, however, was on policy questions involving using force in foreign policy. In this area the percentage of "don't knows" actually increased from 1964 to 1983, from 5.2 to 5.4 percent, the highest percentage of "don't knows" for any policy area.[60] Several researchers report similar finding concerning the lack of knowledge among women on nuclear weapons and foreign policy and politics more generally.[61] Shapiro and Mahajan speculated that women's lesser knowledge of foreign policy views reflected a lack of emphasis on international issues on the part of the Women's Movement. Another possible explanation may, however, lie in the public's perception that foreign policy, unlike domestic concerns, are more properly the interest and concern of men. Women's lack of military experience may also contribute to a hesitancy to express an opinion or take a hawkish position on war. Schreiber, for instance, reported veterans of U.S. wars to be more supportive of the military, military spending, and the use of force in international affairs than were nonveterans.[62]

Our examination of citizen-level public opinion on foreign policy thus reveals a mixed picture. First, while the results generally show a gender gap in the use of force, an examination of foreign policy views more broadly does not always find a disparity in male and female views. Second, the differences that exist are generally modest at best, especially when controls for ideology, partisanship, and feminism are introduced. Third, on many foreign policy questions women are more reluctant to express an opinion, or are less knowledgeable than men. It is at least possible that if women were as knowledgeable or opinionated as men, the gap might diminish. It is equally probable that it might increase. Thus in forming a hypothesis about the gender differences between men and women in the State and Defense Departments, we might predict a gender gap, or we might expect no gap given the similarity between the men and women in our sample. The data on elites, our third source of hypotheses, is most supportive of the second of these predictions.

In contrast to the proliferation of studies examining the gender gap in mass politics, there has been relatively little written specifically addressing the question of foreign policy differences among elites. Probably most well known are the studies conducted by Ole R. Holsti and James N. Rosenau in 1976, 1980, 1984 and 1988, examining foreign policy beliefs of people in leadership positions.[63] Their data was derived from mail surveys of America's leaders, within and outside government, including persons from the fields of education, media, business, law, foreign service, public officials and the military. Their analysis based on the 1976 survey found only limited support for a gender gap. Foreign policy beliefs were categorized into three major areas: Cold War internationalism; post-Cold War internationalism; and post-Cold War isolationism. In terms of overall "Cold War axioms," they found differences between men and women on only four of 20 questions. Women proved to be slightly more "dovish" than men, specifically in opposing the use of the CIA to undermine hostile governments and being less likely than men to see the Soviet Union as expansionist. However, in examining their "post-Cold War internationalist axioms," systematic differences between men and women did not appear, leading them to conclude that, "On many of the issues that have dominated foreign policy discourse during the post-World War II era, differences among men and women are substantially less impressive than are the similarities."[64]

Holsti and Rosenau's third cluster of questions concerned post-Cold War isolationism. It was only in this series of questions that a pattern of differences between men and women emerged, with variances in eight of the eleven items. Here, "women were inclined to favor a more restricted international role for the United States."[65] Seeking to explain the origins of these differences, Holsti and Rosenau noted that there were significant differences between their male and female leaders in terms of their occupations, with women:

> clustered in two occupations (educators [26.8 percent] and media leaders [14.7 percent]), whose members are more likely to take a 'dovish' or isolationist position on international issues, whereas a high proportion of male leaders, are to be found in the more 'hawkish'/interventionist occupations (military officers [24.3 percent] and business executives [13.4 percent]).[66]

The female leaders also tended to be younger, more Democratic, and more liberal. After controlling for occupation, few if any gender differences survived (women still being somewhat more isolationist), leading Holsti and Rosenau to conclude that "the dominant lines of cleavage among this sample of respondents are those defined by occupation. Military officers and business executives, including both men and women, provide the strongest support for Cold War issues."[67] While in a later study there was some indication of some emerging gender-based differences, the conclusion that gender is less important than ideology, partisanship, or occupation as a predictor of foreign policy beliefs among elites strengthens the conclusion of citizen-level studies which reported a diminished gender gap when these variables were controlled.[68]

Research by Wittkopf and Maggiotto on an even narrower elite sample reinforced Holsti and Rosenau's conclusion.[69] Their study relied on a mass sample and a leadership sample of "Americans in leadership positions with the greatest influence upon and knowledge about foreign relations."[70] They found that elites and masses both structured the foreign policy arena using the same issue dimensions, however, they often held different views on these dimensions with the leaders tending to be more liberal.[71] Leaders were more likely to be found in the internationalist and accomodationist categories, while the masses were more isolationist.[72] Examination of the role of gender, more importantly, found no influence. Among the leader and mass samples, political philosophy, and for the elite, party identification, were most strongly correlated with foreign policy views. Gender, however, was not.[73] Moreover, the differences between the foreign policy beliefs of the two samples (elite and mass) were also largely explained by discrepancies in position (elite-mass), political philosophy, and party identification of the two groups with a gender-race variable adding marginally to the explanation.[74] Similarly, a study of Carter appointees by Carroll and Geiger-Parker found that though women were slightly more liberal than men concerning military strength, the differences were more of a degree than of a fundamental conflict between the sexes.[75]

Thus the data from the elite studies, in possible contrast to the surveys of citizens, suggests we should anticipate no or few differences between the men and women at State and Defense. Extrapolating from the research of Holsti and Rosenau and Wittkopf and Maggiotto, we would predict that the similarity in occupation and position, and possibly political philosophy and knowledge, would lead to little divergence in the foreign policy beliefs of the men and women in our elite sample of Insiders.

The Gender Gap Among Foreign Policy Decision-Makers

> Despite the fact that since the 1930s national opinion polls have demonstrated the existence of a "gender gap" on foreign policy that crosses class and race lines, one should not risk the conclusion that the existence of a different climate of opinion among women will significantly change U.S. diplomacy in the future any more than it has in the past. Some women (and men) . . . forget that most of the women who reach high level positions within the Foreign Service have, to date, thought more like their male colleagues at State than they have like women peace advocates—at least in this century.
>
> *Joan Hoff-Wilson*[76]

In attempting to answer the question of whether women in foreign policy decision-making positions hold different views from men in those same positions, we first asked respondents whether they saw themselves as having different priorities in foreign policy than their counterparts of the opposite sex. Most of the respondents reported that they did not see any differences. Men were especially likely to think their views were similar, with only six percent seeing a difference. Among women, one out of five reported differences from their male colleagues, but few of the answers given in the follow-up question focused on specific policy questions. Rather, those women and men seeing differences were more likely to mention management style issues. Only a few gave any response which might be called policy differences, and even these were quite vague. For instance, a few of the respondents noted women were more likely to be concerned about people. One woman in the State Department, appearing to respond to the stereotypical view that women have different priorities, drew a line between women inside the State Department who do not hold different views from the men in State and those women outside who might have different priorities from men:

> The line now—at least ten years ago—the line was women ought to have a different role in international affairs. The international agenda for women was the environment, planned parenthood or no planned parenthood, desertification of Africa and drought, and the lack of nutrition around the world. I just found that self-defeating. Now I think there are some women who organize around that and you'll hear speeches but. . . . Maybe it's self-selecting. Those of us who are comfortable with a broad agenda don't see it the way people do who have chosen to live a different kind of life.

It is possible however, that the perception of this respondent and of others that women in the foreign policy arena hold the same foreign policy views as men may not reflect reality. To examine this possibility, we asked respondents a lengthy series of questions requiring them to indicate the importance of various foreign policy goals for the United States and their level of agreement with some general statements that have been made concerning U.S. foreign policy. Though the focus of our study is a narrower, more specialized, elite than those in the Holsti and Rosenau study, we saw their leaders as a valid comparison group. Therefore, we utilized a number of questions from the Holsti and Rosenau survey in this part of our interviews. In addition, we asked respondents to give us their opinions toward contemporary (1988) issues in American foreign policy; to classify their general views in political matters, ranging from far right to far left; and to indicate their partisan affiliation.

Looking first at the general political orientation of the respondents, we found that the women in the sample were generally more conservative than the men (see Table 4-1). Among the women, 44.8 percent indicated that they saw themselves as very or somewhat conservative, while only 27.8 percent of the men chose either of these two categories. These figures contrast sharply with those of the general public. As we noted earlier, women in mass public opinion surveys tend to be more liberal. For instance, Alison Cowan reported on a 1989 New York Times public opinion poll which found that 32 percent of the women and 37 percent of the men considered themselves to be conservative.[77] When we subdivided our respondents according to State or Defense Department affiliation and whether they were political appointees or career civil servants, the picture became more complex (see Table 4-2). While there were no significant

Table 4-1. Political views of men and women in the Departments of State and Defense[a]

| | | Overall | | State | | Defense | |
Political Ideology	All	Men	Women	Men	Women	Men	Women
Far Left	0.0	0.0	0.0	0.0	0.0	0.0	0.0
Very Liberal	1.4	2.8	0.0	0.0	0.0	6.3	0.0
Somewhat Liberal	18.9	27.8	10.5	20.0	20.0	37.5	4.3
Middle of the Road	43.2	41.7	44.7	55.0	40.0	25.0	47.8
Somewhat Conservative	27.9	22.2	31.6	25.0	33.3	18.8	30.4
Very Conservative	9.5	5.6	13.2	0.0	6.7	12.5	17.4

[a] Figures represent the percentage of men and women in each of the categories.

differences between men and women in the State Department generally or in the subcategories at State, there were significant differences between men and women in the Defense Department. Overall, women in Defense were more conservative than the men in the Department, with 47.8 percent of the women and 31.3 percent of the men choosing one of the conservative labels. Even among career civil servants at Defense the women were the more conservative of the two genders, with 40 percent of the women and 28.5 percent of the men calling themselves conservative. Moreover, while the number of cases makes generalization difficult,

Table 4-2. Political views by career, department, and gender[a]

Political Ideology	Career— State		Appointee— State		Career— Defense		Appointee— Defense	
	Men	Women	Men	Women	Men	Women	Men	Women
Far Left	0.0	0.0	0.0	0.0	0.0	0.0	0.0	0.0
Very Liberal	0.0	0.0	0.0	0.0	7.1	0.0	0.0	0.0
Somewhat Liberal	20.0	33.3	20.0	11.1	42.9	6.7	0.0	0.0
Middle of the Road	66.7	66.7	20.0	22.2	21.4	53.3	50.0	37.5
Somewhat Conservative	13.3	0.0	60.0	55.6	21.4	26.7	0.0	37.5
Very Conservative	0.0	0.0	0.0	11.1	7.1	13.3	50.0	25.0

[a] Figures represent the percentage of men and women in each of the categories.

women appointees in both Departments tended to be more conservative than the male appointees. Further examination of Table 4-2, reveals that the most conservative of the respondents were the women appointees in both Departments, followed by the men appointees and the career women in the Defense Department. The least conservative members of the foreign policy establishment were the career women at State, although the career men in both Departments were also quite likely to adopt a moderate or liberal label for their political views.

The results for party identification were similar (see Tables 4-3 and 4-4). Overall women were more likely to be Republican, although the difference was not statistically significant. Similarly, in three of the subgroups (career personnel and appointees in Defense, and appointees at State) women were more likely to be Republican. The one reversal was in the State Department, where women in career SES/SFS positions were more likely to be Democrats than men holding similar positions. The results for party identity are particularly striking given national figures that show women to be significantly more likely to identify with the Democratic party. The same New York Times poll of June 1989 which reported women were more liberal, also found that of women, 28 percent were Republican, 35 percent were Democrats and 30 percent Independent, while men were 34 percent Republican, 32 percent Democrats and 27 percent Independent.[78]

Overall differences in the political views between women and men in the foreign policy establishment are, however, only half the picture. Of more importance than general political philosophy or partisan inclination

Table 4-3. Party identification of men and women in the Departments of State and Defense[a]

Party Identity	All	Overall		State		Defense	
		Men	Women	Men	Women	Men	Women
Strong Democrat	7.0	5.7	8.3	0.0	14.3	11.8	4.5
Weak Democrat	14.1	11.4	16.7	5.6	21.4	17.6	4.5
Independent leaning Democrat	14.1	22.9	5.6	27.8	14.3	17.6	0.0
Independent	15.5	20.0	11.1	22.2	7.1	17.6	13.6
Independent leaning Republican	11.3	17.1	5.6	16.7	0.0	17.6	9.1
Weak Republican	12.7	8.6	16.7	11.1	0.0	5.9	27.3
Strong Republican	25.4	14.3	36.1	16.7	42.9	11.8	31.8

[a] Figures represent the percentage of men and women in each of the categories.

Table 4-4. Party identification by career, department, and gender[a]

Party Identity	Career—State		Appointee—State		Career—Defense		Appointee—Defense	
	Men	Women	Men	Women	Men	Women	Men	Women
Strong Democrat	0.0	33.3	0.0	0.0	13.3	0.0	0.0	11.1
Weak Democrat	7.7	33.3	0.0	12.5	20.0	23.1	0.0	0.0
Independent leaning Democrat	23.1	33.3	40.0	0.0	20.0	0.0	0.0	0.0
Independent	30.8	0.0	0.0	12.5	20.0	23.1	0.0	0.0
Independent leaning Republican	15.4	0.0	20.0	0.0	20.0	15.4	0.0	0.0
Weak Republican	7.7	0.0	20.0	0.0	6.7	30.8	0.0	22.2
Strong Republican	15.4	0.0	20.0	75.0	0.0	7.7	100.0	66.7

[a] Figures represent the percentage of men and women in each of the categories.

are the specific foreign policy views of men and women. Table 4-5 reports only those questions on which men and women in the sample held significantly different positions. Overall, only 11 questions (out of a total of 83) revealed statistically significant gender variations. Moreover, no clear picture of a unique women's view was apparent. If there was a pattern, it finds women taking the more conservative position. In the summer of 1988, for instance, women in our sample were more likely to downgrade the policy goals of strengthening the United Nations and preventing the destruction of Israel, and less likely to support relying on the United Nations to settle international disputes. Similarly, women were more in agreement than men that revolutionary forces were controlled by China or the USSR; that détente allowed the USSR to pursue policies that promote conflict; that the government, not the press, tells the truth about foreign policy; and that Third World conflicts jeopardize American interests. That these views paralleled those of the Reagan Administration perhaps explains why these women also agreed with the Administration on the Gulf policy (protect shipping) and the then current success of arms control efforts. The same explanation may also account for the fact that women, more than men, graded the performance of Margaret Thatcher highly, since the British Prime Minister was perhaps the strongest sup-porter of the Reagan Administration's foreign policy. Given the findings on political orientations of men and women in our sample of leaders, these results are as expected. That so few significant issue differences separated men and women, moreover, parallels the results of other elite

Table 4-5. Overall policy differences between men and women in the Departments of State and Defense combined[a]

Policy Issue	% Who Disagree or Disagree Strongly		% Who Agree or Agree Strongly	
	Men	Women	Men	Women
Revolutionary forces in the "Third World" countries are usually nationalistic rather than controlled by China or the USSR	26.4	61.5	73.6	38.5
Détente permits the USSR to pursue policies to promote rather than restrain conflict	81.3	57.1	18.8	42.9
It is vital to enlist the cooperation of the UN in settling international disputes	34.2	53.9	65.8	46.2
The press is more likely than the government to report the truth about the conduct of foreign policy	67.7	84.6	32.3	15.4
Third World conflicts cannot jeopardize vital American interests	89.5	97.5	10.5	2.6
The U.S. has a moral obligation to prevent the destruction of Israel	16.2	36.9	83.7	63.1

Continued

Table 4-5. (Continued)

		Men	Women
Current Issues			
American policy in the Persian Gulf should place primary emphasis on:	Protecting shipping	18.8	72.0
	Other policy	81.8	28.0
Evaluation of Policy Performance			
Rating of the job done by Thatcher	Successful	56.8	77.1
	Pretty good/fair/poor/not successful	43.2	22.9
Rating of the Job			
U.S. is doing on arms control	Successful/pretty good	25.0	64.9
	Fair/poor/not successful	75.0	27.1
Protecting the interests of American interests abroad	Successful/pretty good	54.3	81.6
	Fair/poor/not successful	45.7	18.4
Policy Goal			
Strengthening the UN	Not important	31.6	52.6
	Somewhat important	63.2	42.1
	Very important	5.3	5.3

[a] Figures represent the policy positions of all men and women in our sample on policy questions that showed a statistically significant difference.

studies. Our results, however, diverge from what the literature on the gender gap among the public or the maximizer feminists would predict.

An examination of the foreign policy views of men and women in each of the two Departments finds pretty much the same picture. In the State Department, only nine policy questions find men and women taking different stands (figures not reported). Again no clear picture emerged. While the women at State were more likely than the men in the Department to disagree that military aid draws the U.S. into unnecessary wars, they were more likely than the men to endorse the idea that stationing American troops abroad encourages other nations to let us do their fighting and the view that if foreign interventions are undertaken the necessary force should be applied in a short period of time rather than through a policy of gradual escalation. There was also a very slight tendency for women to be more positive in evaluating the success of then current U.S. foreign policy efforts.

In the Defense Department more questions separated men and women and the pattern is clearer (figures not reported). Women, more so than the men, were likely to take the hard-line or Administration viewpoint. For instance, women were more likely to disagree on the need to enlist the support of the United Nations in settling international disputes and to reject the desirability of giving foreign aid to poor foreign nations. Similarly, the women in Defense accepted the Cold War view that revolutionary forces were not nationalistic but rather controlled by the USSR or China. These findings were particularly interesting in comparison to the Holsti and Rosenau study, which found that women leaders overall were more likely to favor enlisting the support of the United Nations and were less inclined to see revolutionary forces as being controlled by the USSR or China. Even when they controlled for occupation, their figures for men and women in the military showed women still slightly more likely to perceive revolutionary forces as nationalistic while men in the military tended to disagree, thus seeing them as controlled by the USSR or China.[79] On two other questions the women at Defense seemed to be adopting the position of the Reagan Administration, rejecting the notion that the press is a more truthful recorder of foreign affairs than the government, and accepting the need to send U.S. ships into the Persian Gulf to protect shipping. They were also more positive in evaluating the foreign policy efforts of the Reagan Administration.

In dividing the sample still further between appointees and career civil servants, we have to be tentative, however, in our generalizations because of the problem of diminishing number of cases. With this caveat in mind, we examined the distribution of this further breakdown in Tables 4-6 and 4-7, and again the results were quite revealing. Looking first at the State Department, we found the first evidence of a consistent gender gap between the men and women career civil servants (see Table 4-6, note only statistically significant results are reported). On 17 separate issues, women's views diverged from those of men, and generally in unique ways. We can divide these 17 policy questions into four areas: overall view of foreign affairs; use of force in foreign affairs; policy goals; and methods of implementing goals. With respect to the first of these, we find women were more likely to reject the hard-line or Cold War view of the world: women careerists downgraded containing Communism as a goal, and they were more likely to disagree with propositions that the domino theory is valid and that any Communist victory is a defeat for America's national interests. Similarly, the career women evidenced reluctance to use force to solve international disputes. They were more likely than men to reject the statement that the U.S. should take all steps, including the use of force, to prevent the spread of Communism. However, they did not favor gradual escalation of foreign conflicts, preferring greater use of force initially.

In choosing policy goals for the United States, the career women at State were more likely than the men to favor combatting world hunger and giving foreign aid to poor countries. In selecting strategies for foreign policy implementation, the career women at State favored fostering international cooperation. They also soundly rejected the use of the CIA. Moreover, they gave the U.S. low grades for its the current level of success in fostering international cooperation to solve common problems. These findings are particularly interesting in comparison to both the Holsti and Rosenau leadership data and the general public opinion data. The differences between men and women career government officials State correspond fairly closely to those of Holsti and Rosenau, but the magnitude of difference in our sample was greater. Where they found only modest support for female "dovishness," in terms of opposition to use of the CIA and Soviet expansionism, the difference between men and women in our data was more pronounced. In general, the views of career civil servants in the State Department look like what we might anticipate on the basis of studies of citizen-level opinion.

The picture for political appointees at State, however, is nearly transposed. Women appointees diverged significantly from male appointees on 13 of the policy questions, and on all 13 their views were more conservative (see Table 4-6, note only statistically significant results are reported). They strongly endorsed the Cold War view of an expansionist Soviet Union and the need to contain Communism, even if it means using force. More modern goals like combatting world hunger or protecting the global environment were downgraded, as was the tactic of fostering international cooperation. Instead, we see the policy of using the CIA to undermine

Table 4-6. Policy differences between men and women career and political appointees in the Department of State[a]

Policy Goal	Importance	Career Men	Career Women	Appointee Men	Appointee Women
Containing communism	Not	0.0	16.7	0.0	0.0
	Somewhat	60.0	83.3	60.0	0.0
	Very	40.0	0.0	40.0	100.0
Promoting capitalism	Not	13.3	50.0		
	Somewhat	73.3	50.0		
	Very	13.3	0.0		
Helping to bring a democratic form of government to other nations	Not	6.7	33.3		
	Somewhat	73.3	66.7		
	Very	20.0	0.0		
Combating world hunger	Not	6.7	0.0	0.0	25.0
	Somewhat	66.7	33.3	20.0	50.0
	Very	26.7	66.7	80.0	25.0
Strengthening the UN	Not	13.3	71.4		
	Somewhat	80.0	14.3		
	Very	6.7	14.3		
Protecting the global environment	Not			0.0	12.5
	Somewhat			0.0	25.0
	Very			100.0	62.5
Fostering international cooperation to solve common problems such as food, inflation and energy	Not	0.0	0.0	0.0	0.0
	Somewhat	66.7	14.3	0.0	62.5
	Very	33.3	85.7	100.0	37.5

Continued

205

Table 4-6. (Continued)

Policy Issue		Career Men	Career Women	Appointee Men	Appointee Women
Détente permits the USSR to pursue the policies that promote rather than restrain conflict	% disagree or disagree strongly			100.0	37.5
	% agree or agree strongly			0.0	62.5
If foreign interventions are undertaken, the necessary force should be applied in a short period of time rather than through a policy of gradual escalation	% disagree or disagree strongly	28.6	0.0		
	% agree or agree strongly	71.4	100.0		
There is considerable validity in the "domino theory" that when one nation falls to Communism, others nearby will soon follow similar path	% disagree or disagree strongly	73.4	85.1		
	% agree or agree strongly	26.7	14.3		
An effective foreign policy is impossible when the Executive and Congress are unable to cooperate	% disagree or disagree strongly	6.7	28.6		
	% agree or agree strongly	93.4	71.4		
Any Communist victory is a defeat for America's national interest	% disagree or disagree strongly	60.0	85.7	40.0	0.0
	% agree or agree strongly	40.0	14.3	60.0	100.0
The Soviet Union is generally expansionist rather than defensive in its foreign policy goals.	% disagree or disagree strongly			20.0	0.0
	% agree or agree strongly			80.0	100.0
The U.S. has a moral obligation to prevent the destruction of Israel	% disagree strongly	6.7	57.1		
	% disagree	93.3	42.9		
Third World conflicts cannot jeopardize vital American interests	% disagree or disagree strongly	40.0	85.7		
	% agree or agree strongly	60.0	14.3		
There is nothing wrong with using the CIA to undermine hostile governments	% disagree or disagree strongly	28.6	85.8	80.0	0.0
	% agree or agree strongly	71.4	14.3	20.0	100.0
The U.S. should give economic aid to poorer countries even if it means higher prices at home	% disagree or disagree strongly	50.0	14.3		
	% agree or agree strongly	50.0	85.7		
The U.S. should take all steps including the use of force to prevent the spread of Communism	% disagree or disagree strongly	64.3	100.0		
	% agree or agree strongly	35.7	0.0		

Current Issues		Career Men	Career Women	Appointee Men	Appointee Women
The Defense budget should be	Increased			0.0	12.5
	Maintained			20.0	87.5
	Reduced			80.0	0.0
American policy with respect to Nicaragua should be oriented toward:	Intervening directly			20.0	
	Aiding the contras				80.0
	Supporting the Arias Peace Plan			80.0	20.0
	Aiding the Sandinista Government				

Evaluation of Policy Performance

Current Issues		Career Men	Career Women	Appointee Men	Appointee Women
Promoting and defending human rights in other countries	Successful/pretty good			40.0	100.0
	Fair/poor/not successful			60.0	0.0
Job done by Aquino	Successful/pretty good	50.0	16.7		
	Fair/poor/not successful	50.0	83.4		
Rating of the job the U.S. is doing in fostering international cooperation to solve common problems such as food, inflation, energy	Successful/pretty good	21.4	0.0		
	Fair/poor/not successful	78.6	100.0		
Rating of the job the U.S is doing on arms control	Successful/pretty good			40.0	25.0
	Fair/poor/not successful			60.0	75.0
Job done by Thatcher	Successful			40.0	100.0
	Pretty Good			60.0	0.0

[a] Figures represent the policy positions of men and women, careerists or appointees, on policy questions that showed statistically significant differences, blank cells indicate the difference was not significant.

hostile governments being strongly supported. The women were also more likely to adopt Reagan Administration policies, opposing cuts in the Defense budget and supporting the Contras. Similarly they were more willing to give high marks to the administration's job in human rights and to rate Reagan's favorite ally, Margaret Thatcher, highly. Several possible explanations arise as to why women appointees at State should be so hard-line, especially compared to the women in career positions. One possibility is that there is a greater preponderance of outsiders or political ideologues among the appointees in the Reagan Administration. However, the status of the political appointees in the State Department is clouded by the fact that a number of women appointees were former career Foreign Service Officers. Maybe the difficult struggle to make it as women in that hostile environment has allowed only the solidly doctrinaire to survive, especially to make it to the top of the Department as political appointees. Clearly the more conservative, Republican position of the women appointees at State, compared to both their men and women contemporaries, is another obvious explanation. We shall have more to say about these possible explanations below. One thing is clear. The gender gap at State is complex, and the absence of an overall gap is largely a function of the sharply divergent views *among women* in the Department.

Turning to the Defense Department, we find a neater set of results (see Table 4-7). Among career SES members of the Defense Department, the women differed significantly from the men on only 13 policy questions. As we might expect, given the data in Tables 4-1 and 4-2 which showed the career women at Defense to be both more conservative and Republican than the career men, on almost all these policy differences the women took the more hard-line position. For instance, they were more likely than their male counterparts to reject the idea that revolutionary forces are nationalistic and not under the control of the USSR or China. They also were more likely to downgrade the goals of protecting the global environment or giving aid to poor countries. Similarly, in terms of strategies, they rejected enlisting the United Nations in settling international disputes. They also were more likely to reject the ability of the press to fairly report on foreign policy. Interestingly, they were less likely than men to adopt the foreign policy goal of protecting the jobs of American workers. Support for Reagan Administration foreign policy goals was also apparent, with women more favorably disposed than the men careerists toward Reagan's Persian Gulf and Grenada policies, and his success in achieving worldwide arms control. The women appointees at Defense showed fewer differences from their male colleagues than had the women appointees at State, but where there were significant differences it was mostly a result of the more conservative stance of the women.

Table 4-7. Policy differences between men and women career and political appointees in the Department of Defense[a]

Policy Goal	Importance	Career Men	Career Women	Appointee Men	Appointee Women
Helping to bring a democratic form of government to other nations	Not	12.5	25.0		
	Somewhat	56.3	68.8		
	Very	31.3	6.3		
Protecting the jobs of American workers	Not	7.7	31.3		
	Somewhat	69.2	62.5		
	Very	23.1	6.3		
Protecting the global environment	Not	0.0	0.0		
	Somewhat	20.0	57.1		
	Very	80.0	42.9		

Policy Issue		Career Men	Career Women	Appointee Men	Appointee Women
Revolutionary forces in "Third World" countries are usually nationalistic rather than controlled by the USSR and China	% disagree or disagree strongly	23.1	66.7		
	% agree or agree strongly	77.0	33.4		
It is vital to enlist the cooperation of the UN in settling international disputes	% disagree or disagree strongly	37.5	66.7		
	% agree or agree strongly	62.6	33.3		
The press is more likely than the government to report the truth about the conduct of foreign policy	% disagree or disagree strongly	33.4	75.0		
	% agree or agree strongly	66.7	25.0		
Efforts to protect weaker domestic industries from foreign competition are not a viable strategy	% disagree or disagree strongly			0.0	77.7
	% agree or agree strongly			100.0	22.2
The U.S. has a moral obligation to prevent the destruction of Israel	% disagree or disagree strongly			0.0	55.6
	% agree or agree strongly			100.0	44.4
Third World conflicts cannot jeopardize vital American interests	% disagree or disagree strongly			50.0	88.9
	% agree or agree strongly			50.0	11.1
The U.S. should give economic aid to poorer countries even if it means higher prices at home	% disagree or disagree strongly	26.7	61.5		
	% agree or agree strongly	73.4	38.5		

Continued

Table 4-7. (Continued)

Current Issues		Career Men	Career Women	Appointee Men	Appointee Women
American policy in the Persian Gulf should place primary emphasis on:	Protecting shipping	0.0	63.6		28.6
	Other policy	100.0	36.4		71.4
The U.S. invasion of Grenada was:	Successful in stopping Communism	27.3	8.3		
	Successful in protecting U.S. influence	45.5	91.7		
	Unnecessary	27.3	0.0		

Evaluation of Policy Performance

		Career Men	Career Women	Appointee Men	Appointee Women
Job done by Mitterand	Successful/pretty good			0.0	28.6
	Fair/poor/not successful			100.0	71.4
Job done by Aquino	Successful/pretty good	0.0	50.0		
	Fair/poor/not successful	100.0	50.0		
Rating of the job the U.S. is doing in maintaining a balance of power among nations:	Successful/pretty good	93.3	73.4		
	Fair/poor/not successful	6.7	26.7		
Rating of the job the U.S. is doing in protecting the jobs of American workers:	Successful/pretty good			100.0	50.0
	Fair/poor/not successful			0.0	50.0
Rating of the job the U.S. is doing in protecting the interests of American business abroad:	Successful/pretty good	42.8	87.6		
	Fair/poor/not successful	57.1	12.5		
Rating of the job the U.S. is doing on arms control:	Successful/pretty good	6.7	57.1		
	Fair/poor/not successful	93.4	42.8		

[a] Figures represent the policy positions of men and women, careerists or appointees, on policy questions that showed statistically significant differences; blank cells indicate the difference was not statistically significant.

To summarize our results, only among careerists in the State Department does the gender gap look similar to those expected by the feminist maximizers and found in general public opinion polls. Among career men and women at State we found a strong tendency for women to adopt a more moderate stance on world issues, rejecting many of the hard-line policy views and the use of force or subterfuge in favor of more global concerns and international cooperation. In contrast, women political appointees at State and Defense and women career SES at Defense, in the few instances in which they differed from their male counterparts, seemed to be more hard line and conservative. In the overall sample we discovered few instances of a gender gap, thus paralleling the research of others who have studied the views of elite policy-makers. There are several possible explanations as to why we should get such divergent findings at State and Defense and among career and political appointees.

We can classify these explanations into the three sets of variables we explored in Section I: societal, organizational, and individual. A societal explanation would focus on the lack of preparation and knowledge on the part of women for a career in foreign affairs. We do find some support for this in the greater reluctance of women compared to men to respond to the policy questions. In the sample, as a whole, the women respondents chose "don't know" or "no answer" consistently more frequently than men, often averaging double the percentage of such answers as given by the men for the various foreign policy questions (figures not reported). Interestingly, this was particularly true among the women careerists at State, the very group reflecting the more traditionally expected "women's view" on foreign policy questions. Unlike the results in the national polls, however, we find it difficult to accept that this greater reluctance on the part of women to express a point of view stems from a deficiency in knowledge of foreign policy issues on the part of the women in our sample. Instead we are inclined to believe that men are more reluctant than the women to not have a opinion or to indicate a lack of knowledge on topics about which they "should" have opinions and knowledge. Indeed, we suspect this unwillingness to say "I don't know" or "I have no opinion" may characterize men more generally. Clearly, the pervasiveness of this gender disparity and its close ties to the gender gap suggest further research on the "don't know" gender gap needs to be undertaken.

The second explanation centers around the conflicting political outlooks or organizational climates of the two Departments. Most observers of foreign policy formulation would characterize the Defense Department's position on most foreign policy positions as more hard-line than that of the State Department. While controlling for occupation, Holsti and Rosenau found the military officers took strong "Cold War" positions 16 times while Foreign Service Officers took such stances only twice.[80] Indeed, the battles between State and Defense on foreign policy questions are legend, and only rarely do the Secretaries of State and Defense find themselves on the same side of the foreign policy spectrum for very long. Given the two organizational environments, the socialization experience for women careerists may be quite different. Women coming into Defense may, in their attempt to "fit in" to an overwhelmingly male-dominated organization, overcompensate and become too conservative. Georgia Duerst-Lahti and Cathy Marie Johnson noted this "need to go native to succeed" in their study of women in state government. They conclude that:

> Nonetheless, good top administrators must exhibit masculine traits. Probably from trying to fit preconceptions of native culture, or maybe because they "read" the perquisites for top jobs better, women seem to erase much of the feminine and adhere more closely to the masculine than men do. Women do so selectively though, shying away from all traits which might be deemed negative for women. One outcome of this selectivity is women's tendency to focus on masculine elements that are most important to an organization.[81]

This same argument was voiced by one of the women in Defense, who gave weight to socialization as the determinant of policy preference:

> I think the differences that are there are those that have been *conditioned* based on gender. They are based on how you act as a man, and what policy is the manly thing to be done. These things are behaviors I think have been ground into people. I don't think they are inherent differences. I think you could take any woman, educate her to be Godzilla, if you wanted, or Ghengis Khan. I do think the differences we see are more societal than genetic.

As discussed in Chapter 2, this organizational ethos has a major impact upon women, particularly in the Defense Department, in which women claim to have a difficult time establishing credibility due to their lack of military experience. As one of our women respondents in Defense noted:

> In the Department of Defense, it is much more difficult to be a woman and to be accepted and have people listen to what you have to say. There is a military macho image, so you have to prove yourself. Before they listen to you, you have to prove yourself, over and over and over again.

The same process, though in the opposite direction, may be happening at State. Because of the more internationalist, liberal view of that Department, women wishing to be team players may find it necessary to become more liberal than their male counterparts in order to fit in. It is also possible that the more open environment at State allows women to express their "naturally" greater peacefulness, a peacefulness which has to be repressed at Defense.

A third explanation focuses on individual factors, especially political and partisan views. More specifically, it is possible that women who go into foreign policy self-select into the department where they feel most ideologically "at home," with liberals going to State and conservatives to Defense. Our interviews with the women careerists, however, casts some doubt on this explanation. As we saw in Chapter 3, the women we interviewed rarely gave ideological reasons for choosing a career. Indeed, many of the older women seem to have fallen into their jobs at Defense or State or selected careers in government in preference to the more discriminatory opportunities provided by private industry. However, one of our female Defense careerists did follow this line of argument in explaining the origins of women's foreign policy views:

> I think you'd find that the women in the Department of Defense, as a group, would be more conservative in their outlook than would be people elsewhere, at State, for example. As a group, I think, we are far more skeptical about the Soviets, and far less inclined to give them the benefit of the doubt than others. I think maybe people who go to work at State are more interested in other cultures, seeing thing from other people's perspective. You know, agencies have cultures, too. And Defense is perceived as a more conservative culture vis-à-vis foreign policy issues, or arms control than is State. Despite the fact that it is no longer true, I think people perceive the Arms Control and Disarmament Agency as still the bastion and home front of the liberals.

Our analysis of the political views and partisan affiliations of our subgroups did find conservative Republican women more likely to be at Defense, while moderate or liberal Democratic women were at State. Whether this ideological and partisan distribution reflects self-selection or socialization, however, is not discernable from our data.

Looking at our results on women and men political appointees, the slight tendency of the Reagan woman appointees to be more conservative than the male appointees may reflect similar factors. Women wishing to "fit into" the Republican Party organization, especially into the very conservative Reagan Administration, may have overcompensated in adopting the hard line of the political right. Another possibility is that during the Reagan Administration a selection process was at work which put a special emphasis on checking for the correct conservative views of women. At least one of our respondents suggested this possibility. A member of the White House staff making personnel appointments during Reagan's first term, said she had felt "a lot of pressure to get people with a special view." Indeed, Republican women were extremely critical of the difficult time women had getting political appointments during the Reagan Administration.[82] One woman close to the personnel situation in the Administration noted, "fear of an open conflict with Reagan's views on ERA and abortion is the motivation in precluding women where possible. A woman, merely because of her uniqueness in a male power structure, is extremely visible and therefore is more likely to be asked for her opinion on such issues."[83] Because of both women's outsider status in general and the traditional stereotypes about women's peacefulness, it is possible women appointees were questioned more closely than men on their foreign policy positions with only the Reagan hard-liners being allowed on the "inside."

Thus our data on the policy views of women and men at the top of the foreign policy establishment suggests few differences exist between the women and men in our sample. Paralleling the research of Holsti and Rosenau and others who have looked at elites, organizational position, ideology, or individual factors seem more important than gender. However, the gender gap, in terms of a willingness to express a point of view on such issues, may suggest a residual effect of societal conditioning.

Implications for the Maximizer-Minimizer Debate

> In feminist discourse, a tension keeps forming between finding a useful lever in female identity and seeing that identity hopelessly compromised, unavoidably inert.
>
> *Ann Snitow*[84]

In the introduction to this chapter, we noted that the debate between feminist maximizers and feminist minimizers often involves a disagreement over whether women are more peaceful than men in their views on international affairs. Maximizers opine that women are or should be more pacifist. This position is supported empirically by most of the data from public opinion surveys of average citizens. Minimizers, in contrast, do not expect women to hold foreign policy views distinct from men, and their expectations are borne out by research on the views of elites.

Our data on the foreign policy beliefs of a small group of women and men intimately involved in foreign policy formulation allows us to join the debate between maximizers and minimizers. On one hand, some portions of our research seem to buttress the position of the maximizers. Women careerists at State did appear to fit the expectations of this school as they were more pacifist and less aggressive in their foreign policy beliefs than their male colleagues. In sharp contrast, however, the data on women and men appointees in both Departments and women careerists at Defense found exactly the opposite to what the maximizers would have anticipated, with women adopting the more hawkish positions. Moreover, in the overall sample there were virtually no differences between men and women on the vast majority of issues, buttressing the position of the minimizers and substantiating that found in other studies of elites. Our results, therefore, do not completely confirm or vitiate either the position of the maximizers or the minimizers, although the argument of the minimizers does seem to benefit the most from our findings. As with earlier research on elites and some of the work on the general public, political ideology and occupation appear to be more important than gender in determining foreign policy beliefs. Among men and women in positions of authority in the foreign policy field, where the organizational culture is conducive to liberal or pacifist views, women may exhibit such issue stands. In contrast, where the environment demands conservative or hawkish positions, women may adopt, or already come equipped with, such views. Obviously, our results do not close the maximizer-minimizer debate. They do suggest, however, the need to concentrate further research on elites. Our tentative expectation would be that additional data from this level would reveal a narrow or nonexistent gender gap. In the next chapter, we explore whether women and men view the foreign policy process in the same way. Our expectation, based on the findings in this chapter, would be that, contrary to the expectations of the maximizers, the women and men would both characterize the process in similar terms.

Interview
AMORETTA HOEBER
A Stereotypical Contrast

Amoretta M. Hoeber presents an interesting paradox, an activist feminist and a leading expert on chemical warfare. For most of her professional life, Ms. Hoeber has been employed in "think tanks" doing research for the Defense Department on such topics as strategic arms control, Soviet strategy, theater nuclear warfare, and chemical warfare issues. She is currently working for TRW, an aerospace firm with offices in Fairfax, Virginia, where she is studying environmental issues for the Defense Department. In 1981 she was appointed by Ronald Reagan to the position of Deputy Assistant Secretary for Research and Development for the Army. She was subsequently appointed to the positions of Principal Deputy Assistant Secretary and Deputy Under Secretary of the Army at Defense.

I've been in the defense business all my life. When I graduated from college almost thirty years ago, I went to my favorite professor and said, "This is all very nice and good, but how do I pay my rent?" He sent me to a defense think tank where I got a job. I've been in the defense business ever since. The particular Reagan appointment was really gotten in several ways. There is an art that I call "running for appointed office," and one really does have to run for it. I had been doing the think tank business at several of the defense think tanks, including the Rand Corporation, which is probably the best known of the defense think tanks. I came to Washington and worked for a think tank called System Planning Corporation. I became, through a variety of circumstances, one of the leading experts on chemical warfare which is, generally speaking, an Army problem. . . . This got me very much in touch with Army problems, and so the Army was a logical place to want to go. I was also involved in the Reagan campaign. One of the things that I did in the Reagan campaign was to go around and give speeches to women's groups on why I, as a feminist, was supporting Reagan. Some people considered that a contradiction in terms, but I really didn't, because I felt that the defense problems were more important for the country at that particular point in time. So I did have some campaign connections. I also, through all my defense work, knew a large number of people who were on the Reagan Defense Department transition team. I made it clear to them that I would like a government appointment. After 15 some years in the think tank business, it was clearly time to do a turn at government. . . . So I went around and just talked to people on the Hill, talked to people in the incoming Reagan Administration. One day I got a phone call saying, come in for an interview. That's the way the system works.

It was an experience. I had had no concept of how busy I would be, how much intensity there really would be, it was just completely absorbing. It was almost a 24-hour-a-day job in the sense that I was always thinking of the work, always doing something. The intensity and the number of different subjects that I had to deal with—I jumped from combat boots to ballistic missile defense to helicopters to gas masks to production problems to basic medical research. I jumped from one subject to another every day all day long.

> Despite the problems common among women of having to prove themselves, Ms. Hoeber's expertise in chemical weapons, not commonly seen as a stereotypical female field, gave her an advantage.

I think it's clear that the men in the Pentagon, both the appointees and the uniformed guys, understand that most women have not served in the military, or at least far fewer in terms of percentages, and therefore simply don't have a piece of experience that many of the men have. There was a lot that I needed to absorb in terms of the military culture and the way that works and the way they deal with each other, because I had had no real experience in the same thing. But I don't think it was a disadvantage. I think it's more or less accepted that that is one of the differences.

I think in many ways the military culture helped. The military is very structured, your role is very carefully defined. I mean, you have protocol, you have appointment rank, and your role is well structured that way. I believe when I went in I probably spent at least the first month and maybe somewhat more just proving myself. I mean, there was a lot of "who is this woman and what is she doing here?" reaction. I do believe that after I got through the proving period, I was fine and I don't believe I was treated with discrimination by very many people, although there were a few. And I think it was viewed as a job, not a person. In many ways the role you have in the Pentagon is very much job associated. . . . I think that is an advantage to somebody like me going in, because the people in some sense *have* to work for me, and I have to work for other people, and you have to fulfill the role. So it isn't a matter of the sex of the person or, unfortunately, it's not even a matter of the competency of the person. But it is structured so that one can be comfortable, if you prove that you can do the job. The people who are truly incompetent, who are political appointees, simply get shuffled out of the chain of command, shuffled out of the decision process. They get given the courtesies but not any real role in it. . . .

> Ms. Hoeber's interests in a sense straddle the gender gap. While a staunch advocate of the Reagan buildup, Ms. Hoeber's objectives also included improving the position of women in the Army, a position favored by rights feminists.

The main goal was to help the Army in its buildup, the Reagan buildup. There was a lot of money flowing into the Pentagon at that point in time, and a lot of decisions had to be made on where the money would go and to what sort of purposes. I wanted to focus on some rebuilding of the chemical defense arena. I wanted to focus on rebuilding the strategic defense arena. Those were the two main goals. . . .

[With regards to accomplishments] there were a few other things, like getting the Army to be more conscious of the role of its women in the military. One of my funny stories on that is combat boots. The Army during my time had a plan to buy new combat boots. They went out to the commercial world essentially and said, "here are our requirements, we want new combat boots that will go for so many miles. . . . " Then we were going to have the tests on these commercial combat boots. It turned out that the test group was all to be men, and so I said, "That's ridiculous, because there are women, and women's feet are in fact very different from men's feet." So I made them change the whole test and they got some women in the test, and I believe the results actually came out differently, if you look at the statistics, by incorporating women. To some extent I also played role model for both the uniformed and nonuniformed women in the Army. I was the senior female appointee during my time for the Army, so I did a lot of speeches and a lot of going around to different Army schools, in particular the schools like the chemical warfare school in Fort McClellan, and talking to the women there. . . .

Male mentors have some limited-time utility for professional women, a restriction more severe than with female mentors. One meets a mentor at a particular point in one's career, and the help and guidance that can be given by that mentor is really important, but the male mentor is more likely to not want you to grow "too much." So one can get the help, but only for a little while. When and if one grows "too much" one must leave that mentor relationship and find a new one that can help one up the next step. I think that's less true of female mentors because there isn't that impulse to "use" the mentee in the same sort of way, or at least I certainly don't feel that way about my "mentees." I encourage them to keep on going and keep on going, whether they happen to be working for me or not. There isn't a point at which I "want them to stop." . . .

We had a whole debate when I was in there [the Army Department] on what extent more jobs could be opened up to women. And my consistent argument was that it ought to be physical-characteristic-based not sex-based. It's true that women in general can't throw artillery shells. That's just the way we're built and that's the way it is. On the other hand, some men can't either, and perhaps some women can. So my argument was always if you have to lift 60 pounds, then what you ought to do is say that if you can lift 60 pounds you can have that job, rather than base it on if you are female. Now, I got into lots of philosophical discussions on the whole issue of women casualties, and I think that is a very difficult one. I don't think our culture could handle women casualties as well as they can handle male casualties. On the other hand, assigning women to a limited set of jobs is probably not very related to how many casualties there will be. There is no such thing as a "front line" anymore, in the sense that there were trenches in World War I. So it is not clear to me that distributing jobs addresses that problem. So I got into lots of philosophical discussions, but I don't think I had any real impact on that issue. I think the military is a long ways away from solving that satisfactorily. In fact, I'm not sure what a satisfactory solution really is.

> With her support of rights feminism, Ms. Hoeber's positions are more in line with the minimalists, who see few differences between men and women. Ms. Hoeber generally disagreed with the position of the maximizers and dismissed the possibility of a gender gap at Defense, while arguing that including more women in the process is important.

The gap that occurs in the Defense Department tends to be strictly political, at least among the appointees. The Democratic appointees tend to have a different center for their viewpoint than Republican appointees. I think that's just true. I think that's political, and I don't think it is gender-related.

It's important to include more women at Defense for other reasons, but I don't think it would have much of an impact. In my view, you have to have a wide variety of people in the building in order to get the decisions made well, because it is that sort of a consensus process where you get all different points of view expressed, and women's backgrounds tend to be different than men's backgrounds. Therefore they bring something to the table, in addition to the image sorts of things.

A "serious feminist," Ms. Hoeber has served as Chair of the Northern Virginia Women's Political Caucus and Chair-Elect of the Virginia State Women's Political Caucus. She strongly endorses the main goals of feminism which she broadly defines as "allowing women to determine their own future." The development of her feminism she traces to her first working experiences.

I would argue from the early years of my working professionally, it's been discovering that discrimination really is there, and how you have to fight it. I've chosen to fight it sort of blatantly sometimes. I just try to remind people as gently as possible. One of the things is language. Around here everything is discussed in terms of "man years of effort," and I always keep changing it to "person years." It is just sort of little things like that. Just sort of consciousness-raising.

I hope the status of women will improve. I'm inclined to believe it will probably remain the same. I think the whole feminist movement has made a real difference. Not necessarily in achieving all the objectives, I mean we lost the ERA, we are still fighting on the abortion issue and things like that. But it has made women much more prominent as policy-makers.

It is very slow, you can't change culture overnight. I raised my son with my being a feminist. When he was about five or six, we had moved here from California, and I had been very active politically in California. I had honestly considered running for office, and so when we got back here, I made a comment to him that I regretted the move only in the sense that I couldn't run for Congress in Virginia. It was still unacceptable for women to do that, and I could have had we stayed in California. His instant response, after years of raising him in all this stuff, was "oh gee, can women do that?" I thought, oh dear, if the culture is that deeply ingrained, it just takes a long time to change it.

5

Gender Gap in Attitudes
toward the Foreign Policy Process?

I think the hope of the world is getting women into the policy-making process. I honestly think that if we are ever going to have a world, a rational world, women have got to have a lot more to say about how the world is run.

A Defense Careerist

If women do not necessarily choose different policy options from men, perhaps they hold alternative views about the way foreign policy is made. Cynthia Enloe has argued that current conceptions of what constitutes international politics generally is incomplete, failing to take into account the impact of such policies on women and the impact of women on these policies. "Conventional analyses stop short of investigating an entire area of international relations, an area that women have pioneered in exploring: how states depend on particular constructions of the domestic and international spheres."[1] Feminists, like Enloe, are calling for a new conception of the way foreign policy is made that incorporates the oft-forgotten role of women, be they Third World banana growers or diplomatic wives. Maximizer feminists might expect women in the foreign policy process to be sensitive to Enloe's conception of who makes foreign policy, incorporating a broader perspective of who influences, or makes it. Even if the women on the inside do not yet see the process this broadly, maximizers might at least expect women, because of their maternal upbringing, to view the process in ways distinct from their male colleagues. Minimizer feminists, of course, would not predict that women would characterize the process or its participants differently from similarly influential men. An examination of the perceptions of the foreign policy process by the men and women in our sample allows us to begin to see which viewpoint is closer to reality.

Numerous models have been developed to explain the American foreign policy process. However, most of these models address in one way or another two very distinct and analytically separable questions: who makes foreign policy; and how is it made? In the process of developing his decision-making framework, Jerel Rosati referred to this dichotomy as the decision structure and the decision process.[2] We are going to adopt his terminology and to address these two subject areas separately in an attempt to develop a more detailed picture of the foreign policy process from the perspective of the women and men in our sample of Insiders.

Decision Structure: Who Makes Foreign Policy?

It is instructive to note that the selection of key personnel on the basis of their ability to be loyal team players was the Reagan Administration's approach to overcoming potential bureaucratic intransigence— before it could develop.

Kegley and Wittkopf[3]

In terms of examining the question concerning who makes foreign policy, most authors have pictured the foreign policy process as consisting of a number of concentric circles. The first circle (Circle I) encompasses the President and his or her closest advisors, the Secretary of Defense, Secretary of State, Under Secretaries of both, the CIA Director, the Joint Chiefs of Staff, and the National Security Advisor. The second circle (Circle II) includes the bureaucracies or lower-level bureaucrats in foreign policy agencies. The third circle (Circle III) incorporates Congress, political parties, and interest groups, while the fourth circle (Circle IV) focuses upon the media and public opinion.[4]

For our purposes, there are at least three sub-issues to be examined. First, whether there are significant differences between the degrees of influence of the various bureaucracies. Second, to what extent do the bureaucracies of Circle II have an impact on the political appointees of Circle I? Third, and probably most importantly, which of the circles generally makes foreign policy?

In terms of the relative power of the bureaucracies, it has been estimated that there are at least 16 federal agencies with 36,000 personnel engaged in foreign affairs.[5] The Department of State has traditionally been seen as the focal point of the foreign policy process, but as was described in Chapter 2, recent developments have led to a decline in the Department's influence, and a corresponding rise in the power of the White House and the Pentagon. Duncan Clarke has outlined a number of reasons for this growing dismissal of the State Department, including: unresponsiveness or inertia; insensitivity to domestic political concerns; lack of expertise and quality analyses; clientism; elitism; and intradepartmental disputes. "FSOs are thought of (and think of themselves) as diplomats whose principal duty is to execute, not make, foreign policy."[6]

Another reason for the decline in State is the gap between what Presidents want and expect, and what they come to believe State can or will give them. "Among other things, they expect loyalty, responsiveness to their needs and directives, an opportunity to exercise foreign policy leadership, and sensitivity to their domestic political requirements. No recent president has found the Department able or willing to perform as expected."[7]

> With some exceptions, State devotes little attention to framing its proposals in terms that will draw domestic political support. Presidents soon come to know that they and their staffs can frame decisions in a more politically acceptable manner. When the White House becomes convinced that State is out of touch with politics, the White House staff is well on its way to dominating policy-making.[8]

The criticism from the White House is that the State Department is a "fudge factory" that produces soft, squidgy recommendations and little leadership. It is slow in acting, requiring endless "clearances" from various bureaus and offices before taking action. It is indecisive in the actions it does take, and it rarely provides the other departments and agencies with the strong general leadership that is needed. In exasperation at all these faults, President Kennedy once called the State Department a "bowl of jelly."[9]

In contrast, the Defense Department has fared well. The military is not only powerful, but it also has a legitimate concern in nearly every aspect of U.S. foreign policy. The reasons for its influence include the facts that: it has become a major source of foreign intelligence; its analyses tend to contain specific policy recommendations which are of value to Circle I; and the fact that the Joint Chiefs of Staff members are generally included in the inner circle (whereas the Secretary of State is usually the only representative from the entire State Department).[10] The Pentagon also has great clout "in a policy-making environment where money and personnel mean political influence."[11] In contrast to State, the military also "has natural allies in industries that manufacture weapons, and it has the patriotic appeal, as has the CIA, of being the instrument to 'smite our enemies.' The task of the State Department is not to smite our enemies but to negotiate with them. It deals with foreigners, and foreigners do not vote in American elections."[12] As a result, many theorists have argued that State is becoming almost peripheral to foreign policy formulation.[13] However, with the advent of the Reagan Administration and a President who had little experience in foreign affairs, many felt that the State Department, particularly under Secretary of State Alexander Haig, would experience a revival:

His experience as NATO commander and his service as one of Henry Kissinger's top aides seemed to provide him with a stature sufficient to reverse the decade's long decline of the Secretary of State's position, especially in view of Reagan's intention to downgrade the position of the security adviser.[14]

However, Haig became embroiled in numerous conflicts over bureaucratic turf with Defense, CIA, and the National Security Council (NSC), which led to his replacement by George Shultz. Though Shultz was more effective, State continued to be pushed aside, ultimately by an unusually powerful White House Chief of Staff.[15] Thus, at the time of our interviews, one might assume that the Defense Department would be seen as having at least equal, if not more, foreign policy influence than State.

Our second question concerned the degree to which the bureaucracies of Circle II have an impact on the President and the political appointees of Circle I. Prior to 1980, it was assumed that the bureaucracies were exceedingly powerful due to their possession of important resources such as expertise and tenure. Thus the bureaucracies were seen as influential actors in the policy process. Conversely, political appointees were seen as being in a weak position to challenge these bureaucratic resources primarily due to their transience, low levels of expertise, and the fact that they are caught between the competing demands of their Department and the President's programs.[16] Similarly, a significant amount of research has been devoted to the conflict between the President and Congress over control of the policy process. The "Imperial Presidency" argument contends that the President has increasingly come to dominate the foreign policy process. In contrast, however, are those who argue that Congress controls foreign affairs.[17] These competing demands have been the concern of Presidents from Johnson to Bush, who have consequently placed a priority on gaining control of the administrative apparatus. "Each of these presidents, with varying degrees of success, attempted to centralize policy and implementation decisions in the Executive Office of the President and to politicize the agencies and bureaus of the executive branch by placing political appointees in many top leadership positions."[18] For example, the NSC was originally founded in 1947, with the purpose, not only of centralizing decision-making on national security issues, but also supposedly of being a check against presidential discretion. However, as Spanier and Uslaner have noted, "Most recent presidents have circumvented the NSC as the formal or actual locus of foreign policy decision-making. Instead, they have formed their own informal circle of advisers. ..."[19] As Duncan Clarke has more recently observed; "In any administration, the president's confidence is gained through demonstrated loyalty and competence, which normally come only through daily interaction with the president. Usually only the president's White House advisers, including the NSA, and cabinet officials like the secretary of state can meet this condition. A sprawling bureaucracy cannot."[20] Thus as the power of the departments has declined, the President has increasingly relied on his or her own personal staff and the Executive Office of the President. This struggle for control of the policy process has a number of repercussions, the most obvious of which is probably the growing hostility within the bureaucracy toward the administration and, in particular, its political appointees. This resentment was in evidence in a 1989 study of all SES officials throughout the government. As Table 5-1 demonstrates, the career SES employees rated themselves highly in terms of attributes, but lower in terms of policy influence. However, the careerists paint a very harsh picture of the political appointees in terms of their experience, leadership, and management skills, though they do admit that the appointees have a significant role in policy-making. This negative view of appointees has not been limited to the careerists. During the Senate confirmation hearings on appointments, a number of Senators have shown a resistance to uninformed appointees. As one Senator put it: "Many of them share a fluency in one language. Money."[21] Interestingly, as Table 5-1 reveals, even the appointees do not have an overwhelmingly positive picture of other appointees. Even though they see appointees as very influential, they are rated more modestly in terms of management skills and experience. On the other side of the coin, however, the political appointees have a rather high opinion of the careerists, especially in terms of their experience. Assuming this study to be accurate, we should expect to find both that there is hostility on behalf of the careerists in State and

Table 5-1. How former SES executives rate other SES executives

	Appointees Rate Appointees	Appointees Rate Careerists	Careerists Rate Careerists	Careerists Rate Appointees
Bring valuable experience to their jobs	62%	83%	92%	25%
Have good leadership qualities	54%	54%	68%	18%
Have good management skills	39%	47%	64%	15%
Play an important role in the policy-making of their agencies	88%	78%	59%	76%

Source: Senior Executive Service: Views of Former Federal Executives (Washington, DC: Merit Systems Protection Board, 1989), 20–21.

Defense toward the political appointees, and that this hostility is not necessarily reciprocated. There also may be a difference in the perspectives the two groups have concerning the policy process, particularly in terms of the degree of influence of the bureaucracies.

The final question relates to the degree to which the policy formulation process is centralized or dispersed. In particular, it has been argued that the Reagan Administration was successful in reducing administrative discretion in some of the agencies of the federal government by its politicization and centralization of the bureaucracy.

> Immediately after taking office, Reagan and his inner circle of top White House aides embarked on an ambitious and energetic program designed to seize control of policy-making and implementation in the executive branch . . . key administrative positions in the departments and agencies were staffed with loyal appointees who were philosophically unsympathetic to most forms of government activism; and, political executives were encouraged to exclude career professionals from important policy-making duties and responsibilities.[22]

In particular, the Reagan Administration had favored a "cabinet system" of government in contrast to the "NSC centered" system adopted by several of its predecessors.[23] As a result, the National Security Adviser was to be denied regular access to the President, instead having to report through White House Counselor Edwin Meese.[24] "The NSC itself was not well respected, NSC staffers were lesser-known individuals drawn largely from the academic world."[25] In addition, a number of informal policy groups were established, and below this was a series of interdepartmental groups, chaired by State Department representatives instead of NSC staffers. "By the beginning of his second term, the NSC had lapsed into bureaucratic immobilism and trench warfare."[26] Consequently, policy making devolved to the more informal National Security Planning Group and to Reagan's personal advisers: Meese, Baker and Deaver in the first term; and Donald Regan in the second.[27] This approach was also adopted by the Administration as a means of ensuring that the appointees would not "marry the natives." The appointees were to function as White House emissaries to the departments, not as departmental advocates.[28] As Steven Stehr has noted, such a "transfer of influence in the direction of political appointees challenges many of the prevailing theories of presidential-bureaucratic relations. . . . If the Reagan appointees were successful in reducing the administrative discretion of top bureaucrats, as many observers seem to believe, then our understanding of the dynamics of policy-making in the executive branch needs to be re-examined."[29] Such modifications would perhaps put more emphasis on the President and a small group of personal advisors and on interposing a circle of a single small group between the President in Circle I and the multiple actors of Circle II. Some who have discerned this pattern of the concentration of power have described it as a "principate" of power consisting of the President and his or her immediate cohorts.[30] It has been argued that this informal circle is especially prominent in crisis decision-making, and seems to be becoming increasingly influential over time.

The literature concerning the foreign policy decision structure might lead us to expect several findings; that both State and Defense are instrumental in foreign policy formulation; that there is tension between the careerists and political appointees, or between Circle II and Circle I; and that we should expect an increasing emphasis on policy being made by a small group dominated by the President.

Decision Process: How is Foreign Policy Made?

Edwin Meese, erstwhile coordinator of the system, saw things differently. "We have," Meese insisted, "a highly centralized but participatory decision-making system for policy implementation with specific responsibility and accountability."[31]

In examining the question of how foreign policy is made, theorists have developed a whole variety of decision-making models, positing any number from two to five[32] to 12 different models.[33] Most of the theorists, especially those with large numbers of models, seem to be combining the two separate concepts of decision structure (or who makes policy) with decision process (or how policy is made). Since we see these issues as analytically distinct, we decided to focus upon the three models of decision-making as described by Glenn Snyder and Paul Diesing in their landmark volume *Conflict Among Nations*.[34] The three theories or models of decision-making are:

Rational Actor, in which decisions are made on the basis of the maximization of utility, by which one sets goals, defines the alternatives, calculates the consequences of actions and makes a choice based on maximizing the utility of the alternatives.

Bounded Rationality focuses upon the decision-making process by which one selects an alternative, not that maximizes utility, but which suffices or is good enough.

Bureaucratic Politics sees decision-making as a process of building coalitions and bargaining.

Theorists have debated the extent to which each of the models is successful in explaining actual foreign policy. Though there has been no apparent consensus as to their efficacy, most interest has centered upon discussions of the rational actor and the bureaucratic politics models. In terms of the rational actor model, there recently have been several theorists who have argued that the rational actor model is more an idealized version which could be improved by making the model more complex yet less restrictive.[35] In contrast, other theorists have attempted to explain some of the less rational elements of foreign policy by focusing upon the mental process of decision-making, emphasizing personality disorders, misperceptions, and cognitive process.[36]

In terms of the bureaucratic politics model, one of the more critical complaints is that it essentially ignores the impact of the President and the hierarchical structure of the government.[37] As Bendor and Hammond also noted, the "bureaucratic politics model thus understates the dominance of the President over decision-making in foreign affairs and the degree to which other participants defer to what they assume to be presidential preferences. This evidence seems to require a model accenting hierarchy more and bargaining less."[38] In an attempt to analyze the conflicting claims of the bureaucratic politics model versus the "power of the President" model, Wilfrid Kohl formulated and empirically probed six different models of policy-making. His results bear out the central importance of the attention of the President and his or her top aides, supporting what he described as the "Royal Court" model of decision-making in which the personality and operating style of the President and his or her key court advisor were especially important.[39]

The literature thus has not resolved the question of which of the three decision-making processes best fits reality. In fact, reality may be substantially less precise than the models suggest. The following description may in fact give some indication of the type of process we may expect to find:

> The result is not rationality, with each step taken leading logically to the next in a value-maximizing way, but something that appears quite different—a haphazard, trial-and-error, seat-of-the-pants, decision-making process conducted in a rush, based on "gut it out," best-guess calculations, and influenced strongly by the social context of the process.[40]

There is one final issue which could be raised concerning the foreign policy decision process; whether there are circumstances which alter the decision process. Charles Hermann has offered his well-known hypothesis that the decision-making process changes primarily during a crisis (defined as a situation that has surprise, limited response time, and perceived threats to high-priority goals). In such a situation, it is argued that decision-making will: go to the highest levels; sidestep bureaucratic procedures; put information at a premium; have decisions based more often on analogies; and encourage the centralization of foreign policy.[41] Crises, it would appear, have an impact both on the decision-making structure and the decision-making process, moving the process toward both a smaller decision unit and a less rational process. Thus the implications of crisis situations would appear to be of interest for our survey.

The Reagan Administration, in particular, inserted several new elements into the discussion of the decision process. The first focused on his intention to create a more "cabinet style" of government in which the President would set the goals, yet leave the more specific policy formulation to others.

> The key to the Reagan Presidency was to have the President fuel the policy agenda—to enunciate his goals and sell them rather than watch over operations or intervene obtrusively in the process of decision-making and policy formulation at lower levels. Reagan's style has been distinctively that of a "hands-off" President.[42]

However, for this delegation process to work for a President as ideologically committed as Reagan, it became particularly important that the major positions throughout the executive branch be filled with persons loyal to Reagan's ideas, in other words an ideologically homogeneous group. Bert Rockman refers to this process as the creation of an "administrative presidency," which had as its goal responsiveness to a particular political agenda.[43] Specifically, this was accomplished by an explicit personnel process which utilized a set of five criteria to determine the compatibility with the President's philosophy of the over 3,000 political appointees.[44] This meant that the political appointees in both State and Defense tended to be drawn more extensively from outside the Departments. "By early 1982, a record 50 percent of the ambassadors appointed came from outside the State Department compared to less than 30 percent in the Carter administration."[45] One could hypothesize that such an ideological component might serve to exacerbate the preexisting tensions between the appointees and the careerists, and contribute to a decreased propensity for the careerists in particular to see the policy process in rational terms.

Decision Structure: According to the Insiders

The Reagan Administration style depended very much upon the agencies to come up with proposals, and things bubbled up from that.

Careerist at Defense

In addressing the most significant of our three questions, we attempted to analyze how those within the foreign policy apparatus view the decision-making structure. We first asked respondents to describe the person(s) who make foreign policy. They were given four choices: primarily by the President alone; by a small group of presidential advisors; by a fairly dispersed number of people, or other. Table 5-2 reports the percentage choosing each of the possible answers. One of the most striking things to note about the results is that no one said primarily by the President alone. While this may reflect the narrow wording of the question (the President alone), it may also indicate a desire to describe the American system in general in democratic terms, or it may also be a reflection of the "hands-off" decision-making process followed by the Reagan Administration. Indeed, several of the respondents emphatically rejected the idea that Reagan was directing (primarily or otherwise) U.S. foreign policy. One very Senior Foreign Service officer with a long career at State commented:

> It isn't made by the President. Well it depends on the President, some Presidents are much more involved. I mean I've known Presidents, I've worked under Presidents, who were fairly informed with what's going on, but even they had so much to do that it was very difficult to say that the President more or less followed a set of guidelines. Richard Nixon was probably the President who knew the most details, he had a fantastic grasp and understanding, he liked to engage himself. I don't think President Reagan knows that much. Others were probably in the middle somewhere. Obviously, the President can enter into foreign policy if he wants to and some Presidents do more than others.

This observation about the "who" varying with administrations is reflected throughout the questions dealing with perceptions of the policy process, a point we shall return to later.

Table 5-2.   Who makes foreign policy?[a]

Response	Overall Percentage
Primarily by the President alone	0.0
By a small group of presidential advisors	15.2
By a fairly dispersed number of people	62.0
Other	6.3
Depends (volunteered)	16.5

[a] Responses based on the following question: Overall, how would you describe the person(s) who make foreign policy: Primarily by the President alone? By a small group of presidential advisors? By a fairly dispersed number of people? Other (describe).

Returning to Table 5-2, we see the second option, policy as made by a small group of presidential advisors, was chosen by only a few of the respondents (15 percent). Moreover, several of those who did choose this option hedged their choice by noting this was true only on some important policies, like going to war with Grenada. The most frequent response to the question regarding who makes foreign policy was a fairly dispersed number of people. Sixty-two percent gave this answer. Respondents who elaborated on their choice of "dispersed group" tended to indicate that the participants represented several departments and many agencies depending on the type of policy involved, and varying with administrations. A political appointee with years of experience as a Foreign Service Officer expanded on her choice by noting, "Fairly dispersed number of people, and increasingly that group is becoming more numerous and widespread. It just grows." Another old hand at State expounded:

> There is a stereotype I think on the outside, I think it's understandable, that the top people get together and they decide policy and they take it down to the lower group who then carry out the instructions like you have in the Army. It really isn't like that in the world of ideas. Plans are coming out, this is being knocked off and this is being approved and being carried out and maybe the guy carrying it out does it a little differently or faces some problems. . . . So it's that sort of game.

Nearly one quarter of the respondents rejected the options listed, choosing instead to give their own description, or indicating that the "who" "depends." (6.3 percent said "other," or something else; 16.5 percent said "depends.") For those giving these responses, the most frequent comments revolved around the composition of decision-makers varying with administrations. Another response reflected a common view that the structure depended on the issue area: "Important foreign policy is made by a small group. For less important issues, a fairly dispersed number of people is involved." A careerist at Defense summarized this perspective:

> How the institutions are in fact operated depends a lot on the personalities involved. I think both the current Secretary of State and Secretary of Defense are very powerful, intelligent, knowledgeable men in their own right. In other words, they are competent and eminently qualified for their jobs and do their jobs. The major foreign policy decisions are taken by the top leadership. Those decisions tend to be sort of macrodecisions basically, not real fine points. They tend to take those kinds of decisions only when problems arise the bureaucrats think are insoluble at their level, usually because different agencies have different views about how to solve them. Then those kinds of things get escalated. I don't know, and never have been able to figure out, to what extent there

is a point at which things get done just by chatting in a room at high
levels, or whether the people who chat in the room at high levels have
actually read the briefing papers that they are given. You can't tell that
in any administration. The final decision is made at high levels, by few
people who have access to a lot of information. By the time they get the
information, the salient points hopefully have been identified, and they
can talk through something in a half an hour that a lot of people have
sort of agonized through in different meetings and writing different
papers and so forth.

Several of those who gave long involved answers revealed a process that
engaged a large number of players. A policy-maker at Defense commented
at length, having rejected all three proffered descriptions of "who":

Theoretically a small group of presidential advisors and the President
should be setting the tone. I have served now through Nixon, Ford,
Carter, and Reagan, and I must say it is not a coherent, organized thing.
It is like everything else in this country, in that it reminds me a little bit
of a political convention. You have a general idea of where you want to
go, but having said that, you've said it all. In some instances, you do have
very carefully stated policy. There's a lot of attention paid to it. But two
things happen. One is that an awful lot of things that are significant, but
whose significance isn't recognized early, do not make it up to that level
where policy is made. And the second thing is that you have the age-old
problem of bureaucracy. The bureaucracy can, either through ineptness
or stubbornness, either carry out or not carry out the policy. God help
us all. I don't know a better way.

Another woman at Defense ventured a similar overall view of the wide
variety of participants in the process, but was less sanguine about the
beneficial or neutral results:

Foreign policy is an agglomeration of State Department input, the career
people, modified and adjusted by the National Security Council and
adjusted by a Congress which perceives its role as major in foreign policy.
I don't think we have a foreign policy because of a disjointed effort. Too
many cooks spoiling the broth is the perception I have. My perception
is that policy is much more disjointed than Defense policy is, and Defense
policy is rather disjointed, but not as bad. Where Defense policy is bad
is where it interfaces with State. It's like interfacing with jello.

Interestingly, these last two views do not necessarily reflect the overall
views of their colleagues. Indeed, there was a significant difference between State and Defense Department responses, with the latter more
likely to say the group of decision makers was a small group (20.9 percent

versus 8.3 percent if we exclude those choosing "other" and "depends") (see Table 5-3). At State, the overwhelming majority of respondents (77.8 percent) said those making decisions were a dispersed group. While 48.8 percent of the respondents at Defense also said dispersed, there was clearly a difference in emphasis. One possible explanation for this disparity between the two Departments is that their internal decision making processes may vary. More explicitly, there is some evidence, to be presented below, that decision making at Defense is more hierarchical, with fewer participants involved in the process.

There was no statistically significant difference between women and men in how they characterized who made foreign policy, although there was a slight tendency for men to see the process as more focused in a small group. Among men, 21.1 percent said a small group set policy, while less than half this percentage of women chose this response (see Table 5-3). On the surface, this might suggest some support for the position of Enloe and the maximizers that women are more collegial; however, the responses of the women on the inside did not seem to favor Enloe's notion of a broader base of participants, as slightly fewer women than men chose this option. Rather, the difference between women and men was more a function of women hedging their descriptions by saying it "depends." Women in all the sub-groups, appointees and careerists both

Table 5-3. Who makes foreign policy: Differences by department, position, and sex[a]

	Department		Position		Sex	
	State	Defense	Career	Appointee	Male	Female
Primarily by the President alone	0.0	0.0	0.0	0.0	0.0	0.0
By a small group of presidential advisors	8.3	20.9	14.8	16.0	21.1	9.8
By a fairly dispersed number of people	77.8	48.8	57.4	72.0	65.8	58.5
Other	0.0	11.6	9.3	0.0	5.3	7.3
Depends	13.9	18.6	18.5	12.0	7.9	24.4

[a] Response based on the following question: Overall, how would you describe the person(s) who make foreign policy: Primarily by the President alone? By a small group of presidential advisors? By a fairly dispersed number of people? Other (describe).

at State and Defense, opted in larger numbers than men in the comparable sub-group to say the "who" making foreign policy "depends" on the issue area. While none of these differences were statistically significant, they did suggest one of two possibilities. Either women were less certain than men about who is in charge, or equally likely, women may be making finer distinctions than men about the locus of authority. Except for this minor and statistically insignificant difference, men and women were in general agreement about who makes foreign policy. At least in 1988, a sample of both men and women in the upper echelons of the State and Defense Departments, especially the former, believed the decision-makers were a rather wide ranging group of individuals, organizations, and interests. Similarly, there were only minor differences between the careerists and appointees. Though the appointees were slightly more likely to see policy being made by a small group, the major difference between the two groups was the tendency of the careerists to say "other" or "depends," which could be a reflection of the fact that they have generally been in government longer, and thus could make comparisons among several administrations.

The second area of structure focuses upon the impact of the bureaucracies of Circle II on the President and the appointees of Circle I. We asked our sample of political appointees, Senior Foreign Service, and Senior Executive Service Officers if they thought policy-making occurred at levels below them in the bureaucracy. Interestingly, nearly three in five (58.2 percent) said yes. Respondents in the State Department were especially likely to answer in the affirmative to this question, (66.7 percent versus 51.2 percent for Defense Department respondents). Women were particularly likely to see policy being made below them in the hierarchy. More than 63 percent of all the women in our sample, but only 52.6 percent of men, gave this response. Among women at State, the percentage citing the contributions of those in the lower ranks soared to over 81 percent (85.7 percent for careerists). In comparison, only 55 percent of the men in the Department (53.3 percent of the careerists) saw those in the lower grades making a significant policy contribution. Why the gap between men and women should be so great at State, particularly among careerists, is not clear. (At Defense and among appointees the gap between women and men concerning the evaluation of those in the GS-15 ranks or lower is much narrower). Perhaps the greater sensitivity to those below them in the hierarchy is heightened at State because of the tradition of the foreign service camaraderie, and reduced among those at Defense because of the military chain-of-command structure. Alternatively, one could argue that the perceptions in State are a function of the State Department's own precarious position in the policy process. Those in State tend to see both the number of actors as being more dispersed, and policy-making occurring at lower levels, and thus including more people. As we saw in the Introduction, the position of the State Department itself has been transformed from the major foreign policy agency to being just one of several. Thus, the tendency at State to see the policy structure as more dispersed could merely be a defense mechanism, or wishful thinking, to preclude the Department itself from becoming more marginalized on the periphery. Women careerists at State may just be more conscious of this pattern. As we shall see in Chapter 6, this awareness or sensitivity to one's staff or employees was also reflected in the differences in women's and men's management styles.

When we asked our respondents to detail how those in the lower ranks contributed to policy, most people (46.3 percent) talked about how the knowledge, talent, or skill of those at the lower ranks could often be used to shape policy outcomes. A closely related response, given by 25.9 percent, mentioned the influence of position papers written by those outside the top echelons. Men and women who saw those below them making a contribution were about evenly distributed in their descriptions of the type of influence found among the junior ranks. A few quotes give the flavor of the high praise sung by the superiors of the power of those below them in the hierarchy.

> Policy occurs at the most bottom level for two reasons. One reason is that knowledge is not at the top. The details of any operation occur at the bottom. Therefore, the people at the top don't have the knowledge and they depend upon the people below to be smart. Secondly, there's a million decisions being made every day and they don't all come up, and some of those decisions are policy.

> A nonsupervising person in this agency is a GS-13. They have a strong hand in influencing policy. They gather information, formulate an initial position, and they sell their position. If they are effective in selling it, they can have influence.

Even those who rejected the view that policy is made by those at the lower ranks did often concede that influence on policy was to be expected.

> Policy-making no, but "policy thinking about," yes. A policy officer who makes policy without asking staff what they think or seeing the pros and cons is shooting from the hip. Ultimately, people below my level do frequently get involved in policy-making. It is their thinking that becomes policy.

Although this reasoning and the earlier comments regarding even greater influence by junior officers were widespread, a few of our respondents rejected the notion of influence coming from below, and indeed some even rejected the idea that people at their own level actually made decisions. However, as noted, fewer women (36.6 percent) than men (47.4 percent) dismissed the input of those in the lower ranks. Interestingly, just as the overall survey of SES officials indicated (see Table 5-1), political appointees had a relatively favorable opinion of the middle-rung careerists. Of the appointees, 68 percent reported policy-making occurring below SES/SFS levels, while 53.7 percent of the careerists saw the lower levels being that influential. While some appointees were positive about the influence of those way down the hierarchy from them, other political appointees were more critical: "Sometimes obscure people have too much influence. They are not accountable. The bureaucrats can be sinister. If the bureaucrats have a strong agenda then they can influence policy." Our sample similarly reflected the suspicion with which careerists regard appointees. This hostility particularly was not unexpected, due to the aforementioned desire of the Reagan Administration to wrest control of policy-making from the bureaucracy for ideological reasons. A Senior Executive Service Officer assigned to the State Department drew a picture of the Departmental staff on the outside looking in:

> We are perceived in this building [the State Department] by whomever comes to power as a bunch of bad children because we take on, as bureaucrats, political preferences. We are held in contrast to the Office of Management and Budget in which the bureaucrats there switch gears as an administration switches gears. We in the State Department are considered one of the worst agencies. We have political agendas of our own. "We are the best and the brightest. Why don't you do it our way?" We don't care who is in power. We refuse, they think, to take on the political agenda of the government in power. This creates real havoc in trying to do our business. So you have political appointees who come in and have to figure who they can trust. Especially if they're younger than thirty-five, they are immediately resented by most Foreign Service Officers in the building who feel that they don't even know enough. You have bureaucrats saying "you don't know enough, and I need to tell you everything. You'll go away, and I'll still be here." After awhile, though you get to the point where political appointees and career civil servants make peace with each other, but that can take 18 months to two years. What happens during all that time can be a real dance.

This description of the career officer hostility to inept appointees was reflected at several points in the survey by Senior Executive and Senior Foreign Service Officers who would give examples of appointees whose qualifications were limited. The Reagan appointees were often singled out because of their high ideological profile. Typical is this quote from our interview done with an official at the Defense Department:

Generally I think political appointees, male or female, tend not to be of the caliber of the career civil servants in terms of brains, experience, and dedication, which didn't use to be the case in the Defense Department. One reason is that the Reagan Administration brought in a lot more political appointees than we ever had into lower levels of the organization. Another reason is that in order to get cleared for the White House, to get nominated as a political appointee during the first Reagan Administration, you had to have worked for Reagan in 1960, you had to be ideologically pure.

This same characterization was adopted by another Defense careerist:

The Reagan Administration came in with a Reagan ideology that was very conservative, very hard-line, and included a bunch of ideologues (not everyone, clearly). I think career civil servants tend to be more liberal and see the value of it taking a while to get things done, which was anathema to the political appointees who came in. More so this time than when the Carter people came in, for example. The Reagan political appointees thought they had the Reagan political agenda and the mandate. They were going to come in and give orders and make things happen. They didn't appreciate being told that certain actions were against the law, or violated a regulation.

Similar comments were made by civil servants at State. Thus it seemed that for several of our interviewees, who and how well a person makes policy was clouded by the conflict between entrenched (and perhaps more knowledgeable, depending on one's perspective) civil servants and political appointees who may be resented or ignored because of their lack of expertise.

In trying to tap into the relative foreign policy power of the two agencies, State and Defense, we asked our people in the "upper trenches" how much influence they thought they had. There was no statistically significant difference overall between the participants of the two Departments, although those in Defense tended to see themselves as slightly more influential than our respondents in State, with 11.9 percent of Defense seeing themselves as having a great deal of influence, whereas only 6.5 percent of State fit into this category. Both the political appointees and the careerists saw themselves as having foreign policy influence. There was no statistically significant difference between the two groups, though the appointees did, as expected, on average rank themselves somewhat higher than the careerists, with 17.4 percent of the appointees ranking their authority as seven on a seven-point influence scale, while only six percent of the careerists chose this category. We might speculate that the natural animosity to appointees, especially ideologues noted above, would be exacerbated if the appointee were a women. As we already have seen, women in both Departments, even careerists, felt a need to prove them-selves. Adding appointee status to this perception would lead one to anticipate that it would be very hard for the few women in these positions to exert influence. This resentment was recently in evidence during con-gressional hearings concerning the status of women at State. Mary Lee Garrison, a Co-President of the State Department chapter of the WAO testified:

> Certainly from the standpoint of female Foreign Service Officers, it is galling that historically approximately two-thirds of the female ambassa-dors have been political appointees. . . . We have no qualms about the inclusion of qualified women from outside the State Department ranks as ambassadors, but if you look at those women who have been appointed from outside the Foreign Service ranks to ambassadorial appointments, in most cases their lack of qualifications is stunning.

However, despite this negative impression, in both Departments, women appointees were as likely as male appointees to rate their own influence on foreign policy highly. Moreover, they were less likely than career women in each Department to think being a woman limited their influ-ence on the policy process. Indeed, the group of women most likely to think that being a women limited their influence were the career women at Defense, 53.3 percent of whom said their sex restricted their power. The appointees at Defense were next at 33.3 percent, followed by careerists at State at 28.6 percent and appointees at State at 12.5 percent. The impor-tance of women's credibility at Defense is clear.

To summarize, in defining who makes foreign policy, most of those on the inside of the structure saw the group of decision-makers as rather large. This was particularly true at the State Department, especially among women, where most saw the participants as a broad group stretching not only across agencies, but also deep into the bureaucratic layers of the Department. Moreover, while most of our Insiders rated their own influ-ence highly, there was evidence that women at Defense were having a more difficult time having an input than the men in the Department or the women at State. We will explore this possibility more fully in Chapter 6. The process that these decision-makers actually follow in formulating policy is the topic of the next section.

The Foreign Policy Decision Process:
According to Insiders

> A principal cause of this power shift has been the triumph of politics and ideology over foreign policy.
>
> *Destler, Gelb, and Lake*[46]

There has been, during this administration [under Reagan], more severe problems initially because a number of ideologues with no experience in government were brought in and were antagonistic to the people in the civil service. We wasted an enormous amount of energy with "enemies lists" and that sort of nonsense.

A Careerist at Defense

Turning from who to how, our next line of questions attempted to examine the Snyder-Diesing models more directly by asking our sample: "Which of the following processes best describes the way overall foreign policy is made?" Respondents were given four options:

(1) By a rational process of examining the options, probabilities of success outcomes, and selecting the most beneficial option for the country;

(2) By a process that attempts to rationally pick the best option for the country but is based on less than perfect information; or

(3) By bureaucratic politics; by a group of people, each trying to promote or defend only the interests of their own specific organization without considering what's best for the country.

(4) Some "other" process.

A majority of respondents created a fifth option, which was a "combination" of two or more of the above descriptions. Table 5-4 reports the frequency of each of the options. If we restrict our examination to the three descriptions of process drawn from Snyder-Diesing, we found the most common response centered on bounded rationality, chosen by 19.2 percent of the sample. The bureaucratic politics model was second with 12.8 percent, and the rational model third, with only 10.3 percent selecting it as the best description of the process. Those indicating that the process was rational often elaborated on their selection. A woman at Defense commented: "It is by a rational process to the extent number one [rational] is possible. That is the goal. The aim is number one." At State, a woman said "I think it is very rational and very broad-based." However, some of

Table 5-4. Foreign policy process: Overall

Responses	Overall Percentage
Rational	10.3
Bounded Rationality	19.2
Bureaucratic	12.8
Other	3.8
Combination	53.8

those who chose the rational model added qualifiers. This extensive quote from a State Department SFS dealing with policy on the Middle East gives a good overview of the "normal," almost textbook-quality rational process, and the perhaps equally common process under crisis situations, that is not so rational:

> Working on the Middle East is sort of an anomaly. If you have the luxury of time to work on an issue, there is a process and it's kind of orderly. You do studies, starting basically at a working level, which is below me and then they come up to my level, and then they go up to the Assistant Secretary level. In this process you start out with a basic study laying out all the facts, intelligence assessment and all of that, the likely outcomes and implications for the U.S., and then you provide some options and recommendations. Then as it goes up the layer, to the smart working level, you pick the option that everybody's going to endorse. You then go up to higher level meetings, ultimately culminating in an NSC meeting with the President. That is when you have the luxury of time, for example, when new administrations come in. However, most of what we do here is crisis policy, reactive policy, how you respond to a certain situation or event that occurs. In these situations, the highest levels are called in and they make the decisions, while we're sitting like everybody else in America watching TV, and it's like, oh my God, look at what we're doing now! The one thing I have discovered is that you really don't have the luxury of time to plan, to do preemptive planning. The area is so unpredictable that every administration comes in and tries as hard as they might to say we're going to have a policy that will adjust. But it doesn't work that way. You end up by default having to react because the area is so volatile and unpredictable.

Those saying the process was bureaucratic often were quite positive about the give and take involved. Typical is this description by an official who helps formulate National Security policy:

> It's good that you have conflict among and between department agencies. It's important, that's how the best decisions are made so by working through those conflicts. Perhaps the Department of Commerce would have one very strong view and the Defense Department would have quite another, the State Department might be somewhere in between. The intelligence community supports probably the Department of Defense and you have the private sector supporting the Department of Commerce and you have congressional interests supporting everybody. You have those people who feel strongly because of the information, and the policies and the issues and the constituencies that they serve. That's the way you want it, you don't want a monolithic kind of decision-making process ever. I think that the development of foreign policy in the United States today is pretty healthy.

Individually, the three models proposed by Snyder-Diesing, however, capture less than half of our respondents' views on the foreign policy process. As the data in Table 5-4 makes clear, 3.8 percent chose to describe the process in their own words and fully 53.8 percent rejected the neat dividing lines between the models, claiming that one, two, or all three of the models, combined, were more accurate descriptions of the process. This would seem to be a reflection of Snyder's view that rationality, bounded rationality and bureaucratic politics are complementary.[47] The first thing that is noteworthy about the combination/other responses is that of the 40 persons who said this, the single largest group (20) indicated that all three descriptions applied. Typical of the descriptions given were the following:

> All of these. There is no standard way. Sometimes a brilliant flash, all the way to a lengthy study team. It depends on the agency, subject matter, personalities.

> All three, but light on number three [bureaucratic]. Never with perfect information. Short-term decision-making is number two [bounded rationality]. Long-term is more one [rational].

> By all three. Depends on aggressiveness of players.

> Depends on time. All apply. Number three [bureaucratic] most prevalent.

> Any of these, depends on the situation.

> All of these. Starts as rational, but then influenced by politics and ideology.

Of those who did not say all three, the most common combinations were bounded rationality and bureaucratic (eight people), and rational and bureaucratic (six people). Indeed, only three of the 40 respondents saying "combination" did *not* indicate bureaucratic politics was part of the process. However, the respondents often disagreed over the extent to which bureaucratic politics was necessarily self-interested politics, or whether it could be seen more in terms of coalition politics. A woman at the Defense Department made this point:

> A combination of two [bounded rationality] and three [bureaucratic] and four [other]. Certainly bureaucratic policies comes into play. No getting around that. I think, in general, people would like to think they're taking a rational approach, but they're always dealing with imperfect information. There is no way to have perfect information. Also the syndrome of the blind men and the elephant comes into play. Everyone does it from their own perspective, and not just bureaucratic politics. There can be

competing national objectives where there has to be some trade-offs made between national objectives.

A political appointee at State also argued that everyone believes they represent the national interest, yet emphasized the more negative aspects of the bureaucratic game:

> It's a combination of those, I mean, obviously policy is affected by day-to-day decisions made all over town. I can suddenly find, while we are talking, that somebody in the Agriculture Department has cut off a shipment of grain to somebody just as we're in the middle of base negotiations. Policy is made, and we may lose a base. I draw the extreme but that could happen because of this wide, dispersed group of people, not all of whom look at the global questions or the regional questions or indeed even at a national relationship between the United States and France for instance. This is the only place in town that keeps track of all of those pieces when they are colliding. Sometimes we do not know everything and things will collide. I don't think there's an absence of information, but there are strong views on subjects like this, and to that extent, it is a weakness. It leads to cheating in the argumentation, not in the facts. In the presentation of the arguments, words have values, words like compromise. I can tell you that you better not ever use the word compromise, it's a weak word. You can say finding the middle ground, finding a convergence, finding an accommodation, but for God's sake don't say "compromise." If you say "this option represents a good compromise," then someone else comes in and says "this is a compromiser's option." I'll tell you how it's going to end. Cheating is also there, and much of the cheating represents a desire to win, and that desire to win is the expression of an institution. There are institutions colliding, I mean there are mind-sets colliding, and the starting point of each is different. But I'm sure that each side would be insistent that it is acting in the national interest.

Another political appointee at State described different elements of bureaucratic politics, emphasizing bureaucratic inertia:

> Combination of one [rational] and three [bureaucratic]. I definitely think everyone starts with the intent of the first one. That's the way it begins and it breaks down, which is a human thing to happen when you have a large bureaucracy. There's also a certain amount of inertia in a large bureaucracy. And it's not out of bad motivation. But if you have to go through six offices like mine, it's going to lay in everyone's in-basket for a day or two, and it may take two weeks in a couple of offices. Then a third guy suggests alterations, and it has to be sent back. It is an agonizingly slow process. The up side is that snap decisions aren't made without considering all the options.

Several subgroup differences surfaced on the question of policy process. Table 5-5 reports the breakdown by Department, sex, and political appointee/career official. The political appointees were more likely to see the process as rational than were the careerists, though the differences are not statistically significant. This is no doubt partially a function of their higher position within the process and corresponding desire to see the process in as beneficial a light as possible. On the other hand, the careerists tended to see the process as more bureaucratic, which may, at least on some level, be tied to their desire to see themselves as having a significant policy making role. However, the only statistically significant differences were found in comparing the results from State and Defense. While a total of 44.5 percent of State officials characterized the process as at least aiming at rationality [rational plus bounded rationality], only 16.6 percent of Defense officials classify the process this way. Foreign policy decision-making may look rational to those at State, but for those at Defense, the whole process apparently looked quite bureaucratic. In other words, when forced to interface with other agencies in setting U.S. foreign policy, the interface may seem like "jello" compared to the hierarchy of the decision-making process at the Pentagon. However, not too much should be made of this distinction, given that a combination of the three models is the most common choice in both Departments. An examination of sex differences finds, in contrast to what the maximizer feminists might have anticipated, that women's characterization of the process was not statistically different from that of men's. Moreover, there was no hint of a gender pattern in the responses of the women in our sample.

The Decision Process Within The Bureaucracy

In addition to asking respondents how they characterized the foreign policy process, we also asked which of the three models best described

Table 5-5. Foreign policy process overall: Differences by department, position, and sex

Response	Department		Position		Sex	
	State	Defense	Career	Appointee	Male	Female
Rational	13.9	7.1	5.7	20.0	5.4	14.6
Bounded Rationality	30.6	9.5	20.8	16.0	27.0	12.2
Bureaucratic	2.8	21.4	17.0	4.0	10.8	14.6
Other	2.8	4.8	3.8	4.0	2.7	4.9
Combination	50.0	57.1	52.8	56.0	54.1	53.7

Table 5-6. Policy process in respondent's own organization[a]

Response	Overall Percentage
Rational	40.3
Bounded Rationality	24.7
Bureaucratic	1.3
Other	6.5
Combination	27.3

[a] Responses based on following question: In your organization, which of these responses best describes the way policy is made. Is it made (1) By a rational process? (2) By limited rationality? (3) By bureaucratic policies? (4) Other. Combination category includes those who said the process involved a combination of two or more of the options listed.

how policy was made within their own organization. Table 5-6 reports the results of this question. The most striking aspect of the results is how few of the respondents believed the decision-making process in their own Department was bureaucratic. Less than two percent saw it as bureaucratic, while 40.3 percent saw it as rational, and 24.7 percent as bounded rationality. Moreover, unlike the overall process, most people were content to use the three categories, with only 27.3 percent of the sample saying a combination of the processes and 6.5 percent saying yet another description explained policy-making in their arena. Perhaps we should not be surprised by these results. It may be human nature to see what one does as rational and straight-forward, while the larger world or arena in which we work is irrational, bureaucratic, or complex. Indeed, several of the extended responses to the question drew this contrast between policy-making in their agency and the larger foreign policy arena. A few representative quotes give an indication of the view of those saying the process was rational: "Rational. That's the way it is here." "Systematic procedures for recommending up the hierarchy." However, not all respondents claimed that their own Department was more rational than the overall process, and a few cited evidence of bureaucratic influence within their area of decision-making:

Again I would say it's a combination of two and three. I think that we would like to think that we are more rational. But we all have two hats we wear, we wear our Center hats sometimes and then we wear our Department hats at other times. When we are wearing our Department hats, we are fighting for resources for our Department to do its job. And since the resources are limited and there's some trade-off going on and there are times you'll see bureaucratic positioning, so it's a combination of the two. I don't think you'll ever get away from that. I would think you would be asking people to be something less than human, frankly, I think the job requires it to an extent.

Moreover, those saying "other" or "combination" also generally conceded bureaucratic influence in the decision-making process, although they sometimes reported that their organization was less bureaucratic than elsewhere or overall. A man at State described the Department's decision-making as follows:

Inside the organization it's really a combination of one and two. You either know what you're doing or you're not quite sure of what you're doing but you still have to make a decision. The State Department actually has a pretty effective process. I've been in five government agencies in my career and of all of them the State Department is by far the best at making decisions. Unlike a lot of places, you can generate a paper here, get it around to a bunch of people, get clearances or views or whatever, have a quick meeting and you can move papers very quickly, all the way to the Secretary. And if something is urgent, you can literally put a red tag on it and have it on the Secretary's desk in 45 minutes. There is no place in government, outside the Presidency, where I know of, where you can do that.

This view from State was probably pretty reflective of many in the Department. As an examination of sub-group differences reported in Table 5-7 shows, the most frequent response from State was bounded rationality. However, as the data in the table reveals, at Defense the most common response was rational. Fully 50 percent of the respondents at

Table 5-7. Policy process in respondent's own organization: Differences by department, position, and sex[a]

Response	Department		Position		Sex	
	State	Defense	Career	Appointee	Male	Female
Rational	28.6	50.0	37.7	45.8	42.1	38.5
Bounded Rationality	40.0	11.9	30.2	12.5	31.6	17.9
Bureaucratic	0.0	2.4	1.9	0.0	0.0	2.6
Other	2.9	9.5	3.8	12.5	2.6	10.3
Combination	28.6	26.2	26.4	29.2	23.7	30.8

[a] Responses based on the same question as Table 5–6.

the Pentagon judged the process as rational in their area. This difference with State was statistically significant. Although appointees were more likely than nonappointees to see the process in their area as rational, a finding that parallels our results on characterization of the overall process, the difference was not significant. Again there was no statistical significant difference between women and men, although women overall and within the sub-groups did show a slight tendency to downgrade the level of rationality in their own agency.

Why Defense would view the process in their Department as so rational is not entirely clear. Most likely it reflects the chain-of-command structure and the more rigid hierarchy at the Pentagon, both products of the influence of the military on the decision-making process. Indeed, several of the respondents referenced the hierarchy in claiming rationality. As noted earlier, this structured decision-making at Defense may be responsible for our earlier results that found people at the Pentagon characterizing the overall process as more confusing ("interfacing with jello"). Similarly, the tight command structure, or the belief that a tight command structure should exist, may lead to the perception that a small group makes final decisions on foreign policy (or at least in national security policy). This view may be reinforced by crises and other events that alter the decision-making process. As we shall see in the next section, in such cases we have some evidence the decision-making team gets even narrower at Defense.

To summarize, when examining the models of Snyder-Diesing, none of the three in isolation describes the process for a majority of our interviewees. The favored response was to see foreign policy decision-making as involving elements of all three models. However, it should be noted, if we analyze the responses of those saying "combination," the one common theme in most is the inclusion of descriptions of, or references to, the bureaucratic model. Indeed, more than 58.7 percent of our respondents either said the process was bureaucratic, or involved elements of the bureaucratic and other models, when referring to the overall process, although they saw decision-making in their own Department as quite rational. Our findings would thus seem to coincide with two major trends in the literature: firstly, the recurring emphasis on some aspects of bureaucratic politics; secondly, our findings would also seem to support the general description of a process which aims at rationality, but which ends up being less than completely so.

Crises and Other Events that Alter
the Foreign Policy Process

In the discussion up to this point, we have focused on policy-making in normal conditions, however, at a later point in the interview, we did raise the question: "Does the foreign policy decision-making in your Department change during an international crisis?" Not surprisingly, an overwhelming majority (73.3 percent) said yes. For those who answered in the affirmative, we asked how the process changed. Table 5-8 reports the answers of our respondents. The results are as anticipated. Of those saying the process changed, the two most common sets of answers follow what the literature would have led us to expect. Crises shorten the time frame for decision-making (52.7 percent) and narrow the range of decision-makers (38.2 percent). A few representative quotes convey the view by Insiders of decision-making in crises:

> Only in sense decisions are quicker, they don't get lost in the bureaucracy.

> It becomes closed-in more, because they have to make a decision in a hurry, because you can't take a year to staff out which way to go.

Several of those citing the shortened time frame noted that this often had negative consequences. To quote from a State Department interview:

> Yes, of course things change. Decision-making is compressed—often on less than complete information. Lines of authority are breached; and occasionally, in the name of expediency or reaction, mistakes are made— albeit well intentioned.

Several (4 percent) of the respondents indicated that when a crisis developed, their Department had standard procedures (crisis management procedures, establishment of task forces, etc.) that were generally set up to deal with such emergencies. A few of the surveys from State Department

Table 5-8. Crisis decision-making: How the process changes

Responses	Overall percentage
No	24.7
Yes	73.3
Responses of those saying yes[a]	
Shorter time frame/quicker action	52.7
Smaller group/fewer decision makers	38.2
Rely on intuition/not rational	4.0
Crisis management/task force	4.0
Other	12.7

[a] Multiple responses possible; figures do not add to 100 percent.

officials stationed abroad gave conflicting pictures as to how crises are handled by an overseas embassy:

> It becomes faster and less is referred to Washington—much more is decided in the field.

> More centralized, small decisions are taken at higher levels. More gets done on the phone, but peripheral players outside the direct chain of command have much less influence.

> Formality declines; less paper; more verbal consultation.

While respondents at State and Defense both gave roughly comparable answers, there was some indication that the process was more likely to be perceived as faster and more closed at Defense. Forty percent of Defense Department officials, compared to 36 percent of State, indicated that a smaller group of decision-makers was active during a crisis. Furthermore, when asked to indicate what happened to *their own* influence during a crisis, our respondents at Defense were statistically more likely than those at State to say their influence declined (30 percent versus 7.4 percent) or remained the same (56.7 percent versus 48.1 percent). This reduction of influence during a crisis may be related to the perception, noted earlier, of our Defense Department respondents, that a small group of persons make foreign policy decisions. Another interesting difference was the greater propensity of career officials to see the process as changing during a crisis. Over 80 percent of the careerists but only 60 percent of the appointees thought the process changed (a statistically significant difference). A possible explanation may be the greater experience of career officials with crises. Alternatively, appointees may assume that they are involved in all circumstances, and thus perhaps they are less aware of the layers of bureaucracy that are cut out of decision making during a crisis. Indeed, the appointees were more likely than career officials to say their influence remained the same (63.2 percent versus 47.4 percent) or increases (31.6 percent versus 26.3 percent) during a crisis, while only a few of the appointees (5.3 percent) as opposed to 26.3 percent of the careerists said their influence declines. Although these differences are not statistically significant, they are in the direction to be expected and may suggest why crisis decision-making looks somewhat different from the perspective of the two groups of officials.

When we looked at the responses of men and women to crises, we find once again no difference in the recognition that such events alter the decision process. However, when women were asked what happened to their own influence in a crisis, we did find several statistically significant patterns. Most notable was the much larger percentage of women at Defense who said their authority declined or remained the same during a crisis. Overall none of the women at Defense saw their influence increase, in contrast to 31 percent of the men in the Department who said their influence increased during a crisis. Among both appointees and careerists at Defense the pattern was the same. The picture at State was nearly the opposite. Among appointees and careerists, although the relationship was not statistically significant, women were more likely than men to anticipate a rise in their own power during an international crisis. We can not be sure about what factors explain this contrary set of results, but we expect it reflects both the difficulty women at Defense generally have in influencing policy already noted earlier, and the more peripheral position of women at Defense. As we discussed in Chapter 2, women at Defense are more likely to be found in the support fields (personnel, manpower) and not in the line positions. Crises are less likely to involve these areas, indeed crises may push these fields off to the side while more pressing issues take the floor.

In addition to crises, we also asked the people at State and Defense if there were situations other than a foreign policy crisis that altered the decision-making process. Interestingly, over 80 percent said "yes." As the figures in Table 5-9 indicate, the most commonly cited factor bringing about a change was domestic politics, specifically increased public awareness, media attention and/or interest group involvement. Nearly one-third of the sample's responses fell into this category. Typical were the following descriptions of factors producing change:

Table 5-9. Situations other than crises altering the decision-making process[a]

Response	Overall Percentage[b]
No	15.9
Yes, domestic crisis	31.9
Yes, congressional action/ Congress	13.0
Yes, personalities	15.9
Yes, different administrations/White House, President	10.3
Yes, other	13.0

[a] Responses based on the following question: Are there situations other than a foreign policy crisis that alter the decision-making process? Yes, no. If yes, what are these other situations?

[b] Multiple responses possible, figures do not add to 100 percent.

If we have an international domestic crisis, things like AIDS in the military or drug abuse. A lot of these are international domestic problems, but they can become a crisis.

Issues that affect special interest groups and that could have domestic political implications.

Public opinion. When I say public, it's the public at large. It's our constit- uents, the universities, in particular. Their view of DOD, of how we're doing our job.

Often domestic considerations were linked to Congress. For instance, a State official complained: "When Congress or interest groups get involved, although their level of interest tends to be proportioned to the crisis level they perceive in any particular situation." Several of the officials at Defense mentioned the procurement scandals, noting the impact of these on both public opinion and Congress. Budget battles with Congress were also a common theme, again especially from Defense. The White House was also cited as a factor that could alter the policy process. More specifically, heightened interest in an issue by the President, or a change in the administration, or administration policy were mentioned by 10 percent of those interviewed as variables that could alter business as usual. For nearly 16 percent of the sample, a factor that could change the process was the personalities and preferences of decision-makers.

When comparing sub-groups on what they saw as factors altering the situation, again the major difference of note was between Defense and State. Those at State were more likely to name something that altered the process (90.9 percent versus 77.8 percent). In addition, domestic consider- ations loomed large at Defense (41.7 percent versus 21.2 percent), while at State personalities and domestic issues both topped the list (cited by 24.2 percent and 21.2 percent respectively). Interestingly, in contrast to crises, where many of our interviewees, especially career people, saw their influence decline or remain the same, other situations that alter the policy process were much more likely to produce an increase in authority. More than 40 percent of our respondents reported their own influence increased in noncrisis situations, while only 28.1 percent saw their influ- ence rise in an international crisis. There were no significant sub-group differences with respect to influence changes in noncrisis situations, although women careerists, but not appointees, at Defense were again more likely than the men in the Department to anticipate a decline in authority.

Thus, it seems that both domestic considerations and international crises can alter the decision-making process. The latter is especially interesting in light of the three models proposed by Snyder and Diesing, because in international crises the bureaucratic model, the popular choice in explaining the day-to-day foreign policy process, appears to give way, at least temporarily, to a process that is less influenced by layers of bureaucratic players. Furthermore, in the context of our question regarding who makes policy, crises also narrow the field of players. We can see this in the answers to how the process changes during a crisis and in our interviewees' reports of their own influence in crisis. This was particularly true for the women at Defense whose tenuous position becomes even more so when crises or other events intrude on business as usual.

Implications for American Foreign Policy

In the literature there appear to be two conflicting analyses of President Reagan's policy process. On the one hand, he has been characterized as having a very detached policy process, which allowed for a great dispersal of policy-making power. For example, Ronald Reagan had promised to restore leadership on U.S. foreign policy by organizing it in a more coherent way. He at first pledged to involve the State Department and the cabinet more in decision-making.[48] "Reagan's choice of Alexander Haig as Secretary of State was spotlighted as an indication of the new president's desire to relocate primary control over foreign policy making in the State Department and to downgrade the role of the National Security Advisor."[49] Additionally, as a result his own personality and partially as a by-product of the Iran-Contra scandal, Reagan became perceived as disinterested and uninvolved in foreign policy.

> President Reagan had relatively little interest in foreign affairs, and his ignorance of the subject, compounded by a poor memory, concerned even his most senior policy advisers. Few presidents were more passive in policy formulation. . . . Whereas Nixon overcentralized authority in the White House, Reagan delegated authority excessively, in what he called "cabinet government" . . . the consequent insufficient degree of White House centralized discipline contributed to a perhaps unprecedented fragmentation of policy.[50]

On the other hand, Reagan has also been seen as part of a trend which increasingly concentrated power in the hands of the President's staff and immediate advisors at the expense of the cabinet and the bureaucracies. In particular, the National Security Planning Group (NSPG), which consisted of the President's closest personal advisors, emerged as a kind of "executive committee" of the NSC.[51] Within this group, Secretary of Defense Casper Weinberger appeared to enjoy greater influence due to his personal friendship with the President.[52] In terms of the contest between career bureaucrats and political appointees in the Reagan Administration, it has been argued from this perspective that the power of the appointees definitely increased. Appointees were selected on the basis of their ability to be loyal team players, and the NSPG was especially seen as having a strong ideological bent:

> Ronald Reagan is the most ideologically oriented president to have occupied the White House in the post-World War II era. . . . Washington's key policy-making roles have come to be occupied by those subscribing to conservative political values in greater proportion than at perhaps any other time in the preceding half century.[53]

The judgment has been that the Reagan appointees were successful in reducing the discretion or policy power of the top bureaucrats.[54] Career executives were excluded from important decision-making responsibilities and influence increasingly shifted in the direction of political appointees.

This bifurcation in evaluating the Reagan Administration's foreign policy process was also reflected in the responses of our interviewees. Though they clearly rejected a dominant role for Ronald Reagan, with no one saying that foreign policy was made by the President alone, there was some disagreement as to whether foreign policy was being made by a small group of presidential advisors (NSPG), or whether there was a more open system, with significant input from the bureaucracies. As Table 5-2 indicated, overall 62.0 percent of our respondents saw policy being made by a fairly dispersed number of people. Though this was especially true of those at State (see Table 5-3), even in the Defense Department a vast number of policy-makers saw the system as more open. Their evaluation of Reagan's "cabinet style" of leadership focused upon its benefits, particularly in terms of providing the careerists with an avenue for impact. As one Defense career official noted, "Reagan depended very, very much upon the agencies to come up with proposals, and things bubbled up from that. You knew always where to go if you had an idea, and how to put it in the process."

On the other hand, there was among the careerists in Defense and among the political appointees in both Departments, a significant proportion who saw policy being made by a small group of presidential advisors. Our interviews were replete with comments concerning the power of a select few political appointee insiders whose ideological bent fueled the antagonism between the careerists and the appointees. In discussing one such appointment to a very important position for foreign policy, one respondent commented:

> This is a key job for foreign policy in the Department today. There was nothing in this individual's background that would appear to be qualifications for that position. But sometimes the politics of the political deck becomes the most important aspect. The process is political, a lot more political than you would like to think it is.

Though complaints concerning the power and qualifications of appointees are not new, those who felt that the Reagan Administration relied on them to a greater extent than previous administrations, argued that this exclusionary process entailed significant costs. For example, the Iran-Contra affair was cited as illustrating the dangers of giving power to those who were selected on the basis of ideology, not qualifications. Additionally, these costs included a devaluation of the contributions career government officials could make. As one careerist concluded:

> There is a high cost of this policy. The cost is that the career service is not being nurtured. They are not getting rid of ineffective people, and are not encouraging the good people. They are allowed to just stagnate, which is too bad for the country. They lose a lot of productivity that way.

There are a number of ways of trying to explain or reconcile these two competing judgements of the Reagan policy process. Perhaps the key is in the type of issue. Day-to-day issues may have been dispersed to a larger circle of participants, while crises or ideologically important policies were the province of a visible, small circle. Our respondents seemed to agree with this view in their descriptions of the policy process under stress and of the factors which altered the policy-making process. Alternatively, one could argue that this divergence is merely a reflection of organizational bias. In DOD, 20.9 percent of the respondents saw policy being made by a small group, while this was true of only 8.3 percent of those in State. Conversely, 77.8 percent of those in State saw decisions being made by a dispersed group, while only 48.8 percent of those at DOD characterized the process in those terms (see Table 5-3). Thus the difference in perspective might be tied to a preference for the more hierarchical, closed, chain-of-command philosophy which is more common in DOD than State. In a contradictory vein, one could argue that the administration was merely an aberration. Reagan's personality and "hands-off" management style was a respite (which allowed a little more latitude to the bureaucracy) from the historical trend of increasingly concentrating foreign policy power in the White House. Subsidiarily, one could posit that the tendency of our respondents to see the process as fairly dispersed just reflected wishful thinking on their part: an attempt to see themselves as playing an important role in decision-making against a hierarchy which was content to exclude them.

In terms of the overall significance of these perspectives for the American foreign policy process, it is unlikely that both of these contradictory trends and/or judgements could continue. In fact, it appears that the Bush Administration has relied on the more closed model of policy-making in which authority has crept up the chain of command, though the ideological emphasis has not remained the same.[55]

Implications for the Maximizer-Minimizer Debate

In Chapter 4 we found only minor differences between women and men in their foreign policy views. Those differences we did uncover were largely explainable by reference to organizational and individual factors. Our examination in this chapter of how the foreign policy process was described by Insiders has revealed even fewer gender disparities. Indeed, there were *no* statistically significant differences between the women and men in our sample in how they described the "who" or the "how" of the foreign policy process. The key variable again was not gender but organization or position, with those at Defense more often describing decision-making as involving a small group; and with appointees seeing policy-making as more rational. Similarly our Insiders at State were more willing to portray the process as rational, than were the women and men at Defense. Indeed, the one area where gender differences did appear most dramatically was also largely explained by reference to organizational factors. More specifically, women at Defense evidenced considerable doubts about their own ability to influence foreign policy in crises in particular. This fits with what we have already come to expect. Defense is a tough arena for women to seek credibility.

While organizational factors dominated, there was some suggestion that individual factors were also important. Careerists and appointees occasionally diverged in describing the process, with women appointees and women civil servants sometimes choosing different options. Possible evidence of the effects of societal factors might be seen in the greater willingness of women to credit the contributions of those below them in the hierarchy, although again organizational and individual factors were important, with women careerists at State the most conscious of the contributions of those in the ranks beneath them.

Our results, thus, do little to support the position of the maximizers. As the minimizers would lead us to expect, women on the inside of the foreign policy process are no different from the men on the inside in how they describe the way U.S. international affairs are conducted. Which Department a person is in and what position they hold appear to be more important than their sex in shaping their views. This is not to say that sex is without significance. Women may describe the game the same way as men do, but as the women in Defense are so keenly aware, women encounter problems when they attempt to play it. In the next chapter we shall examine in more detail the problems women encounter and the management styles they adopt as they attempt to shape foreign policy.

Interview

JENONNE WALKER

Privy to Policy-Making

Jenonne Walker had a nearly 30 year career in American foreign policy institutions, including positions in both the Central Intelligence Agency and the State Department. Her latest government position, as the Director of the State Department office responsible for European and United Nations' arms control issues during the Reagan Administration, provided Ms. Walker with valuable insights into the ways in which American foreign policy is formulated. When we interviewed her in January 1991, Ms. Walker was a Senior Associate with the Carnegie Endowment for International Peace, researching European security and U.S.-European relations. She is widely published on the subject of American foreign policy, including a recent article, "Keeping America in Europe," which appeared in the Summer 1991 volume of *Foreign Policy.*

I started in the CIA as an analyst. ... The particular office in which I wanted to work at the CIA had never had a woman, except secretaries, and it took me three years to get into it, but that was the early sixties. ... The CIA is a great learning experience because the whole job, or the analytical part of it, is to explain to whoever is in the White House how foreigners see issues, and why they see them the way they do, and how they are likely to respond to developments or possible U.S. policy changes. There came a time when I wanted to say what U.S. policy should be, which one couldn't do there. Working at the State Department gives one a chance to recommend what American policy ought to be, and I was very lucky having jobs where I got a real hearing for my ideas. I was extremely lucky in the jobs I had in the State Department. State sounds like a big, impersonal bureaucracy, but in fact it's not at all. I was already fairly senior when I went there, which helped. I was first on the Policy Planning Staff, and the two Secretaries of State under whom I worked used the Policy Planning Staff as their substantive cabinet, so we were at the center of things. We had fantastic access. Then, during the years I was in the Politico-Military Bureau, I was chairing several interagency groups that were at the center of things. That's not the case now. Now the NSC staff is chairing the groups and it's been back and forth from administration to administration. So in State, I always felt that I had wonderful support and access, no complaints at all, and very, very happy with relations with the European Bureau, and in the human rights' years, with the Latin American Bureau, the African Bureau, and the other bureaus that human rights' policy affected more than the European Bureau. . . . One part of the arms control job was chairing the interagency groups that tried to make policies on my issues. The CFE [Conventional Forces in Europe] treaty and the INF [Intermediate-range Nuclear Forces] treaty were my major accomplishments. I would like to have had a chemical weapons [CW] convention. I did not expect to because most people in the Reagan Administration did not want *our own* proposal to be accepted, and therefore we were not negotiating it very actively. But I would like to have changed Washington's mind on the CW treaty. I did not. One of the few people who agreed with me on the CW ban was the then Vice-President, now President. So Washington's position has changed, but not because I did it. I think I kept us from backsliding even more than we did away from the CW proposals. So I helped mark time in a relatively nondamaging way.

> Owing to the interagency role she had, Ms. Walker was in a position which afforded her a vista of foreign policy formulation, both in terms of decision structure: "who makes foreign policy?" but also in terms of decision process: "how foreign policy is made." In response to our question: "Is foreign policy primarily made by the President alone, or by a small group of presidential advisors, or by fairly a dispersed number of people?" Ms. Walker responded:

American foreign policy is made by a *very* diverse number of people. There are so many issues that don't seem important, that certainly never get through to the President or not even to his top advisors, not even to the Secretary of State. A wide, wide range of arms control measures are signed off at the working level. Each member of my interagency groups knew which issues his superiors ought to know about before he signed off for his agency. Obviously, different agencies have a strong interest in different subjects. . . . One of the things I liked about the State Department was that your rank matters to the job that you can have, but it doesn't matter to the way you're treated within a bureau. Not in any of the offices I have worked in, and not within the European Bureau, which I worked very closely with. There is a premium on being outspoken and saying what you really think, and if you're bright and have good ideas, people will listen to you and you will have a lot of influence. There was a critical summer in the CFE negotiations with some of the NATO proposals coming together just as the negotiations opened. Then, because of a series of accidents, the only people working on CFE in the European Bureau were three girl interns who were very, very good. One was a Council of Foreign Policy fellow and the other two were interns. They were superb and had a lot of influence all over town. The front office of the European Bureau knew that was happening and trusted them. It's who you are and how good you are, not what rank you have. There were two new members of my working group, I am thinking of one young man from overseas in particular, who was just so bright that he had a lot of influence on all the rest of us. . . . I was actually very lucky in the people that I worked for. I always worked for people who thought that honest disagreement was the highest loyalty. People who were bright, extremely bright and stimulating, so it was intellectually fun to work with them. I was just very, very lucky with my superiors who also had a sense of humor about disasters that happened. They were fun to work with in every possible way. I had a warm, close, personal relationship every time it counted with my superiors and many of them I count as friends now.

> In terms of the decision process, the traditional debate has focused on whether the process can best be described as: basically a rational one, examining the options and picking the most beneficial option for the country; or whether it is bounded rationality, one in which there is an attempt at rationality which is hampered by less than perfect information; or whether it is dominated by bureaucratic politics. Ms. Walker tends to see it as a combination of these.

The way in which policy is made is different, of course, on different issues and in some ways it's more structured on arms control than others, because everything in arms control is done interagency. The results and guidance, be it proposals you put on the table or guidance telegrams to the negotiating delegation, have to be somewhat more formalized. In my years it was done through interagency committee. In theory, as chairman, I would assign tasks. In practice, that means you talk to the people on the telephone first to make sure that they are going to be happy with the assignments, and divide up the basic analytical work to be done. If you're going into a particular negotiation where the proposals are on a range of things—what will the limits be, what will the definitions be, verifications regimes—you can divide up different pieces of the pie. . . . Somebody has to organize the large numbers of agencies that all have a legitimate voice in arms control. Then there are one or more telegrams to a negotiating delegation everyday. Toward the endgame of the INF treaty, they were in almost constant session in Geneva, and we were too back here, Saturdays, Sundays. We got to the point that people would leave a meeting in Washington and get on the telephone and tell Geneva "Yes, you can do this; no you cannot do this, try this instead," and then try to follow it up with a telegram so there would be a paper trail, so the negotiator would be protected in that kind of thing. You sort of do what works. On things that are not arms control negotiations, that are less formalized, the State Department's role is not totally independent, but it is a lot closer to being independent. There are a good many things that the State can tell an embassy "yes" or "no" on, which means the country desk or the regional bureau in which the country desk is located, has a large voice. The human rights business was another interagency process. Then the Deputy Secretary of State, Warren Christopher, chaired a group of which I was the Executive Secretary. I would have subordinate meetings trying to reach agreement on specific decisions, and the issues we couldn't agree on we would send to his group. Increasingly so many of the issues do concern more than one agency, so there needs to be some mechanism for interagency management. It varies from subject to subject. If you make the process sound well organized and formal like that, though, it is misleading, because so much depends on the interaction of personalities, on mood, on accidental circumstances. I always feel everyone should to be in government, if only for six months to a year. You could never again believe in a conspiracy theory of history. You couldn't run a good conspiracy if you really tried. It's only the "screw up theory of history" that could ever again be plausible. ... [The foreign policy process] is generally the attempt at rationality with less than perfect information, but obviously bureaucratic politics and personalities matter. People who like each other want to do deals, will accommodate each other. People who don't like each other are going to oppose whatever the other says, no matter what.

In the arms control business, the interagency process was handicapped by a weak National Security Council staff. They are the ones that have to adjudicate differences. The task of my interagency working groups was to try to reach agreement on policy issues, and 98 percent of the time we did, but it is the 2 percent that are really hard issues obviously. ... So the fact that we resolve most of the issues is misleading, it's the hard ones that are important. They need to be adjudicated and, in theory, it is the President who decides, or the National Security Advisor. In practice that is almost always on the advice of a NSC staff member. The quality was not what it should have been in the Reagan years. Neither in the Reagan years, nor the first Bush year that I was in government, were they prepared to really set deadlines and make clear decisions. There was lot of sabotage in the Reagan years. Some people were so adamantly opposed to any arms control at all that when a presidential decision went against them, there were real efforts to keep the decision from being implemented. We did not have a NSC staff that would impose discipline and say that if you don't have a position by three o'clock on Thursday afternoon, we're going to decide without you. So a lot of delaying tactics, some deliberate I think, and some just sloppy work, were permitted and tolerated. So there was a real problem with the NSC staff. It got better under Bush and it may be better still by now. It was a very weak staff under Reagan.

So far as I know the basic way of making policy hasn't changed, having the NSC staff chair interagency working groups should help, but that is a minor procedural change, and as far as I know there has been no fundamental change. And in the Bush Administration, as you know, the top is very closed, there is an "us-them" attitude between Baker and his inner circle on the one hand, and the career establishment on the other. Shultz drew on the career bureaucracy, he knew its weaknesses as well as its strengths, and he obviously ignored some of the people and used others, but he tried to use the whole building. To my great surprise the Baker people came in with real animosity towards the Reagan *political appointees*, which is strange. They must have felt really mistreated during the vice presidential years. There was a real animosity toward the Reagan political appointees and toward the career people in the State Department. This "us-them" attitude extends even to some of Baker's own political appointees.

There have been women assistant secretaries, but except for Rozanne Ridgway in the European Bureau under Shultz, none in regional bureaus, which is what really matters, or in the Politico-Military, Economic and Business, or International Organization Bureaus. There are a lot of younger women doing very, very well, so it may be a generational thing. But one won't know for maybe ten or 15 years. Some of those women will drop out because of their husband's careers and because they want to raise children, so they will drop out by choice. The ones who don't drop out by choice, it will be very interesting to see what happens to them.

> Ms. Walker's decided in late 1989 to leave government service and to pursue a different avenue through which she could attempt to influence American foreign policy.

I had done all I could expect to do as a civil servant in the State Department. Really, more than I could have expected to do as a civil servant in the State Department. So many of the jobs I would have been interested in were reserved for Foreign Service Officers, and I was a Senior Executive (SES) in the State Department. I could have taken a big demotion and tried to enter the Foreign Service, but I was not prepared to do that.

Partly, I was tired. When I was younger, I felt there would be time to get around to everything. As I got older, every night I was in my office until nine or ten o'clock, which was most nights, I was very aware that there was a friend that I was not seeing, there was not a lot of balance in my life. I had been doing arms control under lots of pressure for five and a half years, and I really had a perfectly fabulous time. But in the summer, or early autumn of 1989, even that early, it was long before most of us realized how completely the Warsaw Pact was collapsing and the Soviet military threat was disappearing, but even without that, it seemed clear that for the next year, arms control was going to be less interesting. Basic proposals were on the table, the CFE and START proposals were on the table, the INF treaty was concluded, and I thought for the next year we would be fine-tuning in the CFE negotiations, fine-tuning the definition of a tank. Those things are important, but not as much fun as the basic conceptual work that you do in the beginning of a negotiation when you are designing an American or NATO proposal. So, I started looking for a place to spend a sabbatical year. I had no intention of leaving government, I thought they would have to drag me out kicking and screaming. One of the first people I called was Tom Hughes here at Carnegie, who said he wasn't really interested in government people on sabbatical because he felt the prospect of going back would affect what they wrote, which was actually true, I realize that now. I got sabbatical, and was debating between two other institutions, and suddenly Tom called back and said, in effect, if you would be willing to leave government, I'd offer you a job. I'm really not sure why it struck me as the right thing to do, to make a fresh start, to write exactly what I think. Sure, also probably wanting a better balance in my life, more time for my personal life. But the freedom of writing what I want to write, and finding somebody to publish it. I have been pretty lucky in that so far. Before, I usually had to clear it with half the population in Washington. I had probably done the most interesting things I would have been able to do in government. Basically, in my gut it seemed the right thing to do. I wondered if it was just a passing mood, but I have found, still over a year later, I have not had a moment's regret. I keep expecting to regret it, not so much to regret it, but to miss being there in the thick of things, but I haven't yet.

I was just so very lucky, I had a wonderful time. I was able to work on issues that really interested me for and with people whom I admired and liked and enjoyed. In large part by accident, I was in positions where my ideas got a hearing, which is all you can ask. I won some arguments and lost some, but I always felt that I got a fair hearing, I never felt muzzled or ignored.

6

Gender Gap in Management Styles?

We would like to be the advocates of political perestroika—a less adversarial and more consensus-built system—that is what we are more comfortable with. But the bottom line in politics is crude and demanding. It's win or lose. Nothing in between. Living with these contradictions is uncomfortable for any woman in a "man's place." That is what is hard, reconciling one's internal self with the demands of the political system, which is based on male traditions and is still largely male defined.

Gov. Madeleine Kunin[1]

Our particular focus in this portion of our study is the extent to which the female-male distinction is significant in studying the leadership styles of persons in decision-making positions. Are there any discernible differences in the way women and men manage, and if so, what factors might contribute to such differences? We are again going to address the same three variables examined in Section I as influencing individuals in organizations. Our focus now shifts to the impact these three variables—societal factors, organizational factors, and individual factors—have on the tactics or methods women utilize in their careers, and in particular, their styles of leadership.

Societal Factors

But the higher you come up that political scale in people's minds, the more it's a question of leadership, strength, and courage—attributes that we usually give to men.

Gov. Barbara Roberts[2]

Our first variable is societal factors, or the societal stereotypes about what a good leader or manager should be. As Georgia Duerst-Lahti observed, and as we discussed in Chapter 1, most studies to date have suggested that men are widely believed to possess the qualities of successful managers and women are not.[3] Masculine traits are overwhelmingly the norm for top-level administrators. Powell agreed and noted that people have described men as more like good managers than women, and good managers as higher in stereotypically masculine traits than stereotypically feminine traits.[4] He also found that these managerial stereotypes have stayed essentially the same despite the considerable increase in women managers in recent years.

These managerial stereotypes generally have formed around the dichotomy of task-oriented and people-oriented types of behavior. Task-oriented behaviors, such as initiating structure, setting goals, and making decisions are those most associated with the masculine stereotype. People-oriented behaviors, including practices such as showing consideration toward subordinates and soliciting of subordinates' ideas, are those most associated with the feminine stereotype.[5] We shall address each of these general stereotypes separately before trying to evaluate their impact upon foreign policy decision-makers.

Task Orientation

> The idea of leadership is not built into our education—school, home, community. If you say the word "politician" or the word "leader" most people see an image of a person in a suit, with short hair—a man.
>
> Ruth Mandel[6]

Studies of leadership have argued that managers vary in terms of a desirable type of leadership behavior referred to as "task orientation" by Duerst-Lahti, or as "initiating structure" by Powell. What they are both referring to is the extent to which the manager initiates activity in the group, organizes it, and defines the way work is to be done. It includes such behavior as insisting on standards and deciding in detail how tasks will be accomplished.[7] Male leaders are seen to be more likely to engage in task-oriented leadership than women, primarily because of their different socialization experiences. For example, it is argued that men are better prepared to be managers because of such factors as their greater participation in team sports during their formative years. As a result, men bring to the management setting a clearer, stronger and more definite understanding of what they have to do if they are to achieve the objectives they set for themselves.[8] Women on the other hand have been socialized into "learned helplessness." This "feminine discounting habit . . . is a culturally learned tendency for women to discount, minimize, discredit their abilities and achievements."[9]

People-Oriented or Consensual Behavior

Another element of leadership style is the way in which leaders work with others, which can be confrontational or consensual. Powell referred to "consideration behavior" as the extent to which the manager works with others and exhibits concern for the welfare of group members.

Consideration-oriented managers take subordinates' ideas into account and devote attention to the subordinates' satisfaction by seeking to build their self-esteem and showing appreciation and credit for work performed well.[10] Managerial gender stereotypes have generally stressed the conclusion that women are more concerned with consensual, or consideration behavior than men. As Gov. Roberts concluded, "Women represent a very different kind of leadership. . . . Women are more direct than men, yet at the same time more willing to work cooperatively toward solving problems."[11] Studies have shown that women prefer a participatory leadership style, rather than an authoritative style preferred by men.[12] Masculine style would emphasize leading from a position of power, relying on control of resources and the authority of the organization. Women pay more attention to personal abilities and tend not to be as goal oriented as men. Service to profession or to others is a primary motivation. Women prefer collaborative, win-win strategies while men avoid conflict by reverting to authority.[13]

There have been several arguments made to explain women's preference for collaborative strategies. It has been suggested that women tend to adopt such consensual tactics in the context of a different definition of task orientation. For women, power may be conceived in terms of "getting things done." This emphasis on achievement becomes more important than a hierarchical emphasis on domination of subordinates. As a result, women leaders are characterized as being able to handle multiple tasks simultaneously, and as stressing leadership through group-oriented activities. Achievement, in itself, is empowering for women as a result. They do not need to dominate another person to feel powerful.[14]

Alternatively, one could argue that leadership style differences between men and women may be more accurately seen as responses to women's position in hierarchical structures. For example, women are seen as more perceptive about, and more caring of people than their male counterparts. One could argue that these management abilities, as well as consensual tactics in general, are management techniques of resource accrual, used by those who have had to work very hard even to begin to move up the hierarchical ladder. They cannot afford to squander any resource, including the good will of one's compatriots. Equally convincingly, it could be argued that consensual tactics are used by people who are already considered outsiders, that is, tokens, in an attempt to keep from being further alienated within the organization.

Whatever their rationalizations, these two gender stereotypes (men as task-oriented and women as people-oriented) continue to dominate the research on leadership styles. As Rita Mae Kelly, Mary Hale, and Jane Burgess concluded, women and men are perceived as having different behavioral styles. Men are seen as more focused on competition, winning, domination, risk-taking, being team players, as well as more assertive, opportunistic, and more impersonal than women. Meanwhile, women are characterized as better at interpersonal relations, being receptive to ideas, encouraging subordinates, and assuming supportive roles.[15] In the same vein, Duerst-Lahti and Johnson utilized these traditional gender stereotypes as a baseline against which to assess patterns of leadership styles.[16]

Implications of Style Stereotypes

Theoretically there are three possible leadership-style responses to these stereotypes: acting in accordance with them; acting in ways to reinforce, yet disprove the stereotypes; or acting in ways to neutralize managerial stereotypes. Various studies have found evidence of each of these types of response. For example, in terms of acting in accordance with stereotypes, Duerst-Lahti found that women were more perceptive about people than men, though that trait could be caused by the fact that the nondominant group always has a greater incentive to be perceptive than the dominant group.[17] She also found that women used stereotypical female tactics, which may be rational, partially because it will be expected and therefore rewarded, and partially because women confront sanctions when they break stereotypical behavior.[18] Kelly et al., also found support for gender-stereotypical behavior. "Recent research suggests that viable, gender-based behavioral styles, distinct from either assimilationist or an-drogynous styles, are developing. Those leaders who display sex-role behavior, regardless of whether they are male or female, have been found to be more effective managers by their subordinates."[19] However, Kelly et al., do admit that the implications of their findings are limited due to the lack of repetition of the same fact patterns among the mid-level women. Thus they conclude that there are still gender differences due to societal sex roles, but since these differences are neither based on physiological sex differences nor unique to gender differences as grounded in child-hood socialization, that such variations will not continue forever.[20]

In contrast, other theorists argue that in fact anti-stereotypes operate, with some women accepting the conclusions of the stereotype that "mas-culine" behavior is more appropriate for managerial behavior, and adopt-ing "masculine" leadership styles, or portraying themselves as masculine. As Powell noted: "Support for a stereotype of the 'good manager' as masculine has remained steady among men and women, who as manag-ers see themselves as masculine on the whole."[21] Thus, in a sense, anti-stereotypes operate. Women adopt more masculine elements in their style and avoid feminine traits more than men, especially those traits that might be construed as negative.[22] In some instances, this process is so complete that women appear to hold to a more masculine standard than do men:

> Women adopt a greater number of masculine behaviors significantly more than men, four to one. While this is not surprising given the dearth of female stereotypes in a bureaucratic context, that women "out-male" the men is instructive. Women cross gender stereotypes on the characteristics task oriented, managerial, assertive, and straightforward and frank.[23]

It has been argued that women may adopt a male orientation for a number of different reasons, ranging from expedience to socialization. "If reward structures are consistent with dominant perspectives, women who wish to succeed in the public realm may find it advantageous to learn them and act consistently with those perspectives, even when they do not believe in them."[24] Similarly, as Powell has noted, women who pursue the nontraditional career of managers have motives, values, and behaviors similar to those of men who pursue managerial careers. This may be due to self-selection, or it may also be due to a similarity in socializing experiences within the managerial role.[25] Since bureaucratic training is created by men, women may have been resocialized, overcoming feminine characteristics. This reversal may occur because women leaders have had to be exceptional in order to compensate for their early socialization experiences and their socialization experiences within organizations. This is in fact the conclusion of Georgia Duerst-Lahti who found, contrary to stereotype, that it is women who seem to be, and who *have to be,* more focused on task orientation or "getting things done" than men in equivalent positions.[26]

The third theoretical response mechanism is the creation of an androgynous leadership style. Women attempt to neutralize the impact of managerial stereotypes by adopting leadership styles which include elements of both masculine and feminine behavior. Such tactics for women might include more moderate responses to poorly performing subordinates, more subtle influence strategies, and increased accessibility to others.[27] Tactics of this type have been referred to as an "inclusive approach" and studies have indicated that female public executives tend to employ an inclusive approach more than their male counterparts (though this approach is not unique to women, nor do all women adhere to it).[28] In fact Duerst-Lahti's study had indicated that: "for all ten respondents it was not a question of either task or people. Rather, they perceived themselves, and women in general, as concerned with both—by socialization, choice, and necessity."[29] Subsequently, a study by Duerst-Lahti and Johnson concluded that both men and women are no longer tied to gender stereotypes in assessments of good administrators.[30] Furthermore, they concluded that gender-neutral traits are those which are valued most, and contrary to expectations, male traits do not dominate.[31] Similarly, in their study of the Carter Administration, Carroll and Geiger-Parker found that both men and women rejected the conclusion that men make better managers than women. Of their sample, 98.5 percent of women and 82.3 percent of men disagreed or disagreed strongly.[32] Most women administrators believe that stereotypical "female" people-oriented approaches, when combined with attention to task, are optimal for managerial success.[33] A similar acceptance of a more androgynous style was found by Sally Hillgessen. In her study of four female executives, *The Female Advantage*, she concluded that these women have developed ways of leading which break the traditional hierarchical mold, by creating a more "web style" structure which is more flexible and which is responsive to other employees and society at large.[34]

Findings of this nature, indicating that gender stereotypes are changing with more traits being deemed gender neutral, are supported by a study from the Center for Creative Leadership. It found few statistically significant sex differences, with men and women being essentially similar in terms of dominance, capacity for status, sociability, social presence, self-acceptance, good impression, achievement, and intellectual efficiency.[35] Similarly, research by Donnell and Hall found that better managers are in fact not masculine nor feminine, but androgynous, combining task-oriented and people-oriented behavior:

> Managers in their [Donnell and Hall] study who were high achievers successfully integrated their concerns for task and people, average achievers concentrated on the task at the expense of the people performing it, and low achievers showed little concern for either task or people. To paraphrase their results in sex role identity terms, high achievers were androgynous, average achievers were masculine, and low achievers were undifferentiated.[36]

Societal Factors in State and Defense

Task Orientation in State and Defense

> Women have that sense of having to work harder. I had a boss who once said that given two equal candidates, he would always choose the woman because she would work harder.
>
> *Defense Appointee*

Though we were not able to directly observe the men and women in our sample while they were actually managing their offices, we relied on their own self-evaluations. As we shall see, from these reports we gained a picture of women who in general have either tried to adopt masculine behavior or who have adopted an androgynous leadership style, combining task-oriented and people-oriented behaviors.

In an attempt to test the first stereotype of men as task-oriented managers, we looked at several indicators of task orientation or goal motivation. Initially, we asked our respondents a series of questions regarding their policy goals and accomplishments. We first asked if the respondent had a policy goal they hoped to achieve when they took their present position. As the figures in Table 6-1 indicate, men and women were virtually equally likely to have goals, with 71.1 percent of the men and 75.6 percent women saying they had a goal or goals.

When asked to describe their goals, women were slightly more likely to list foreign policy and management goals. The differences with men were not statistically significant, with the exception that Defense career women were more likely to list foreign policy goals than men, 42.9 percent versus 0 percent (breakdown not included in Table). The task orientation of the women was reflected in this quote from a woman at Defense who had only been in the job a year:

> With only one year, the accomplishment has been to set a direction, to build a team, to acquire the assets, to get the money, and to formulate

Table 6-1.   Goals of women and men in the State and Defense Departments

	Men %	Women %
Had a policy goal[a]	71.1	75.6
Foreign policy goal[b]	35.5	45.7
Policy goal (not foreign)[b]	22.6	28.6
Management goal[b]	35.5	45.7
Other goal[b]	6.5	8.6
Achieved goal[c]		
Totally	70.8	54.8
Partially	29.2	35.5

[a] Responses based on the following question: "Did you have any specific policy goals you hoped to achieve when you took this position?"

[b] Multiple responses possible, figures do not add to 100%.

[c] Responses based on the following question: "Have you been able to achieve your policy goal?"

a plan that will work. If you have 50 high-achieving military officers and civilians, you can't be too vague about what you want. So really the accomplishment is to figure out what you want to do and to do it.

Not only were the women as goal-oriented as the men, they were almost as likely as men to achieve the goals, although the women did report more partial successes. This was particularly true for career women in both Departments, especially in Defense where only 23.1 percent of them achieved their goals completely (76.9 percent had partial or complete success). This compared with 63.6 percent of the men indicating complete success and 90.9 percent partial or complete goal attainment. In the State Department 33.3 percent of career women said they had complete success (66 percent partial or complete), while the figures for career men were 63.6 percent and 96.9 percent for complete and at least partial goal achievement, respectively. Among political appointees, the differences were small, with all the women and men reporting total or partial success, generally the former. There was, however, some evidence to support the hypothesis that women might have a different definition of task-orientation, one which focuses upon "getting things done." As one Defense careerist explained:

> I guess it comes to how you reach solutions to problems. Women have different ways of solving problems and I don't mean the nurturing approach so much, I mean the reasoning approach. I find that women have far more patience in exploring alternatives and in having a participative form of consultation than many men. Women are not insecure in admitting that they don't know everything, a lot of men are. I think one of women's great strengths is the willingness, that they have the confidence in their capability to stand up and say "hey, I don't know what's happening, let's get me educated so I can make sure I do a right job." To me that is not a weakness, it's a strength, truly.

There was also some evidence that women's task-orientation was influenced by their status in hierarchical organizations and that the barriers we described in the sections above do limit women's ability to achieve all they hoped to accomplish. A quote from a woman at Defense conveys some of the difficulties encountered by women, "But your job is much more difficult. You have to beat them at their own game. They go around you, and it is a game. It takes longer for you to defeat them at the game and to get anything done. But unfortunately that is the way it works."

Despite the women decision-makers' positive evaluation of their leadership skills, societal stereotypes do persist within the agencies as to women's unsuitability for leadership positions. A few male leaders mentioned the inability of women to make decisions. One man, for instance noted:

> Women in the SFS [Senior Foreign Service] are treated as equal colleagues. Their influence is probably proportionate to their numbers. I might add, and you'll love this, that based on my observations of my wife's all-female office, that women in general get bogged down on appearances, trivialities, perquisites, and petty garbage. Sorry, but I hear it from my wife [a Foreign Service Officer].

This same man in another part of the survey also noted:

> My experience with female colleagues is that they are excellent at under-standing and formulating policy issues, they are quite good at seeing nuances, quite good at laying out the problem and issues, but they are not at all good when it comes to getting a solution to the problem or offering options: where we should go, why we should do it, here is what we should do. That is not universally true, but it is so frequently true that I think it is time to mention it.

Most of the men we interviewed were not so blunt. Perhaps they did not hold stereotypes about women, or perhaps they were unwilling to express them to two women interviewers.

Consensual Behavior at State

Having established that women are as task-oriented as men, the next question becomes whether they are more people-oriented. Do they per-form along the lines of gender-stereotyped concern for others, or do they combine feminine and masculine traits into an androgynous management style? To test this question, we asked respondents to list policy achieve-ments other than their initial goals, and other accomplishments, not necessarily in the area of policy, that they had achieved in their current position. These figures are reported as Achievements and Accomplish-ments respectively, in Table 6-2 (multiple responses were possible for both questions).

With respect to the first area, we still found no significant differences between men and women, although there was a tendency for men to mention foreign policy achievements and women other policy achieve-ments. This difference may be a function of the types of jobs held by men and women, although in answer to another question in the survey women were as likely as men to say their job involved foreign policy.

The interesting results came in the area of accomplishments, where we found a number of significant differences. While men were more likely to continue to mention other policy accomplishments, women more frequently mentioned success in the areas of management and human relations (establishing collegial relations). A couple of examples from the

Table 6-2. Achievements and accomplishments

	Men %	Women %
Foreign policy achievement	58.8	41.7
Other policy achievement	23.5	38.9
Other management policy achievement	29.4	33.3
Management accomplishment	31.4	63.2
Women accomplishment	5.7	18.4
Human development accomplishment	31.4	28.9
Human relations accomplishment	8.6	24.3
Policy accomplishment	31.4	13.2
Other accomplishment	20.0	13.2

responses give a flavor of the things of which the women were proud. In the area of management women mentioned: "efficient management," "good manager of people," "turned back the tide on auditors," "reorganized the Department, made it more efficient." Human relations comments included: "more interagency cooperations," "quality of life improved," "improvement in employee morale."

As the responses indicated, there was evidence here for both goal-oriented activity and people-oriented activity. In the area of management accomplishments, nearly two-thirds (63.2 percent) of the women, as opposed to 31.4 percent of the men, talked about such things as establishing a good staff and improving the organization of the office, activities that fall in the category of "initiating" goal-oriented strategies. This relationship was true, moreover, for all groups of men and women in both Departments. This would seem to negate any hypothesis that contends that women do not focus on management or are not successful at it. Yet there was also evidence of a people orientation. While fewer women listed successes in the area of human relations (collegiality) than they did in management, (24.3 percent and 63.2 percent respectively) they were, by their own reports, more successful with people issues than were men (24.3 percent to 8.6 percent). Women in Defense were particularly likely to mention both these activities. A possible exception to this was human development (staff training) concerns, which men and women seemed equally likely to cite as areas of accomplishment (although the State career women were significantly more likely than State career men to cite success in this area—60 percent versus 15.4 percent).

Part of the discrepancy between men and women in listing human relations and women successes may be tied to the respondents' job titles, as more women than men, especially in Defense, were found in the personnel offices. However, there was some additional evidence in the survey that women were, or at least saw themselves as, more concerned with people issues. We asked respondents (women and men) if there were any special traits they as women or men brought to the job, and if adding more women to the Department would change the way policy is made. Answers to both these questions, and at other points in the interviews, found women mentioning the following qualities: ability to listen; receptivity to the views of others; having intuition, or people sense; having the capacity to get people to talk or negotiate; and sympathy with the people working for them. With respect to the first of these, listening ability, one woman commented regarding women's special traits: "Better listening skills and communication skills. Not inherent in women, but due to socialization (the way society treats men and women)." Receptivity to the views of others is reflected in this quote: "more insight into what opposite numbers see, but maybe that is because I have dealt with some very obtuse men." Several women mentioned intuition or sensitivity to what was happening in negotiations. Examples of this sentiment were reflected in these quotes: "Women are more sensitive to the vibes in the room." "I have an innate feeling for character. I can see beneath the facade of the personality. I have a good people sense." "Intuitive sense is very important. One of the reasons Henry Kissinger was so effective was that he had a very female sense of intuition." More than one woman referred to her capacity of being able to get people to talk or negotiate: "If there is a macho man in the room who can lead others to take the macho position, I can sometimes call their bluff and settle them down to a serious discussion of the issues." This last trait parallels our findings in Chapter 5 that women were more aware of the contributions made by those below them to the policy process. Our women interviewees also evidenced some acceptance of the win-win management style as witnessed in this quote from a woman at Defense in describing her accomplishments:

> Should I personally take credit? I don't see it that way. The way this office functions, we really reinforce each other. So even though you may have priorities, in terms of taking credit, I see it as a collaborative-cooperative effort, at least in this bureau.

If we combine these people skills with the management skills noted earlier, we see that the women in the highest ranks of the foreign policy establishment appeared to display the qualities ascribed to the androgynous leader: concerned about both goals *and* people, and an effective manager too.

There was, however, some suggestion in the data that many of our women respondents found that combining male and female management styles, especially in adopting the aggressive-assertive style more commonly attributed to men, did present some particular problems. On the one hand, women had to avoid the traditional stereotype of women as nonassertive or unable or unwilling to speak up, a perception which is detrimental to the woman in leadership positions. As one man noted, the perceived inability to present one's views was, from his perspective, a reason why some women were less able to influence the policy decisions of the Department of State. The issue for the women in our study, however, generally was not merely how to be more assertive but how to finesse the fine line drawn by sexual stereotypes between assertive and aggressive behavior. The quandary was described by one woman as follows, "Well, I am a little bit too strong. My strong personality has given me whatever I have tried in life. This is not my normal way of being, but I have learned to fight to get what I want in this office. Sometime it isn't too pleasant." Thus, women who want to be successful have to be able to be aggressive, must express opinions and attempt to convince others to follow their suggestions, while hoping to avoid the negative fallout from crossing gender stereotypes. As one woman explained, society often views the successful woman as one who has adopted behaviors inappropriate for her sex:

> People who don't know you, they tend to assume if you're a woman and you got where you are, you are naturally aggressive. Sometimes they think you're going to be naturally confrontational. People believe that in order to be here you have to be very aggressive and acerbic. They generally don't think of you as the person they'd like to be waiting home with dinner.

As both women indicated, assertiveness, real or assumed, places a woman manager in the category of a person at, or over, the boundary of acceptable behavior for a woman companion, although totally within the bounds of appropriate, and indeed required, style for a successful male decision-maker.

Even more problematic for the women we interviewed, and for the same reasons, was the expression of anger and the use of profanities, which like aggression are acceptable for men, but not for women. One woman described the reaction she received to her anger as follows, "When I lose my temper, as I have occasionally, and I have a man as a boss, then it's because I'm a woman. They can lose their temper and it's all right." Another woman told us she was reprimanded for saying "damn" when the men in her group used much worse language. The inability to express anger or to use profanity can be a handicap, at least from the vantage point of one sympathetic male who described the way he could, and women could not, control a meeting.

I'm over six foot tall. I'm over 200 pounds. I have a deep voice. I have a
certain rank and I can gain immediate attention and respect. With some
males, and definitely with women who are smaller in stature, who are
not as vociferous or assertive, if they stand up for what they believe they
are just being bitchy or they're overreaching, not looking at it in a rational
way. If I pound the table or start screaming, I guarantee I get the effect
I want, I do that for calculated purpose—to get what I need. I really
believe if a woman did that she would lose credibility instantaneously.
I think that is unfortunate.

Obviously not all men employ the tactics described, and not all women
are mild-tempered, but the line is apparently broader for men than
women. Societal stereotypes about appropriate behavior for women did
hamper or impinge upon our women managers to the extent that they
were perceived as crossing some invisible "style" boundary. Thus these
social limitations do present some restrictions on the leadership styles of
women in the foreign policy arena.

Organizational Factors

Women as a group may not fit organizations based on male values,
but individual women may be recruited because they "fit" (or are
willing to fit) the existing system.

Georgia Duerst-Lahti[37]

The next issue concerns the extent to which the structure of an organization will impact upon women's leadership styles. As described in Chapter 2, a major difference between men and women decision-makers is
the environment in which they operate. Research has suggested that
situations in which there is a lack of fit between the characteristics of the
employees, and the characteristics of the organization within which they
work, could frustrate careers in a number of ways, or may require that an
employee modify his or her traits, styles, or behaviors.[38] Most organizations can be characterized as projecting a gender ethos favorable for men,
and thus women must either adapt to this ethos or see their careers
hindered. "Women as a group attempting to act in powerful ways in
organizational power positions may be round pegs in square holes,"
unless they are able to "share, or at a minimum be knowledgeable in and
behave in accordance with, the culture of the organization. This may
require adopting habits and values which run counter to those which
they prefer."[39] As we saw in Chapter 2, gender ethos is a reflection of an
organization's historical forces, the ecological context, internal topography, and social demography. An organization's imbalanced sex ratio and

hierarchical structure impact particularly on women, especially those in top management levels.[40] The interesting question thus becomes, in what ways do women respond differently to these organizational characteristics?

As we described earlier, the imbalanced sex ratios in the Departments of State and Defense have relegated women to Kanter's "token" status, and this status has major implications for women's leadership styles. The token status of women is most clearly seen in response to a question concerning the number of women colleagues a respondent had. We found that on average women had less than four (3.8) women co-workers, while men reported even fewer (2.3). Many of the women (19.4 percent) and men (18.5 percent) had *no* women with whom they worked as equals. These numbers convey a sense of the paucity of women in these ranks and the near-isolation of the women in the upper echelons of the two Departments. In order to gauge our respondent's perceptions of women's token status, we asked them if they felt there were "too many," "too few," or "just about the right number of" women in their Department. Tables 6-3 and 6-4 report their responses. Stating the obvious, no one responded that there were too many women in their Department. However, beyond that, the answers show a vast difference in perception between men and women, elements of which are statistically significant. Overall, 25.8 percent of the men, and only 2.8 percent of the women judged that there were adequate numbers of women in their Department, and the difference was even greater at State. However the breakdowns by types of position on Table 6-4 show the greatest disparities. While virtually 100 percent of the women in all categories believed that there were too few women in their Departments, 50 percent of the male appointees at State and 100 percent of the male appointees at Defense saw the number of women as

Table 6-3.   Number of women in the Department[a]

	Too Few	About Right	Too Many
All men	74.2	25.8	0.0
All women	97.2	2.8	0.0
Men at State	73.3	26.7	0.0
Women at State	100.0	0.0	0.0
Men at Defense	75.0	25.0	0.0
Women at Defense	95.7	4.3	0.0

[a] Responses based on the following question: "Do you think the number of women in the Department of State [Defense] is about right, or are there too few women or too many women?"

Table 6-4. Number of women in Department[a]

	Too Few	About Right	Too Many
Career men at State	81.8	18.2	0.0
Career women at State	100.0	0.0	0.0
Appointee men at State	50.0	50.0	0.0
Appointee women at State	100.0	0.0	0.0
Career men at Defense	85.7	14.4	0.0
Career women at Defense	92.9	7.1	0.0
Appointee men at Defense	0.0	100.0	0.0
Appointee women at Defense	100.0	0.0	0.0

[a] Responses based on the same question as in Table 6–3.

sufficient. The polarities with the appointee women are striking. Such findings would seem to indicate that resistance to the inclusion of women increases as one moves up the hierarchical levels. It also again reinforces the impression that women in Defense face a much more difficult position than do those at State.

One might also speculate that the divergence in male and female perceptions must exacerbate the effects of women's token status. Kanter argued that tokens are in a disadvantageous situation in three respects: they are subject to increased performance pressure; they are confronted with boundary-heightening activities by the dominants; and they have a greater probability of being classified according to stereotypes.[41] Token women may react to such pressure in two ways; they may try to over-achieve relative to their peers, or they may seek to become "socially invisible." This latter is particularly difficult, because by their very presence, tokens also make dominants more aware of what dominants have in common, while at the same time posing a threat to that commonality.

> For example, if "boys will be boys," dominant males are even more so when token females are present. They may try to highlight what they can do in personal, sexual, and business affairs as men, in contrast to what women can do. They also do not want women around at all times, choosing to exclude them from certain secretive activities.[42]

Kanter calls this process boundary-heightening, and as Powell observed, token women are left with only two responses to boundary-heightening activities by men: they may accept isolation, opting for friendly but distant relations with male members; or they may try to become insiders by defining themselves as exceptional members of their sex and turning against other women who attempt to join the group. This would account for the "queen bee syndrome" where women ostracize or avoid other women in social settings if men are present.[43] Finally, token women have few options for responding to role encapsulation. They may accept a stereotypical role, which could limit their participation in policy-making, and which might lead to programmed male responses. If they try to fight being assigned a stereotypical role, they risk being classified as "iron maidens" and face rejection by the group. Alternatively, they may deliberately attempt not to exhibit any characteristics that might support the stereotypes. As Susan Carroll and Ella Taylor noted, this pressure to conform to male norms is greatest in situations in which the proportion of women is small.[44]

The impact of token status can also be amplified by other elements of gender ethos, particularly hierarchical structure and elements of social demography which define the organization's mission. In skewed organizations, women are marginalized by their token status. In hierarchical organizations, women are marginalized in the lower levels by lack of opportunity and sex segregation, because they supposedly do not have the same characteristics as those who dominate the structure. In both circumstances, women have to exert more effort in order to have their contributions to departmental decisions taken seriously. Duerst-Lahti described the dynamic as follows:

> Yet, this . . . case suggests that women still take more medicine than men
> to achieve a similar state of health in bureaucratic power politics. Most
> of the medicine comes in the form of extra effort to achieve the same
> end with few of the men recognizing the dynamic occurs.[45]

Women must also work harder and accomplish more in situations in which they have less initial credibility. On one level, this is true for all women in senior level positions. For example, a study of federal employees in SES positions uncovered the stereotypical opinion that women generally were not qualified for management positions:

> Perceptions regarding the qualifications of female senior executives also
> vary according to sex and race of respondents. . . . 20 percent of females
> and 5 percent of males indicated that women were more qualified; 23
> percent of males compared to 6 percent of females say women are less
> qualified.[46]

This lack of credibility would be even more pervasive in situations in which the mission of the organization has been traditionally seen as being one for which women were not suited, or about which they were considered not to be knowledgeable, such as foreign policy. In such situations, studies have indicated that the process of gaining credibility often took over a year. During the "noncredible" time period, women felt that they had to work harder, know more, and constantly be on guard. Credibility thus was an issue for the women in a way few of the respondents believed it was for a man.[47] Women thus have to develop different strategies to build credibility. In her interviews, Duerst-Lahti questioned whether women use different tactics to have their contributions to the department taken seriously, and she found that 69 percent of women and 23 percent of men perceived that different tactics were utilized.[48] Tactics which can be employed to build credibility include: planning extensively; doing "homework" to be thoroughly prepared; presenting a logical and well-documented argument; and maneuvering behind the scenes. These tactics directly reflect the perception that women have a harder time, but they are not stereotypical "female" approaches. Tactics differ by gender only to the extent that women need to put forth this additional effort and most men do not. As one female respondent in Duerst-Lahti's study put it, "We need to be very capable, have a superior knowledge base and work hard. Men do less of all of these." As another said, "Male deadweights are shoveled to the corner; it's made obvious for a woman." These tactics require women to invest more time and effort than men for similar results, but they do not fall within gender stereotypes.[49] The task of developing credibility is important for women not only in their relationships with their peers and superiors, but in regards to their subordinates as well. Few managers can maintain a style of leadership that does not yield the desired responses from their employees. Thus even subordinates have an influence on the leadership styles of the managers. Subordinates who engage in gender stereotyping are likely to have different expectations of female and male managers, to reinforce different behaviors from them and to behave differently themselves to male and female managers.[50]

Organizational Factors at State and Defense

The review of the literature suggested some disagreement over the management style of women in the context of skewed organizations. Our data allows us to explore this question in some detail as regards women in the field of foreign policy. As we saw earlier, one of the key leadership traits of our women managers was high achievement motivation. They perceived that they work harder than men and must continuously strive to prove themselves. This was particularly true in Defense where the combined factors of token status and a military, macho environment continually threatened women's credibility.

Not surprisingly, given this overview and Kanter's hypothesis, being a token presented some special problems for women in senior management in the two Departments. Indeed, nearly one-third (31.7 percent) of the women reported that being one of only a few women in a position of authority in their Department affected their job performance. Interestingly, all of the women who evaluated their power in this way could be found in the Department of Defense, where more than half of the women (52 percent) claimed they were so restricted. The problem seemed an issue for both career and political appointees with 56.3 percent and 44.4 percent, respectively, agreeing that their gender limited their influence. A related question showed a similar divergence between the two Departments. When women were asked if being female limited their ability to influence foreign policy, 35.9 percent felt it did, although the vast majority of women did not feel so limited. In the State Department one in five (20 percent) answered in the affirmative. However among women in the Defense Department, the figure was closer to one in two (45.8 percent). (See Table 6-5.)

The responses to both questions revealed some of the problems women face in managing in the Departments. One woman explained her problems as follows: "It makes it tougher. You really have to know your environment well. There are barriers and you have to overcome them." For several of the other women respondents the barriers also seemed in evidence:

I think I would have been in a better position as a guy. I don't think I would have been in the same position as long as I have, if I had been a

Table 6-5. Being a woman limits ability to influence foreign policy[a]

	Limited For Women	
	Yes	No
Women Overall	35.9	64.1
Women in State	20.0	80.0
Women in Defense	45.8	54.2
Men Overall	16.7	83.9
Men in State	22.2	77.8
Men in Defense	7.7	92.3

[a] Responses are based on the following questions: (Women only) Do you think being a women limits your ability to influence foreign policy decisions? (Men only) Do you think your female counterparts have less influence on foreign policy decisions?

man. At the same time, if I had been a man, I would have been much more forceful about getting myself that job. I have done very well. But then I stop and think, if I were a man would I be here? I would have done other things.

Still another woman commented that being a woman resulted in "lack of career development, lack of promotions, discrimination with respect to jobs, discrimination with respect to being used in a powerful capacity." For a woman at Defense the problem was one of credibility:

> The way society is, a man is assumed competent till he opens his mouth and proves he isn't. A woman is assumed she isn't until she opens her mouth and proves she is. Very subtle kind of thing, but it requires energy and time to overcome. So it keeps us from being as effective as we might be.

Not all the respondents agreed that their own influence was limited, but often their negative answers to the question suggested otherwise. One woman replied no to the question and then went on to describe how when she was first appointed to the position, a man had used her gender as a reason for not sending her to Japan to do work for the Department.

Awareness of the fact, that being the only woman (or one of a handful) can affect their job performance, was also reflected in the responses, as the following quotes from senior women at Defense clearly show: "Probably initially I was very self-conscious about being the only woman in the room. Now that doesn't phase me." "Because we stand out like sore thumbs, you recognize you are always on parade." Conscious of their "oneness," or of being the first or lead woman, (as Kanter hypothesized) many women in both Departments indicated that they feel pressure to work harder and to prove themselves. More specifically, in response to the question of whether they have to work harder than men, 68.3 percent of the women in our survey said yes. This was particularly true for career women in both Departments. More than 85 percent of the career women at State and 69 percent of the similarly situated women at Defense said they had to work harder. One women, in answering the question, also commented, "They [women] have to work smarter because of the way the culture is now." A senior woman a State elaborated, "It's always been my theory that when you start off in a job and you are a woman, you always work ten percent harder." Another woman described her response to being one of few senior women by noting:

> You feel like you try harder. You wouldn't want to embarrass your sex. So I think you are conscious of that. Gosh, sometimes you walk in the room and you're the only woman and the room is filled with all these

biggies. It makes you conscious. So you better look right, act right, be right.

As a result, women need to prove themselves in order to prove that a woman can do the job. This requirement is often explicitly stated by the male superiors for whom the women work. A senior woman at Defense described her experience as follows:

> When I was appointed, it was the first time a woman had held this position officially in the DOD. Women just don't hold these positions and it has worked out. The fellow who hired me, the Assistant Secretary at that time, let me know that if I wanted to keep this job I had to cut it. I let him know, in no uncertain terms, that if I couldn't cut it, he would be the first to know. That's how I was greeted here. There was a question if I was going to be able to hold my own, and I think I have and then some.

Many of the women felt they needed to continue to prove themselves in every new situation and with every new group of men:

> I think being a women partly limits my ability to influence Navy policy but it doesn't completely restrict it. It takes longer to build rapport and establish capabilities. You come with no certificates that say you know something and so you have to continue to prove to each new guy who comes in every three years that you do in fact have some knowledge.

For at least some of the women the need to prove themselves was linked to the consciousness that they are cutting a path for other women to follow. When asked if being one of a few women affected her performance, a career woman at Defense replied:

> Only in the sense one feels a responsibility to ensure you do it well because of all the young women who will be coming up behind you. There have certainly been a lot of people who have had good influences on me, and they mostly have been women.

As noted earlier, Kanter hypothesized that as tokens, women in male-dominated organizations, confronted with additional performance pressures, have two strategies: overachieving or becoming socially invisible. As the quotations above indicate, most of the women found that as one of few, invisibility was not an option. Rather they continually tried to prove themselves and to establish their credibility and visibility. As one senior woman at State commented:

> I don't go anywhere I'm not prepared. I am willing to work hard. I'm willing to put in the stamina—the actual physical stamina. I really don't have any airs and some days I really wish I had them. I watch people become famous, and you really need airs. You've got to become a personality and I don't have it. That's what makes you an effective bureaucrat. The same thing that makes you an effective bureaucrat disqualifies you [from being famous]. I think I have a decent sense of humor. I'm not afraid of men. When I see a group of men, competition bells don't go off. But I'm not a quiet performer. *I want credit.* There is another group of women out there who take great perverse pride in sort of being the librarian in the back room and just getting patted on the head. It has been an unfortunate, generational thing. But if I come in and say something off-the-wall, I usually get somebody's attention because I'm not an off-the-wall kind of person.

As this quote exemplifies, very few of our women made any reference to aiming for the second option of social invisibility. Although one did note, "Men need an external manifestation of their power and there are women who don't need, are content to be effective quietly as opposed to advertising it." She placed herself in this latter category.

As noted, token women also confront a variety of boundary-heightening activities by men intended to reinforce the bonds among the dominant group and to exclude the tokens. For instance, a quarter of our women respondents felt that male colleagues often interrupt them when they are talking, which has proven to be a problem for women in other settings. As we saw in terms of stereotypes in general, women have the option of either accepting or confronting these boundaries. For example, in an attempt to bridge boundary-heightening measures, one woman at Defense, a fast-rising political appointee, played a great game of golf, which a sister appointee felt was a factor in the former's success (a strategy the second appointee soundly rejected, as one she would not adopt). There was also some evidence of other women consciously rejecting assigned stereotypical roles and adopting mannerisms they believed would make them "fit in." To quote one woman at Defense:

> I have always been conscious of the fact that I was in a statistical minority and that bad action on my part had an implication greater than perhaps for a male counterpart. So I am probably more reserved and more careful. Very conscious of not wanting to be perceived with any of the bad characteristics that are sometimes associated with women in authority, for example the power-trip type in the grey pin stripe suit with the Ivy League button-down shirt.

Male boundary building and stereotyping seems more prominent in Defense, and the atmosphere for women in the Defense Department seemed to most closely fit the expectations of Kanter concerning tokens, Though these activities are not absent in State, it does appear that at State that gender is less of a hindrance than at Defense.

In an attempt to evaluate the effects of women's token status in reference to the minimizer-maximizer debate, we asked our policy-makers if having more women in their Department would affect the content of foreign policy or the way in which policy is made. As the data in Table 6-6 indicate, the vast majority of both men and women claimed it would make no difference. Though women were more likely than men to indicate that it would make a difference, again we see significant differences between State and Defense. At State both men and women overwhelmingly reject the notion that employing more women would affect policy or policy implementation. It was really only the women in Defense, particularly the career women, who anticipated that increasing the number of women would have an impact, which may be an additional reflection of the barriers women face in that Department. Thus the differences between

Table 6-6. Would having more women in the Department impact on foreign policy or the way policy is made?[a]

	No	Yes
All Men	91.4	8.6
All Women	75.0	25.0
Men at State	94.4	5.6
Women at State	93.8	6.3
Men at Defense	88.2	11.8
Women at Defense	60.0	40.0
Career men at State	92.3	7.7
Career women at State	100.0	0.0
Appointee men at State	100.0	0.0
Appointee women at State	88.9	11.1
Career men at Defense	86.7	13.3
Career women at Defense	46.2	53.8
Appointee men at Defense	100.0	0.0
Appointee women at Defense	85.7	14.3

[a] Responses based on the following question, "Do you think having more women in the Department of State [Defense] would have an impact on foreign policy and/or the way policy is made?"

men and women on these issues seemed to be more a function of career, rather than being gender-driven. As one woman in Defense explained: "I don't think gender would make a difference in policy. I just think it would be good for women to have more women here."

The third impact of token status is the increased reliance on sexual stereotypes. As was noted earlier, gender stereotyping is more prevalent in hierarchical organizations and in organizations in which there is a skewed sex ratio. These characteristics fit both the State and Defense Departments, and thus one could speculate that women might adopt strategies to make themselves "invisible," or conversely women might be convinced of the necessity of working even harder. The impact of such stereotypes has proven to be related to several characteristics of the individual utilizing these generalizations. Older individuals, or those who hold more traditional attitudes towards women and their role in society, are more likely to see working women in stereotypical terms. Additionally, persons who have been isolated from women, or who have not worked with women in the past will tend to rely more on stereotypes.[51]

This increased reliance on stereotypes is a characteristic not only of one's hierarchical peers or superiors, but can also be common among a decision-maker's subordinates as well. When subordinates engage in such gender stereotyping, they will judge managers whose behavior fits the stereotype more favorably than those who adopt varying patterns of behavior. For example, female managers are judged more favorably when their behavior fits the feminine stereotype: women using a personal approach will be judged more favorably than one using a task-oriented approach. If one agrees with Powell that subordinates' responses do have a major impact on the leadership styles of managers, then one would assume that such an impact would be most prevalent in situations in which gender stereotyping is high.

We have some evidence of this phenomenon of increased reliance on stereotyping from both superiors and subordinates in the volunteered comments of our respondents. One woman recalled that "Over the course of the years, I have been in an authoritative position over men and that's a real problem for some men." One characterized the unease of men who work for a woman, "There is an attitude that one's prestige with one's male colleagues is negatively affected by working with or for a woman." At the other end of the spectrum, one woman noted, when she was confronted with a superior officer who could not accept taking advice from a woman, she used to send information to him through her male assistants. The problem seems more notable in Defense where women must confront men with military backgrounds or who are currently still officers in a branch of the service. Three high-ranking women in Defense described the situation as follows: "It makes it very much harder to deal with the military because the military is very much male-oriented." "In terms of military requirements, in terms of military manpower, being a civilian and being a woman is a disadvantage." "Particularly in dealing with the Pentagon and the military, I sometimes have difficulty in getting taken seriously." Another woman, when asked whether she had ever experienced discrimination, described direct sabotage attempts by an admiral who worked with her as follows:

> One person, out of six. He requested I be removed from the job. After spending six months deliberately undermining everything I did: counter-manding my orders to my officers, encouraging them to set me up so I would not look good. I'd be briefing the boss and the wrong slides would come up, and I found out afterwards he'd have them changed at the last minute and not tell me. That sort of thing. There were two problems with him. One was his basic belief woman's place was in the home, barefoot and pregnant. And the other, he was threatened by intelligence. Not real sharp as admirals go—most are real sharp. He just didn't under-stand Washington. He just wasn't capable of dealing with the system.

Not all the women felt that their authority as a woman manager-boss was weakened by the military presence at the Department, rather they reported the military tradition of following orders of superiors reinforced their authority over the military officers who worked for them. Though one woman indicated some resistance on the part of subordinates, she felt "the hierarchical structure of the military would make it easier to be a woman in that structure because you just do away with a lot of the hundred ways to *not do* something you ask somebody to do." Not all the women interviewed believed being a woman means diminished credibil-ity. A political appointee said flatly, "No, once you get a job at this level, you get it because of your qualifications and you are judged on [that]. I would hate to see a woman get a job because she is a woman." Another referred to a different kind of advantage:

> I've had some advantages and disadvantages. When I'd come through with a very creative solution to a problem, when I was early into the position, I would get double credit for it because, "my God, she can think." However, they might not have asked me because they might have assumed, "well she wouldn't know." But once you came through you'd get more credit than a man would have gotten. Now because I've been around for a long time, that has evened out.

Indeed, several women reported that their sex could be an advantage in influencing the decisions in their Departments because they were remembered more readily than their male colleagues or because of their uniqueness. However, one problem with being unique is that you cannot be mediocre. As one appointee noted:

> Another thing I resent, but it is so true. A woman who is very good at her job gets a lot of credit. Sometimes she's considered an exception, but people can't accept that men don't have a corner on mediocrity. There are mediocre women too. Women have a right to fail.

While the women at State and Defense confront a number of problems in trying to exercise leadership, overall they reported that the people who work for them like them, respect them, and follow their lead. Thus it seems that the difficulty of being a woman boss can be negated somewhat, if a woman blends her people- and task-oriented skills, thus inspiring those who work for her.

Sexual Discrimination

> Here is a person who is in charge of protecting rights of women and other groups in the workplace and he is using his position of power for personal gain . . . and he did it in a very ugly and intimidating way.
>
> *Anita Hill*[52]

As discussed in Chapter 2, the elements of organizational ethos combine to create a situation which has in the past and continues in the present to discriminate against women in leadership positions. Such discrimination not only hinders women's influence and their career advancement, but it also serves as a key source of stress, in women's already stressful situations. Through organizational decisions and practices, men perpetuate outmoded stereotypes about female behavior, asserting differences where none exist, and then using these alleged differences as justifications for the status quo and their privileged position therein.[53] The focus here is on examining the types of leadership styles women adopt in response to the organizational practices which have tended to, and continue to, discriminate against them.

There are several ways in which women can respond to discriminatory practices: they can deny that they exist (or deny that they apply to them); they can accept them as either legitimate, or at least unassailable at that point in time; or they can challenge them. Denial is the basis of what Roberta Sigel and Lauren Burnbauer refer to as the "Not-Me Syndrome." Though women may admit that women in general are discriminated against, they perceive of themselves as exceptions, exceptions who are treated equitably.[54]

Alternatively, some women respond to stereotypical practices by accepting the validity of the masculine stereotype and practices, and attempting to conform to the dictates of such stereotypes. This tactic has been found to be most prevalent in women managers with less than five years of experience.[55] Once women managers have gained experience, and begun to feel more secure in their positions, this tactic becomes less appealing. This tactic can also be adopted by those who recognize the effects of discriminatory practices, but who are also cognizant of the costs (both personal and professional) involved in challenging such practices, and are simply unwilling to suffer the consequences of such resistance.

Most studies have found, however, that when faced with discriminatory practices, women in leadership positions tended to put even greater emphasis on achievement or success, rather than respond by giving in. For example, Donnell and Hall found that in comparison with men, women managers were more concerned with opportunities for growth, autonomy, and challenge. The women managers exhibited a higher-achieving motivational profile than the male managers. They argued that women have chosen this leadership style because they have had to overcome stereotypical attitudes about their unsuitability for management.[56] Another tactic women have adopted as a means of resisting discriminatory practices is to try to work to end such practices and to assist other women in order to ameliorate the effects of discrimination. Women in leadership positions act in ways which are sensitive to the needs of women and which attempt to bring issues which are of particular interest to women to the forefront. Such behavior meets feminist expectations that women officials will be conscious of and/or responsive to women's life experiences and their concerns, and that women officials will "act for" other women by working to insure that public policy adequately reflects women's interests.[57]

Discrimination at State and Defense

As discussed earlier, discriminatory practices have persisted in both Departments, and nearly half of all the women in our sample report having experienced discriminatory treatment. However, how women handle this form of behavior varies. The strategy of denial of discrimination comes through in a number of the interviews, especially with older women and political appointees. A woman who fit both categories and who had been in the State Department for over 40 years said simply, in response to whether she had ever experienced discrimination, "No. Not that I'm personally aware of." Though the Department had faced lawsuits in which the courts generally agreed that sex discrimination existed in the Department, perhaps she simply did not think these issues affected her directly. Another woman at State expressed this sentiment when in response to the same question she commented:

> No, I've done so well in my career. I came here in April 1971 as a GS-11 and I was promoted to the senior ranks in 1986, 15 years later. And I may have been discriminated against and I probably have been but, on the other hand, I don't know of any way it has affected my life.

Many of the career women in both Departments who have risen in the ranks have apparently also been successful in dealing with discrimination by ignoring it, or in their early years on the job simply not seeing it. One "old hand" at State, for example, saw the past practice of limiting women's assignments abroad as an example of chivalry, not discrimination. Another woman described her reaction to discrimination by noting, "It is something you deal with. If you carry it on your shoulder, it will weigh you down."

Confronted with a series of stereotypes about one's ability to function in a male-dominated arena, many of the women did note the need to be prepared and to work harder than men. A senior woman commented:

> But you still have to work harder to earn, to work your way up. Men work very hard too so it is hard to say what the extra dimension is—but you do have to prove yourself quickly. Reputations are formed quickly and they're very hard to get rid of. Do you want a reputation as a hard worker, who thinks on your feet, and is at the right place at right time? Reputations are established at the junior level, and I think it is harder for a woman to correct a bad impression than it is for a man.

Consequently, a political appointee noted that extra effort and being the only woman could actually work to her advantage. "People who have influence are people who have done their homework and are not afraid to speak up. In the enforcement community, being a female helps you stick out. Sometimes an asset, because you're not a middle-aged white guy in a gray suit."

It is probable that the responses exemplified by these women are what is needed if you want to move up the ranks, at least that seems to be the position of many of our interviewees. Although several did note that because of discrimination, the move up those ranks had been slower. At least one woman reported a novel solution. The secret for her present success in dealing with, or eliminating male discriminatory practices, was for both her male colleagues and her to have a woman boss. "Having a woman boss makes a lot of men with whom I deal pay attention. These are the same men who I've regularly seen put down women. But they can't be very successful at it now, because they have a woman boss." Only a few women responded to discriminatory personnel policies by filing lawsuits, for example, Alison Palmer at State. As the profile in Chapter 2 detailed, Ms. Palmer and others who chose this route often have done so at great personal cost to themselves financially, personally, and professionally. After her first suit was filed, Alison Palmer was warned that her complaint might "mitigate against her chances for promotion."[58] To cover the costs of the second lawsuit, Ms. Palmer has sent half her pension to the attorneys, and had spent over $200,000.[59] The ramifications of the decision to fight discrimination and harassment were also seen in the recent Anita Hill-Clarence Thomas hearings. The hearings not only demonstrated the problem women face demonstrating credibility, but subjected Ms. Hill to numerous personal attacks as well. A wider repercussion of this debacle appeared soon thereafter, when three women who were purported victims of non-governmental discrimination refused to testify before the Senate, fearing the same type of grilling and criticism to which Ms. Hill was subjected.[60] Thus, it seems that the ability to respond to discriminatory treatment by ignoring it or in other low-key ways, while not a useful strategy for eliminating the practices themselves, have helped many of the women in our sample to make it to the top of the management team in both Departments.

Individual Factors

As was discussed in Chapter 3, women have to deal with a unique set of "stressors," in terms of individual factors, that men encounter less often.[61] In particular, men seldom experience conflicting demands of career and family life because they traditionally have not been expected to stay home with their families. These conflicting demands can lead to increased stress for women, forcing them to develop coping strategies of one sort or another. The effects of this conflict were reflected in the statistics that demonstrated that fewer female managers than male managers are married or have children. For those who have these conflicting demands these problems can be acute. Women may have to restrict career opportunities or delay advancement based on family demands. At this point, the aspect of this conflict between professional and personal requirements which is important is the extent to which these individual factors affect the management styles of women in leadership positions.

Individual Factors in State and Defense

Management styles can have two interrelated functions: tactics which leaders apply to their own careers, and tactics utilized in relating to subordinates. As has been pointed out in a number of other chapters, the primary tactic women have adopted in response to societal and organizational factors has been to work harder. This has been equally true in response to individual factors, however in this realm, the costs and/or benefits accrue more personally. For example, the time devoted to work decreases the time available for private personal activities. A few representative quotes give the flavor of these women's lives: "When I was younger, I was working long hours and not able to pick up my child from child-care on time." "I was tired all the time. You feel you aren't doing anything well. No free time." "You must be willing to deal with tiredness and no leisure." In this vein, one Defense careerist described women in leadership positions:

> They think they have to. Their whole feeling, their psyche tells them that, "I have to be twice as good as he is in order to be rated equal to him." So therefore they will work longer hours, take less time off, will not go take two hours at lunch to go do their jogging, they'll do that during the dark hours. There is still a tendency on the part of many women to do that.

On the other hand, working harder can also produce personal benefits. A woman appointee in Defense felt that it contributed to increased stamina:

> I think that women emotionally are much tougher, maybe intellectually. I am in danger of generalizing in ways that probably aren't wise. But emotionally we have more stamina certainly than men. Intellectually perhaps we are more logical, but that may be the accident of my experience, rather than a valid generalization.

In particular, in Chapter 3 the primary focus was upon the extent to which individual factors impacted upon women's career paths or the management of their own careers. However, at this juncture, the subsequent question becomes whether having to function under these increased stressors alters the ways in which women managers relate to their subordinates.

We have some evidence that the impact of individual factors goes beyond one's personal career and consequently gives women managers more interest in and understanding of the impact of these variables upon their subordinates. The more significant impact of individual factors on the management styles of women (as compared to men) was initially in evidence when we asked women to list the goals they had when taking their positions. Women were more likely than men (45.7 percent to 35.5 percent) to list management goals (see Table 6-1). Women's greater interest in staff management was also indicated in their ratings of their own accomplishments: 28.9 percent of the women listed human development accomplishments; 24.3 percent listed human relations accomplishments; and 18.4 percent described women's issue accomplishments (see Table 6-2). Women's issues included attempts to increase the number and status of women in the Departments: human relations issues included not only establishing good relations with subordinates and improving employee morale, but also promoting equal employment standards and opportunities. Human development responses focus on development and training for staff.

Women's concern for subordinates has two sub-elements, extending both to an awareness of their hard work the contributions they can make, but also to their personal problems as well. Women managers thus act in ways to reinforce the positive elements in their staff and in ways to ameliorate the negative impacts of these factors. At one level, women tend to be more open to allowing subordinates greater influence in policy-making. As discussed in Chapter 5, women were more likely than men (63 percent to 52.6 percent) to see policy-making occurring below them in the hierarchy. This was particularly true for women at State, over 81 percent of whom saw those in lower grades making policy. Women also tired to encourage subordinates through mentoring activities. As was discussed in Chapter 3, women frequently espoused on obligation to mentor others, frequently younger women, in an attempt to assist them in overcoming institutional and societal barriers. In this same vein, a careerist in Defense noted that she tried to acknowledge women's hard work whenever possible, "Women are much easier to work with. I promote people on the basis of competence, and the women have been *much* more competent, the rating isn't even close."

At another level, women tend to be more sympathetic to subordinates' personal problems as well. As one of our respondents explained she considered herself as:

> More sympathetic to people who work under me and around me. More sympathetic to their foibles than men. Men tend to be more punitive. That makes me better liked by the people who want my opinion and don't feel I will be vindictive. People like to work for me because of that.

Thus, overall the additional influence of personal factors has served to sensitize women and make them managers who are more committed to promoting less stressful working conditions for their subordinates (see the following interview with Sheila Buckley).

Conclusion

The focus of this analysis has been the leadership styles of women in foreign policy formulation, specifically addressing the factors which determine or influence the selection of leadership styles. In particular, societal factors (gender stereotypes), organizational ethos, and individual factors have all been found to impact upon the ways in which women behave in organizations. This analysis of the management styles of the women in senior executive positions in both Departments was somewhat encouraging. While women face a number of stressors that should limit their managerial skills, the data suggests most were able to overcome these limitations, at least to a large degree. These women rated their management successes highly; and their ability to combine people skills and task orientation facilitated their rise to positions of authority. Moreover, there was evidence that these people-task-orientation attributes have allowed these women to make significant contributions to our nation's foreign policy. As we saw earlier, the women were more likely than the men to have a foreign policy goal, and were nearly as likely to list it as an area of achievement. Further when asked to rate their own influence in the foreign policy arena on a seven point scale, we found women's scores were virtually as high as those of men.

All was not completely equal, however. There was a somewhat disturbing tendency for women to report less than complete success in obtaining their goals. Possibly the limitations discussed in the earlier sections have a dampening affect on women's management achievements relative to public policy in both Departments, but especially in Defense. However, either in compensation for these problems, or because of a special interest, women reported more success than men in managing their staffs and dealing with people. In sum, our women managers appeared to be able to overcome the limitations of being in rather inhospitable environments. Indeed, they seemed to bring a special dimension to the management arena: a dimension that allowed them to have successes where none or few might be expected.

In terms of the maximizer-minimizer debate, the results in this chapter were most compatible with the maximizer school. Our women managers seemed to adopt a leadership style, particularly in terms of people-orientation and support for subordinates, that was uniquely, or more generally, female. There was, however, also support for the minimizer school in that the women were equally likely as men to be goal oriented. Whether the differences between the men and women in our sample were "inborn" or socialized responses to a foreboding environment was not discernable from our data. What was clear was that the Departments do shape the perceptions of women as to the problems or difficulties they face as managers. Women at Defense were painfully conscious of their token status, the limits this placed on their influence, and their need to continually strive to overcome them.

Interview

SHEILA R. BUCKLEY

The "Personal" Manager

Sheila Buckley has served within the Office of the Secretary of Defense (OSD) in several staff and managerial positions, covering Latin American and African Affairs, Security Assistance, and long range Security Policy Planning. She is now working on arms control issues as the Director for Multilateral Negotiations in the Office of the Assistant Secretary of Defense for International Security Policy. In 1990, as a result of her work in chemical weapons arms control, Ms. Buckley was awarded the Department of Defense Distinguished Civilian Service Award. She serves on the Advisory Board of the professional society Women in International Security and is a member of the International Institute for Strategic Studies.

My attention was first turned to international politics by the Hungarian revolution in 1957. I graduated from Pomona College with a major in international relations in 1961. By that time, most of us in that field were excited by the appealing idealism of the Kennedy policy visions. Moreover, at that time government service was seen as the place to be to make good things happen. After earning a Masters at Johns Hopkins, I came into OSD as a career civil servant in 1963. My OSD tenure has included welcome interludes, such as two years at the National War College (student and then faculty), further graduate study, and a year at the State Department's Senior Seminar. For the last decade I've worked on arms control.

The Office of International Security Policy provides, for Defense, an interface with other agencies within the National Security Council (NSC) system having security planning responsibilities, such as the Department of State and the Arms Control and Disarmament Agency. My subject areas are chemical and biological weapons arms control, U.S. policies at the Geneva-based Conference on Disarmament and at the United Nations First Committee, and implementation issues associated with several multilateral treaties, such as the Antarctic Treaty, the Seabeds Convention, the Limited Nuclear Test Ban Treaty, and the Environmental Modification Convention.

There appear to be more women in arms control than in other national security fields. I suspect that is because arms control became a particularly active area over the same time period (the 70s and 80s) that women began to be considered for higher-level policy jobs. Also, some women out of the political science community, at least in my generation, tended to feel that if they went into security related areas at all, they would be more comfortable in arms control than in the "hardware" and military strategy arenas. Finally, it is my perception and experience that men (the hirers and assigners) sometimes see arms control as "soft," less important, and therefore as territory that can be left to women.

> In addition to concluding that women have been segregated and self-segregated by the internal topography (or subject areas) of the organization, Ms. Buckley has also concluded that women may indeed have distinctive management styles. In fulfilling her responsibilities of manager, negotiator, and policy analyst, she exercises a "personal" management style. She conjectures that such a style may be more characteristic of women.

What do I do? I spend considerable time writing and defending policy "options" papers. These typically analyze and make recommendations on particular U.S. negotiating positions. They may become decision documents for the senior leadership, including the President. I also engage in multilateral and bilateral international negotiations, principally with key allies and the Russians.

My management style is based on the conviction that people want to, and should, "stretch." Having done so, one of the few rewards in the government is being able to carry your own product. It is satisfying to get the credit, if there is any, and important to learn to stand up to and learn from the criticism, if you can. In trying to provide an environment where that can happen, I spend a good deal of time just interacting with the six or seven military and civilian professionals on the staff, each of whom has a full plate of projects and concerns that it is important to air. Necessary as it is, of course, time so spent does not produce a tangible product.

One of my accomplishments is that I have successfully brought several young people along, giving them responsibilities that they might not have had elsewhere, letting them stretch. If they fall short, I try to back them up. I've done it for many years and I believe it is a manager's responsibility. Many of these persons, who are now in high-level positions themselves, have said that I have contributed. So, personally, it's gratifying. I know they have stayed in government, despite financial and other pressures to leave, partly because of values I have shared with them. If good people stay in government service, a part of my job is being done.

My style is, I guess, "personal" also because the quality of the relationships I have with my colleagues matters to me. If a relationship is troubled, I seek to find out why and resolve it. I would not assert that this is a universally correct approach—some would argue that it can be inefficient—but I find it's the best for me. An element of this approach is my belief that it is very important to promote staff. How much you see the boss does affect how well you do professionally, if you're good. If the boss associates your ideas with you, then he or she thinks about you when it comes time for bonuses, or interesting projects, or who should go along to see the Secretary of Defense. "Face time" is important to all of us; as a manager, I try to create opportunities for this kind of visibility for my staff.

I think probably women do come at the substantive issues a little differently. Women are negotiators, options finders, conflict avoiders. Right after Desert Storm started, I was in a gathering of professional women who were talking about the kinds of options they would have explored earlier. The war was on, yet, they still wanted to talk options. Though they did not oppose the war, it was very hard for many of them to say "I support fighting." They would say things like, "I want to be sure Saddam doesn't get his way." Bringing no expertise whatsoever to the question, I suspect that this tendency to conflict avoidance may indeed turn out to be a survival strategy having to do with the physical weakness of women. Whatever its explanation, it seems to be fundamental, and to have something to do with how—not whether—women succeed in the tasks and responsibilities of modern society.

> Ms. Buckley has also considered the possibility that women's personal management style may be an adaption or response to the barriers women face.

From what I've read, and listening to the kinds of concerns my women friends have, I think women will tend to be less aggressive in professional relationships and tend to pursue goals through personal manipulations more than through direct order kinds of power plays. However, some of my women colleagues are "succeeding" by behaving in ways I would not. In terms of using power directly and "toughly," they surpass many men. I have no opinion on whether this is a chance phenomenon or whether they have been driven to those behaviors by the experiences they have been through.

Have I had negative career experiences? Of course. But my approach is not to dwell on them; I do so here only to respond to the purposes of this interview. During the course of my career I have been denied opportunities and used ineffectively. In the early years, I was one of so very few professional women that I represented little or no threat to my male colleagues. Oddly they and I were thus able to enjoy a certain relaxed collegiality. I have been directed not to attend inter-agency meetings because "a woman shouldn't represent the office." I have had a personnel manager casually note that my promotion was delayed for nine months "because I was a woman." Upon completing an important training assignment, I was informed that I had qualified as a "distinguished graduate," but would not be so designated because another woman was even more deserving and the institution did not wish to honor more than one "female" from any graduating class.

What about the glass ceiling? I do not believe that I have been the subject of seriously discriminatory action or attitudes during the last ten years. And the earlier instances, though hurtful in career terms, were infrequent. It is a measure of the progress made by women that even those few negative experiences seem, by today's standards, almost unbelievable. In considering the barriers that remain, we should remember that the leadership generation, which is in its forties and fifties, was shaped in a world where it was simply not correct for women to be doing most jobs. Moreover, it cannot be denied that all of us draw on our personal ties and are shaped by our backgrounds. The current leaders for example have the camaraderie created of having shared undergraduate and graduate educations at the top American institutions—institutions then closed to women of the same generation, my own. Nevertheless, the bureaucratic culture has dramatically improved, reflecting attitude changes that I believe are genuine, and there is institutional censure for falling back to old prejudices and practices. But it is also true that there are actually no institutional rewards for making the extra efforts that could contribute to eliminating the glass ceiling. Most of us—whatever the area—are going to channel our energies toward that which interests us and/or that for which we will be professionally rewarded. It is understandable that the ceiling remains and that women had best not rely on men to remove it. At the same time, at least in my workplace, the vast majority of men are trying to be increasingly principled and sensitive. We women should respond, in my view, by minimizing our tendency to be defensive and resentful of past wrongs.

The traits I described, valuing personal relationships in a professional setting, trying to be a problem solver and consensus builder, have caused me to be less threatening to male colleagues in an environment where most power is exercised differently. Again, generational differences are undoubtedly at work in both my perceptions and others' responses. Nowadays, what I might see as a reasonable response in a difficult situation, a twenty-five year old woman might call a cop-out. But the culture of 20 or 30 years ago was simply different. Then, being tough did not mean telling off a male supervisor. Being tough meant not quitting your job under the pressures of prejudice.

There is also the matter of professional credibility. Though dramatically reduced, that remains a workplace problem. Women can establish their credibility fairly quickly, but it is not granted to them automatically. And they must establish it rather impressively, because it is still harder to be a merely competent woman than a merely competent man. Finally, while the culture has changed significantly, individual's feelings about sexual roles are as deeply relevant as ever. Women and men both, for example, are very conflicted over the question of child-rearing. Many of us believe it is a civil right of women to work outside the home, but also believe that it is actually *not* okay to have children in child-care centers ten or 12 hours a day. Women and men both would never consider returning to the days of discriminatory remarks, foul language, and hands-on, as it were, office behavior. But many of us are sort of nostalgic for the days when a professional colleague could give or receive a kiss on the cheek without first analyzing the possible consequences.

In sum, the prejudices seem very much on the wane and women are moving at a reasonable pace toward achieving the necessary equities in the American workplace. I believe the next steps toward those equities involve accounting for other social needs, particularly the needs of children for parenting by persons, male or female, whose jobs do not consume their physical and emotional energies.

Conclusion

There is still a sense in government that the traditional fields of national security, defense, nuclear policy and intricate diplomacy are just not things that women do. Women do social policy. Women do environment. Women do humanitarian things.

Maureen Dowd[1]

Closed out of the foreign policy process for generations, women in the last two decades have begun to make agonizingly slow progress entering the domain of international politics. Our sample of women in leadership positions in the State and Defense Departments is testimony both to the difficulties women confront in breaking down the barriers constructed to keep women from coming "inside," and to the contributions women can make once they do surmount the blockades that have been set in their way. As we have discovered, the three main determinants that limit or condition the entrance and success of women in foreign affairs are societal, organizational, and individual factors. Our review of these three variables in Chapters 1, 2, and 3 suggests some limited optimism about the permeability of the foreign policy process to women. Moreover, the examination in Chapters 4, 5, and 6 of the policy viewpoints and management strategies of our women "Insiders" gives us a basis for projecting the potential impact of having women constructing foreign policy on an equal footing with men.

The most pervasive variable limiting the entrance of women to the foreign policy arena, and often the one most difficult to concretely identify, is the legacy of societal values, which have since perhaps the beginning of recorded time, identified politics, especially foreign policy politics, as one realm for which only men possess the proper credentials. This societal stereotype was effectively used until this century to keep foreign policy-making completely restricted to men. In the modern era, this cultural cliché is still manifested in questions concerning the credentials and the abilities of women to manage the affairs of nation-states. Whether this cultural attitude is based on outmoded ideas about the biological attributes of women or on a limited analysis of the power of socialization experiences, our exploration of this cliché finds it alive, if not so well, among the public and in both the Departments of State and of Defense. Society at large continues to doubt that women can be equally as effective as men in leadership positions that involve direct dealing with other nations or other nationals. Tied as this idea is to the legacy of the soldier-citizen, women are seen as particularly ill-suited for war preparation and war fighting. However, as we saw in Chapter 1, this stereotype about women is increasingly under challenge.

Both the Panama conflict and Desert Storm, fought by the volunteer army with its heavy reliance on women, did much to undermine the narrow picture of the soldier as male and replace it with new ideas about modern war and the role of women in such conflicts. The change is perhaps best manifested in the way commentators referred to the participants in the Persian Gulf conflict. For the first time, the phrase "our fighting men" was replaced with the oft heard refrain "our fighting men and *women*." The real breakthrough may come when, and if, the combat exclusion rule is eliminated. Moreover, it is possible that the more pervasive and limiting cultural conception linking politics and war-fighting ability may also come under serious challenge as the generation of women and men who came of age during the Vietnam War begin to assume leadership positions in the political arena. It is at least probable that this generation, whose best and brightest contain many who avoided service in Vietnam or who actively helped others avoid service, and who collectively protested the war, will hold very different notions about the necessity of war fighting as a prerequisite to proving your ability to be a good citizen or government official. In the 1991 Democratic Party presidential nominating contests this issue was displayed in the revelation that Governor Bill Clinton, ultimately the party nominee, had attempted to avoid the Vietnam draft. While the 1991 Clinton attempted to explain what he had done, a statement from his 1969 letter to an ROTC officer probably best captures the sentiment of his generation, "To many of us, it is no longer clear what is service and what is disservice."[2]

Other cultural stereotypes about women's abilities, while on the decline, still restrict women's influence. For instance, while few today question the right of married women to work, it is still true that the public has yet to grant that work may be as important in the lives of women as it is for men. Similarly, while women managers are slowly becoming accepted, and traditional notions of leadership and management are under serious challenge, women in such positions still confront ancient notions about women's abilities to give orders.

The legacy of discriminatory societal values has been institutionalized in the two main organizations constructing and conducting foreign policy. Both the State Department and the Defense Department have been and continue to be under legal and societal pressure to change their traditional practices of covert and overt discrimination against women. The more than 20 year battle to eliminate sexually discriminatory practices at State is beginning to bear fruit. The Foreign Service exam, and the way it is scored, is under review to make it fairer to the thousands of women who take it. Moreover, as we saw in some of our profiles, women in the Department are being compensated for the discriminatory practices they and others of their sex have faced in the past. However, it is clear that many of the same organizational factors persist, leading to continued discrimination at State. In 1989, the General Accounting Office report found that the State Department did not meet Equal Employment Opportunity goals and did not have a satisfactory affirmative action plan.[3] This report became the focus of Congressional hearings,[4] which concluded that: "The State Department is dramatically out of compliance with the Foreign Service Act, which specifically requires an active minority recruitment and hiring plan and equal representation of all American groups in the American Foreign Service."[5] As testimony by Clarence E. Hodges (previously Deputy Assistant Secretary for Equal Employment Opportunity) revealed, the dissatisfaction with the situation in State is evidenced in the growing number of EEO complaints, 30 percent of which were based on sex discrimination.[6] The data on employment in State continues to show the exclusion of women from the policy-making positions. As of March, 1991, they filled only 7.8 percent of the SFS positions.[7]

The recent treatment of April Glaspie is also revealing of the continuing problems women face. Ms. Glaspie, a career Foreign Service Officer with extensive training and experience in the Middle East, was appointed the first woman ambassador to a Middle Eastern country. However, due to the fact that she met with Saddam Hussein just prior to the Iraqi invasion of Kuwait, Ms. Glaspie has in essence been blamed by Congress for taking a conciliatory approach to Hussein, virtually giving a green light for the invasion.[8] In contrast, many analysts see Ms. Glaspie as merely having followed the Administration's policy of cooperation with Iraq, and thus consider her as being made into a "scapegoat for a failed policy."[9] Not only did the Bush Administration not defend Ms. Glaspie, it put her out to pasture, at an academic post, and she is unlikely to get another ambassadorship. The lingering devaluation of women's abilities is reflected in this comment about Ms. Glaspie's performance made by a senior male State Department official, reported by one of our interviewees:

He said "We have some lessons to learn. The first is don't send women as Ambassadors." Isn't that fascinating that that is the inference he drew.

> That is a dramatic example of the sheer prejudice and level of resistance
> to women.

At the Defense Department, the legacy of the soldier-citizen continues perhaps more strongly than at State to shape Departmental policies on women. The still strongly held cultural notion that only men can engage the enemy, as manifested in the combat exclusion rule, continues to hamper the ability of women to assume an equal participatory role with men in the Department. If the restrictions on women's roles in the military are eliminated it will help the generations of women who might fight alongside men in this nation's future wars, it will not eliminate the power of this stereotype, however, for the generations of women who could not do so. Women still are not prominently represented in the upper echelons at Defense. Overall in DOD in 1991, SES women constituted only 6.15 percent, while in the particular agencies, women were 8.6 percent of SES in OSD, 6.2 percent of SES in the Air Force, 5.7 percent of the SES in the Army and only 3.6 percent of the SES in the Navy.[10]

As a product of the culture which has historically tied politics, international relations, work, leadership and war fighting with maleness, women have often relied upon these same stereotypes about their sex in choosing and managing their own careers. We discussed the impact of this typecasting or pigeon-holing on women as individual factors. Paralleling the other two sets of factors, individual factors also evidenced improvements for the better on the horizon. Our data, for instance, suggest that women in an earlier era often did not so much plan a career as fall into one. For at least some of the older women in the two Departments, the choice of a career in the foreign policy arena was often the lesser of two evils, selected as the better alternative in a highly sex-discriminatory world. Among the younger women there is substantial evidence that a political position in foreign policy was a long-held goal, influencing even their choice of major while in college. However, one of the continuing problem areas for women as individuals wishing a career in the foreign policy establishment is the persistence of educational differences with men. This is manifested in the level and nature of the degrees obtained by the women in our study and women more generally. For women to obtain an equal footing with men, several things will need to happen. First, women will have to achieve advanced education beyond the undergraduate degree. Second, the degrees women obtain can not be limited to the less technical fields. Women and their teachers and advisors must not underestimate the abilities of women to do well in the sciences and math. A recent report conducted by the American Association of University Women suggests this may not be easy. The study found widespread

sexism in the nation's schools. The disparity in the educational performance of girls was widest in the sciences, with even the young women
who took courses in this area and who did well in them, being less likely
to pursue a college degree in the sciences or in engineering than a
comparable group of young men.[11] Whether the blames rests with the
schools or with a culture that tells women they lack the ability to do well
in these fields, the results are the same. This is a particularly damaging
phenomena for the prospects of women in the defense field, which recruits heavily from those with backgrounds in engineering or science.

The other individual factor that presents a hurdle to women's prospects
in the foreign policy field is the same set of problems that confront all
women, namely the difficulty, if not the impossibility, of combining a
high-powered career with marriage and a family. In a nation which assigns
responsibility for homemaking and child rearing to women while at the
same time providing very little support in the way of day-care or family
leave, the choice of so many of our women interviewees to avoid marriage
and/or a family becomes more understandable. In order to become equal
participants, future generations of women must either include even more
women who are willing to forego these traditional life-options, or society
will have to make it easier for women and men to combine the worker,
spouse, and parent roles. There is reason to hope the latter is increasingly
likely. Not only are government officials actively considering a Family and
Medical Leave Act, but the younger men in our sample seem increasingly
willing to take some responsibility in this area. The strain on them, and
the other men of their generation, as they attempt to combine roles
may provide the impetus, when added to the long-standing demands of
women, to break the policy and societal logjam preventing a solution to
the problem.

Our biggest source of hope that the influence of the three barriers of
societal, organizational and individual factors are waning is the presence
of so many powerful and influential women at the State and Defense
Departments. The women we interviewed in 1988 and the women we
profiled in each chapter are testimony that as rigid and seemingly imper-
meable as the barriers have been in the past, many exceptional women
have been able to overcome the limitations placed in their way by society,
the Departments, and their own backgrounds. In these women we can
also begin to see how the same three factors, societal, organizational and
individual, shape their attitudes toward, and their management of, the
foreign policy process.

Overall, the data contained in Chapters 4, 5, and 6 give little evidence
that the women already on the inside have a distinctly "women's perspective" on either the major international issues of the day or on a conceptual-
ization of how the process of forging foreign policy works. We did, how-

ever, see some indication that perhaps women bring to the management of their agencies a style of leadership that is somewhat different from that of their male colleagues. A new androgynous manager was revealed in the greater concern women expressed about those who worked for them. It is our expectation that this style difference may make the women we interviewed more effective than they might otherwise have been in the often-challenging environments in which they found themselves. As we discovered, most of the differences we did find between the women and men in the study were traceable to the influence of societal, organizational, or individual factors. This was perhaps most in evidence in the examination of policy and process differences in Chapters 5 and 6, where organizational and individual factors loomed large as explanatory variables. Women and men in the State Department were more likely to differ with the women and men at Defense than they were with each other. Position and ideological variables were also often better at predicting attitudes and opinions than was gender. Because of the limited nature of our study, we do not want to overstate the lack of differences between the women and men in our study, but these results do have some suggestive implications for the possible future role of women in shaping foreign policy, and for the maximizer-minimizer debate among feminists.

The question that provided the focus for our research was whether adding women to the foreign policy process would change the output of that process. When we asked the men and women in our study whether having more women in the Departments of State and Defense would have an impact on foreign policy, 74.7 percent of our respondents replied in the negative. Even in instances in which a change was anticipated, it was not of major proportions. "Policy wouldn't be different, but a better cross section would give a wider range of opinions, lead to more diversity." Women are not seen as having a united or "women's" position on foreign policy. At the time when we did our analysis, women could be found at both ends of the foreign policy issue spectrum. Which of the various "women's views" might be influential in the process will depend on the nature of how foreign policy is actually constructed, the relative power of the two Departments in that process, and the locus and influence of women within the Departments.

As was noted in Chapter 5, the foreign policy process during the Reagan Administration showed a bifurcation in its characteristics, delegatory versus concentration of power. It was not assumed that this split would continue, and our follow-up interviews in January 1991 allow us to make several brief comparisons between the Reagan and Bush Administrations. The public perception of Bush as virtually captivated by foreign affairs is the opposite of Reagan's disinterested approach. The tighter, more restricted model of foreign policy-making has apparently attracted Bush, who continues to shift policy-making out of State to an increasingly small group of decision-makers. Indeed, the popular press has been replete with reports of Bush Administration attempts at concentrating power in the hands of a very small group at the expense of the careerists. *Time* magazine even named Bush "*Men* of the Year," partially due to his mastery of foreign affairs, which was based on his penchant for secrecy and "hatching backstage deals with a small group of leaders whose confidence he has carefully cultivated over the years."[12] "In addition, Bush and Baker often bypass Foreign Service Officers in favor of direct contacts and personal relationships with other heads of state."[13]

This shift in power away from the bureaucracy can also be seen in the President's ambassadorial appointments. In the first ten months of his Administration, 57 percent of the ambassadorial appointments went to Bush's political friends, seven of whom had contributed more than $100,000 to the Republican Party. Bush has cut the number of ambassadorial posts to careerists to 43 percent (down from 63 percent under Reagan).[14] As a result, "The estrangement between the politicians and the professionals is getting worse."[15] Even former Secretary of State Baker deliberately snubbed the Foreign Service Officers and relied on non-Foreign Service aides. As Evans and Novak concluded, Baker has a deep suspicion of any outsider entering the closed circle of his intimate advisers. None of his policy-makers was from the Foreign Service or ever had served at State before. As one Insider observed:

> I think that's too bad. The career bureaucracy has, God knows, lots and lots of faults. It's the job of the Secretary to make the decisions in the end, but he does himself a disservice if he doesn't listen to his career people first, and then decide against their advice if he wants to. But they are also excluded, including some of his own appointees, which I think is very unfortunate.

This trend indicates a radical change in the foreign policy process between the Reagan and Bush Administrations, perhaps requiring an alteration in the political science literature's emphasis on the bureaucratic politics model. Indeed, in our 1991 interviews with current and past Senior Foreign Service and Executive Officers (results not reported here), a very different description of the decision-making powers was presented. Close observers of the Bush foreign policy process were in general agreement that the "in-group" (Bush, Cheney, Baker, Powell, and Scowcroft), were *the* decision-making body on many of the questions of foreign policy. By contrast, in 1988, the notion of a small group of foreign policy decision-makers was rejected by most of those who had front row seats to the process. As one of our senior executives in the Department of Defense noted in describing the Bush foreign policy process:

> It's a very different style, for example, from the Reagan Administration style. Reagan depended very, very much upon the agencies to come up with ... proposals, and things bubbled up from that. You knew always where to go if you had an idea, and how to put it in the process. Much more now comes from the NSC, it is a conscious decision to not have the kinds of working groups ... but to do things on an ad hoc basis. And I think that comes out of a decision of wanting to control, much more control. ... I think in terms of the things that are really important, ... those decisions are made by a much, much smaller group, with much less participation by the career staff.

As a result, Bush's inner sanctum has a fraternity air, what one top Republican calls "a male prep school, locker-room atmosphere."[16] This trend of concentration of policy-making in the hands of Presidential intimates has a negative impact on women who have generally been excluded from such groups. The degree to which women can influence policy will depend on how much those in the SES/SFS ranks are allowed to influence the policies of the Department, something that the Secretary of State under President Bush often seems reluctant to let them do.

Another important variable in predicting women's influence may be the relative power of women in the two Departments. We have noted that after years of discriminatory behavior, the State Department, in particular, is under court pressure to allow women a wider role in the Department. Thus, women might be more able to press their point of view at State. Similarly there are a larger percentage of women moving up through the ranks at State when compared with the Defense Department. Other aspects of the ethos in both Departments appear to make State more permeable to women's views (although by no means are women treated equally or equitably at State or are their views given equal hearing). Thus, we might expect women to have a greater opportunity to have a say at State. In a positive vein, 48.1 percent of our respondents felt that the influence of women in the Departments will increase in the future, (30.4 percent thought it would remain the same and 6.3 percent felt it depended upon future changes in administrations). Unfortunately, there is always the possibility that administration officials who might not favor the participation of women, might shift decision making in foreign policy even more to male appointees in the Departments, or to other executive agencies in which women may be having an even more difficult time exercising influence. The future role of women in the foreign policy process is thus highly contingent, particularly in the near term, on the way in which foreign policy is formulated in a given administration. In the long term, we would hope that women and men would be equally represented in each of the Departments and in all ranks, including the innermost circle of presidential advisors. Perhaps this will happen when we have a woman

President. For this to occur, however, the remaining legacies of societal and individual factors will also have to have disappeared. In these circumstances, the addition of women to the foreign policy process will probably not alter policy outcomes.

This conclusion, of course, is based on our finding of limited gender differences in foreign policy views, a conclusion to which those feminists who believe women are distinct from men in their foreign policy beliefs would strongly object. Indeed, we have speculated at several stages in our analysis on the implication of our results for the maximizer-minimizer debate among feminists. As we outlined in the Introduction, feminists are engaged in an often-heated discussion over whether women's unique roles as daughters and mothers provide them with a perspective that is sharply divergent from that of the views of men. The maximizer feminists, or course, believe such a difference exists, while the minimizer feminist doubt a unique "women's perspective" will remain after controlling for situational and demographic differences between men and women. Our results, based on a limited sample in a single time frame, give most support to the position of the minimizers. While there are differences between the women and men in our study, the differences are small and readily explained by the three dimensions of social, organizational, and individual factors. Paralleling the expectations of Cynthia Fuchs Epstein, we are thus inclined to speculate that in the future, when societal attitudes toward the abilities of women and men are the same, and organizational barriers are eliminated, and the backgrounds of women and men are more nearly identical, even the few differences we uncovered in our sample of foreign policy "Insiders" will vanish. Then the role of women in the foreign policy process will depend more on who they are as individuals, and their right to be participating along side men, than on their gender.

Notes

Notes to Introduction

1. Hans J. Morgenthau, *Politics Among Nations: The Struggle for Power & Peace*, 6th ed. (New York: Alfred A. Knopf, 1985), 31, 38.

2. Hans J. Morgenthau, "Another 'Great Debate': The National Interest of the United States," in *Classics of International Relations*, 2nd ed., ed. John A. Vasquez (Englewood Cliffs, NJ: Prentice Hall, 1990), 132.

3. Patricia Schroeder, "Women's Role in National Peace Politics," in *Women and Peace: An International Conference*, ed. Ketayuh H. Gould, Janice Hartman, and Nancy Weinberg (Urbana-Champaign, IL: University of Illinois, 1989), 46.

4. Jean Bethke Elshtain, *Women and War* (New York: Basic Books, 1987), 7; Cynthia Enloe, *Bananas, Beaches, and Bases: Making Feminist Sense of International Politics* (Berkeley: University of California Press, 1989).

5. Edward P. Crapol, ed., *Women and American Foreign Policy: Lobbyists, Critics, and Insiders* (New York: Greenwood, 1987), 1–18, 91–118, 137–152.

6. C. Roland Marchand, *The American Peace Movement and Social Reform 1898–1918* (Princeton: Princeton University Press, 1972), 182.

7. Amy Swerdlow, "Ladies' Day at the Capitol: Women Strike for Peace Versus HUAC," *Feminist Studies* 8 (3): 493–518; Amy Swerdlow, "Pure Milk, Not Poison: Women Strike for Peace and the Test Ban Treaty of 1963," in *Rocking the Ship of State: Toward a Feminist Peace Politics*, ed. Adrienne Harris and Ynestra King (Boulder, Co: Westview, 1989).

8. Bella Abzug and Mim Kelber, *Women's Foreign Policy Council Directory* (New York: Women's Foreign Policy Council, 1987), iii.

9. Women for Meaningful Summits, "Statement of Purpose," n.d.

10. Nancy E. McGlen and Karen O'Connor, "Women and Peace: The Connections" (Presented at the Women and Peace Conference, University of Illinois, 1989).

11. Alice Stone Blackwell, cited in Aileen Kraditor, *The Ideas of the Women's Suffrage Movement, 1890–1920* (Garden City, NY: Anchor Books, 1965), 50.

12. McGlen and O'Connor, "Women and Peace."

13. Helen Caldicott, *Missile Envy: The Arms Race and Nuclear War* (New York: Bantam, 1985), 322.

14. Linda Smith as quoted in "It is a Women's Role to Save the Species," *USA Today*, April 14, 1986, 11a.

15. Caldicott, *Missile Envy*.

16. McGlen and O'Connor, "Women and Peace," 23–24.

17. Betty Bumpers quoted in "Peace Links Organized," *New York Times*, May 26, 1982, 26.

18. Kathleen Jones, "Dividing the Ranks: Women and the Draft," *Women & Politics* 4 (4): 80; Ruth Roach Pierson, "'Did Your Mother Wear Army Boots?' Feminist Theory and Women's Relation to War, Peace and Revolution," in *Images of Women in Peace and War*, ed. Sharon MacDonald, Pat Holden and Shirley Ardener (Madison: University of Wisconsin Press, 1988), 225.

19. Pat Reuss quoted in "Plan Given Cautious Approval by Women's Groups," *New York Times*, February 9, 1980, 9.

20. "Women of War," *Congressional Quarterly* 49 (19): 1210.

21. Elshtain, *Women and War*, xiii.

22. Pierson, "'Did Your Mother Wear Army Boots?" 221.

23. Catherine R. Stimpson, as cited in Ann Snitow, "A Gender Diary," in *Rocking the Ship of State*, ed. Adrienne Harris and Ynestra King (Boulder, CO: Westview Press, 1989), 41.

24. Snitow, "A Gender Diary," 41.

25. Ibid., 41–42.

26. Ibid., 42–43.

27. Ibid., 48.

28. Nancy Chodorow, *The Reproduction of Mothering* (Berkeley: University of California Press, 1978), 166–167.

29. Carol Gilligan, *In a Different Voice: Psychological Theory and Women's Development* (Cambridge, MA: Harvard University Press, 1982), 73–74, 156, 161–162.

30. Ibid., 164–165.

31. Sara Ruddick, "Preservative Love and Military Destruction: Reflections on Mothering and Peace," in *Mothering: Essays in Feminist Theory*, ed. Joyce Treblicot (Totowa, NJ: Littlefield Adams, 1983b), 231–262.

32. Sara Ruddick, "Feminist Questions on Peace and War: An Agenda for Research, Discussion, Analysis, Action," *Women's Studies Quarterly* 12 (2): 8–11.

33. Sara Ruddick, "The Rationality of Care," in *Women, Militarism, and War*, ed. Jean Bethke Elshtain and Sheila Tobias (Savage, MD: Rowman and Littlefield, 1990), 229–254.

34. Ruddick, "Preservative Love and Military Destruction," 233.

35. Ruddick, "The Rationality of Care," 249–51.

36. Nancy Hartsock, "Masculinity, Heroism, and the Making of War," in *Rocking the Ship of State*, 133–152.

37. Ibid., 138–39.

38. Ibid., 148.

39. Betty Reardon, *Sexism and the War System* (New York: Teachers College Press, 1985);

Birgit Brock-Utne, *Educating for Peace: A Feminist Perspective* (New York: Pergamon Press, 1985).

40. J. Ann Tickner, *Gender in International Relations: Feminist Perspectives on Achieving Global Security* (New York: Columbia University Press, 1992); Enloe, *Bananas, Beaches, and Bases*.

41. Sara Ruddick, "Pacifying the Forces: Drafting Women in the Interest of Peace," *Signs* 8 (3): 486–87; Mary Lou Kendrigan, "The Use of Force: Feminist and World Peace" (Presented at the Annual Meeting of the American Political Science Association, Washington, DC, 1987); Mary Lou Kendrigan, "The 'Mom's War' or What Effect Will Women Warriors Have on the Move Towards Greater Equality for Women?" (Presented at the Annual Meeting of the American Political Science Association, Washington, DC, 1991); Kathleen Jones, "Dividing the Ranks: Women and the Draft," *Women & Politics* 4 (4): 84–85.

42. Snitow, "A Gender Diary," 41–42, 44.

43. Joan Tronto, "Beyond Gender Differences to a Theory of Care," *Signs* 12 (4): 646.

44. Linda Kerber, "May All Our Citizens Be Soldiers and All Our Soldiers Citizens: The Ambiguities of Female Citizenship in the New Nation," in *Women, Militarism, and War*, ed. Jean Bethke Elshtain and Sheila Tobias, 309–310.

45. Micaela di Leonardo, "Morals, Mothers, and Militarism: Antimilitarism and Feminist Theory," *Feminist Studies* 11 (3): 612.

46. Ibid., 615.

47. Janet Radcliffe Richards, "Why the Pursuit of Peace Is No Part of Feminism," in *Women, Militarism, and War*, ed. Jean Bethke Elshtain and Sheila Tobias, 211–225.

48. Ibid., 223.

49. Ibid., 224.

50. See comments of the women soldiers in David H. Hackworth, "War and the Second Sex," *Newsweek*, August 5, 1991: 24–29; "Women Have What It Takes," *Newsweek*, August 5, 1991: 30.

51. Dean Jaros and Elizabeth S. White, "Sex, Endocrines, and Political Behavior," *Women & Politics* 3 (2/3): 131.

52. Cynthia Fuchs Epstein, *Deceptive Distinctions: Sex, Gender, and the Social Order* (New Haven: Yale University Press, 1988), xii.

53. Sharon MacDonald, "Drawing the Lines—gender, peace and war: an introduction," in *Images of Women in Peace & War*, ed. Sharon MacDonald, Pat Holden and Shirley Ardener (Madison, WI: University of Wisconsin Press, 1988), 1.

54. Snitow, "A Gender Diary," 52–56.

55. Snitow, "A Gender Diary," 37.

56. For a review of this literature as it relates to politics, see Denise L. Baer and David A. Bostis, "Biology, Gender, and Politics: An Assessment and Critique," *Women & Politics* 3 (2/3): 29–66. This whole double issue of *Women & Politics* is devoted to the topic of Biopolitics and Gender.

57. Epstein, *Deceptive Distinctions*.

58. Ibid., 1.

59. Ibid., 240.

60. Lincoln Bloomfield, *The Foreign Policy Process: A Modern Primer* (Englewood Cliffs, NJ: Prentice-Hall, Inc., 1982), 42–43.

61. Gene Rainey, *Patterns of American Foreign Policy* (Boston: Allyn and Bacon, 1975), 179.

62. Charles Kegley and Eugene R. Wittkopf, *American Foreign Policy: Pattern and Process*, 3rd ed. (New York: St. Martin's Press, 1987), 388.

63. Georgia Duerst-Lahti, "Gender, Power Relations in Public Bureaucracies" (Ph.D. diss., University of Wisconsin-Madison, 1987a); Gary N. Powell, *Women & Men in Management* (Newbury Park: Sage Publications, 1988).

Notes to Section I

1. Georgia Duerst-Lahti, "Gender, Power Relations in Public Bureaucracies" (Ph.D. diss., University of Wisconsin-Madison, 1987a), 64.

2. Ibid., 63.

3. Ibid., 70.

4. Gary N. Powell, *Women & Men in Management* (Newbury Park: Sage Publications, 1988), 189.

5. Ibid., 71–72.

6. Ibid., 185.

7. Ibid., 13.

8. Ibid.

Notes to Chapter 1

1. Robert K. Merton, cited in Cynthia Fuchs Epstein, *Deceptive Distinctions: Sex, Gender, and the Social Order* (New Haven: Yale University Press, 1988), 15.

2. Georgia Duerst-Lahti, "Gender, Power Relations in Public Bureaucracies" (Ph.D. diss. University of Wisconsin-Madison, 1987), 64.

3. Ibid., 36.

4. Georgia Duerst-Lahti, "Gender, Position and Perception: Communicating Power in State Organizations" (Presented at the Annual Meeting of the Midwest Political Science Association, Chicago, 1985), 20.

5. As cited in Epstein, *Deceptive Distinctions*, 42.

6. Duerst-Lahti, "Gender, Position and Perception," 2.

7. Constantina Safilios-Rothschild, *Sex Role Socialization and Sex Discrimination: Synthesis and Critique of the Literature* (Washington: National Institute of Education, 1979), 125.

8. Epstein, *Deceptive Distinctions*, 8–10.

9. Ann Snitow, "A Gender Diary," in *Rocking the Ship of State*, ed. Adrienne Harris and Ynestra King (Boulder: Westview Press, 1989), 42.

10. Virginia Sapiro, "Biology and Women's Policy: A View from the Social Sciences," in *Women, Biology, and Public Policy*, ed. Virginia Sapiro (Beverly Hills: Sage Publications, 1985), 57.

11. Betty Friedan, *The Feminine Mystique* (New York: Dell Publishing, 1963), 37.

12. Gary N. Powell, *Women & Men in Management* (Newbury Park: Sage Publications, 1988), 37.

13. Meredith Watts, "Introduction: Biopolitics and Gender," *Women & Politics* 3 (2/3): 1–28.

14. Dean Jaros and Elizabeth S. White, "Sex, Endocrines, and Political Behavior," *Women & Politics* 3 (2/3): 129–145.

15. Glendon Schubert, "The Biopolitics of Sex: Gender, Genetics, and Epigenetics," *Women & Politics* 3 (2/3): 120; Michael Ruse, *Is Science Sexist?* (Holland: D. Reidel, 1981); James C. Neely, *Gender: The Myth of Equality.* (New York: Simon & Schuster, 1981).

16. Powell, *Women & Men in Management*, 25; Epstein, *Deceptive Distinctions*.

17. Sapiro, "Biology and Women's Policy," 57.

18. Epstein, *Deceptive Distinctions*, 10.

19. Powell, *Women & Men in Management*, 29–30.

20. Ibid., 64.

21. Ibid., 668–72.

22. Janet Shibley Hyde, "Meta-analysis and the Psychology of Gender Differences," *Signs* 16 (1): 64–67.

23. Denise L. Baer and David A. Bositis, "Biology, Gender, and Politics: An Assessment and Critique," *Women & Politics* 3 (2/3): 30–52.

24. Powell, *Women & Men in Management*, 48.

25. Epstein, *Deceptive Distinctions*, 79.

26. Duerst-Lahti, "Gender, Power Relations," 20.

27. Epstein, *Deceptive Distinctions*, 84.

28. Powell, *Women & Men in Management*, 65, 84.

29. Epstein, *Deceptive Distinctions*, 137.

30. Hazel Erskine, "The Polls: Women's Role," *Public Opinion Quarterly* 35 (2): 282.

31. Ibid., 283.

32. Lewis Lord, "America on the Eve of Conflict," *U.S. News & World Report*, August 27–September 3, 1990, 57.

33. Ibid., 58.

34. Francine D. Blau, "The Data on Women Workers, Past, Present and Future," in *Working Women*, ed. Ann H Stromberg and Shirley Harkess (Palo Alto, Ca., Mayfield, 1978), 58.

35. Rita J. Simon and Jean M. Landis, "The Polls: A Report on Women's and Men's Attitudes About a Woman's Place and Role," *Public Opinion Quarterly* 53 (2): 270.

36. Ibid.

37. Duerst-Lahti, "Gender, Power Relations," 14.

38. *The 1990 Virginia Slims Poll*, data distributed by The Roper Center for Public Opinion Research.

39. Ibid.

40. "Work and Families," *Public Perspective*, 1990, 1 (6): 92.

41. Yolanda Woodlee, "Diploma doesn't ensure pay equity," *Detroit News*, September 20, 1991, 1B.

42. Lisa Belkin, "Bars to Equality of Sexes Seen as Eroding, Slowly," *New York Times*, August

20, 1989, A26; Alison Leigh Cowan, "Women's Gains on the Job: Not Without a Heavy Toll," *New York Times*, August 21, 1989, A14.

43. *New York Times/CBS Poll*, June 20–25, 1989.

44. "Work Experience," *Public Perspective* 1 (6): 86.

45. Ibid.

46. Ibid.

47. Epstein, *Deceptive Distinctions*, 155.

48. Erskine, "The Polls," 279.

49. Ibid., 281.

50. Jean Bethke Elshtain, *Women and War* (New York: Basic Books, 1987), 4.

51. Ibid., 140–142.

52. Ibid., 4.

53. Antonia Fraser, *The Warrior Queens* (New York: Alfred A. Knopf, 1988), 7.

54. Ibid., 12.

55. Elshtain, *Women and War*, 47.

56. Ibid., 53–56; Epstein, *Deceptive Distinctions*, 3–4.

57. Elshtain, *Women and War*, 70.

58. Ibid., 58.

59. Ibid., 62.

60. Ibid., 75.

61. Linda Kerber, "May All Our Citizens Be Soldiers and All Our Soldiers Citizens: The Ambiguities of Female Citizenship in the New Nation," in *Women, Militarism, and War*, ed. Jean Bethke Elshtain and Sheila Tobias (Savage, MD: Rowman and Littlefield, 1990), 90.

62. Pauline Schloesser, "Republican Motherhood, Modern Patriarchy, and the Question of Woman Citizenship in Post-Revolutionary America" (Presented at the Annual Meeting of the American Political Science Association, Washington, DC, 1991).

63. *The 1990 Virginia Slims Poll*.

64. James A. Davis, Jennifer Lauby, and Paul B. Sheatsby, *Americans View the Military* (Chicago: National Opinion Research Center, 1983), 32.

65. Ibid., 34.

66. Ibid.

67. "Women in Combat," *Public Perspective* 2 (3): 87.

68. Barbara Kantrowitz, Eleanor Clift and John Barry, "The Right to Fight," *Newsweek*, August 5, 1991, 23. and "Opinion Watch: On the Front Lines," *Newsweek*, August 5, 1991, 27.

69. "On the Front Lines," 27.

70. Quoted in Kantrowitz, Clift and Barry, "The Right to Fight," 22.

71. Quoted in Pat Towell, "Breaking the Gender Barrier," *Congressional Quarterly* 49 (31): 2183.

72. Ibid.

73. Quoted in Elizabeth A. Palmer, "Senate Debates Rights, Role of Women Warriors," *Congressional Quarterly* 49 (25): 1687.

74. Pat Towell, "Women's Combat Role Debated as Chiefs Denounce Sex Bias," *Congressional Quarterly*, 50 (31): 2292.

75. Sheila Tobias, "Shifting Heroisms: The Uses of Military Service in Politics," in *Women, Militarism, and War*, ed. Jean Bethke Elshtain and Sheila Tobias, 173, 177–79.

76. Joanne Edgar, "Women Who Went to the Summit," *MS*, February, 1986: 84.

77. Ibid.

78. Quoted in *New York Times*, October 12, 1984, B6.

79. Kathleen Frankovic, "The 1984 Election: The Irrelevance of the Campaign," *P.S.* 18 (1): 44–45.

80. *The 1990 Virginia Slims Poll*.

81. Ibid.

82. Powell, *Women & Men in Management*, 22.

83. Ann Snitow "A Gender Diary," in *Rocking the Ship of State*, ed. Adrienne Harris and Ynestra King, 35.

84. Snodgrass in Powell, *Women & Men in Management*, 106.

85. Erskine, "The Polls," 287.

86. Simon and Landis, "The Polls: A Report," 271.

87. Ibid.

88. *The 1990 Virginia Slims Poll*.

89. *New York Times/CBS Poll*, June 20–25, 1989.

90. Ibid.

91. James J. Kilpatrick, "Women still shortchanged in top jobs," *Buffalo News*, September 19, 1991.

92. Bureau of Labor Statistics, "Employment in Perspective: Women in the Labor Force," 796 (Washington, DC: U.S. Department of Labor, 1990).

93. Rosabeth Moss Kanter, *Men and Women of the Corporation* (New York: Basic Books, 1977), 210.

94. *New York Times/CBS Poll*, June 20–29, 1989.

95. Ibid.

96. *The 1990 Virginia Slims Poll*.

97. Ibid.

98. Epstein, *Deceptive Distinctions*, 148.

99. For a brief profile see Judith Ewell "Barely in the Inner Circle: Jeane Kirkpatrick" in *Women and American Foreign Policy*, ed. Edward P. Crapol (Greenwood Press, N.Y. 1987), 153–171. For a detailed description of her tenure at the UN, see Allan Gerson, *The Kirkpatrick Mission: Diplomacy Without Apology*, (Free Press, N.Y. 1991).

Notes to Chapter 2

1. W. V. Rouse, *Evaluation at the Equal Employment Opportunity Program: U.S. Dept. of State* (Evanston, IL: W. V. Rouse & Co., 1977), 32.

2. Georgia Duerst-Lahti, "Gender, Position and Perception: Communicating Power in State Organizations" (Presented at the Annual Meeting of the Midwest Political Science

Association, Chicago, 1985); "Organizational Ethos and Women's Power Capacity: Perceived and Formal Structure in State Administrative Organizations" (Presented at the Annual Meeting of the American Political Science Association, Washington, DC, 1986); "Gender, Power Relations in Public Bureaucracies" (Ph.D diss. University of Wisconsin-Madison, 1987).

3. Duerst-Lahti, "Gender, Power Relations in Public Bureaucracies," 101.

4. Gary N. Powell, *Women & Men in Management* (Newbury Park: Sage Publications, 1988), 71–72.

5. Duerst-Lahti, "Gender, Power Relations in Public Bureaucracies," 8.

6. *Putting Women in Their Place: The Federal Women's Program* (Pm1.2:W84) (Washington, DC: Federal Women's Program, 1979).

7. Commission on Civil Rights, *Equal Opportunity in the Foreign Service* (Washington, DC: Office of Management, 1981), 9.

8. For a discussion of this issue, see Mady Wechsler Segal, "Social Representation in the Military: The Case of Gender" (Presented at the Annual Meeting of the Inter-University Seminar on Armed Forces and Society, Baltimore, 1989).

9. Quoted in David Coleman, "Woman wins 21 year legal battle," *Wellfleet Oracle*, April 27, 1989, 6.

10. Quoted in Barbara Gamarekian, "Women gain, but slowly, in the Foreign Service," *New York Times*, July 28, 1989.

11. Homer Calkin, *Women in the Department of State: Their Role in American Foreign Affairs* (Washington, DC: Department of State, 1978), 6.

12. Ibid., 68–69.

13. Ibid., 69.

14. Ibid., 70.

15. Ibid., 81–85.

16. Ibid., 105–106.

17. Ibid., 125.

18. Ibid., 127.

19. Commission on Civil Rights, *Equal Opportunity in the Foreign Service*, 3.

20. *State Department: Minorities and women are underrepresented in the Foreign Service* (Washington, DC: General Accounting Office, 1989), 13.

21. Calkin, *Women in the Department of State*, 145.

22. Benjamin Welles, "Women Winning State Department Case," *New York Times*, Feb. 28, 1972.

23. Herman Nickel, "Sex and the Foreign Service," *Time*, August 27, 1971.

24. Calkin, *Women in the Department of State*, 149–150.

25. Ibid., 229.

26. Commission on Civil Rights, *Equal Opportunity in the Foreign Service*, 5.

27. Philip Habib, "Report to the Committee to Review Recruitment and Examination for Foreign Service" (Washington, DC: Dept. of State, 1979).

28. Commission on Civil Rights, *Equal Opportunity in the Foreign Service*, 20.

29. Ibid., 1.

30. W. V. Rouse, *Evaluation at the Equal Employment Opportunity Program*.

31. Mary S. Olmsted, Bernice Baer, Jean Joyce and Georgiana M. Prince, *Women at State: An Inquiry into the Status of Women in the United States Department of State* (Washington, DC: Women's Research and Education Institute of the Congressional Caucus for Women's Issues, 1984), vi.

32. Olmsted et al., *Women at State*, 25.

33. Ibid., 26, 29.

34. Ibid., 30.

35. Office of Equal Employment and Civil Rights, *Update of the Affirmative Action Plan and Annual Accomplishment Report of Equal Employment Activities for Fiscal Year 1987* (Washington, DC: Department of State, 1988), 17–18.

36. James Baker, "Overseas Cable to all Posts" (Washington, DC: Department of State, April 17, 1989), 1–3.

37. Gamarekian, "Women gain, but slowly, in the Foreign Service."

38. *Palmer, et al. v. Baker*, 1987, 662 Federal Supplement: 1551; Baker, "Overseas Cable to all Posts," 1–2.

39. Department of State, *Multi-Year Affirmative Action Plan: FY 1990–92* (Washington, DC: Department of State, 1991), 62.

40. Gamarekian, "Women gain, but slowly, in the Foreign Service."

41. Conversation with Monica Wagner, esq., August 8, 1992.

42. National Women's Studies Association, "Thousands of Unknown Claimants Eligible for Damages: Search Underway for Female Applicants to VOA, Radio Marti, and Asia," 1989.

43. John M. Goshko, "2 Reports Urge Overhaul of Foreign Service," *Washington Post*, May 31, 1989, A21.

44. Jeanne Holm, Maj. Gen. USAF (Ret.), *Women in the Military: an Unfinished Revolution* (Novato, CA: Presidio, 1982), xv.

45. Ibid., xvi.

46. Ibid., 5; Jean Bethke Elshtain, *Women and War* (New York: Basic Books, 1987).

47. Holm, *Women in the Military*, 6.

48. *Going Strong: Women in Defense* (Washington, DC: DOD, 1984), 27.

49. Holm, *Women in the Military*, 8.

50. Ibid., 9.

51. Ibid., 11.

52. Ibid., 13.

53. *Going Strong: Women in Defense*, 27.

54. Holm, *Women in the Military*, 10.

55. American Forces Press Services, *Women in the Armed Forces* (Washington, DC: Department of Defence, 1976).

56. Holm, *Women in the Military*, 17.

57. Ibid., 22.

58. American Forces Press Services, *Women in the Armed Forces*.

59. Holm, *Women in the Military*, 100.

60. Ibid., 92.

61. Ibid., 50.

62. Ibid.

63. Ibid., 62.

64. Ibid., 93.

65. Rita Victoria Gomez, "Black WAC's and Bad Times in the Good War," *Washington Post*, Nov. 10, 1991, C5.

66. Holm, *Women in the Military*, 102.

67. Gene Rainey, *Patterns of American Foreign Policy* (Boston: Allyn and Bacon, 1975), 146.

68. Ibid.

69. Holm, *Women in the Military*, 130.

70. American Forces Press Services, *Women in the Armed Forces*.

71. *Going Strong: Women in Defense*, 7.

72. Holm, *Women in the Military*, 178.

73. Judith Hicks Stiehm, *Arms and the Enlisted Woman* (Philadelphia: Temple University Press, 1989).

74. *Going Strong: Women in Defense*, 28.

75. Ibid..

76. Stiehm, *Arms and the Enlisted Woman*.

77. Martin Binkin, *Military Technology and Defense Manpower* (Washington, DC: Brookings Institute, 1986), 116.

78. Holm, *Women in the Military*, 274.

79. Ibid., 387.

80. Stiehm, *Arms and the Unlisted Woman*.

81. Ibid., 65.

82. Holm, *Women in the Military*, 398.

83. *Going Strong: Women in Defense*, 5.

84. Task Force on Women in the Military, *Report of the Task Force on Women in the Military* (Washington, DC: Department of Defense, 1988).

85. *Women on the Way Up: The Federal Women's Program* (Washington, DC: OPM, 1980), 1.

86. Duerst-Lahti, "Organizational Ethos and Women's Power Capacity."

87. Duerst-Lahti, "Gender, Power Relations in Public Bureaucracies," 100.

88. Ibid., 23–24.

89. Ibid., 121–122.

90. Rosabeth Moss Kanter, *Men and Women of the Corporation* (New York: Basic Books, 1977), 208.

91. Ibid., 210.

92. Ibid., 210–211.

93. Ibid., 211.

94. Ibid., 212.

95. Ibid., 210–221.

96. Ibid., 221–230.

97. Ibid., 230–237.

98. *Annual Report on the Employment of Minorities, Women and Handicapped in the Federal Government Fiscal Year 1983* (Washington, DC: EEOC, 1983).

99. Ibid., 56.

100. *Federal Civilian Workforce Statistics* (Washington, DC: OPM, 1984), 4.

101. Office of Equal Employment and Civil Rights, *Update of the Affirmative Action Plan and Annual Accomplishment Report of Equal Employment Activities for Fiscal Year 1987*.

102. *Federal Civilian Workforce Statistics* (Washington, DC: OPM, 1988).

103. *Annual Report on the Employment of Minorities, Women and Handicapped*, 56.

104. Calkin, *Women in the Department of State*, 151; Office of Equal Employment and Civil Rights *Update of the Affirmative Action Plan and Annual Accomplishment Report of Equal Employment Activities for Fiscal Year 1987*; and Herman Nickel, "Sex and the Foreign Service," *Time*, Aug. 27, 1971.

105. Department of State, *Multi-Year Affirmative Action Plan: FY 1990–1992*, 46b.

106. Calkin, *Women in the Department of State*, 115; Olmsted, *et al.*, *Women at State*, 29; Office of Equal Employment and Civil Rights, *Update of the Affirmative Action Plan*.

107. *Federal Civilian Force Statistics, Equal Employment Opportunity Statistics* (Washington, DC: OPM, November 1979 & 1986); and *Selected Manpower Statistics* (Washington, DC: Department of Defense, September 1987).

108. Susan J. Carroll, "New Strategies To Increase The Number Of Women Appointed To Recent Presidential Administrations In The United States" (Presented at the Vater Staat Und Seine Frauen Conference, Berlin, West Germany, 1988).

109. Rita Mae Kelly and Mary E. Guy et al., "Public Managers in the States: A Comparison of Career Advancement by Sex," *Public Administration Review*, 51 (5): 403–404.

110. Duerst-Lahti, "Gender, Power Relations in Public Bureaucracies," 157.

111. Ibid., 177.

112. *Senior Executive Service* (Washington, DC: OPM, 1980), 1.

113. Ibid., 1.

114. *Annual Report to Congress on the Federal Equal Opportunity Recruitment Program for Fiscal Year 1990* (Washington, DC: OPM, 1991), 27.

115. *Women on the Way Up: The Federal Women's Program* (Washington, DC: OPM, 1980), 1.

116. Duerst-Lahti, "Gender, Power Relations in Public Bureaucracies," 197.

117. Cynthia Fuchs Epstein, *Deceptive Distinctions: Sex, Gender, and the Social Order* (New Haven: Yale University Press, 1988), 154.

118. Powell, *Women & Men in Management*, 92.

119. Ibid., 17.

120. Ibid., 92.

121. Ibid., 91.

122. Ellen Boneparth and Emily Stoper, eds., *Women, Power and Policy*, 2nd ed. (New York: Pergamon Press, 1989), 55.

123. Quoted in Barbara Gutek and Laurie Larwood, eds., *Women's Career Development* (Newbury Park: Sage Publications, 1989), 107.

124. Duerst-Lahti, "Gender, Power Relations in Public Bureaucracies," 154.

125. Franklin and Sweeney, in Ellen Boneparth and Emily Stoper, eds., *Women, Power and Policy*, 2nd ed. (New York: Pergamon Press, 1989) 48.

126. Epstein, *Deceptive Distinctions*, 160–164.

127. Duerst-Lahti, "Gender, Power Relations in Public Bureaucracies," 112.

128. Ibid., 115.

129. "WAO's 20th Anniversary," 3.

130. *State Department: Minorities and Women*, 22.

131. Ibid.

132. Calkin, *Women in the Department of State*, 116.

133. Office of Equal Employment and Civil Rights, *Update of the Affirmative Action Plan*.

134. *Palmer v. Baker*, 662 Federal Supplement (1987): 1571.

135. *State Department: Minorities and Women*, 12.

136. *Palmer v. Baker*, 662 Federal Supplement (l987): 1573.

137. Richard Havemann, "State Dept. Sex-Bias Case Reopened," *Washington Post*, May 12, 1990.

138. Conversation with Monica Wagner, esq., August 18, 1992.

139. Olmsted et al., *Women at State*, 4.

140. Ibid.

141. Ibid., 12.

142. Office of Equal Employment and Civil Rights, *Update of the Affirmative Action Plan*.

143. "WAO's 20th Anniversary," 4.

144. *State Department: Minorities and Women*, 36.

145. *Joint Hearing Before the Subcommittee on International Operations of the Committee on Foreign Affairs and Subcommittee on the Civil Service of the Committee on Post Office and Civil Service* (DOC. Y4.F76/1: P43/11) (Washington, DC: US Printing Office, 1990).

146. *State Department: Minorities and Women*, 2–3.

147. Ibid., 4.

148. Olmsted et al., *Women at State*, 13–15.

149. *Palmer v. Baker*, 662 Federal Supplement (1987), 1560.

150. Conversation with Monica Wagner, esq., August 18, 1992.

151. *Palmer v. Baker*, 662 Federal Supplement (1987), 1561.

152. Olmsted et al., *Women at State*, 24.

153. Charles Kegley and Eugene R. Wittkopf, *American Foreign Policy: Pattern and Process*, 3rd ed. (New York: St. Martin's Press, 1987), 374.

154. W. V. Rouse, *Evaluation of the Equal Employment*.

155. Olmsted, *et al.*, *Women at State*, 25.

156. *State Department: Minorities and Women*, 35.

157. Molly Moore, "Open Doors Don't Yield Equality," *Washington Post*, Sept. 24, 1989, A16.

158. American Forces Information Service, *Defense '87 Almanac* (Washington, DC: Department of Defense, 1987).

159. Paul Kattenburg cited in Charles Kegley and Eugene R. Wittkopf, *American Foreign Policy: Pattern and Process*, 2nd. ed. (New York: St. Martin's Press, 1982), 367.

160. Carolyn Becraft, *Women in the Military, 1980–1990* (Washington, DC: Women's Research and Education Institute, 1990), 2.

161. Ibid.

162. American Forces Information Service, *Defense '87 Almanac*.

163. Defense Manpower Commission, *Defense Manpower:The Keystone of National Security*, 250.

164. Figures from Office of Personnel Management, August 1991.

165. Office of Equal Employment and Civil Rights, *Update of the Affirmative Action Plan*.

166. Ibid.

167. Ibid.

168. *State Department: Minorities and Women*, 32.

169. Office of Equal Employment and Civil Rights, *Update of the Affirmative Action Plan*.

170. *Palmer, et al. v. Baker*, 662 Federal Supplement (1987), 1558.

171. Conversation with Monica Wagner, esq., August 18, 1992.

172. *State Department: Minorities and Women*, 4.

173. *Palmer, et al. v. Baker*, Plaintiffs' Brief on Remand to the District Court (l987), 2.

174. Office of Equal Employment and Civil Rights, *Update of the Affirmative Action Plan*, 5.

175. Statement of Mary Lee Garrison, Deputy Division Chief, Developing Countries and Trade Organizations, Department of State in "Hearing before the Subcommittee on the Civil Service of the Committee on Post Office and Civil Service, House of Representatives" (Serial No. 101–28) (Washington, DC: U.S. Printing Office, Sept. 22, 1989), 41.

176. *Selected Manpower Statistics* (Washington, DC: Department of Defense, September, 1987).

177. *Selected Manpower Statistics* (Washington, DC: Department of Defense, September, 1980).

178. American Forces Information Service, *Defense '87 Almanac*.

179. *Selected Manpower Statistics* (Washington, DC: Department of Defense, September, 1987).

180. Stiehm, *Arms and the Enlisted Woman*.

181. Jay Matthews, "Hill decries female powerlessness," *Buffalo News*, Nov. 17, 1991, A10.

182. Duerst-Lahti, "Gender, Power Relations in Public Bureaucracies," 137.

183. Ibid., 144.

184. Ibid., 144, 279.

185. Ibid., 23.

186. *Federal Employee Attitude: Phase 1 Baseline Survey* (Washington, DC: OPM, 1979).

187. *Federal Employee Attitudes Phase 2: Follow-up Survey* (Washington, DC: OPM, 1980), 33.

188. Powell, *Women & Men in Management*, 119.

189. Kanter, *Men and Women of the Corporation*, 58.

190. Quoted in Marlene Cimons, "Bias Brought Home in Foreign Service Case," *Los Angeles Times*, Feb. 13, 1972, 1.

191. Kegley and Wittkopf, *American Foreign Policy*, 2nd ed., 357.

192. Ibid., 358.

193. Office of Equal Employment and Civil Rights, *Update of the Affirmative Action Plan*, 17–18.

194. Department of State, *Multi-Year Affirmative Action Plan: FY 1990–92*, 68.

195. Powell, *Women & Men in Management*, 116.

196. Mike Causey, "Hero of the (Older) Ages," *Washington Post*, August 28, 1989, D2.

197. Powell, *Women & Men in Management*, 118.

198. Department of State, *Multi-Year Affirmative Action Plan: FY 1990–92*, 15.

199. Desda Moss, "U.S. Agencies Vow to Fight Harassment" *USA Today*, July 1, 1988, 4.

200. Anson Shupe, "Family violence and the nation's military complex," *Buffalo News*, Dec. 4, 1991, B3.

201. Kegley and Wittkopf, *American Foreign Policy*, 2nd ed., 367.

202. Defense Manpower Commission, *Defense Manpower: The Keystone of National Security*, 250.

203. Becraft, *Women in the Military, 1980–1990*, 3.

204. Causey, "Hero of the (Older) Ages."

205. *Report on Pre-Complaint Counseling and Complaint Processing Data Submitted by Federal Agencies for Fiscal Year 1984* (Washington, DC: Equal Employment Opportunity Commission).

206. "67 Female Navy Workers Win Sex Bias Lawsuit," *Niagara Gazette*, Nov. 27, 1991.

207. Holm, *Women in the Military*, 70.

208. Task Force on Women in Military, *Report of the Task Force on Women in the Military*; Desda Moss, "U.S. Agencies Vow to Fight Harassment"; and Felicity Barringer, "4 Reports Cite Naval Academy for Rife Sexism," *New York Times*, October 10, 1990, A12.

209. Eric Schmitt, "2 out of 3 Women in Military Study Report Sexual Harassment Incidents," *New York Times*, September 12, 1990, A22.

210. Ibid.

211. Anne J. Stone, "1987 in Review," in *The American Woman 1988–89* ed. Sara E. Rix, (New York: W.W. Norton), 44.

212. Richard Halloran, "Study Finds Servicewomen Harassed," *New York Times*, Feb. 21, 1989, A18.

213. Rep. Beverly B. Byron in Molly Moore, "Attitudes of Male-Oriented Culture Persist as Grievances go Unreported," *Washington Post*, Sept. 25, 1989, A9.

214. Ibid.

215. Eloise Salholz with Douglas Waller, "Tailhook: Scandal Time," *Newsweek*, July 6, 1992, 40–41.

216. Pat Towell, "Women's Combat Role Debated as Chiefs Denounce Sex Bias," *Congressional Quarterly*, 50 (31): 2292–2293.

217. Quoted in Ibid., 2292.

218. Ibid., 2292.

219. David H. Hackworth, "War and the Second Sex," *Newsweek*, August 5, 1991, 29.

220. John Lancaster, "24 Women Assaulted on Gulf Duty: Perpetrators Often Were Higher-Ranking Soldiers, Army Says, *Washington Post* July 21, 1992, A1.

221. Shupe, "Family Violence."

Notes to Chapter 3

1. Carolyn R. Dexter, "Women and the Exercise of Power in Organizations," in *Women and Work: An Annual Review*, ed. Laurie Larwood, Ann H. Stromberg, and Barbara Gutek (Beverly Hills: Sage, 1985), 245.

2. Edward P. Crapol, ed., *Women and American Foreign Policy: Lobbyists, Critics, and Insiders* (New York: Greenwood, 1987), xii.

3. Judith Buber Agassi, *Comparing Work Attitudes of Women and Men* (Lexington: Lexington, Mass., 1982), 4.

4. Esther E. Diamond, "Theories of Career Development and the Reality of Women at Work," in *Women's Career Development*, ed. Barbara A. Gutek and Laurie Larwood (Newbury Park: Sage, 1989), 15–16.

5. Gary N. Powell, *Women & Men in Management* (Newbury Park: Sage, 1988), 178–182.

6. Ibid., 179.

7. Bureau of Labor Statistics, "Employment in Perspective: Women in the Labor Force, Report 805" (Washington: Department of Labor, 1990), 1.

8. Diamond, "Theories of Career Development," 16–19; Powell, *Women & Men in Management*, 178–182.

9. Barbara A. Gutek and Laurie Larwood, ed. *Women's Career Development* (Newbury Park: Sage, 1989), 172.

10. Ibid., 173.

11. Ibid., 174.

12. Ibid., 174–175.

13. Ibid., 175.

14. Ibid., 176.

15. Ibid., 177.

16. Powell, *Women & Men in Management*, 188–190.

17. Ibid., 190–191.

18. Ibid., 194–196.

19. Ibid., 194–196, 201–203.

20. Ibid., 191–194, 196–198.

21. Ibid., 190–191.

22. Sharlene Hesse, "Women Working: Historical Trends," in *Working Women and Families*, ed. Karen Wolk Feinstein (Beverly Hills: Sage, 1979), 51–54.

23. Valerie Kincade Oppenheimer, *The Female Labor Force in the United States: Demographic and Economic Factors Governing its Growth and Changing Composition* (Berkeley: Institute of International Studies, 1970), Ch. 5.

24. Sara E. Rix, ed. *The American Woman, 1990–1991* (New York: W.W. Norton, 1990), 376; and

Bureau of Labor, "Employment in Perspective: Women in the Labor Force, Report 801" (Washington: Department of Labor, 1990), 1.

25. "Work and Families," *Public Perspective* 1 (6): 92.

26. Francine D. Blau and Marianne A. Ferber, "Women in the Labor Market: The Last Twenty Years," in *Women and Work: An Annual Review* Vol. 1, ed. Laurie Larwood, Ann H. Stromberg, and Barbara Gutek (Beverly Hills: Sage, 1985), 30–41.

27. Bureau of Labor Statistics, "Employment in Perspective: Women in the Labor Force, Report 796" (Washington: Department of Labor, 1990), 1.

28. Powell, *Women & Men in Management*, 195.

29. Ibid., 194.

30. Thomas R. Dye and Julie Strickland, "Women at the Top: A Note on Institutional Leadership," *Social Science Quarterly* 63 (2): 337–338.

31. Jerry A. Jacobs, "Sex Segregation in American Higher Education," in *Women and Work: An Annual Review*, Vol 1, ed. Laurie Larwood et al., 206–212.

32. Constantina Safilios-Rothschild, *Sex Role Socialization and Sex Discrimination: Synthesis and Critique of the Literature* (Washington: National Institute of Education, 1979), 32–44, 52–53.

33. Powell, *Women & Men in Management*, 194.

34. Laurie Larwood and Urs E. Gattiker, "A Comparison of the Career Paths Used by Successful Women and Men," in *Women's Career Development*, ed. Barbara A. Gutek and Laurie Larwood, 136–137.

35. Ibid., 139–150.

36. Susan K. Boardman, Charles C. Harrington, and Sandra V. Horowitz, "Successful Women: A Psychological Investigation of Family Class and Education Origins," in *Women's Career Development*, ed. Barbara A. Gutek and Laurie Larwood, 66–85; Safilios-Rothschild, *Sex Role Socialization and Sex Discrimination*, 36, 44, 48; Powell, *Women & Men in Management*, 57–58.

37. Powell, *Women & Men in Management*, 58–61; and Gaye Tuchman, "The Impact of Mass-Media Stereotypes Upon the Full Employment of Women," in *Women in the U.S. Labor Force*, ed. Ann Cahn (New York: Praeger, 1979), 249–268.

38. Dye and Strickland, "Women at the Top," 339.

39. Ibid., 337.

40. State Department, *Minorities and women are underrepresented in the Foreign Service* (Washington, DC: General Accounting Office, 1989), 46.

41. Meredith Reid Sarkees and Nancy E. McGlen, "Confronting Barriers: The Status of Women in Political Science" forthcoming *Women & Politics*; and Marilyn Marks Rubin, "Women in ASPA: The Fifty-Year Climb Toward Equality," *Public Administration Review* 50 (2): 281.

42. James L. Perry and Lois Recascino Wise, "The Motivational Basis of Public Service," *Public Administration Review* 50 (3): 371–372.

43. Powell, *Women & Men in Management*, 201–203.

44. Ibid., 201.

45. Ibid.

46. Roberta T. Anderson and Pauline Ramey, "Women in Higher Education: Development Through Administrative Mentoring," in *Women in Higher Education*, ed. Lynne Welch (New York: Praeger, 1990), 183.

47. Ibid., 183–184.

48. Project on the Status and Education of Women, *Academic Mentoring for Women Students and Faculty: A New Look at an Old Way to Get Ahead* (Washington, D.C.: Association of American Colleges, 1983), 2.

49. Powell, *Women & Men in Management*, 186.

50. Rita May Kelly and Mary E. Guy et al., "Public Managers in the States: A Comparison of Career Advancement by Sex," *Public Administration Review* 51 (5): 408.

51. Anderson and Ramey, "Women in Higher Education," 183–190.

52. Cited in Anderson and Ramey, "Women in Higher Education," 184.

53. Powell, *Women & Men in Management*, 185.

54. Kelly and Guy, "Public Managers in the States," 409.

55. Project on the Status of Women, *Academic Mentoring for Women Students and Faculty*, 2.

56. Ibid., 2.

57. Ibid., 4.

58. Ibid., 5.

59. Berenice Fisher, "Wandering in the Wilderness: The Search for Women Role Models," in *Reconstructing the Academy: Women's Education and Women's Studies*, ed. Elizabeth Minnich, Jean O'Barr and Rachel Rosenfeld (Chicago: University of Chicago Press, 1978) 245.

60. Project on the Status of Women, *Academic Mentoring for Women Students and Faculty*, 4.

61. Ronnie Braun, "The Downside of Mentoring," in *Women in Higher Education: Change and Challenges*, ed. Lynne B. Welch, 195.

62. Fisher, "Wandering in the Wilderness," 246.

63. Ibid., 234–235.

64. Ibid., 238.

65. Ibid., 236.

66. Ibid., 240

67. Ibid., 240–241.

68. Braun, "The Downside of Mentoring," 191–198.

69. Dowling, 1981 cited in Anderson and Ramey, "Women in Higher Education," 188.

70. Fisher, "Wandering in the Wilderness," 251.

71. Ibid., 254.

72. Priscilla Burnaby and Agnes K. Missirian, "Two Fast-Track Business Professors Tell the Secrets of Their Success," in *Women in Higher Education: Changes and Challenges*, ed. Lynne B. Welch, 258.

73. Powell, *Women & Men in Management*, 46–47; and Cynthia Fuchs Epstein, *Deceptive Distinctions: Sex, Gender, and the Social Order* (New Haven: Yale University Press, 1988), 78–80.

74. Kay Deaux, "From Individual Differences to Social Categories: Analysis of a Decade of Research on Gender," *American Psychologist* 39 (2): 105–1116.

75. Powell, *Women & Men in Management*, 49.

76. Brenda Majors, Untitled lecture at The State University of New York at Buffalo, April 1981.

77. Mary Lee Garrison, Testimony, "Hearing before the Subcommittee on the Civil Service of the Committee on Post Office and Civil Service, House of Representatives," (September 22, 1989) (Serial No. 101–28) (Washington, D.C.: U.S. Printing Office), 49–50.

78. Powell, *Women & Men in Management*, 71–72; and Gutek and Larwood, *Women's Career Development*, 10.

79. Roberta Valdez and Roberta A. Gutek, "Family Roles: A Help or a Hindrance for Working Women?" in *Women's Career Development*, ed. Roberta A. Gutek and Laurie Larwood, 163; and Dye and Strickland, "Women at the Top," 340.

80. Diamond, "Theories of Career Development," 23.

81. Powell, *Women & Men in Management*, 159.

82. Valdez and Gutek, "Family Roles," 163.

83. Gutek and Larwood, *Women's Career Development*, 166.

84. Kelly and Guy, "Public Managers in the States," 410–411.

85. Ibid., 164; and Teresa M. Cooney and Peter Uhlenberg, "Family-Building Patterns of Professional Women: A Comparison of Lawyers, Physicians, and Postsecondary Teachers," *Journal of Marriage and Family* 51 (3): 756–757.

86. Powell, *Women & Men in Management*, 159.

87. Gutek and Larwood, *Women's Career Development*, 164.

88. Ibid., 158.

89. Ibid.

90. Rosabeth Moss Kanter, *Men and Women of the Corporation* (New York: Basic Books, 1977), 76, 216–217, 220.

Notes to Chapter 4

1. Jean Bethke Elshtain, *Women and War* (New York: Basic Books, 1987), 232–233.

2. Pamela Johnston Conover, "Feminists and the Gender Gap," *Journal of Politics* 50 (4): 1004.

3. Betty Reardon, *Sexism and the War System* (New York: Teachers College Press, 1985); Birgit Brock-Utne, *Educating for Peace: A Feminist Perspective* (New York: Pergamon, 1985); Sara Ruddick, "Maternal Thinking," *Feminist Studies* 6 (2): 342–367; Sara Ruddick, "Pacifying the Forces: Drafting Women in the Interest of Peace," *Signs* 8 (3): 471–489; Sara Ruddick, "Preservative Love and Military Destruction: Reflections on Mothering and Peace," in *Mothering: Essays in Feminist Theory*, ed. Joyce Trebilcot (Totowa, NJ: Littlefield Adams, 1983), 231–262; Sara Ruddick, "Feminist Questions on Peace and War: An Agenda for Research, Discussion, Analysis, Action," *Women's Studies Quarterly* 12 (2): 8–11; Sara Ruddick "Maternal Work and the Practice of Peace," *Journal of Education* 167 (3): 97–111. Sara Ruddick, "Mothers and Men's Wars," in *Rocking the Ship of State*, ed. Adrienne Harris and Ynestra King (Boulder, CO: Westview Press, 1989), 75–92; and Sara Ruddick, "The Rationality of Care," in *Women, Militarism, and War*, ed. Jean Bethke Elshtain and Shelia Tobias (Savage, Md.: Rowman and Littlefield, 1990), 229–254.

4. Nancy Chodorow, *The Reproduction of Mothering* (Berkeley: University of California, 1978); and Carol Gilligan, *In a Different Voice: Psychological Theory and Women's Development* (Cambridge, MA: Harvard University Press, 1982).

5. Ruddick, "Pacifying the Forces," 478–479.

6. Ruddick, "The Rationality of Care," 249–251.

7. Ruddick, "Mothers and Men's Wars," 81.

8. Conover, "Feminists and the Gender Gap," 983–1010; and Betty Friedan and Midge Dector, "Are Women Different Today?" *Public Opinion* 5 (20): 41.

9. Joan Tronto, "Beyond Gender Differences to a Theory of Care," *Signs* 12 (4): 644–663.

10. Elshtain, *Women and War*, ch. 5; and Antonia Fraser, *The Warrior Queens* (New York: Alfred Knopf).

11. Elshtain, *Women and War*, 134.

12. Carol M. Mueller, ed., *The Politics of the Gender Gap* (Newbury Park: Sage, 1988); and Conover, "Feminists and the Gender Gap," 985–986.

13. Susan J. Carroll, "Women's Autonomy and the Gender Gap: 1980 and 1982," in *The Politics of the Gender Gap*, ed. Carol M. Mueller (Newbury Park: Sage, 1988), 236–257; Kathleen Frankovic, "Sex and Politics-New Alignments, Old Issues," *P.S.* 15 (3): 439–448; Henry C. Kenski, "The Gender Factor in the Changing Electorate," in *The Politics of the Gender Gap*, ed. Carol M. Mueller (Newbury Park; Sage, 1988), 28–60; Celinda Lake, "Guns, Butter, and Equality: The Women's Vote in 1980" (Presented at the Annual Meeting of the Midwest Political Science Association, Milwaukee, 1982); and Arthur H. Miller, "The Emerging Gender Gap," *Election Politics* 1 (Winter); Arthur H. Miller, "Gender and the Vote: 1984," in *The Politics of the Gender Gap*, ed. Carol M. Mueller, 258–282.

14. Carol M. Mueller, "The Empowerment of Women: Polling and the Women's Bloc Voting," in *The Politics of the Gender Gap*, 16.

15. Carol Matlack, "Women at the Polls," *National Journal*, December 19, 1987, 3205.

16. "The Exit Poll Results" *Public Opinion*, January/February, 1989, 25.

17. Daniel Wirls, "Reinterpreting the Gender Gap," *Public Opinion Quarterly* 50 (3): 322.

18. Everett Carl Ladd, "The National Electorate," *Public Opinion*, January/February, 1989, 3.

19. Wirls, "Reinterpreting the Gender Gap," 319; "Changes in Party Identification," *Public Perspective* 2 (4): 92.

20. Miller, "Gender and the Vote: 1984," 268–277.

21. Robert Y. Shapiro and Harpreet Mahajan, "Gender Differences in Policy Preferences: A Summary of Trends from the 1960s to the 1980s," *Public Opinion Quarterly* 50 (1): 50.

22. Arthur H. Miller, "Gender and the Vote: 1984," 264–268; Susan Carroll, "Gender Schema and Mass Politics" (Presented at the Annual Meeting of the Midwest Political Science Association, 1985): 16–21; and Ethel Klein, *Gender Politics: From Consciousness to Mass Politics* (Cambridge, MA: Harvard University Press, 1984).

23. Conover, "Feminists and the Gender Gap," 994–995; and Shapiro and Mahajan, "Gender Differences in Policy Preferences," 51.

24. Miller, "Gender and the Vote: 1984," 270–279; and Conover, "Feminists and the Gender Gap," 999–1002.

25. Frankovic, "Sex and Politics," 445–446; Lake, "Guns, Butter, and Equality"; and Miller, "Gender and the Vote: 1984," 277–279.

26. Frankovic, "Sex and Politics," 444–446.

27. "Worth Noting," *Public Opinion*, January/February, 1989: 33.

28. Tom W. Smith, "The Polls: Gender and Attitudes Toward Violence," *Public Opinion Quarterly* 48 (1B): 384.

29. Shapiro and Mahajan, "Gender Differences in Policy Preferences," 49.

30. Ibid.

31. Ibid., 50.

32. Ibid.

33. Ibid., 54.

34. David Fite, Marc Genest and Clyde Wilcox, "Gender Differences in Foreign Policy Attitudes," *American Politics Quarterly* 18 (4): 500.

35. "Women and the Use of Force," *The Public Perspective* 2 (3): 85–86; and Fite, Genest, and Wilcox, "Gender Differences in Foreign Policy Attitudes," 497–502.

36. Sandra Baxter and Marjorie Lansing, *Women and Politics: The Visible Majority*, 2nd ed. (Ann Arbor, MI: The University of Michigan Press, 1983), 57–59: "Women and the Use of Force," 85–86; and Shapiro and Mahajan 1986, "Gender Differences in Policy Preferences," 51.

37. John M. Benson, "The Polls: U.S. Military Intervention," *Public Opinion Quarterly* 46 (4): 595.

38. Colleen Roach, "Feminist Peace researchers, culture and communications," *Media Development* 28 (2): 6.

39. "Women and the Use of Force," 86.

40. Ibid.

41. Ibid.

42. Ibid.

43. Frankovic, "Sex and Politics," 445.

44. Frankovic, "Sex and Politics," 444.

45. Nancy E. McGlen and Karen O'Connor, "The Societal Impact of the American Women's Peace Movement" (Presented at the Annual Meeting of the International Political Science Association, Washington, D.C., 1988), 6.

46. Patricia A. Gwartney-Gibbs and Denise H. Lach, "Sex Differences in Attitudes Toward Nuclear War," *Journal of Peace Research* 28 (2): 168.

47. Ibid.

48. Daniel Yankelovich Group, *Americans Talk Security: A Series of Surveys of American Voters' Attitudes Concerning National Security Issues*, No. 3 (1988), 2, 36.

49. Barbara Bardes and Robert Oldendick, "Beyond Internationalism: A Case for Multiple Dimensions in the Structure of Foreign Policy Attitudes," *Social Science Quarterly* 59 (3): 505; see also Eugene Wittkopf, "The Structure of Foreign Policy Attitudes: An Alternative View," *Social Science Quarterly* 62 (1): 108–123 .

50. Wirls, "Reinterpreting the Gender Gap," 320.

51. Fite, Genest, and Wilcox, "Gender Differences in Foreign Policy Attitudes," 498.

52. Conover, "Feminists and the Gender Gap," 987–89.

53. Gwartney-Gibbs and Lach, "Sex Differences in Attitudes Toward Nuclear War," 171.

54. Mark P. Jensen, "Gender, Sex Roles, and Attitudes Toward War and Nuclear Weapons," *Sex Roles* 17 (5/6): 260–61.

55. Fite, Genest, Wilcox, "Gender Differences in Foreign Policy Attitudes," 507.

56. Conover, "Feminists and the Gender Gap," 987–89.

57. Ibid., 1004.

58. Elizabeth Adell Cook and Clyde Wilcox, "Feminism and the Gender Gap—A Second Look," *The Journal of Politics* 53 (4): 1117–1121. For the two other groups, potential feminists and nonfeminists, attitudes toward nuclear war also distinguished women and men.

59. Fite, Genest, and Wilcox, "Gender Differences in Foreign Policy Attitudes," 508.

60. Shapiro and Mahajan, "Gender Differences in Policy Preferences," 56–58.

61. James W. Tankard, "Nuclear Weapons Literacy and Its Correlates," *Peace Research* 16 (1): 32–33; and Barbara Bardes, "Gender and Foreign Policy: A Comparative Perspective" (Presented at the Annual Meeting of the American Political Science Association, Washington, D.C., 1986), 7; and Michael X. Delli Carpini and Scott Keeter, "The Gender Gap in Political Knowledge," *Public Perspective* 3 (5): 23–26.

62. E. M. Schreiber, "Enduring Effects of Military Service? Opinion Differences Between U.S. Veterans and Nonveterans" *Social Forces* 57 (3): 830–831.

63. Ole R. Holsti and James N. Rosenau, "The Foreign Policy Beliefs of Women in Leadership Positions," *The Journal of Politics* 43 (2): 326–347; Ole R. Holsti and James N. Rosenau, *American Leadership in World Affairs* (Boston: Allen & Unwin, 1984); Ole R. Holsti and James Rosenau, "The Domestic and Foreign Policy Beliefs of American Leaders," *Journal of Conflict Resolution* 32 (2): 248–294; and Ole R. Holsti, "Gender and Political Beliefs of American Leaders, 1976–1988," (Presented at the Annual Meeting of the International Studies Association,Washington, D.C., 1990).

64. Holsti and Rosenau, "The Foreign Policy Beliefs of Women," 337–338.

65. Ibid., 339.

66. Ibid., 332.

67. Ibid., 342.

68. Holsti, "Gender and Political Beliefs of American Leaders."

69. Eugene R. Wittkopf and Michael A. Maggiotto, "Elites and Masses: A Comparative Analysis of Attitudes Toward America's World Role," *The Journal of Politics* 45 (2): 303–334.

70. Ibid., 308.

71. Ibid., 312, 319.

72. Ibid., 321–322.

73. Ibid., 324.

74. Ibid., 326, 328.

75. Susan Carroll and Barbara Geiger-Parker, "Women Appointed to the Carter Administration: A Comparison with Men" (Rutgers: Center for the American Woman and Politics), 55, 60.

76. Joan Hoff-Wilson, "Conclusion: Of Mice and Men," in *Women and American Foreign Policy: Lobbyist, Critics, and Insiders*, ed. Edward P. Crapol (New York: Greenwood Press,1987), 185.

77. Alison Leigh Cowan, "Women's Gains on the Job: Not Without a Heavy Toll," *New York Times*, August 21, 1989, sec. A.

78. Ibid.

79. Holsti and Rosenau, "The Foreign Policy Beliefs of Women," 338, 346.

80. Ibid., 346.

81. Georgia Duerst-Lahti and Cathy M. Johnson, "Gender, Style, and Bureaucracy: Must Women Go Native To Succeed?" (Presented at the Annual Meeting of the American Political Science Association, Atlanta, 1989), 20.

82. For a discussion of the Reagan appointment process, see "10 Weeks to Put It All Together," *U.S News and World Report*, November 17, 1980; Joel Havemann, "Inside the Reagan Administration," *National Journal*, April 25, 1981, 675–677; and Hedrick Smith, "Conservatives Cite Gains in Top Posts," *New York Times*, March 3, 1981, 1.

83. Quoted in Monica Langley, "Reagan Men Learn What GOP Women Really Want: Jobs," *Wall Street Journal*, July 7, 1981.

84. Ann Snitow, "A Gender Diary," in *Rocking the Ship of State*, ed. Adrienne Harris and Ynestra King (Boulder, CO: Westview, 1989), 45.

Notes to Chapter 5

1. Cynthia Enloe, *Bananas, Beaches and Bases: Making Feminist Sense of International Politics* (Berkeley: University of California Press, 1989), 197.

2. Jerel A. Rosati, "Developing a Systematic Decision-Making Framework: Bureaucratic Politics in Perspective," *World Politics* 33 (2): 234–252.

3. Charles Kegley and Eugene R. Wittkopf, *American Foreign Policy: Pattern and Process*, 3rd ed. (New York: St. Martin's Press, 1987), 589.

4. See John Spanier and Eric M. Uslaner, *How American Foreign Policy is Made* (New York: Holt Rinehart and Winston/Praeger, 1978), 49–50.

5. Ibid., 339.

6. Duncan L. Clarke, *American Defense and Foreign Policy Institutions* (New York: Harper & Row Publishers, 1989), 89–91.

7. Ibid., 83.

8. Ibid., 86.

9. Roger Hilsman, *The Politics of Policy Making in Defense and Foreign Affairs: Conceptual Models and Bureaucratic Politics* (Englewood Cliffs: Prentice-Hall, 1987), 187.

10. Spanier and Uslaner, *How American Foreign Policy is Made*, 62.

11. Kegley and Wittkopf, *American Foreign Policy*, 3rd ed., 340.

12. Hilsman, *The Politics of Policy Making*, 187.

13. Duncan L. Clarke, "Why State Can't Lead," in *The Conduct of American Foreign Policy Debated*, ed. Herbert M. Levine and Jean Edward Smith (New York: McGraw Hill, 1990).

14. James A. Nathan and James K. Oliver, *Foreign Policy Making and the American Political System*, 2nd ed. (Boston: Little, Brown and Company, 1987), 82.

15. Ibid., 101.

16. Steven D. Stehr, "Top Bureaucrats and the Distribution of Influence in Reagan's Executive Branch" (Presented at the Annual Meeting of the American Political Science Association, Atlanta, 1989), 6.

17. L. Gordon Crovitz, "Micromanaging Foreign Policy," *The Public Interest*, 100 (Summer): 102–115.

18. Stehr, "Top Bureaucrats and the Distribution of Influence in Reagan's Executive Branch," 1.

19. Spanier and Uslaner, *How American Foreign Policy is Made*, 53.

20. Clarke, *American Defense and Foreign Policy Institutions*, 84.

21. Tom Bowman, "Critics set diplomacy aside in rapping Bush nominees for envoy," *Buffalo News*, July 16, 1989, A10.

22. Stehr, "Top Bureaucrats and the Distribution of Influence in Reagan's Executive Branch," 1.

23. Nathan and Oliver, *Foreign Policy Making*, 95.

24. Ibid., 85.

25. Ibid.

26. Ibid., 92.

27. Kegley and Wittkopf, *American Foreign Policy*, 3rd ed., 344.

28. Peter M. Benda and Charles H. Levine, "Reagan and the Bureaucracy: The Bequest, The Promise, and the Legacy" in *The Reagan Legacy*, ed. Charles O. Jones (Chatham, NJ: Chatham House Publishers, Inc., 1988), 109.

29. Stehr, "Top Bureaucrats and the Distribution of Influence in Reagan's Executive Branch," 2.

30. Hilsman, *The Politics of Policy Making in Defense and Foreign Affairs*, 314.

31. Nathan and Oliver, *Foreign Policy Making*, 87.

32. Wilfrid L. Kohl, "The Nixon-Kissinger Foreign Policy System and U.S.-European Relations: Patterns of Policy Making," *World Politics* 28(1): 1–43.

33. Dan Caldwell, "Bureaucratic Foreign Policy-Making," *American Behavioral Scientist* 21(1): 87–110.

34. See Glenn H. Snyder and Paul Diesing, *Conflict Among Nations* (Princeton: Princeton University Press, 1977), 340–350 for a more complete description.

35. Gregory M. Herek, Irving L. Janis, and Paul Huth, "Decision Making During International Crises," *Journal of Conflict Resolution* 31(2): 203–226.

36. Martha L. Cottam, *Foreign Policy Decision Making: The Influence of Cognition* (Boulder: Westview Press, 1986).

37. Lori Helene Gronich, "The Cognitive Processing Theory of Decision-Making: A New Explanation for Policies of War and Peace" (Presented at the Annual Meeting of the American Political Science Association, Atlanta, 1989), 6.

38. Jonathan Bendor and Thomas H. Hammond, "Rethinking Allison's Models" (Presented at the Annual Meeting of the American Political Science Association, Atlanta, 1989), 33.

39. Kohl, "The Nixon-Kissinger Foreign Policy System," 41.

40. Paul Anderson cited in Kegley and Wittkopf, *American Foreign Policy*, 3rd ed., 476.

41. Cited in Kegley and Wittkopf, *American Foreign Policy*, 3rd ed., 561–562.

42. Bert A. Rockman, "The Style and Organization of the Reagan Presidency," in *The Reagan Legacy*, ed. Charles O. Jones, 9.

43. Ibid., 10.

44. Benda and Levine, "Reagan and the Bureaucracy," 107.

45. Nathan and Oliver, *Foreign Policy Making*, 83–84.

46. Quoted in Kegley and Wittkopf, *American Foreign Policy*, 3rd ed., 363.

47. Snyder and Diesing, *Conflict Among Nations*, note on p. 408.

48. Kegley and Wittkopf, *American Foreign Policy*, 3rd ed., 341.

49. Ibid., 357.

50. Clarke, *American Defense and Foreign Policy Institutions*, 7.

51. Kegley and Wittkopf, *American Foreign Policy*, 3rd ed., 359.

52. Ibid., 359.

53. Ibid., 574–75.

54. Stehr, "Top Bureaucrats and the Distribution of Influence in Reagan's Executive Branch," 2.

55. Institute for the Study of Diplomacy, *The Foreign Service in 2001* (Washington, DC: Georgetown University, 1992), 53; and Colin Campbell and Bert A. Rockman, eds. *The Bush Presidency: First Appraisals* (Chatham, NJ: Chatham House Publishers, Inc., 1991).

Notes to Chapter 6

1. Quoted in Ellen Goodman, "Women's Meeting Poses Question: Is it Worth Getting into Public Service?" *Niagara Gazette*, October 20, 1989, 4A.

2. Quoted in Brad Knickerbocker, "Ms. Roberts Goes to the Statehouse," *Christian Science Monitor*, February 15, 1991, 10.

3. Georgia Duerst-Lahti, "Gender, Position and Perception: Communicating Power in State Organizations" (Presented at the Annual Meeting of the Midwest Political Science Association, Chicago, 1985), 10.

4. Gary N. Powell, *Women & Men in Management* (Newbury Park: Sage Publications, 1988), 149.

5. Ibid., 167.

6. Quoted in Elizabeth A. Brown, "Why Most Public Officials Are Still Men," *Christian Science Monitor*, Feb. 15, 1991, 11.

7. Powell, *Women & Men in Management*.

8. Ibid., 151.

9. Susan Schenkel cited in Cynthia Hanson, "Fitness for Leadership," *Christian Science Monitor*, Feb. 15, 1991, 12.

10. Powell, *Women & Men in Management*, 153.

11. Paraphrased by Brad Knickerbocker, "Ms. Roberts Goes to the Statehouse," *Christian Science Monitor*, Feb. 15, 1991, 10.

12. Rita Mae Kelly, Mary M. Hale, Jayne Burgess, "Gender and Managerial/Leadership Styles," *Women & Politics* 11(2): 22.

13. Ibid., 23.

14. Duerst-Lahti, "Gender, Position and Perception," 24.

15. Kelly et al., "Gender and Managerial/Leadership Styles," 19–20.

16. Georgia Duerst-Lahti and Cathy Marie Johnson, "Gender and Style in Bureaucracy," *Women & Politics* 10 (4): 67–120.

17. Duerst-Lahti, "Gender, Power Relations in Public Bureaucracies," 296.

18. Ibid., 354–55.

19. Kelly et al., "Gender and Managerial/Leadership Styles," 22.

20. Ibid., 34.

21. Powell, *Women & Men in Management*, 241.

22. Georgia Duerst-Lahti and Cathy M. Johnson, "Gender, Style, and Bureaucracy: Must Women Go Native to Succeed?" (Presented at the Annual Meeting of the American Political Science Association, Atlanta, 1989), 17, 100.

23. Ibid., 11.

24. Duerst-Lahti and Johnson, "Gender and Style in Bureaucracy," 70.

25. Powell, *Women & Men in Management*, 151.

26. Georgia Duerst-Lahti, "Gender, Position and Perception," 17; Georgia Duerst-Lahti and Cathy M. Johnson, "Gender, Style, and Bureaucracy," 20.

27. Powell, *Women & Men in Management*, 155.

28. Duerst-Lahti, "Gender, Power Relations in Public Bureaucracies," 5.

29. Duerst-Lahti, "Gender, Position and Perception," 17.

30. Duerst-Lahti and Johnson, "Gender, Style and Bureaucracy," 84.

31. Ibid., 77.

32. Susan J. Carroll and Barbara Geiger-Parker, "Women Appointed to the Carter Administration: A Comparison with Men," (Rutgers, NJ: CAWP), 48.

33. Duerst-Lahti, "Gender, Power Relations in Public Bureaucracies," 6.

34. Cited in Catherine Foster, "A Different Track to Managing People," *Christian Science Monitor*, Feb. 15, 1991, 13.

35. Kelly et al., "Gender and Managerial/Leadership Styles," 21.

36. Cited in Powell, *Women & Men in Management*, 16.

37. Duerst-Lahti, "Gender, Power Relations in Public Bureaucracies," 109.

38. Duerst-Lahti and Johnson, "Gender and Style in Bureaucracy," 67–68.

39. Duerst-Lahti, "Gender, Power Relations in Public Bureaucracies," 108–109.

40. Powell, *Women & Men in Management*, 165–166.

41. Rosabeth Moss Kanter, *Men and Women of the Corporation* (New York: Basic Books, 1977), 210–230.

42. Powell, *Women & Men in Management*, 113.

43. Ibid.

44. Susan J. Carroll and Ella Taylor, "Gender Differences in Policy Priorities of U.S. State Legislators" (Presented at the Annual Meeting of the American Political Science Association, Atlanta, 1989), 6.

45. Duerst-Lahti, "Gender, Power Relations in Public Bureaucracies," 23.

46. *Federal Employee Attitudes Phase 1 Baseline Survey*, Washington, D.C.: OPM, 24.

47. Duerst-Lahti, "Gender, Position and Perception: Communicating Power in State Organizations," 13.

48. Duerst-Lahti, "Gender, Power Relations in Public Bureaucracies," 289.

49. Georgia Duerst-Lahti, "But Women Play the Game Too: Gender Power Dynamics in Administrative Decision Making" (Presented at the Annual Meeting of the American Political Science Association, Chicago, 1987), 7.

50. Powell, *Women & Men in Management*, 144.

51. Ibid., 110.

52. "Notable and Quotable," *San Diego Union*, Oct. 13, 1991, C–6.

53. Ellen Boneparth and Emily Stoper, eds., *Women, Power and Policy*, 2nd. ed. (New York, Pergamon Press, 1989), 53.

54. Roberta Sigel and Lauren D. Burnbauer, "The 'NOT ME' Syndrome. A Paradox in Search of An Explanation" (Presented at the Annual Meeting of the American Political Science Association, Atlanta, 1989), 2.

55. Powell, *Women & Men in Management*, 146.

56. Ibid., 157.

57. Carroll and Taylor, "Gender Differences in Policy Priorities of U.S. State Legislators," 1.

58. Benjamin Welles, "Women Winning State Department Case," *New York Times*, February 28, 1972.

59. See interview with Alison Palmer, Chapter 2.

60. Judith Barra Austin, "Women won't testify on job discrimination," *Niagara Gazette*, October 24, 1991, 5A.

61. Powell, *Women & Men in Management*, 161.

Notes to Conclusion

1. Maureen Dowd, "Women at White House find it's still a man's world," *Detroit Free Press*, May 21, 1991, A4.

2. Quoted in Bill Turque with Eleanor Clift, Howard Fineman, and Ginny Carroll, "Reliving the '60s," *Newsweek*, February 24, 1992, 22.

3. *State Department: Minorities and women are underrepresented in the Foreign Service* (Washington, DC: General Accounting Office, 1989), 4–5.

4. "Hearing before the Subcommittee on the Civil Service of the Committee on Post Office and Civil Service, House of Representatives" (Washington, DC: U.S. Printing Office, 1989); *Joint Hearing Before the Subcommittee on International Operations of the Committee on Foreign Affairs and Subcommittee on the Civil Service of the Committee on Post Office and Civil Service* (Washington, DC; U.S. Printing Office, 1990).

5. Ibid., 2.

6. Ibid., 10.

7. Conversations at the Office of Personnel Management, August 1991.

8. Roxanne Roberts, "The Silence of the Diplomat," *Washington Post*, March 15, 1991, C1.

9. Elaine Sciolino, "Deskbound in the U.S. The Envoy to Iraq is called Scapegoat for a Failed Policy." *New York Times*, September 12, A19.

10. Figures from interviews at OPM, August 1991.

11. A recent study, supported by the American Association of University Women, found widespread sexism in this nation's classrooms. Barbara Kantrowitz with Pat Wingert and Patrick Houston, "Sexism in the Schoolhouse" *Newsweek*, February 24, 1992, 62.

12. George Church, "Men of the Year," *Time*, January 7, 1989, 20.

13. Roberts, "The Silence of the Diplomat," C6.

14. Elaine Sciolino, "Friends as Ambassadors: How Many is Too Many?" *New York Times*, November 7, 1989, A8.

15. Margaret Garrard Warner, "A 'Drone Class' of American Diplomacy?" *Newsweek*, October 30, 1989, 62.

16. Dowd, "Women at White House find it's still a man's world," 1A.

Selected Bibliography

Aberbach, Joel D. 1991. "The President and the Executive Branch." In Colin Campbell and Bert A. Rockman, eds. *The Bush Presidency: First Appraisals*. Chatham, NJ: Chatham House Publishers, Inc.

Abzug, Bella with Mim Kelber. 1984. *Gender Gap*. Boston: Houghton Mifflin.

Abzug, Bella and Mim Kelber. 1987. *Women's Foreign Policy Council Directory*. New York: Women's Foreign Policy Council.

Agassi, Judith Buber. 1982. *Comparing the Work Attitudes of Women and Men*. Lexington, MA: Lexington Books.

Alexander, Doreene Ward. 1990. "An Exploration of Attributes Present in a Mentor/Protégé Relationship in Nursing Education Administration." In Lynne Welch, ed. *Women in Higher Education:Changes and Challenges*. New York: Praeger.

Allison, Graham T. 1971. *Essence of Decision*. Glenview, IL: Scott, Foresman and Company.

American Forces Information Service. 1987. *Defense '87 Almanac*. Washington, DC: Department of Defense.

American Forces Press Services. 1976. *Women in the Armed Forces*. Washington, DC: Department of Defense.

Anderson, Roberta T. and Pauline Ramey. 1990. "Women in Higher Education: Development Through Administrative Mentoring." In Lynne Welch, ed. *Women in Higher Education: Changes and Challenges*. New York: Praeger.

Annual Report. 1979. (DOC PM 1.1979) Washington, DC: OPM.

Annual Report on the Employment of Minorities, Women and Handicapped in the Federal Government Fiscal Year 1983. Washington, DC: EEOC.

Annual Report to Congress on the Federal Equal Opportunity Recruitment Program for Fiscal Year 1989. Washington, DC: OPM.

Austin, Judith Barra. 1991. "Women won't testify on job discrimination." *Niagara Gazette*. October 24, 5A.

Baer, Denise L. and David A. Bositis. 1985. "Biology, Gender, and Politics: An Assessment and Critique." *Women & Politics*. 3 (2/3): 29–66.

Baker, James. 1989. "Overseas Cable to all Posts." Washington, DC. April 17, 1–3.

Bardes, Barbara and Robert Oldendick. 1978. "Beyond Internationalism: A Case for Multiple Dimensions in the Structure of Foreign Policy Attitudes." *Social Science Quarterly*. 59 (3): 496–508.

Bardes, Barbara. 1986. "Gender and Foreign Policy: A Comparative Perspective." Presented at the Annual Meeting of the American Political Science Association, Washington, DC.

Barringer, Felicity. 1990. "4 Reports Cite Naval Academy for Rife Sexism." *New York Times*. October 10, A12.

Battle, Dolores. 1976. *Women in the Defense Establishment*. Washington, DC: Defense Manpower Commission.

Baxter, Sandra and Marjorie Lansing. 1983. *Women and Politics: The Visible Majority*. 2nd ed. Ann Arbor, MI: The University of Michigan Press.

Becraft, Carolyn. 1990. *Women in the Military, 1980–1990*. Washington, DC: Women's Research and Education Institute.

Belkin, Lisa. 1989. "Bars to Equality of Sexes Seen as Eroding, Slowly." *New York Times*. August 20, sec. A.

Benda, Peter M. and Charles H. Levine. 1988. "Reagan and the Bureaucracy: The Bequest, The Promise, and the Legacy." In Charles O. Jones, ed. *The Reagan Legacy*. Chatham, NJ: Chatham House Publishers Inc.

Bendor, Jonathan and Thomas H. Hammond. 1989. "Rethinking Allison's Models." Presented at the Annual Meeting of the American Political Science Association, Atlanta.

Benson, John M. 1982. "The Polls: U.S. Military Intervention." *Public Opinion Quarterly*. 46 (4): 492–598.

Binkin, Martin. 1986 *Military Technology and Defense Manpower*. Washington, DC: Brown Institution.

Blau, Francine D. 1978. "The Data on Women Workers, Past, Present, and Future." In Ann H. Stromberg and Shirley Harkess, eds. *Women Working*. Palo Alto, CA: Mayfield.

Blau, Francine D. and Marianne A. Ferber. 1985. "Women in the Labor Market: The Last Twenty Years." In Laurie Larwood, Ann H. Stromberg, and Barbara Gutek, eds. *Women and Work: An Annual Review*. Vol. 1. Beverly Hills: Sage.

Blitz, Mark. 1990. "Letter from America: President Bush's Foreign Policy." *Government and Opposition*. 25 (2): 219–230.

Bloomfield, Lincoln. 1982. *The Foreign Policy Process: A Modern Primer*. Englewood Cliffs, NJ: Prentice-Hall, Inc.

Boardman, Susan K., Charles C. Harrington and Sandra Horowitz. 1987. "Successful Women: A Psychological Investigation of Family Class and Education Origins." In Barbara A. Gutek and Laurie Larwood, eds. *Women's Career Development*. Newbury Park: Sage.

Boneparth, Ellen and Emily Stoper, eds. 1989. *Women, Power and Policy*. 2nd ed. New York: Pergamon Press.

Bowman, Tom. 1989. "Critics set diplomacy aside in rapping Bush nominees for envoy." *Buffalo News*. July 16, A10.

Braun, Ronnie. "The Downside of Mentoring." In Lynne Welch, ed. *Women in Higher Education: Changes and Challenges*. New York: Praeger.

Brock-Utne, Birgit. 1985. *Educating For Peace: A Feminist Perspective*. New York: Pergamon Press.

Brown, Elizabeth A. 1991. "Why Most Public Officials Are Still Men." *Christian Science Monitor.* February 15, 11.

Bureau of Labor Statistics. 1990. "Employment in Perspective: Women in the Labor Force." Report 796. Washington, DC: U.S. Department of Labor.

Bureau of Labor Statistics. 1990. "Employment in Perspective: Women in the Labor Force." Report 801. Washington, DC: U.S. Department of Labor.

Bureau of Labor Statistics. 1991. "Employment in Perspective: Women in the Labor Force." Report 805. Washington, DC: U.S. Department of Labor.

Burnaby, Priscilla and Agnes K. Missirian. 1990. "Two Fast-track Business Professors Tell the Secrets of Their Success." In Lynne Welch, ed. *Women in Higher Education: Changes and Challenges.* New York: Praeger.

Caldicott, Helen. 1985. *Missile Envy: The Arms Race and Nuclear War.* New York: Bantam.

Caldwell, Dan. 1977. "Bureaucratic Foreign Policy-Making." *American Behavioral Scientist.* 21 (1): 87–110.

Calkin, Homer. 1978. *Women in the Department of State: Their Role in American Foreign Affairs.* Washington, DC: Department of State.

Campbell, Colin. 1991. "The White House and Cabinet under the 'Let's Deal' Presidency." In Colin Campbell and Bert A. Rockman, eds. *The Bush Presidency: First Appraisals.* Chatham, NJ: Chatham House Publishers, Inc.

Carpini, Michael X. Delli and Scott Keeter. 1992. "The Gender Gap in Political Knowledge." *The Public Perspective.* 3(5): 23–26.

Carroll, Susan J. 1985. "Gender Schema and Mass Politics." Presented at the 1985 Annual Meeting of The Midwest Political Science Association, Chicago.

Carroll, Susan J. 1988. "Women's Autonomy and the Gender Gap: 1980 and 1982. In Carol Mueller, ed. *The Politics of the Gender Gap.* Newbury Park: Sage.

Carroll, Susan J. 1988. "New Strategies To Increase The Number Of Women Appointed To Recent Presidential Administrations In The United States." Presented at the Vater Staat Und Seine Frauen Conference, Berlin, West Germany.

Carroll, Susan J. and Barbara Geiger-Parker. 1983. "Women Appointed to the Carter Administration: A Comparison with Men." Rutgers: Center for the American Woman and Politics.

Carroll, Susan J. and Ella Taylor. 1989. "Gender Differences in Policy Priorities of U.S. State Legislators." Presented at the Annual Meeting of the American Political Science Association, Atlanta.

Causey, Mike. 1989. "Hero of the (Older) Ages." *Washington Post.* August 28, D2.

"Changes in Party Identification." 1991. *The Public Perspective.* 2 (4): 92–93.

Chodorow, Nancy. 1978. *The Reproduction of Mothering.* Berkeley: University of California Press.

Church, George. 1991. "Men of the Year." *Time.* January 7.

Cimons, Marlene. 1972. "Bias Brought Home in Foreign Service Case." *Los Angeles Times.* February 13, 1.

Clarke, Duncan L. 1989. *American Defense and Foreign Policy Institutions.* New York: Harper & Row Publishers.

Clarke, Duncan L. 1990. "Why State Can't Lead." In Herbert M. Levine and Jean Edward Smith, eds. *The Conduct of American Foreign Policy Debated.* New York: McGraw Hill.

Coleman, David. 1989. "Woman wins 21 year legal battle." *Wellfleet Oracle.* April 27, 6.

Commission on Civil Rights. 1981. *Equal Opportunity in the Foreign Service*. Washington, DC: Office of Management.

Columbia Broadcasting Systems. 1989. "60 Minutes." July.

"Congress was deceived on warning to Saddam." 1991. *Buffalo News* July 21, A1, A7.

Conover, Pamela Johnston. 1988. "Feminists and the Gender Gap." *Journal of Politics*. 50 (4): 985–1010.

Cook, Elizabeth Adell and Clyde Wilcox. 1991. "Feminism and the Gender Gap—A Second Look." *The Journal of Politics*. 53 (4): 1111–1122.

Cottam, Martha L. 1986. *Foreign Policy Decision Making; The Influence of Cognition*. Boulder, CO: Westview Press.

Cowan, Alison Leigh. 1989. "Women's Gains on the Job: Not Without a Heavy Toll." *New York Times*. August 21, sec. A.

Cooney, Teresa M. and Peter Uhlenberg. 1989. "Family-Building Patterns of Professional Women: A Comparison of Lawyers, Physicians, and Postsecondary Teachers." *Journal of Marriage and Family*. 51 (3): 749–758.

Crapol, Edward P., ed. 1987. *Women and American Foreign Policy: Lobbyists, Critics, and Insiders*. New York: Greenwood.

Crovitz, L. Gordon. 1990. "Micromanaging Foreign Policy." *The Public Interest*. 100 (Summer): 102–115.

Dalson, Delaer L. 1989. "A Comparison of the Impact of Women and Men's Attitudes on their Legislative Behavior: Is what they say what they do?." Presented at the Annual Meeting of the American Political Science Association, Atlanta.

Daniel Yankelovich Group. 1988. *Americans Talk Security: A Series of Surveys of American Voters' Attitudes Concerning National Security Issues*. No. 3.

Davis, James A., Jennifer Lauby, and Paul B. Sheatsley. 1983. "Americans View the Military." Chicago: National Opinion Research Center.

Deaux, Kay. 1984. "From Individual Differences to Social Categories: Analysis of a Decade's Research on Gender." *American Psychologist*. 39 (2): 105–116.

Defense Manpower Commission. 1976. *Defense Manpower: The Keystone of National Security*. Washington, DC: Department of Defense.

Department of Defense. 1987. *Defense 87*. Washington, DC: Government Printing Office.

Department of State. 1991. *Multi-Year Affirmative Action Plan: FY 1990–92*. Washington, DC: Department of State.

Department of State. 1992. "List of Chiefs of Mission as of March 31, 1992." Washington, DC: Department of State.

Dexter, Carolyn R. 1985. "Women and the Exercise of Power in Organizations." In Laurie Larwood, Ann H. Stromberg and Barbara A Gutek, eds. *Women and Work: An Annual Review*. Vol. 1. Beverly Hills: Sage.

Diamond, Esther E. 1989. "Theories of Career Development and the Reality of Women at Work." In Barbara A. Gutek and Laurie Larwood, eds. *Women's Career Development*. Newbury Park: Sage.

di Leonardo, Micaela. 1985. "Morals, Mothers, and Militarism: Antimilitarism and Feminist Theory." *Feminist Studies*. 11 (3): 599–617.

Dowd, Maureen. 1989. "Spokeswoman on Foreign Affairs: a Behind-the-Scenes Player is Up Front." *New York Times*. September 20, A18.

Dowd, Maureen. 1991. "Women at White House find it's still a man's world." *Detroit Free Press*. May 21, 1A, 4A.

Duerst-Lahti, Georgia. 1985. "Gender, Position and Perception: Communicating Power in State Organizations." Presented at the Annual Meeting of the Midwest Political Science Association, Chicago.

Duerst-Lahti, Georgia. 1986. "Organizational Ethos and Women's Power Capacity: Perceived and Formal Structure in State Administrative Organizations." Presented at the Annual Meeting of the American Political Science Association, Washington, DC.

Duerst-Lahti, Georgia. 1987a. "Gender, Power Relations in Public Bureaucracies." Ph.D. diss. University of Wisconsin-Madison.

Duerst-Lahti, Georgia. 1987b. "But Women Play the Game Too: Gender Power Dynamics in Administrative Decision Making." Presented at the Annual Meeting of the American Political Science Association, Chicago.

Duerst-Lahti, Georgia and Cathy M. Johnson. 1989. "Gender, Style, and Bureaucracy: Must Women Go Native to Succeed?" Presented at the Annual Meeting of the American Political Science Association, Atlanta.

Duerst-Lahti, Georgia and Cathy Marie Johnson. 1990. "Gender and Style in Bureaucracy." *Women & Politics*. 10 (4): 67–120.

Duffy, Michael. 1991. "A Case of Doing Nothing." *Time*. January 7, 28–32.

Dye, Thomas R. and Julie Strickland. 1986. "Women at the Top: A Note on Institutional Leadership." *Social Science Quarterly*. 63: 333–341.

Edgar, Joanne. 1986. "Women Who Went to the Summit." *Ms*. February, 60–63, 84.

Elshtain, Jean Bethke. 1987. *Women and War*. New York: Basic Books.

Elshtain, Jean Bethke and Sheila Tobias, eds. 1990. *Women, Militarism, and War: Essays in History, Politics, and Social Theory*. Savage, MD: Rowman and Littlefield.

Enloe, Cynthia. 1989. *Bananas, Beaches, and Bases: Making Feminist Sense of International Politics*. Berkeley: University of California Press.

Epstein, Cynthia Fuchs. 1988. *Deceptive Distinctions: Sex, Gender, and the Social Order*. New Haven: Yale University Press.

Evans, Rowland and Robert Novak. 1991. "Summer played key role in Thomas' nomination." *Buffalo News*. July 10, B3.

Erskine, Hazel. 1971. "The Polls: Women's Role." *Public Opinion Quarterly*. 35 (2): 275–290.

Farr, Patricia Aylward. "The Mentor Relationship: Application of Theory to the Practice of Social Work." In Lynne Welch, ed. *Women in Higher Education:Changes and Challenges*. New York: Praeger.

Federal Civilian Workforce Statistics. 1984. Washington, DC: OPM.

Federal Civilian Workforce Statistics. 1986. Washington, DC: OPM.

Federal Civilian Workforce Statistics. 1988. Washington, DC: OPM.

Federal Civilian Workforce Statistics: Affirmative Employment Statistics. 1986. Washington, DC: OPM. September.

Federal Civilian Force Statistics: Equal Employment Opportunity Statistics. 1979. Washington, DC: OPM. November.

Federal Civilian Force Statistics, Equal Employment Opportunity Statistics. 1980. Washington, DC: OPM. November.

Federal Employee Attitudes Phase 1 Baseline Survey. 1979. Washington, DC: OPM.

Federal Employee Attitudes Phase 2: Follow-up Survey. 1980. Washington, DC: OPM.

Feinstein, Karen Wolk, ed. 1979. *Working Women and Families.* Beverly Hills: Sage.

Fisher, Berenice. 1978. "Wandering in the Wilderness: The Search for Women Role Models." In Elizabeth Minnich, Jean O'Barr and Rachel Rosenfeld, eds. *Reconstructing the Academy: Women's Education and Women's Studies.* Chicago: University of Chicago Press.

Fite, David, Marc Genest, and Clyde Wilcox. 1990. "Gender Differences in Foreign Policy Attitudes: A Longitudinal Analysis." *American Politics Quarterly.* 18 (4): 492–513.

Foster, Catherine. 1991. "A Different Tack to Managing People." *Christian Science Monitor.* February 15, 13.

Frankovic, Kathleen. 1982. "Sex and Politics—New Alignments, Old Issues." *P.S.* 15 (3): 439–448.

Frankovic, Kathleen A. 1985. "The 1984 Election: The Irrelevance of the Campaign." *P.S.* 18 (1): 39–47.

Fraser, Antonia. 1988. *The Warrior Queens.* New York: Alfred A. Knopf.

Friedan, Betty. 1963. *The Feminine Mystique.* New York: Dell Publishing.

Frieden, Betty and Midge Dector. 1982. "Are Women Different Today?" *Public Opinion.* 5 (20): 41.

Gamarekian, Barbara. 1989. "Women gain, but slowly, in the Foreign Service." *New York Times.* July 28, A10.

Gilligan, Carol. 1982. *In a Different Voice: Psychological Theory and Women's Development.* Cambridge, MA: Harvard University Press.

Going Strong: Women in Defense. 1984. Washington, DC: DOD.

Gomez, Rita Victoria. 1991. "Black WAC's and Bad Times in the Good War." *Washington Post.* November 10, C5.

Goodgame, Dan. 1991. "What if We Do Nothing?" *Time.* January 7, 22–27.

Goodman, Ellen. 1989. "Women's Meeting Poses Question: Is it Worth Getting into Public Service?" *Niagara Gazette.* October 20, 4A.

Goshko, John M. 1989. "2 Reports Urge Overhaul of Foreign Service." *Washington Post.* May 31, A21.

Gould, Ketayuh H., Janice Hartman, and Nancy Weinberg, eds. 1989. *Women and Peace: An International Conference.* Urbana-Champaign, IL: University of Illinois.

Gronich, Lori Helene. 1989. "The Cognitive Processing Theory of Decision-Making: A New Explanation for Policies of War and Peace." Presented at the Annual Meeting of the American Political Science Association, Atlanta.

Gutek, Barbara and Laurie Larwood, eds. 1989. *Women's Career Development.* Newbury Park: Sage Publications.

Gwartney-Gibbs, Patricia A. and Denise H. Lach. 1991. "Sex Differences in Attitudes Toward Nuclear War." *Journal of Peace Research.* 28 (2): 161–174.

Habib, Philip, Chairman. 1979. "Report of the Committee to Review Recruitment and Examination for the Foreign Service." Washington, DC: Department of State.

Hackworth, David H. 1991. "War and the Second Sex." *Newsweek.* August 5, 24–29.

Halloran, Richard. 1989. "Study Finds Servicewomen Harassed." *New York Times.* February 21, A18.

Hanson, Cynthia. 1991. "Fitness for Leadership." *Christian Science Monitor*. February 15, 12.

Harris, Adrienne and Ynestra King, eds. 1989. *Rocking the Ship of State*. Boulder: Westview Press.

Hartsock, Nancy. 1989. "Masculinity, Heroism, and the Making of War." In Adrienne Harris and Ynestra King, eds. *Rocking the Ship of State*. Boulder, CO: Westview Press.

Havemann, Joel. 1981. "Inside the Reagan Administration." *National Journal*. April 25, 675–677.

Havemann, Richard. 1990. "State Dept. Sex-Bias Case Reopened." *Washington Post*. May 12, A14.

Herek, Gregory M., Irving L. Janis and Paul Huth. 1987. "Decision Making during International Crises." *Journal of Conflict Resolution*. 31 (2): 203–226.

"Hearing before the Subcommittee on the Civil Service of the Committee on Post Office and Civil Service, House of Representatives." 1989. (September 22) (Serial No. 101–28). Washington, DC: U.S. Printing office.

Hermann, Margaret G. and Charles F. Hermann. 1989. "Who Makes Foreign Policy Decisions and How; an Empirical Inquiry." *International Studies Quarterly*. 33 (4): 361–388.

Hesse, Sharlene J. 1979. "Women Working: Historical Trends." In Karen Wolk Feinstein, ed. *Working Women and Families*. Beverly Hills: Sage.

Hilsman, Roger. 1987. *The Politics of Policy Making in Defense and Foreign Affairs: Conceptual Models and Bureaucratic Politics*. Englewood Cliffs: Prentice-Hall, Inc.

Hoff-Wilson, Joan. 1987. "Conclusion: Of Mice and Men." In Edward P. Crapol, ed. *Women and American Foreign Policy: Lobbyist, Critics, and Insiders*. New York: Greenwood Press.

Holm, Jeanne. Maj. Gen. USAF (Ret.). 1982. *Women in the Military: An Unfinished Revolution*. Novato, CA: Presidio.

Holsti, Ole R. 1990. "Gender and Political Beliefs of American Leaders, 1976–1988." Presented at the Annual Meeting of the International Studies Association, Washington, DC, April 10–14.

Holsti, Ole R. and James N. Rosenau. 1981. "The Foreign Policy Beliefs of Women in Leadership Positions." *The Journal of Politics*. 43 (2): 326–347.

Holsti, Ole R. and James N. Rosenau. 1984. *American Leadership in World Affairs*. Boston: Allen & Unwin.

Holsti, Ole R. and James Rosenau. 1988. "The Domestic and Foreign Policy Beliefs of American Leaders." *Journal of Conflict Resolution*. 32 (2): 248–294.

Hoynes, William and David Croteau. 1989. "Are You on the Nightline Guest List?" *Extra*. January/February.

Hyde, Janet Shibley. 1990. "Meta-analysis and the Psychology of Gender Differences." *Signs*. 16 (1): 55–73.

Institute for the Study of Diplomacy. 1992. *The Foreign Service in 2001*. Washington, DC: Georgetown University.

"It is a Women's Role to Save the Species." 1986. *USA Today*: April 14, 11a.

Jacobs, Jerry A. 1985. "Sex Segregation in American Higher Education." In Laurie Larwood, Ann H. Stromberg, and Barbara A. Gutek, eds. *Women and Work: An Annual Review*. Vol. 1. Beverly Hills: Sage.

Jaros, Dean and Elizabeth S. White. 1983. "Sex, Endocrines, and Political Behavior." *Women & Politics*. 3 (23): 129–145.

Jensen, Mark P. 1987. "Gender, Sex Roles, and Attitudes Toward War and Nuclear Weapons." *Sex Roles*. 17 (5/6): 253–267.

Joint Hearing Before the Subcommittee on International Operations of the Committee on Foreign Affairs and Subcommittee on the Civil Service of the Committee on Post Office and Civil Service. 1990. DOC. Y4.F76/1: P43/11. Washington, DC: U.S. Printing Office.

Jones, Kathleen. 1984. "Dividing the Ranks: Women and the Draft." *Women & Politics*. 4 (4): 75–87.

Kanter, Rosabeth Moss. 1977. *Men and Women of the Corporation*. New York: Basic Books.

Kantrowitz, Barbara with Eleanor Clift and John Barry. 1991. "The Right to Fight." *Newsweek*. August 5, 22–23.

Keene, Karlyn 1991. "'Feminism' vs. Women's Rights." *Public Perspective*. 3 (1): 3–4.

Kegley, Charles and Eugene R. Wittkopf. 1982. *American Foreign Policy: Pattern and Process*. 2nd ed. New York: St. Martin's Press.

Kegley, Charles and Eugene R. Wittkopf. 1987. *American Foreign Policy: Pattern and Process*. 3rd ed. New York: St. Martin's Press.

Kelly, Rita Mae and Mary E. Guy, *et al*. 1991. "Public Managers in the States: A Comparison of Career Advancement by Sex." *Public Administration Review*. 51 (5): 402–411.

Kelly, Rita Mae, Mary M. Hale and Jayne Burgess. 1991. "Gender and Managerial/Leadership Styles." *Women & Politics*. 11 (2): 19–39.

Kendrigan, Mary Lou. 1987. "The Use of Force: Feminist and World Peace." Presented at the Annual Meeting of the American Political Science Association, Washington, DC.

Kendrigan, Mary Lou, 1991. "The 'Mom's War' or What Effect Will Women Warriors Have on the Move Towards Greater Equality for Women?" Presented at the Annual Meeting of the American Political Science Association, Washington, DC.

Kenski, Henry C. 1988. "The Gender Factor in a Changing Electorate." In Carol M. Mueller, ed. *The Politics of the Gender Gap*. Newbury Park: Sage.

Kerber, Linda. 1990. "May All Our Citizens Be Soldiers and All Our Soldiers Citizens: The Ambiguities of Female Citizenship in the New Nation." In Jean Bethke Elshtain and Sheila Tobias, eds. *Women, Militarism, and War*. Savage, MD: Rowman and Littlefield.

Kilpatrick, James J. 1991. "Women still shortchanged in top jobs." *Buffalo News*. September 19.

Klein, Ethel. 1984. *Gender Politics: From Consciousness to Mass Politics*. Cambridge, MA: Harvard University Press.

Knell, Susan and Gerald Winer. 1979. "Effects of Reading Content on Occupational Sex Role Stereotypes." *Journal of Vocational Behavior*. 14: 78–87.

Knickerbocker, Brad. 1991. "Ms. Roberts Goes to the Statehouse." *Christian Science Monitor*. February 15, 10.

Kohl, Wilfrid L. 1975. "The Nixon-Kissinger Foreign Policy System and U.S.-European Relations: Patterns of Policy Making." *World Politics*. 28 (1): 1–43.

Kraditor, Aileen. 1965. *The Ideas of the Women's Suffrage Movement: 1890–1920*. Garden City, New York: Anchor Books.

Ladd, Everett Carl. 1989. "The National Election." *Public Opinion*. January/February: 2–3, 60.

Lake, Celinda. 1982. "Guns, Butter, and Equality: The Women's Vote in 1980." Presented at the Annual Meeting of the Midwest Political Science Association, Milwaukee.

Lancaster, John. 1992. "24 Women Assaulted on Gulf Duty: Perpetrators Often Were Higher-Ranking Soldiers, Army Says." *The Washington Post*. July 21, A1.

Landrum, Cecile S. "The Development and Utilization of Women in the Department of Defense." Washington, DC: Defense Manpower Commission.

Langley, Monica. 1981. "Reagan Men Learn What GOP Women Really Want: Jobs." *Wall Street Journal*. July 7.

Larwood, Laurie and Urs E. Gattiker. 1987. "A Comparison of the Career Paths Used by Successful Women and Men." In Barbara A. Gutek and Laurie Larwood, eds. *Women's Career Development*. Newbury Park, NJ: Sage.

Larwood, Laurie, Ann H. Stromberg and Barbara A. Gutek, eds. 1985. *Women and Work: An Annual Review*. Vol. 1. Beverly Hills: Sage.

Lepper, Mary M. 1974. "A Study of Career Structures of Federal Executives: A Focus on Women." In Jane L. Jaquette, ed. *Women in Politics*. New York: John Wiley & Sons.

Leveritt, Mara. 1985. "An Ounce of Dissention." *Arkansas Times*. August, 51–54, 79–80. Reprint.

Lord, Lewis. 1990. "America on the Eve of Conflict." *U.S. News & World Report*. August 27–September 3, 44–58.

MacDonald, Sharon. 1988. "Drawing the Lines—Gender, Peace and War: An Introduction." In Sharon MacDonald, Pat Holden and Shirley Ardener, eds. *Images of Women in Peace and War*. Madison: University of Wisconsin Press.

MacDonald, Sharon, Pat Holden and Shirley Ardener, eds. 1988. *Images of Women in Peace and War*. Madison, WI: University of Wisconsin Press.

Majors, Brenda. 1981. Untitled lecture State University of New York at Buffalo. (April).

Marchand, C. Roland. 1972. *The American Peace Movement and Social Reform 1898–1918*. Princeton: Princeton University Press.

Mathews, Jay. 1991. "Hill decries female powerlessness." *Buffalo News*. November 17, A10.

Matlack, Carol. 1987. "Women at the Polls." *National Journal*. December 19: 3208–3215.

McGlen, Nancy E. and Karen O'Connor. 1988. "The Societal Impact of the American Women's Peace Movement." Presented at the Annual Meeting of the International Political Science Association, Washington, DC.

McGlen, Nancy E. and Karen O'Connor. 1989. "Women and Peace: The Connections." Presented at the Women and Peace Conference, University of Illinois.

McGlen, Nancy E. and Meredith Reid Sarkees. 1989. "Foreign Policy Bureaucracies and Women's Influence: Rules and Structure." Presented at the Annual Meeting of the American Political Science Association, Atlanta.

McGlen, Nancy E. and Meredith Reid Sarkees. 1991. "The Unseen Influence of Women in the State and Defense Departments." *Gender and Policymaking: Studies of Women in Office*. Rutgers: Center for the American Woman and Politics.

McGlen, Nancy E. and Meredith Reid Sarkees. 1992. "Foreign Policy Decision Makers: The Impact of Gender." *Women in Leadership*. Rutgers: Center for the American Woman and Politics.

Military Women in the Department of Defense. 1987. Washington, DC: Office of the Secretary of Defense.

Miller, Arthur H. 1983. "The Emerging Gender Gap in American Politics." *Election Politics*. 1 (Winter): 7–12.

Miller, Arthur H. 1986. "Gender Politics in the United States." Presented at the 1986 ECPR Joint Workshops, Gothenburg, Sweden.

Miller, Arthur. 1988. "Gender and the Vote: 1984." In Carol M. Mueller, ed. *The Politics of the Gender Gap*. Newbury Park: Sage.

Minnich, Elizabeth, Jean O'Barr and Rachel Rosenfeld, eds. 1978. *Reconstructing the Academy: Women's Education and Women's Studies*. Chicago: University of Chicago Press.

Moore, Molly. 1989. "Attitudes of Male-Oriented Culture Persist as Grievances go Unreported." *Washington Post*. September 25, A1, A8, A9.

Moore, Molly. 1989. "Open Doors Don't Yield Equality." *Washington Post*. September 24: A1, A16, A17.

Morgenthau, Hans J. 1985. *Politics Among Nations: The Struggle for Power & Peace*. 6th ed. New York: Alfred A. Knopf.

Morgenthau, Hans J. 1990. "Another 'Great Debate': The National Interest of the United States." In John A. Vasquez. *Classics of International Relations*. 2nd ed. Englewood Cliffs, NJ: Prentice Hall.

Moss, Desda. 1988. "U.S. Agencies Vow to Fight Harassment." *USA Today*. July 1, 4.

"Most in poll see sexual harassment as serious issue." 1991. *Buffalo News*. November 23, A3.

Mueller, Carol M., ed. 1988. *The Politics of the Gender Gap*. Newbury Park, CA: Sage.

Mueller, Carol M. 1988. "The Empowerment of Women: Polling and the Women's Voting Bloc." In Carol Mueller, ed. *The Politics of the Gender Gap*. Newbury Park, CA: Sage.

Nathan, James A. and James K. Oliver. 1987. *Foreign Policy Making and the American Political System*. 2nd ed. Boston: Little, Brown and Company.

National Women's Studies Association. "Thousands of Unknown Claimants Eligible for Damages: Search Underway for Female Applicants to VOA, Radio Marti, and Asia." 1989.

"Navy Clamps down on sexual harassment." 1992. *Buffalo News*. February 10, A15.

Neely, James C. 1981. *Gender: The Myth of Equality*. New York: Simon & Schuster.

New York Times/CBS Poll. Reprint of articles published August 21, 1989 and August 22, 1989.

Nikel, Herman. 1971. "Sex and the Foreign Service." *Time*. August 27.

"Notable and Quotable." 1991. *San Diego Union*. October 13, C6.

Office of Equal Employment and Civil Rights. 1987. *Secretary's Annual Report to Congress on Equal Employment Opportunity Efforts Fiscal Year 1987*. Washington, DC: Department of State.

Office of Equal Employment and Civil Rights. 1988. *Update of the Affirmative Action Plan and Annual Accomplishment Report of Equal Employment Activities for Fiscal Year 1987*. Washington, DC: Department of State.

Olmsted, Mary S., Bernice Baer, Jean Joyce and Georgiana M. Prince. 1984. *Women at State: An Inquiry into the Status of Women in the United States Department of State*. Washington, DC: Women's Research and Education Institute of the Congressional Caucus for Women's Issues.

"Opinion Watch: On the Front Lines?" 1991. *Newsweek*. August 5, 27.

Palmer, Elizabeth A. 1991. "Senate Debates Rights, Role of Women Warriors." *Congressional Quarterly*. 49 (25): 1687.

Palmer, et al. v. Baker. 1987. Plaintiffs' Brief on Remand to the District Court.

Palmer, et al. v. Baker. 1987. Defendant's Brief on Remand from the Court of Appeals.

Palmer, et al. v. Baker. 1987. 662 Federal Supplement. (D.D.C) 1551–1575.

Palmer, et al. v. Baker. 1989. Remedial Order, United States District Court for the District of Columbia.

"Peace Links Organized." 1982. *New York Times*. May 26, 26.

Pear, Robert. 1987. "Number of Blacks in Top Jobs In Administration Off Sharply." *New York Times*. March 22, 1, 30.

Perry, James L. and Lois Recascino Wise. 1990. "The Motivational Basis of Public Service." *Public Administration Review*. 50 (3): 367–372.

Pierson, Ruth Roach. 1988. "'Did Your Mother Wear Army Boots?' Feminist Theory and Women's Relation to War, Peace and Revolution." In Sharon MacDonald, Pat Holden and Shirley Ardener, eds. *Images of Women In Peace and War*. Madison, WI: University of Wisconsin Press.

"Plan Given Cautious Approval by Women's Groups." 1980. *New York Times*. February 9, A9.

Powell, Gary N. 1988. *Women & Men in Management*. Newbury Park: Sage Publications.

Project on the Status and Education of Women. 1983. *Academic Mentoring for Women Students and Faculty: A New Look at an Old Way to Get Ahead*. Washington, DC: Association of American Colleges.

Putting Women in Their Place: The Federal Women's Program. 1979. (PM1.2: W84). Washington, DC: Federal Women's Program.

Rainey, Gene. 1975. *Patterns of American Foreign Policy*. Boston: Allyn and Bacon.

Reardon, Betty. 1985. *Sexism and the War System*. New York: Teachers College Press.

Report on Pre-Complaint Counseling and Complaint Processing Data Submitted by Federal Agencies for Fiscal Year 1984. Washington, DC: Equal Employment Opportunity Commission.

Richards, Janet Radcliffe. 1990. "Why the Pursuit of Peace Is No Part of Feminism." In Jean Bethke Elshtain and Sheila Tobias, ed. *Women, Militarism, and War*. Savage, MD: Rowman and Littlefield.

Rix, Sara E., ed. 1988. *The American Woman 1988–89*. New York: W.W. Norton and Company for the Women's Research and Education Institute.

Rix, Sara E. 1990. *The American Woman, 1990–1991*. New York: W.W. Norton.

Roach, Colleen. 1991. "Feminist Peace researchers, culture and communication." *Media Development*. 28 (2): 6.

Roberts, Roxanne. 1991. "The Silence of the Diplomat." *Washington Post*. March 15, C1, C6.

Rockman, Bert A. 1988. "The Style and Organization of the Reagan Presidency." In Charles O. Jones, ed. *The Reagan Legacy*. Chatham, NJ: Chatham House Publishers, Inc.

Rockman, Bert A. 1991. "The Leadership Style of George Bush." In Colin Campbell and Bert A. Rockman, eds. *The Bush Presidency: First Appraisals*. Chatham, NJ: Chatham House Publishers, Inc.

Roper Institute. 1980. *The 1980 Virginia Slims Poll*. Storrs, CT: Roper Institute.

Rosati, Jerel A. 1981. "Developing a Systematic Decision-Making Framework: Bureaucratic Politics in Perspective." *World Politics*. 33(2): 234–252.

Rouse, W.V. 1977. *Evaluation at the Equal Employment Opportunity Program: U.S. Department of State*. Evanston, IL: W.V. Rouse & Co.

Rubin, Marilyn Marks. 1990. "Women in ASPA: The Fifty-Year Climb Toward Equality." *Public Administration Review* 50 (2): 277–287.

Ruddick, Sara. 1980. "Maternal Thinking." *Feminist Studies*. 6 (2): 342–367.

Ruddick, Sara. 1983a. "Pacifying the Forces: Drafting Women in the Interest of Peace." *Signs*. 8 (3): 471–489.

Ruddick, Sara. 1983b. "Preservative Love and Military Destruction: Reflections on Mothering and Peace." In Joyce Trebilcot, ed. *Mothering: Essays in Feminist Theory*. Totowa, NJ: Littlefield Adams.

Ruddick, Sara. 1984. "Feminist Questions on Peace and War: An Agenda for Research, Discussion, Analysis, Action." *Women's Studies Quarterly*. 12 (2): 8–11.

Ruddick, Sara. 1985. "Maternal Work and the Practice of Peace." *Journal of Education*. 167 (3): 97–111.

Ruddick, Sara. 1989. "Mothers and Men's Wars." In Adrienne Harris and Ynestra King, ed. *Rocking the Ship of State*. Boulder, CO: Westview Press.

Ruddick, Sara. 1990. "The Rationality of Care." In Jean Bethke Elshtain and Sheila Tobias, eds. *Women, Militarism, and War*. Savage, MD: Rowman and Littlefield.

Ruse, Michael. 1981. *Is Science Sexist?* Holland: D. Reidel.

Safilios-Rothschild, Constanina. 1979. *Sex Role Socialization and Sex Discrimination: Synthesis and Critique of the Literature*. Washington: National Institute of Education.

Salholz, Eloise with Douglas Waller. 1992. "Tailhook: Scandal Time." *Newsweek*. July 6, 40–41.

Sapiro, Virginia. 1985. "Biology and Women's Policy: A View from the Social Sciences." In Virginia Sapiro, ed. *Women, Biology, and Public Policy*. Beverly Hills: Sage Publications.

Sarkees, Meredith Reid and Nancy E. McGlen. 1989. "Women in Foreign Policy Formulation." Presented at the Annual Meeting of the Northeastern Political Science Association, Philadelphia.

Sarkees, Meredith and Nancy E. McGlen. 1991. "Confronting Barriers: The Status of Women in Political Science." *Women & Politics* (Forthcoming).

Schloesser, Pauline. 1991. "Republican Motherhood, Modern Patriarchy, and the Question of Woman Citizenship in Post-Revolutionary America." Presented at the Annual Meeting of the American Political Science Association, Washington, DC.

Schmitt, Eric. 1990. "2 out of 3 Women in Military Study Report Sexual Harassment Incidents." *New York Times*. September 12, A22.

Schreiber, E. M. 1978. "Education and Change in American Opinions on a Woman For President." *Public Opinion Quarterly*. 42 (Summer): 171–182.

Schreiber, E. M. 1979. "Enduring Effects of Military Service? Opinion Differences Between U.S. Veterans and NonVeterans." *Social Forces*. 57(3): 824–839.

Schroeder, Patricia. 1989. "Women's Role in National Peace Politics." In Ketayuh H. Gould, Janice Hartman and Nancy Weinberg, eds. *Women and Peace: An International Conference*. Urbana-Champaign, IL: University of Illinois.

Schubert, Glendon. 1983. "The Biopolitics of Sex: Gender, Genetics, and Epigenetics." *Women & Politics*. 3 (2/3): 97–128.

Sciolino, Elaine. 1989. "Baker's Staff Incomplete 6 Weeks Into Bush Era." *New York Times*. March 3, A12.

Sciolino, Elaine. 1989. "Friends as Ambassadors: How Many is Too Many?" *New York Times*. November 7, A1, A8.

Sciolino, Elaine. 1990. "Deskbound in U.S. The Envoy to Iraq is called Scapegoat for a Failed Policy." *New York Times*. September 12, A19.

Segal, Mady Wechsler. 1989. "Social Representation in the Military: The Case of Gender." Presented at the Annual Meeting of the Inter-University Seminar on Armed Forces and Society, Baltimore.

Selected Manpower Statistics. Washington, DC: Department of Defense. September 1980.

Selected Manpower Statistics. Washington, DC: Department of Defense. September 1987.

Senior Executive Service. 1980. (DOC. PM12 SE5). Washington, DC: OPM.

Senior Executive Service. 1988. (DOC. PM1.10: SES–88–01). Washington, DC: OPM.

Senior Executive Service: Views of Former Federal Executives. 1989. Washington, DC: Merit Systems Protection Board.

Shapiro, Robert Y. and Harpreet Mahajan. 1986. "Gender Differences in Policy Preferences: A Summary of Trends from the 1960s to the 1980s." *Public Opinion Quarterly*. 50(1): 42–61.

Shupe, Anson. 1991. "Family violence and the nation's military complex." *Buffalo News*. December 4, B3.

Sigel, Roberta S. and Lauren D. Burnbauer. 1989. "The 'NOT-ME' Syndrome. A Paradox in Search of An Explanation." Presented at the Annual Meeting of the American Political Science Association, Atlanta.

Simon, Rita J. and Jean M. Landis. 1989. "The Polls—A Report on Women's and Men's Attitudes About a Woman's Place and Role." *Public Opinion Quarterly*. 53(2): 265–276.

"67 Female Navy Workers Win Sex Bias Lawsuit." 1991. *Niagara Gazette*. November 27.

Smeal, Eleanor. 1984. *Why and How Women Will Elect the Next President*. New York: Harper and Row.

Smith, Hedrick. 1981. "Conservatives Cite Gains in Top Posts." *New York Times*. March 3.

Smith, Linda. 1986. Quoted in "It is Women's Role to Save This Species." *USA Today*. April 14, 11A.

Smith, Tom W. 1984. "The Polls: Gender and Attitudes Toward Violence." *Public Opinion Quarterly*. 48(1B): 384–96.

Snitow, Ann. 1989. "A Gender Diary." In Adrienne Harris and Ynestra King, ed. *Rocking the Ship of State*. Boulder, CO: Westview Press.

Snyder, Glenn H. and Paul Diesing. 1977. *Conflict Among Nations*. Princeton: Princeton University Press.

Spanier, John and Eric M. Uslaner. 1978. *How American Foreign Policy is Made*. New York: Holt Rinehart and Winston/Praeger.

State Department: Minorities and women are underrepresented in the Foreign Service. 1989. Washington, DC: General Accounting Office.

Status of the Senior Executive Service. 1989. Washington, DC: Office of Personnel Management.

Stehr, Steven D. 1989. "Top Bureaucrats and the Distribution of Influence in Reagan's Executive Branch." Presented at the Annual Meeting of the American Political Science Association, Atlanta.

Stiehm, Judith Hicks. 1989. *Arms and the Enlisted Woman*. Philadelphia: Temple University Press.

Stone, Anne J. 1988. "1987 in Review." In Sara Rix, ed. *The American Woman, 1988–89*. New York: W. W. Norton and Company, for the Women's Research and Education Institute.

Swerdlow, Amy. 1982. "Ladies' Day at the Capitol: Women Strike for Peace Versus HUAC." *Feminist Studies*. 8(3): 493–518.

Swerdlow, Amy. 1989. "Pure Milk, Not Poison: Women Strike for Peace and the Test Ban Treaty of 1963." In Adrienne Harris and Ynestra King, ed. *Rocking the Ship of State: Toward a Feminist Peace Politics*. Boulder, CO: Westview.

Swerdlow, Amy. 1990. "Motherhood and the Subversion of the Military State: Women's Strike for Peace Confront the House Committee on Un-American Activities." In Jean Bethke Elshtain and Sheila Tobias, eds. *Women, Militarism, and War*. Savage, MD: Rowman and Littlefield.

Tankard, James W. 1984. "Nuclear Weapons Literacy and Its Correlates." *Peace Research*. 16(1): 30–34.

Task Force on Women in the Military. 1988. *Report of the Task Force on Women in the Military*. Washington, DC: Department of Defense.

"10 Weeks to Put it All Together." 1980. *U.S. News and World Report*. November 17.

"The Exit Poll Results." 1989. *Public Opinion*. January/February, 24–26.

The 1990 Virginia Slims Poll. Data distributed by The Roper Center for Public Opinion Research.

Tickner, J. Ann. 1989. "Redefining Security: A Feminist Perspective." Presented at the Annual Meeting of the Northeastern Political Science Association, Philadelphia.

Tickner, J. Ann. 1992. *Gender in International Relations: Feminist Perspectives on Achieving Global Security*. New York: Columbia University Press.

Tobias, Sheila. 1990. "Shifting Heroisms: The Uses of Military Service in Politics." In Jean Bethke Elshtain and Sheila Tobias, eds. *Women, Militarism, and War*. Savage, MD: Rowman and Littlefield.

Towell, Pat. 1991. "Breaking the Gender Barrier." *Congressional Quarterly*. 49 (31): 2183.

Towell, Pat and Elizabeth Palmer. 1991. "Women of War." *Congressional Quarterly*. 49 (19): 1210.

Towell, Pat. 1992. "Women's Combat Role Debated As Chiefs Denounce Sex Bias." *Congressional Quarterly*. 50 (31): 2292–2293.

Tronto, Joan C. 1987. "Beyond Gender Differences to a Theory of Care." *Signs*. 12 (4): 644–663.

Tuchman, Gaye. 1979. "The Impact of Mass-Media Stereotypes Upon the Full Employment of Women." In Ann Foote Cahn, ed. *Women in the U.S. Labor Force*. New York: Praeger.

Valdez, Roberta and Barbara A. Gutek, 1987. "Family Roles: A Help or a Hindrance for Working Women?" In Barbara A. Gutek and Laurie Larwood, eds. *Women's Career Development*. Newbury Park, NJ: Sage.

Wagner, Monica, esq. from the law firm of Terris, Edgecombe, Hecker, & Wayne. 1989. Phone Conversation.

Wagner, Monica, esq. from the law firm of Terris, Edgecombe, Hecker, & Wayne. 1992. Phone Conversation.

"WAO's 20th Anniversary: Legacy of the Past-Challenges for the Future." 1990. Washington, DC: Women's Action Organization.

Warner, Margaret Garrard. 1989. "A 'Drone Class' of American Diplomacy?" *Newsweek*. October 30, 62–63.

Watts, Meredith W. 1983. "Biopolitics and Gender." *Women & Politics*. 3 (2/3): 1–29.

Welch, David A. 1989. "Crisis Decision Making Reconsidered." *Journal of Conflict Resolution*. 33 (3): 430–446.

Welch, Lynne B., ed. 1990. *Women in Higher Education: Changes and Challenges*. New York: Praeger.

Welles, Benjamin. 1972. "Women Winning State Department Case." *New York Times*. February 28.

Wirls, Daniel. 1986. "Reinterpreting the Gender Gap." *Public Opinion Quarterly*. 50 (3): 316–330.

Wittkopf, Eugene. 1981. "The Structure of Foreign Policy Attitudes: An Alternative View." *Social Science Quarterly*. 62 (1): 108–123.

Wittkopf, Eugene R. and Michael A. Maggiotto. 1983. "Elites and Masses: A Comparative Analysis of Attitudes Toward America's World Role." *The Journal of Politics*. 45 (1): 303–334.

"Women and the Use of Force." 1991. *Public Perspective*. 2(3): 85–86.

Women for a Meaningful Summit (Women for Meaningful Summits). n.d. "Statement of Purpose."

"Women Have What it Takes." 1991. *Newsweek*. August 5, 30.

"Women in Combat." 1991. *Public Perspective*. 2 (3): 87.

"Women of War." 1991. *Congressional Quarterly*. 49 (19): 1210.

Women on the Way Up: The Federal Women's Program. 1980. (DOC. PM1.2: W84/2). Washington, DC: OPM.

Woodlee, Yolanda, 1991. "Diploma doesn't ensure pay parity." *Detroit News*. September 20, 1B.

"Work and Families." 1990. *Public Perspective*. 1 (6): 90–92.

"Work Experience." 1990. *Public Perspective*. 1 (6): 85–87.

"Worth Noting." 1989. *Public Opinion*. January/February: 33–34.

Zeidner, Rita L. 1990. "Shroeder Blasts 'Glass Ceiling.'" *Federal Times*. December 3.

INDEX